I0011859

NASA Software Safety Guidebook
NASA-GB-8719.13 – Effective Date: March 31, 2004

This document has been issued to make available to software safety practitioners a guidebook for assessing software systems for software's contribution to safety and techniques for analyzing and applying appropriate safety techniques and methods to software. Software developers and software safety engineers are the primary focus; however, software assurance (SA) engineers, project managers, system engineers, and system safety engineers will also find this guidebook useful.

This is an excellent primer on software safety and a classic!

Why buy a book you can download for free? We print this book so you don't have to.

If you find a good copy, you could print it using a network printer you share with 100 other people (typically its either out of paper or toner). If it's just a 10-page document, no problem, but if it's 250-pages, you will need to punch 3 holes in all those pages and put it in a 3-ring binder. Takes at least an hour. It's much more cost-effective to just order the latest version from Amazon.com. This book includes original commentary which is copyright material. Note that government documents are in the public domain. We print these large documents as a service so you don't have to. The books are compact, tightly-bound, full-size (8 ½ by 11 inches), with large text and glossy covers. 4th Watch Publishing Co. is a HUBZONE SDVOSB. https://usgovpub.com **www.usgovpub.com**

List of Applicable Publications:

NASA RCM	NASA Reliability-Centered Maintenance (RCM)
SP-2016-6105	NASA Systems Engineering Handbook
Probabilistic Risk Assessment Procedures Guide for NASA Managers and Practitioners	
NASA-STD-8719.9B	NASA Lifting Standards
UFC 4-010-06	Cybersecurity of Facility-Related Control Systems
NIST SP 800-82	Guide to Industrial Control Systems (ICS) Security
Whitepaper	NIST Framework for Improving Critical Infrastructure Cybersecurity
NISTIR 8170	The Cybersecurity Framework
FC 4-141-05N	Navy and Marine Corps Industrial Control Systems Monitoring Stations
UFC 3-430-11	Boiler Control Systems
NISTIR 8089	An Industrial Control System Cybersecurity Performance Testbed
NIST SP 800-12	An Introduction to Information Security
NIST SP 800-18	Developing Security Plans for Federal Information Systems
NIST SP 800-31	Intrusion Detection Systems
NIST SP 800-34	Contingency Planning Guide for Federal Information Systems
NIST SP 800-35	Guide to Information Technology Security Services
NIST SP 800-39	Managing Information Security Risk
NIST SP 800-40	Guide to Enterprise Patch Management Technologies
NIST SP 800-41	Guidelines on Firewalls and Firewall Policy
NIST SP 800-44	Guidelines on Securing Public Web Servers
NIST SP 800-47	Security Guide for Interconnecting Information Technology Systems
NIST SP 800-48	Guide to Securing Legacy IEEE 802.11 Wireless Networks
NIST SP 800-53A	Assessing Security and Privacy Controls
NIST SP 800-61	Computer Security Incident Handling Guide
NIST SP 800-77	Guide to IPsec VPNs
NIST SP 800-83	Guide to Malware Incident Prevention and Handling for Desktops and Laptops
NIST SP 800-92	Guide to Computer Security Log Management
NIST SP 800-94	Guide to Intrusion Detection and Prevention Systems (IDPS)
NIST SP 800-97	Establishing Wireless Robust Security Networks: A Guide to IEEE 802.11i
NIST SP 800-137	Information Security Continuous Monitoring (ISCM)
NIST SP 800-160	Systems Security Engineering
NIST SP 800-171	Protecting Controlled Unclassified Information in Nonfederal Systems
NIST SP 1800-7	Situational Awareness for Electric Utilities
NISTIR 7628	Guidelines for Smart Grid Cybersecurity
DoD	Energy Manager's Handbook
FEMP	Operations & Maintenance Best Practices
UFC 4-020-01	DoD Security Engineering Facilities Planning Manual
UFC 4-021-02	Electronic Security Systems by Department of Defense
GSA	GSA Courtroom Technology Manual
Draft NISTIR 8179	Criticality Analysis Process Model
NISTIR 8144	Assessing Threats to Mobile Devices & Infrastructure
NISTIR 8151	Dramatically Reducing Software Vulnerabilities
NIST SP 800-183	Networks of 'Things'
NIST SP 800-184	Guide for Cybersecurity Event Recovery

NOT MEASUREMENT
SENSITIVE

**National Aeronautics and
Space Administration**

NASA-GB-8719.13
March 31, 2004

NASA Software Safety Guidebook

NASA TECHNICAL STANDARD

This document has been issued to make available to software safety practitioners a guidebook for assessing software systems for software's contribution to safety and techniques for analyzing and applying appropriate safety techniques and methods to software. Software developers and software safety engineers are the primary focus; however, software assurance (SA) engineers, project managers, system engineers, and system safety engineers will also find this guidebook useful.

The document:

> Provides an overview of general software safety and good software engineering practices which contribute to software system safety.

> Provides the means to scope and tailor the software safety and software engineering activities to obtain the most cost effective, best quality, and safest products.

> Provides analyses, methods and guidance which can be applied during each phase of the software life cycle. Multiple checklists and examples are provided as well as specific instructions for applying FMEA/CIL and FTA to software.

> Includes development approaches, safety analyses, and testing methodologies that lead to improved safety in the software product.

Procuring NASA Enterprise Programs or Centers shall review this document for applicability to NASA contracts as well as for applicability to its internal activities.

Questions concerning the application of this publication to specific procurements or requests should be referred to the NASA Enterprise Program or Center.

This guidebook cancels NASA-GB-1740.13-96, NASA Guidebook for Safety Critical Software Analysis and Development.

/s/

Bryan O'Connor
Associate Administrator for
Safety and Mission Assurance

Foreword

This guidebook was created to provide specific information and guidance on the process of creating and assuring safe software. In our modern world, software controls much of the hardware (equipment, electronics, and instruments) around us. Sometimes hardware failure can lead to a loss of human life. When software controls, operates, or interacts with such hardware, software safety becomes a vital concern

The audience for this guidebook is diverse. Software developers and software safety engineers are the primary focus. Software assurance (QA) engineers, project managers, system engineers, and system safety engineers will also find this guidebook useful. Section 1.5 of the Introduction provides guidance on sections of particular interest to the various disciplines.

This guidebook is meant to be more than just a collection of development techniques and analyses. The goal is to open the reader to new ways of thinking about software from a safety perspective. This guidebook points out things to look for (and look out for) in the development of safety-critical software. The guidebook includes development approaches, safety analyses, and testing methodologies that lead to improved safety in the software product.

While the focus of this guidebook is on the development of software for **safety-critical** systems, much of the information and guidance is also appropriate to the creation of **mission-critical** software.

Table of Contents

Chapter 11   Software Development Issues 205

Figures

Tables

Chapter 1 Introduction

This NASA Software Safety Guidebook was prepared by the NASA Glenn Research Center, Safety and Assurance Directorate, under a Center Software Initiative Proposal (CSIP) task for the National Aeronautics and Space Administration.

NASA-STD-8719.13A, "NASA Software Safety Standard," [1] prepared by NASA Headquarters addresses the "who, what, when and why" of software safety analyses. This Software Safety Guidebook addresses the "how to."

Section 1.5 provides a roadmap to using this guidebook. The roadmap describes the information in each chapter and shows software developers, project managers, software assurance personnel, system engineers, and safety engineers which sections are relevant for their disciplines.

1.1 Scope

The focus of this document is on analysis, development, and assurance of safety-critical software, including firmware (e.g. software residing in non-volatile memory, such as ROM, EPROM, EEPROM, or flash memory) and programmable logic. This document also discusses issues with contractor-developed software. It provides guidance on how to address creation and assurance of safety-critical software within the overall software development, management, risk management, and assurance activities.

Techniques and analyses are described in varying levels of detail throughout the guidebook, depending on the amount of information available. For techniques or analyses are that are new, the guidebook attempts to give a flavor of the technique or procedure and provides sources for more information. Opinions differ widely concerning the validity of some of the various techniques, and this guidebook attempts to present these opinions without prejudging their validity. In most cases, there are few or no metrics as of yet, to quantitatively evaluate or compare the techniques. This guidebook addresses the value added versus cost of each technique with respect to the overall software development and assurance goals. Without strong metrics, such evaluations are somewhat subjective and should not be taken as the definitive answer. Each technique or analysis should be considered in the context of the specific project.

This guidebook is meant to be more than just a collection of development techniques and analyses. The goal is to encourage the reader to think about software with "an eye for safety." Some familiarity with the NASA methodologies for system safety analysis and software development will assist in following this guidebook, though no experience with either is assumed or required. Acronyms and definitions of terminology used in this guidebook are contained in Appendix B.

1.2 Purpose

The purpose of this guidebook is to aid organizations involved in the development and assurance of safety-critical software. Software developers will find information on the creation of safer software, as well as introduction to the NASA process for system (and software) safety. Software safety personnel are given an introduction to the variety of techniques and analyses available for assuring that the software is safer, as well as information on good development practices. Project managers, system safety, software assurance engineers, and systems engineers may also find this guidebook useful. Some knowledge of software development processes is helpful in understanding the material presented in this guidebook.

This guidebook concentrates on software development and acquisition and the associated tasks and analyses. While the focus is on the development of software for **safety-critical** systems, much of the information and guidance is also appropriate to the creation of **mission-critical** software. Guidance on the acquisition of software, either commercial off-the-shelf or created under contract, is given in Chapter 12.

1.3   Acknowledgments

Much of the material presented in this Guidebook has been based directly or indirectly on a variety of sources (NASA, government agencies, technical literature sources), as well as containing original material previously undocumented. All the sources are too numerous to list here, but are appropriately referenced throughout.

A special acknowledgment is owed to engineers of the NASA/Caltech Jet Propulsion Laboratory of Pasadena, California, whose inputs and suggestions have been used verbatim or slightly modified in several sections of this Guidebook.

We also thank:

- The Software Productivity Consortium for permission to reproduce "The Frameworks Quagmire" diagram.

- Rick Hower for permission to use information from his website on "Software QA and Testing Frequently-Asked-Questions", http://www.softwareqatest.com/.

- Denis Howe for permission to quote from "The Free On-Line Dictionary of Computing", http://foldoc.doc.ic.ac.uk/foldoc/index.html

- Philip J. Koopman for permission to quote from "A Brief Introduction to Forth."

- Paul E. Bennett for permission to reproduce his "Design for Safety" checklist.

Our gratitude goes to the many NASA engineers and contractors who reviewed drafts of the guidebook and provided input and advise as well as encouragement.

1.4   Associated Documents

Documents detailing software safety standards, software development standards, and guidebooks are listed in Appendix A.2: Information. Included are NASA standards for software, as well as IEEE and military standards.

1.5   Roadmap of this Guidebook

This guidebook provides information for several diverse disciplines: software development, system and software safety, software assurance, project management, and systems engineering. Each of these disciplines has an associated graphic symbol, used throughout the document to assist the reader in locating relevant information. When an entire section is appropriate for a specific discipline, the symbol will be placed after the section title. When a paragraph within a section is applicable, the symbol will be placed to the left of the paragraph. In addition, tailoring information will be indicated by this symbol:

Section 1.5.1 provides the symbols that are associated with each discipline, along with a brief description of the discipline. Section 1.5.2 provides a brief description of the contents of each Chapter in this guidebook.

1.5.1 Disciplines and Symbols

Discipline/Symbol	Responsibilities
Software Development	The task of developing safe software falls squarely on the shoulders of the software developer (also referred to as the software engineer), who creates the "code" that must be safe. Almost all sections of this guidebook are relevant to the software development discipline.
Software Safety (including System Safety)	The software safety tasks may be performed system safety personnel, software assurance personnel, or by a separate software safety engineer. The goal is to assure that the final software, when integrated into the system, is safe. This goal is accomplished through education of project team members, analysis of the software products, test verification, and other techniques. Almost all sections of this guidebook are relevant to the software safety discipline.
Software Assurance	Software assurance personnel make sure that the software produced meets the applicable quality standards. Standards include both process (how the software was developed) and product (how good is the actual software). The software assurance engineer may perform some of the safety analyses, if that is negotiated by the project.
Project and/or Software Management	Developing a safe system requires informed involvement of the project manager. A culture where good practices are rewarded and "systems thinking" is encouraged helps in the creation of a safe system. Many of the topics in this guidebook are technical and detailed. The project manager is pointed to sections that are more general in nature. In addition, sections that point out potential problems, difficulties, or concerns are also flagged for the project manager.
Systems Engineering	A systems engineer may wish to read this guidebook for a better understanding of how software fits into the entire system.

1.5.2   Chapter Description

Chapter 2 describes the concepts of system safety and the role of software in safety-critical systems. The chapter provides software developers and others with an understanding of the system safety process. System safety engineers may wish to review this chapter for information on the various types of software that should be considered in a system safety context.

Chapter 3 gives a more in-depth look at software safety. It provides guidance on how to scope the safety effort and tailor the processes and analyses to the required level of effort.

Chapter 4 provides an overview of the software development process. System safety engineers and project managers unfamiliar with the software development process will find this chapter useful. Software developers, software assurance engineers, and software safety engineers should review the chapter to make sure they are familiar with all the concepts. Other discipline experts may wish to skim the chapter, or use the table of contents to locate specific subsections of interest.

Chapters 5 through 10 describe development activities and assurance analyses for each lifecycle phase. While this guidebook uses the waterfall lifecycle phases (Concept, Requirements, Design, Implementation, Test, and Operations) to describe associated software safety activities, this guidebook does not imply a strict adherence to that lifecycle. The ideas of concept (planning the project), requirements (deciding what to build), design (deciding how to build it), implementation (actually building the software/system), test (making sure it works) and operations (using what was built) apply to all lifecycles. Maintenance of software is viewed as a reduced scope of all these phases with good configuration management of problems and upgrades as well as appropriate root cause analyses and corrective action when required. Retirement of safety critical software is a phase not often thought of but perhaps should be.

Chapter 5 focuses on activities performed during the concept phase of the project. Activities and analyses for both development and safety are discussed.

Chapter 6 focuses on activities performed during the requirements phase of the project. Activities and analyses for both development and safety are discussed. Requirements management, determination of critical requirements, and other very important concepts are included in this chapter.

Chapter 7 focuses on activities performed during the design phase of the project. Activities and analyses for both development and safety are discussed.

Chapter 8 focuses on activities performed during the implementation phase of the project. Activities and analyses for both development and safety are discussed.

Chapter 9 focuses on activities performed during the testing phase of the project. Activities and analyses for both development and safety are discussed.

Chapter 10 focuses on activities performed during the operations and maintenance phase of the project. Activities and analyses for both development and safety are discussed.

Chapter 11 is a collection of specific problem areas. Selection of programming language, operating system, and development tools is one such area. Innovative technologies, such as distributed computing, autonomous systems, and embedded web, are also included. Much of this chapter will be of interest to software developers. Safety and software assurance engineers may wish to skim this chapter to obtain a better understanding of software issues.

Chapter 12 discusses the acquisition of software. Both COTS/GOTS (commercial and government off-the-shelf) software and software created under contract are considered.

Chapter 13 provides a look ahead to some evolving areas of software safety.

Appendix A contains reference and resource information.

Appendix B provides definitions of commonly used terms and a list of acronyms.

Appendices C through G provide details on five analysis techniques (Software Fault Tree Analysis, Software Failure Modes and Effects Analysis, Requirements State Machine, Preliminary Hazard Analysis, and Reliability Modeling).

Appendix H contains a collection of checklists.

Chapter 2   Software and System Safety
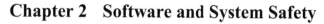

Safety is not the sole responsibility of the System Safety engineer. Creating a safe system is a team effort and safety is everyone's responsibility. Software is a vital part of most systems. It controls hardware and provides mission-critical data. Software must be safe.

But how do you know if any of your software is "safe" or "unsafe"? What are the hazards that software may contribute to, or that software may control? Why should you even care about software safety?

When a device or system can lead to injury, death, the destruction or loss of vital equipment, or damage to the environment, system safety is paramount. The system safety discipline focuses on "hazards" and the prevention of hazardous situations. Hardware or software that can lead to a hazard, or is used to control or mitigate a hazard, comes under that category. Software has become a vital and integral part of most systems. Software can respond quickly to potential problems, provide more functionality than equivalent hardware, and can even be changed in flight! The promise of software, however, must be tempered with the consequences of its failure. The software safety discipline expands beyond the immediate software used in hazard control or avoidance to include all software that can impact hazardous software or hardware. All such software is "safety-critical".

Project managers, systems engineers, software engineers, software assurance personnel, and system safety personnel all play a part in creating a safe system.

2.1   Hazardous and Safety-critical Software

"Software does not fail – it just does not perform as intended." Dr. Nancy Leveson, MIT

2.1.1   What is a Hazard?

A <u>hazard</u> is the presence of a potential risk situation that can result in or contribute to a mishap. Every hazard has at least one cause, which in turn can lead to a number of effects (e.g., damage, illness, failure).

A <u>hazard cause</u> may be a defect in hardware or software, a human operator error, or an unexpected input or event which results in a hazard. A <u>hazard control</u> is a method for preventing the hazard, reducing the likelihood of the hazard occurring, or the reduction of the impact of that hazard . Hazard controls use hardware (e.g. pressure relief valve), software (e.g. detection of stuck valve and automatic response to open secondary valve), operator procedures, or a combination of methods to avert the hazard.

For every hazard cause there must be at least one control method, usually a design feature (hardware and/or software) or a procedural step. Examples of hazard causes and controls are given in <u>Table 2-1</u> *Hazard Causes and Controls - Examples*. Each hazard control will require verification, which may be via test, analysis, inspection, or demonstration. For NASA, critical hazard causes require two independent controls. Catastrophic hazard causes require three independent controls.

Software can be used to detect and control hazards, but software failures can also contribute to the occurrence of hazards. Some software hazard causes can be addressed with hardware hazard controls, although this is becoming less and less practical as software becomes more complex. For example, a hardwired gate array could be preset to look for certain predetermined hazardous words (forbidden or unplanned) transmitted by a computer, and shut down the computer upon detecting such a word. In practice, this is nearly impossible today because thousands of words and commands are usually sent on standard buses.

Table 2-1 Hazard Causes and Controls - Examples

Cause	Control	Example of Control Action
Hardware	Hardware	Pressure vessel with pressure relief valve.
Hardware	Software	Fault detection and safing function; or arm/fire checks which activate or prevent hazardous conditions.
Hardware	Operator	Operator opens switch to remove power from failed unit.
Software	Hardware	Hardwired timer or discrete hardware logic to screen invalid commands or data. Sensor directly triggering a safety switch to override a software control system. Hard stops for a robotic arm.
Software	Software	Two independent processors, one checking the other and intervening if a fault is detected. Emulating expected performance and detecting deviations.
Software	Operator	Operator sees control parameter violation on display and terminates process.
Operator	Hardware	Three electrical switches in series in a firing circuit to tolerate two operator errors.
Operator	Software	Software validation of operator-initiated hazardous command. Software prevents operation in unsafe mode.
Operator	Operator	Two crew members, one commanding and the other monitoring.

2.1.2 How Can Software be Hazardous?

Software, by itself, cannot injure you. But software does not exist by itself. It operates in an electronic system (computer) and often controls other hardware. Software is hazardous if it can directly lead to a hazard or is used to control a hazard.

- Hazardous software includes all software that is a hazard cause.
- Is a hazard control.
- Provides information upon which safety-critical decisions are made.
- Is used as a means of failure/fault detection.

2.1.3 What is Safety-Critical Software?

Safety-critical software includes hazardous software (which can directly contribute to, or control a hazard). It also includes all software that can influence that hazardous software.

Software is considered safety-critical if it controls or monitors hazardous or safety-critical hardware or software. Such software usually resides on remote, embedded, and/or real-time systems. For example, software that controls an airlock or operates a high-powered laser is hazardous and safety-critical. Software that monitors a fire-detection system is also safety-critical.

Software that provides information required for a safety-related decision falls into the safety-critical category. If a human must shut down a piece of hardware when the temperature goes over a threshold, the software that reads the temperature and displays it for the human operator is safety-critical. All the software along the chain, from reading the hardware temperature sensor, converting the value to appropriate units, to displaying the data on the screen are safety-critical.

Software that performs off-line processes may be considered safety-critical as well. For example, software that verifies a software or hardware hazard control must operate correctly. Failure of the test software may allow a potential hazard to be missed. In addition, **software used in analyses that verify hazard controls or safety-critical software** must also function correctly, to prevent inadvertently overlooking a hazard. Modeling and simulation programs are two types of off-line software that may be safety-critical. Very often we rely on our software models and simulators to predict how part or all of a system may react. The system may be modeled to represent stressed or "normal" operations. Based on those modeled reactions, changes may be made in the design of the hardware, software, and/or operator procedures. If the system model fails to properly depict safety critical situations, design errors may go undetected.

 If the **software resides with safety-critical software on the same physical platform**, it must also be considered safety-critical unless adequately partitioned from the safety-critical portion. Non-safety-critical software (such as a data massaging algorithm) could lock up the computer or write over critical memory areas when sharing a CPU or any routines with the safety-critical software. Techniques such as firewalls and partitioning can be used to ensure that the non-safety-critical software does not interrupt or disrupt the safety-critical functions and operations.

In summary, software is safety-critical if it performs any of the following:

- o Controls hazardous or safety-critical hardware or software.
- o Monitors safety-critical hardware or software as part of a hazard control.
- o Provides information upon which a safety-related decision is made.
- o Performs analysis that impacts automatic or manual hazardous operations.
- o Verifies hardware or software hazard controls.
- o Can prevent safety-critical hardware or software from functioning properly.

2.1.4   How Does Software Control Hazards?

In the past, hardware controls were the primary method used to control (i.e. prevent) hardware hazards. Today, because of the complexity of systems, it may not be feasible to have *only* hardware controls, or to have any hardware controls at all. Now, many hardware hazard causes are addressed with software hazard controls. Often this is because of the quick reaction time needed to respond to a failure or the complexity of detecting possible faults and errors before they become failures.

Some examples of software controls are:

- Monitor hazardous hardware (via instrumentation) and execute a corrective action if deviations are outside of established limits. For example, turn off a power supply (or reduce power) when it is in an over-voltage condition.

- Monitor potential hazardous conditions (e.g. temperature) and warn operators. For example, sound an alarm when the pressure goes above a predefined threshold.

- Inhibit certain activities in operational states that could lead to a hazardous event, such as preventing a chamber door from being opened during experiment sequences while toxic gases are present.

2.1.5 Relationship Between Software and Hardware Controls

NASA relies primarily on hardware controls, in conjunction with software controls, to prevent hazards. Hardware controls are well known and understood, and have a better "track record" than software. However, software is often the first line of defense, monitoring for unsafe conditions and responding appropriately. The software may perform an automatic safing operation, or provide a message to a human operator, for example. The hardware control is the backup to the software control. If the software fails to detect the problem or does not respond properly to alleviate the condition, then the hardware control is triggered.

Using a pressurized system as an example, the software monitors a pressure sensor. If the pressure goes over some threshold, the software would respond by stopping the flow of gas into the system by closing a valve. If the software failed, either by not detecting the over-pressurization or by not closing the valve, then the hardware pressure relief valve would be triggered once the pressure reached a critical level.

 While software controls can be, and are, used to prevent hazards, they must be implemented with care. Special attention needs to be placed on this software during the development process. When there are no hardware controls to back up the software, the software must undergo even more rigorous development and testing. This guidebook provides guidance for the development, analysis, and testing of all such software. The amount of effort to develop and assure safety-critical software will be determined by the degree of criticality of the software, as described in Chapter 3.

2.1.6 Caveats with Software Hazard Controls

When software is used to control a hazard, some care must be made to isolate it from the hazard cause it is controlling. For a hazard cause outside of the computer-processing arena (e.g. stuck valve), the hazard control software can be co-located with the regular operations software. Partitioning of the hazard control software is recommended. Otherwise, all of the software must be treated as safety-critical because of potential "contamination" from the non-critical code.

If the hazard cause is erroneous software, then the hazard control software can reside on a separate computer processor from the one where the hazard/anomaly might occur. Another option would be to implement a firewall or similar system to isolate the hazard control software, even though it shares the same processor as that where the potential hazard cause may occur.

If the hazard cause is a processor failure, then the hazard control *must* be located on another processor, since the failure would most likely affect its own software's ability to react to that CPU hardware failure. This is a challenging aspect of software safety, because multiprocessor architectures are costly and can add significant complexity (which in itself can increase the possibility of software failures). A single computer is inherently zero failure tolerant. Many system designers believe that computers fail safe, whereas NASA experience has shown that computers may exhibit hazardous failure modes. Another fallacy is to believe that upon any fault or failure detection, the safest action is always to shut down a program or computer automatically. Instead, this action could cause a more serious hazardous condition. Consider shutting down a computer which is your only means of monitoring, detecting, or controlling many potential hazards due to one program or module failure. Self detection and isolation of the problem area may be much less hazardous, allowing the problem to be corrected or mitigated.

2.1.7 What is Fault or Failure Tolerance?

A fault is any change in the state of an item which is considered anomalous and may warrant some type of corrective action. A failure is the inability of a system or component to perform its required functions within specified performance requirements.

- A fault may or may not lead to a failure.
- One or more faults can become a failure.
- All failures are the result of one or more faults.

Fault tolerance is the ability of the system to withstand an unwanted event and maintain a safe and operational condition. It is determined by the number of faults that can occur in a system or subsystem without the occurrence of a failure. Fault and failure tolerance are often used synonymously, though they are different.

Fault tolerance usually is concerned with detecting and recovering from small defects before they can become larger failures. Error detection and handling is one example of fault-tolerant coding practices. Failure tolerance is concerned with maintaining the system in a safe state despite a failure within the system. Creating failure tolerance requires a system-wide approach to the software and hardware design, so that a failure does not lead to an unsafe state. Depending on the failure and the failure tolerance mechanism, the system may operate normally or with reduced functionality.

System failure or fault tolerance is often described as the number of failures or faults the system can handle and continue functioning at some level. A one failure tolerant system can continue functioning after a single failure has occurred. A second failure would lead to a failed system or the system in an unsafe state. Likewise, a two failure tolerant system requires three failures before the system becomes unsafe or fails to continue normal operations.

While a failed system is not good, it may still be safe. Failure tolerance becomes a safety issue when the failures occur in hazard controls. To prevent a hazard, at least one control must be functioning at all times. NASA, based on extensive experience with spacecraft flight operations, has established levels of failure tolerance based on the hazard severity level necessary to achieve acceptable levels of risk.

- Catastrophic Hazards must be able to tolerate two hazard control failures.
- Critical Hazards must be able to tolerate a single hazard control failure.

2.2   *The System Safety Program*

A System Safety Program Plan is a prerequisite to performing development or analysis of safety-critical software. The System Safety Program Plan outlines the organizational structure, interfaces, and the required criteria for analysis, reporting, evaluation, and data retention to provide a safe product. This safety plan describes forms of analysis and provides a schedule for performing a series of these system and subsystem level analyses throughout the development cycle. It also addresses how the results of safety analyses will be communicated and the sign-off/approval process for all activities. A Safety Program Plan is usually created and maintained at an organizational or "programmatic" level. Within NASA, a program may have one or many projects. At the project level, there should also exist a safety plan which describes for that project how it will incorporate the programmatic plan requirements as well as those specific to the project.

Figure 2-1 Hazard Analysis

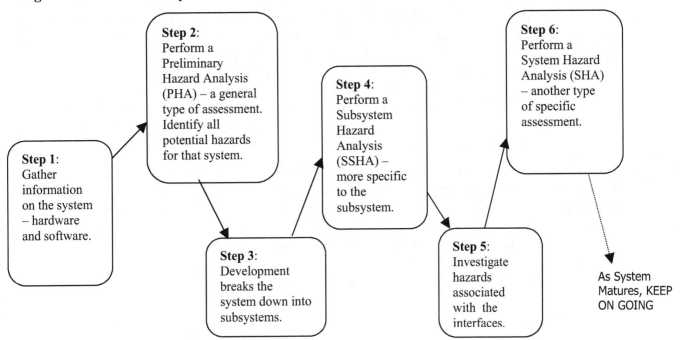

2.2.1   System Safety Process

System safety analyses follow the life cycle of the system development efforts. The system is comprised of the hardware, the software, and the interfaces between them (including human operators). What generally happens in the beginning of project development is that the hardware is conceived to perform the given tasks and the software concept is created that will operate and/or interact with the hardware. As the system develops and gains maturity, the types of safety analyses go from a single, overall assessment to ones that are more specific.

While software is often considered a subset of the complete system (a subsystem), it is actually a "coexisting" system, acting with and upon the hardware system. Because software often commands, interprets, stores and monitors the system functions, it should always be considered in a systems context.

The System Safety Project Plan should describe interfaces within the assurance disciplines as well as the other project disciplines. In practical terms, that means that all parties involved in the project should decide who is doing what analyses. Depending mostly on where the expertise resides, different organizations may be responsible for performing the necessary analyses. For instance, the software assurance engineer may perform all the software safety analyses and the software developer will perform any software development analyses. In a larger organization, or for a very critical project, there will usually be a separate software safety engineer who performs the software safety and development analyses. If the project uses an Independent Verification and Validation (IV&V) team, they will review the analyses plus possibly perform some additional analyses. All analyses and tasks should be complementary and supportive, regardless of which group (development, assurance, safety, IV&V) has the responsibility. The analyses and tasks may be distributed between the groups, and within each discipline, according to the resources and expertise of the project personnel. The project manager along with the appropriate safety and mission assurance organization must assure coverage and support for the needed safety tasks.

 Concurrent engineering can help to provide better oversight, allowing information and ideas to be exchanged between the various disciplines, reduce overlapping efforts, and improve communications throughout the project. Safety and assurance personnel bring a safety "point of view" to a project, and should be included at the earliest possible stage. The information obtained and rapport established by being an early member of the team will go a long way in solving problems later in the project. Designing in safety from the beginning is far easier, more elegant, and cheaper than late-stage alterations or additions intended to work the safety features in after the rest of the system is designed.

The Software System Safety Handbook [7] produced by the Department of Defense has an excellent reference to system safety from a risk management perspective. Chapter 3 of that document goes into detail about how risk and system safety are intertwined. Chapter 4 describes planning a software safety program, including hazard analyses. Appendix E of that document details generic requirements and guidelines for software development and test.

2.2.2 System Safety and Software Development

System safety within NASA has its own set of tasks, independent of the software development lifecycle. These tasks include:

- Creating Safety Data Packages that describe the instrument (hardware, software, and operations) and provide information on any safety hazards, controls, or mitigations.

- Conducting safety reviews through out the system lifecyle, usually Phase 0/1, Phase II, and Phase III. For all Shuttle and ISS sub-systems as well as their payloads, these reviews are conducted at Johnson Space Center before the Shuttle or ISS Safety Panel. However, local review panels may be established as pre-cursors as well as for other programs, facilities and projects.

- Conducting safety verification activities, including completing the Safety Verification Tracking Log prior to launch. The completed log shows that all safety features, controls, and fail safes are working as required.

Software safety engineers, as well as other members of the project team, will provide information and input to the system safety engineer.

Figure 2-2 illustrates the relationship between the basic System Safety life cycle (on top), the system lifecycle, and the software lifecycle. Although the tasks shown in this slide are specifically shown against the backdrop of the waterfall lifecycle, the information is still quite usable for any lifecycle model. Figure 2-2 is a pictorial representation only and should not be used to determine time, length of, or relationship in size for the various phases.

Figure 2-2 Safety, System and Software Timeline

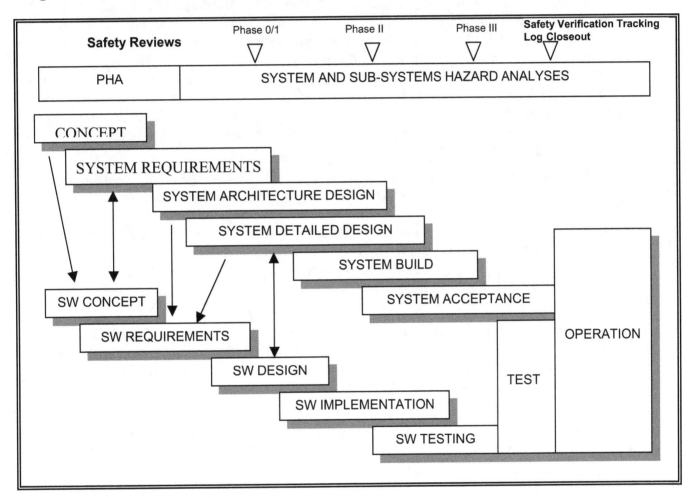

System safety activities are discussed in the next section in general terms. For more information on the NASA Space Shuttle and ISS system safety process, see NSTS 1700.7B, Safety Policy and Requirements for Payloads Using the Space Transportation System; NSTS 22254, Methodology for Conduct of Space Shuttle Program Hazard Analyses; NSTS 18798, Interpretations of NSTS Payload Safety Requirements; and JSC 26943, Guidelines for the Preparation of Payload Flight Safety Data Packages and Hazard Reports.

2.3 Safety Requirements and Analyses

The first step to any safety analysis is asking the right questions: What could go wrong? Why won't it? What if it did? Everyone involved in each activity throughout the life cycle of the system should think about all the ways the system or software can fail, how to prevent the failure from occurring, and how to prevent or mitigate an accident if the failure occurred.. Everyone has a different viewpoint and will see different hazards, different ways the system can fail, and new ways to prevent failures from occurring.

Depending on the program or project, there are many applicable safety requirements. In general, there are two types of safety requirements: 1) imposed by standards and regulations and 2) technically specific to the project and its operating environments. The requirements levied from standards, either established internally by the organization, or externally by government or industry must be sited within the project documentation as well as any tailoring for the specific project. These should be specifically written into any contracts or sub-contracts. Such requirements provide the minimum boundaries that must be met to ensure that the system is safe and will not cause harm to people, itself, other systems, or the environment. Safety requirements can include those specific to NASA, the FAA, the Department of Transportation (DOT), and even the Occupational Health and Safety Administration (OSHA).

Once the regulatory and standard safety requirements have been identified, the available specific system information is gathered to determine the project specific safety requirements. Usually, these will be derived from the first safety analysis performed during system concept and beginning requirements phase. A common assessment tool used during this beginning activity is the Preliminary Hazard Analysis (PHA). This analysis tool will be discussed in more detail in *Section 2.3.1* and *Appendix F*. The results of the PHA are a list of hazard causes and a set of candidate hazard controls, that are taken forward as inputs to the system and software safety requirements flow-down process.

 System hazard controls should be traceable to system requirements. If controls identified by the PHA are not in the system specification, safety requirements to control the hazards should be added to that document, to assure that the software specification derived from the system specification will include the necessary safety requirements.

At least one software requirement is generated for each software hazard control. Each requirement is incorporated into the Software Requirements Specification (SRS) as a safety-critical software requirement.

> **Any software item identified as a potential hazard cause, contributor, control, or mitigation, whether controlled by hardware, software or human operator, is designated as safety-critical, and subjected to rigorous software quality assurance, analysis, and testing. Safety-critical software is also traced through the software safety analysis process until the final verification. Thus, safety critical requirements need to be identified as such to insure future changes, as well as verification processes, take them into appropriate consideration.**

2.3.1 Preliminary Hazard Analysis (PHA)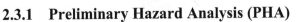

Before any system with software can be analyzed or developed for use in hazardous operations or environments, a system PHA must be performed. Once initial system PHA results are available, safety requirements are derived and flow down into the hardware and software requirements. As the specifications and design take shape, subsystem and component hazard analyses can begin. The PHA is the first source of "specific" system safety requirements and may even go so far as to point to specific software safety requirements (i.e., unique to the particular system architecture). It is a prerequisite to performing any software safety analysis as it defines the overall hazards for the system.

It is then a matter of determining software's role in potentially contributing to those hazards, or in controlling or mitigating them. When performing a PHA, it is important to consider how the software interacts with the rest of the system. Software is the heart and brains of most modern complex systems, controlling and monitoring almost all operations. When the system is decomposed into sub-elements, how the software relates to each component should be considered. The PHA should also look at how components may feed back to the software (e.g. failed sensor leading the software to respond inappropriately).

The PHA is the first of a series of system level hazard analyses, whose scope and methodology is described in NPG 8715.3, NASA Safety Manual [4], and NSTS-22254, Methodology for Conduct of Space Shuttle Program Hazard Analyses [6].

Appendix F describes the PHA process in more detail. Software safety engineers or others who may be assisting in a PHA should read that appendix. The software developer should skim the appendix, noting the information on software hazard controls and must work/must not work functions.

Note that the PHA is not a NASA-specific analysis, but is used throughout industry. IEEE 1228, Software Safety Plans, also requires that a PHA be performed.

2.3.2 Risk Levels

Hazard analyses, such as the PHA, are not primarily concerned with whether the hazard is likely to occur or not. All hazards are bad, even if their occurrence is highly improbable. However, unlimited time and money are usually not available to address all possible hazards. The hazards must somehow be prioritized. This prioritization leads to the concept of **risk**.

Risk is the combination of 1) the probability (qualitative or quantitative) that a program or project will experience an undesired event such as safety mishap, compromise of security, or system component failure; and 2) the consequences, impact, or severity of the undesired event were it to occur.

Each project or program needs to define a set of "hazard severity" levels, using definitions prescribed in Agency policy, procedures, and standards. Organization-wide definitions should be used, if available and appropriate. Having a common language helps when team members from different disciplines discuss the system and software hazards, causes, and controls. The following definitions of hazard severity levels in Table 2-2 are from NPG 8715.3 and are included as an example.

Table 2-2 Risk Definitions

Hazard Severity Definitions	Catastrophic	Critical
	Loss of human life or permanent disability; loss of entire system; loss of ground facility; severe environmental damage	Severe injury or temporary disability; major system or environmental damage
	Moderate	**Negligible**
	Minor injury; minor system damage	No injury or minor injury; some system stress, but no system damage

Likelihood of Occurrence Definitions	Likely	Probable
	The event will occur frequently, such as greater than 1 out of 10 times.	The event will occur several times in the life of an item.
Possible	**Unlikely**	**Improbable**
Likely to occur some time in the life of an item.	Remote possibility of occurrence during the life of an item.	Very rare, possibility is like winning the lottery

As with the hazard severity definitions, each project or program needs to define the "likelihood of occurrence" of the hazard. Likelihood may be expressed in quantified probabilities or as a qualitative measure. Keep in mind that the possibility that a given hazard may occur is usually based on engineering judgment and not on hard numbers, especially where software is concerned. The definitions of likelihood of occurrence in Table 2-2 are provided as an example only, and are based on NPG 8715.3 and "Software Safety Hazard Analysis"[8].

Combining these two concepts (severity and likelihood) leads to a single *risk index* value for the hazard. This allows hazards to be prioritized and risks to be managed. Highly likely and severe hazards require a rigorous development and analysis environment. Improbable and negligible hazards require little or no extra attention, beyond the good engineering, programming, and assurance practices used by the project team.

 The System Risk Index, based on the above severity levels and likelihood of occurrence, is shown in Table 2-3 *Hazard Prioritization - System Risk Index*. This is an example only. Each program, project, or organization should create a similar risk index, using their definitions of severity and likelihood.

Table 2-3 Hazard Prioritization - System Risk Index

Severity Levels	Likelihood of Occurrence				
	Likely	Probable	Possible	Unlikely	Improbable
Catastrophic	1	1	2	3	4
Critical	1	2	3	4	5
Moderate	2	3	4	5	6
Negligible	3	4	5	6	7

1 = Highest Priority (Highest System Risk), 7 = Lowest Priority (Lowest System Risk)

Prioritizing the hazards is important for determining allocation of resources and acceptance of risk. For NASA, hazards with the highest risk, Level 1, are not permitted in a system design. A system design exhibiting "1" for hazard risk index must be redesigned to eliminate or mitigate the hazard probability of occurrence and/or severity level to within an acceptable range. The lowest risk indices, "5" and above, require minimal, if any, safety analysis or controls. For the Levels 2, 3, and 4, the amount of safety analysis required increases with the level of risk. The extent of a safety effort is discussed within Chapter 3, where three levels of safety analysis - Minimum, Moderate, and Full - are described. The three levels of safety analysis correspond to risk as follows:

Table 2-4 System Risk Index

System Risk Index	Class of Safety Activities Recommended
1	Not Applicable as is (Prohibited)
2	Full
3	Moderate
4,5*	Minimum
6,7	None (Optional)

*Level 5 systems fall between Minimum and Optional, and should be evaluated to determine the class of safety activities required.

2.3.3 NASA Policy for Hazard Elimination and Control

The NASA policy towards hazards of Risk Index 2, 3 or 4/5 is defined in NPG 8715.3, paragraph3.4. Hazards are mitigated according to the following stated order of precedence:

- **Eliminate Hazards**

   Hazards are eliminated where possible. This is best accomplished through design, such as by eliminating an energy source. For example, software could have the ability to affect a pressure control. If software access to the control is not needed, and malfunctioning software could lead to a hazard, then preventing software's access to the control removes the possibility of software's contribution to the hazard. From a system perspective, hazard elimination would be in the form of choosing a design solution that does not require hazardously high pressure.

- **Design for Minimum Hazards**

  Hazards that cannot be eliminated must be controlled. For those hazards, the PHA evaluates what can cause the hazards, and suggests how to control them. Control by design is preferred. The hazard may be minimized by providing failure tolerance (e.g. by redundancy - series and/or parallel as appropriate), by providing substantial margins of safety, or by providing automatic safing. For example, software verifies that all conditions are met prior to ignition of rocket engines.

- **Incorporate Safety Devices**

  An example of a safety device is a fire detection and prevention system that detects and interacts with a fire event. Software may be a part of these devices, and may also provide one of the triggers for the safety devices, such as turning on a sprinkler system, sounding an alarm, or flooding the area with an oxygen suppression gas.

- **Provide Caution And Warning**

  Software may monitor one or more sensors and trigger a caution or warning alarm or announcement. Any software used in these caution and warning devices is safety-critical.

- **Develop Administrative Procedures and Training**

  Control by procedure is sometimes allowed, where sufficient time exists for a flight crewmember or ground controller to perform a safing action. The concept of "time to criticality" is an important design aspect of the software/hardware/human interaction in controlling safety critical situations.

2.3.4 Software Subsystem Hazard Analysis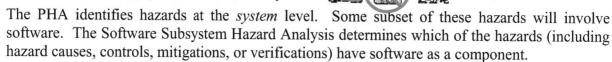

The PHA identifies hazards at the *system* level. Some subset of these hazards will involve software. The Software Subsystem Hazard Analysis determines which of the hazards (including hazard causes, controls, mitigations, or verifications) have software as a component.

 At the beginning of a project, the design is high-level and fluid. While some software functional areas may be identified early on, many more will become apparent as the design matures. It is vital to revisit this analysis regularly, as more detail emerges. Also, a shift of functionality from hardware to software is common during the design process. As the design progresses and possibly changes, system, software, safety and assurance engineering must consider the potential impact to safety. The system and/or software safety engineers update this analysis as the design and implementation progress, or when the system changes.

The procedure for a Software Subsystem Hazard Analysis is fairly simple. The hazards listed on the Preliminary Hazard List (PHL) are examined for a software component. Those that have software as a cause, control, mitigation, or verification are put on a Software Hazard List. The system and software specifications are examined to verify that the software functions identified on the hazard list are included as safety-critical requirements.

Software may impact a hazard in several ways.

- **Software failure may lead to a hazard occurring (hazard cause).** For example, software may incorrectly command a mechanical arm to move past its operational limit, resulting in the arm damaging nearby equipment or causing injury. A failure in a data conversion function could incorrectly report a temperature value, allowing a furnace door to be opened when the temperature inside is at a dangerous level.

- **Failure of a software hazard control may allow a hazard to occur.** Software that monitors pressure and opens a valve when it reaches a threshold may be a hazard control. Failure of that software would allow an over-pressurization of the vessel and a potential for a rupture or other hazard.

- **Software safing mode (move from hazardous to non-hazardous state) may fail.** Failure of the software to detect or shut down a runaway electromechanical device (such as a robotic arm or scan platform) is an example of such an impact.

- **Software used to mitigate the consequences of accident may fail.** As an example, software controlling the purging of toxic gases (which resulted from a failure in some other portion of the system) may fail, allowing the gases to remain in the chamber or be vented inappropriately to the outside air.

- **Software used to verify hazard hardware or software hazard controls may fail.** Failure in this situation would be due to invalid results (either verifying a control when it really failed or failing a control when it actually works). "False positives" may allow a potentially hazardous system to be put into operation.

When conducting the Software Subsystem Hazard Analysis, it is important to consider many types of failures. Examples of failures to consider are:

- Sensors or actuators stuck at some value (all zeros, all ones, some other value)
- Value above or below range
- Value in range but incorrect
- Physical units incorrect
- Wrong data type or data size
- Incorrect operator input
- Overflow or underflow in calculation
- Algorithm incorrect
- Shared data corrupted
- Out of sequence event
- Failure to meet timing requirement
- Memory usage problems
- Data overflow due to inappropriate data packet or data arrives too quickly
- Data sampling rate not sufficient to detect changes
- One task failing to release shared resource
- Deadlocking in a multitasking system
- Effects of either system or computer hardware failures on the software

"Software Safety Hazard Analysis" [94], prepared for the US Nuclear Regulatory Commission, is an excellent reference for details on performing the Software Subsystem Hazard Analysis.

Software safety analyses are conducted throughout the development cycle of the software. **It is important to reexamine software's role and safety impact throughout the system development phases.** Software's role is often altered to accommodate system changes or work around hardware problems. Additions to the system's functionality can result in additions and/or changes to the hazards as well as functionality. As the software changes, hazard contributions may be added, deleted, or their criticality modified. These changes to the safety-critical software functionality must be reflected in the requirements, design, implementation, and verification of the system and software.

The following sections describe these various software safety analyses. Chapter 3 provides guidance on tailoring the number of analyses required to match the risk of the software hazards. Other software safety analyses, such as Software Fault Tree Analysis (SFTA), Software Failure Modes and Effects Analysis (SFMEA), requirements Criticality Analysis (CA), and specification analysis, are described in Chapters 5 through 10.

Chapter 3   Software Safety Planning

If the Preliminary Hazard Analysis (PHA) reveals that any software is safety-critical, a software safety process must be initiated. This chapter describes how to plan the software safety effort, and how to tailor it according to the level of risk of the system and software.

Determination of the level of safety risk inherent in the **system** was presented in Section 2.3.2 *Risk Levels*. This chapter focuses on the risk level of the **software**. Once the risk level is determined (i.e., a risk index is assigned), the amount of effort that must be expended to assure safe software can be estimated.

Figure 3-1 Participants in a Successful Safety Process

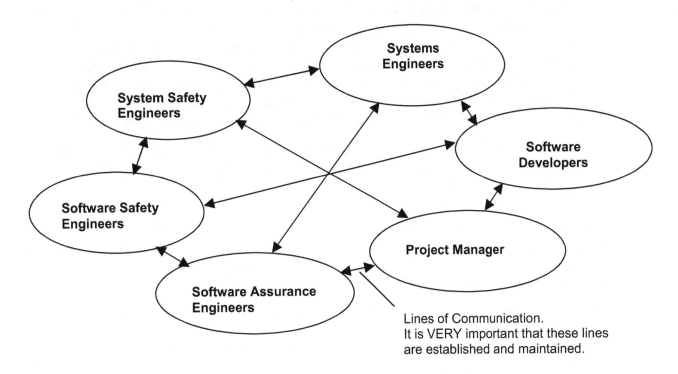

Each discipline involved in the project has a role to play in the creation of safe software.

- The **project manager** maintains a high-level overview of the whole process, works with the team to include the extra software development and analysis tasks in the schedule and budget, and can be called on to help in negotiations between team members. When questions arise as to the necessity of a particular analysis or development technique, the project manager is usually the final authority. Ultimately, the Project Manager determines the amount and types of risk they are willing to accept for their project. They may be required to work with, utilize, and pay for a certain amount of Independent Verification and Validation, but they determine the balance of overall safety analyses, verification, and validation to take place.   SMA and IV&V provide an independent reporting path to assure that an appropriate amount of safety analysis, design and verification does take place.

- **Systems engineers** are responsible for designing the system and partitioning the elements between hardware and software. Because they see the "big picture," they have a unique perspective. System developers can make sure that safety-critical elements are not overlooked in the initial analyses. As system elements shift from hardware to software later in the design process, these engineers can make sure that the criticality of the design component is also transferred.

- **System safety engineers** determine what components of the system are hazardous. They look at the system as a whole entity, but also need to understand how the different elements function (or fail to function).

- **Software safety engineers** build on the work of the system safety engineers. They look closely at the requirements and development process to verify that software safety requirements are present and being designed in. They perform analyses and tests to verify the safety of the software. The software safety engineer works in conjunction with the system safety organization to develop software safety requirements, distribute those safety requirements to the software developers, and monitor their implementation. The software safety engineer also analyzes software products and artifacts to identify new hazards and new hazard causes to be controlled, and provides the results to the system safety organization to be integrated with the other (non-software) subsystem analyses.

- **Software developers** are the "in the trenches" engineers who design, code, and often test the system. They are responsible for implementing all the requirements in the software system. Software developers can have a great impact on the safety of the software by the design chosen and by implementing defensive programming techniques.

- **Software Assurance** engineers work with the software developers and software safety engineers to assure that safe software is created. They monitor development processes, assure the traceability of all requirements, perform or review analyses, witness or perform tests, and provide an "outside view" of both the software process and products.

- **Independent Verification and Validation (IV&V).** For all NPG 7120.5 and all safety critical projects, the project manager is required to perform a self assessment of the project software and report the findings to the NASA IV&V Facility and local SMA organization. (See NPD/NPG 8730.1, Software Independent Verification and Validation Policy/Guidance.) The IV&V Facility may then perform their own review and present the project manager with their estimate for additional analyses. IV&V is in *addition* to software assurance and software safety and not a replacement for those roles.

In a small team, there may not be a separate software safety engineer. The software assurance engineer, the system safety engineer, the system developer, or someone from the software development team may take on this role, depending on the individual's expertise. Several people working cooperatively may also share the software safety role.

Software assurance functions within the overall project and software development processes and can be a key factor in developing safer software. For safety, the objectives of the software assurance process are to:

- Develop software that has fewer defects (and therefore fewer safety-related defects). Software assurance and IV&V can provide guidance on best practices and process improvements that may reduce the required effort to develop the software and/or the number of inherent defects.

- Find the defects earlier in the lifecycle, when they are less costly to correct.

- Assure the safety of the software, contributing to the assurance of system safety.

- Help the project stay within budget and schedule by eliminating problems and risk early on.

- Reduce the software-related risks (safety, reliability, mission success, etc.)

Chapter 4 presents an overview of the software development process, including various life-cycle models. Chapters 5 through 10 discuss the various analysis and development tasks used throughout the software development life cycle. The division of the tasks and analyses into conception, requirements, design, implementation, verification, and maintenance phases does not imply a waterfall lifecycle. These concepts are applicable to all lifecycles, though at different times and to varying degrees.

3.1   Scoping the Software for the Safety Effort

The System Risk Index specified the hazard risk for the system *as a whole*. The software element of the system inherits from the system risk, modified by the extent with which the software controls, mitigates, or interacts with the hazardous elements. In addition, the complexity of the software and the development environment play a role. Merging these two aspects is not an exact science, and the information presented in this section is meant to guide the scoping and then tailoring of the safety effort. The numerous charts provided are to be used only as a starting point when determining the level of safety effort.

The process of scoping the software safety effort begins with the determination of how much software is involved with the hazardous aspects of the system. The PHA, Software Hazard Analysis, Software Risk Assessments, and other analyses provide information for determining whether systems and subsystems should be initially categorized as safety-critical.

Scoping the software safety effort can be accomplished by following three steps:

> 1. Identify safety-critical software
>
> 2. Determine safety-critical software criticality (i.e., how critical is it?)
>
> 3. Determine the extent of development effort and oversight required

The third scoping step actually leaves the project manager with choices in how to meet the needed development and oversight levels. Using the information gained from the scoping process, as well as input from the safety and assurance engineers, the project manager can better tailor the effort and oversight needed for a particular project.

3.1.1   Identify Safety-Critical Software

Before deciding how to apply software safety techniques to a project, it is important to first determine if there is even a safety concern. The initial criteria for determining if software is safety-critical is found in section 2.1.3.

Reliability is also a factor when determining whether software is safety-critical. Most aerospace products are built up from small, simple components to make large, complex systems. Electronic components usually have a small number of states and can be tested exhaustively, due to their low cost, to determine their inherent reliability. Mechanical components have similar means to determine their predictable, usable life span when used within predefined environmental and operational limits. Reliability of a large hardware system is determined by developing reliability models using failure rates of the components that make up the system. Reliability and safety goals of hardware systems can usually be reached through a combination of redundant design configurations and selection of components with suitable reliability ratings.

Reliability of software can be hard to determine, and as yet, is mostly qualitative and not quantitatively expressed. Software does not wear out or break down. It may have a large number of states that cannot be fully tested. For example, an important difference between hardware and software is that many of the mathematical functions implemented by software are not continuous functions, but functions with an arbitrary number of discontinuities. Although mathematical logic can be used to deal with functions that are not continuous, the resulting software may have a large number of states and lack regularity. It is usually impossible to establish reliability values and prove correctness of design by testing all possible states of a medium to large (more than 40,000-50,000 lines of code) software system within a reasonable amount of time.

Much of the software used within NASA is "one-off" code, that is written once for a particular operation/mission and then never used again. That is, there is little to no reuse and thus there is little record of long term use to provide statistics on software reliability. Even code used several times, such as that for the Shuttle operations, is often modified. Reliability estimation requires extensive software testing. Except in the rare cases where formal methods are used to capture the requirements and/or design, testing can only commence after preliminary code has been generated, typically late in the development cycle. At that point, exhaustive testing is not in the schedule or budget. As a result, it is very difficult to establish accurate reliability and design correctness values for software.

If the inherent reliability of software cannot be accurately measured or predicted, and most software designs cannot be exhaustively tested, the level of effort required to meet safety goals must be determined using other characteristics of the system. The following characteristics have a strong influence on the ability of software developers to create reliable, safe software:

- **Degree of Control:** *The degree of control that the software exercises over safety-critical functions in the system.*

  Software that can cause a hazard if it malfunctions is considered safety-critical software. Software which is required to either recognize hazardous conditions and implement automatic safety control actions, provide a safety-critical service, or inhibit a hazardous event, will require more software safety resources and detailed assessments than software which is only required to recognize hazardous conditions and notify a human operator to take necessary safety actions. Human operators must then have redundant sources of data independent of software, allowing them to detect and correctly react to misleading software data before a hazard can occur.

Fatal accidents have occurred involving poorly designed human computer interfaces, such as the *Therac-25 X-ray machine* [9]. In cases where an operator relies only on software monitoring of critical functions, then a complete safety effort <u>is</u> required.

- **Complexity:** *The complexity of the software system. Greater complexity increases the chances of errors.*

  The number of safety related software requirements for hazards control increases software complexity. Some rough measures of complexity include the number of subsystems controlled by software and the number of interfaces between software/hardware, software/user and software/software subsystems. Interacting, parallel executing processes also increase complexity. Note that quantifying system complexity can only be done when a high level of design maturity exists (i.e., detail design or coding phases). Software complexity can be estimated based on the number and types of logical operations it performs. Complexity metrics are further discussed in <u>section 7.4.8</u>.

- **Timing criticality:** *The timing criticality of hazardous control actions.*

  The speed at which a system with software hazard control must react is a major factor. Does control need to be exercised faster than a human or mechanical system can react? With the advent of software control, faults can be detected and countered prior to becoming full failures. Thus, even embedded real-time software systems which need microseconds to react to some critical situations can be designed to detect and avoid hazards as well as control them one they occur. How fast must the system respond? That depends on the system. For example, spacecraft that travel beyond Earth orbit need a turnaround time of possibly hours or days in order to notify a ground human operator of a possible hazard and wait for return commands on how to proceed. That is likely to exceed the time it takes for the hazard to occur. Thus, on-board software and/or hardware must deal with the situation autonomously.

You've determined 1) the function that software is to perform is safety critical, 2) the needed level of control, 3) the system complexity, and 4) the required time to react to prevent a hazard from occurring. The next step is to define the degree of the software criticality, which will translate to the level of software safety effort.

3.1.2 Determine Software Safety- Criticality

Once software has been identified as safety-critical, further analyses such as the Software Failure Modes and Effects Analyses (SFMEA) or Software Fault Tree Analyses (SFTA) will help to determine the criticality rating.

The following sections describe how to determine the **software** risk index. This is an extension of the system risk index shown in <u>Table 2-3</u>. The level of software risk will determine the extent of the software safety effort. Software with low risk will require less effort (analyses, tests, development activities) than software that is high-risk. This exercise will need to be refined as the design architecture and implementation reveal how the functionality is modularized, or not. At first, it may be determined that all the software is safety critical, and that may be the final answer. However, if the safety critical functions can be encapsulated or segregated to some degree within certain routines or objects, then a more refined safety design and analysis approach can be made.

3.1.2.1 Software Control Categories

The degree of control the software exercises over system functions is one factor in determining the extent of the safety effort required. A reference source of definitions for software control categories is from MIL-STD-882C. MIL-STD-882C [10] has been replaced by MIL-STD-882D, which does not reference the software control categories. MIL-STD-882C categorized software according to its degree of control of the system, as follows:

Table 3-1 MIL STD 882C Software Control Categories

Software Control Category	Degree of Control
IA.	Software exercises autonomous control over potentially hazardous hardware systems, subsystems or components without the possibility of intervention to preclude the occurrence of a hazard. Failure of the software, or a failure to prevent an event, leads directly to a hazard's occurrence.
IIA.	Software exercises control over potentially hazardous hardware systems, subsystems, or components allowing time for intervention by independent safety systems to mitigate the hazard. However, these systems by themselves are not considered adequate.
IIB.	Software item displays information requiring immediate operator action to mitigate a hazard. Software failures will allow, or fail to prevent, the hazard's occurrence.
IIIA.	Software item issues commands over potentially hazardous hardware systems, subsystems or components requiring human action to complete the control function. There are several, redundant, independent safety measures for each hazardous event.
IIIB.	Software generates information of a safety-critical nature used to make safety-critical decisions. There are several redundant, independent safety measures for each hazardous event.
IV.	Software does not control safety-critical hardware systems, subsystems or components and does not provide safety-critical information.

Complexity also increases the possibility of errors. Errors lead to the possibility of fault, which can lead to failures. The following chart builds on what we have from MIL-STD 882C and takes into consideration the complexity of the software. The chart also relates back to the system risk index discussed in Section 2.3.2 *Risk Levels* and has already eliminated System Risk Index level 1 (prohibited) and levels beyond 5 (negligible risk). The software category links the complexity of the software, the control that the software exerts on a system, the time to criticality, and the system risk index. This information is used to create a Software Risk Matrix (see Table 3-3).

Table 3-2 Software Control Categories

Software Control Categories	Descriptions
IA (System Risk Index 2)	Partial or total autonomous control of safety-critical functions by software.
	Complex system with multiple subsystems, interacting parallel processors, or multiple interfaces.
	Some or all safety-critical functions are time critical.
IIA & IIB* (System Risk Index 3)	Control of hazard but other safety systems can partially mitigate.
	Detects hazards, notifies human operator of need for safety actions.
	Moderately complex with few subsystems and/or a few interfaces, no parallel processing.
	Some hazard control actions may be time critical but do not exceed time needed for adequate human operator or automated system response.
IIIA & III B* (System Risk Index 4)	Several mitigating systems prevent hazard if software malfunctions.
	Redundant sources of safety-critical information.
	Somewhat complex system, limited number of interfaces.
	Mitigating systems can respond within any time critical period.
IV (System Risk Index 5)	No control over hazardous hardware.
	No safety-critical data generated for a human operator.
	Simple system with only 2-3 subsystems, limited number of interfaces.
	Not time-critical.

Note: System risk index number is taken from Table 2-3 *Hazard Prioritization - System Risk Index*
* A = software control of hazard. B = Software generates safety data for human operator

3.1.2.2 Software Risk Matrix

The Software Risk Matrix is established using the hazard categories for the columns and the Software Control Categories (Table 3-2 above) for the rows. The next matrix relates the software control of a hazard to the system severity levels. A Software Risk Index is assigned to each element of the matrix, just as System Risk Index numbers are assigned in the Hazard Prioritization - System Risk Index (Table 2-3) matrix.

NOTE: The *Software* Risk Index is **NOT** the same as the *System* Risk Index, though the two may appear similar. The difference is mainly that the System Risk Index of 1 (prohibited) has already been eliminated.

Unlike the System Risk Index, a low index number from the Software Risk Matrix does not mean that a design is unacceptable. Rather, it indicates that greater resources need to be applied to the analysis and testing of the software and its interaction with the system.

Table 3-3 Software Risk Matrix

Software Control Category	Hazard Category*			
	Catastrophic	Critical	Moderate	Negligible or Marginal
IA (System Risk Index 2)	1	1	3	4
IIA & IIB (System Risk Index 3)	1	2	4	5
IIIA & IIIB (System Risk Index 4)	2	3	5	5
IV (System Risk Index 5)	3**	4**	5	5

Note: System risk index number is taken from _Table 2-3_ *Hazard Prioritization - System Risk Index*

* Hazard Category definitions are provided in Table 2-2.

** All software in a safety-critical system must be evaluated. If software has the potential to compromise system safety elements, then it must be treated as safety-critical.

 The interpretation of the Software Risk Index is given in Table 3-4. The level of risk determines the amount of analysis and testing that should be applied to the software.

Table 3-4 Software Risk Index

Software Risk Index	Risk Definition
1	High Risk: Software controls catastrophic or critical hazards
2	Medium Risk: Software control of catastrophic or critical hazards is reduced, but still significant.
3-4	Moderate Risk: Software control of less significant hazards
5	Low Risk: Negligible hazard or little software control

Figure 3-2 shows the relationships among the various risk indices and software criteria. The System Risk Index feeds into the Software Risk Index, modified by the software categories. The modification relates to how much control the software has over the hazard, either potentially causing the hazard or in controlling or mitigating the hazard. Note that the Software Risk Index relates to only a subset of the System Risk Index, because the riskiest level (System Index 1) is prohibited, and the levels with the least system risk do not require a safety effort.

Figure 3-2 Relationship of Risk Indices

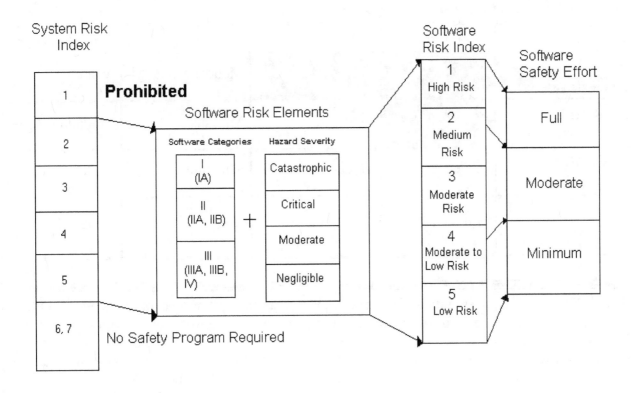

3.1.3 Determine the Safety Effort and Oversight Required

3.1.3.1 Determine Extent of Safety Effort

The Software Risk Index (Table 3-3) determines the level of required software safety effort for a system (Table 3-5 *Required Software Safety Effort*). The mapping is essentially: Software Risk Index 1 = full effort, Software Risk Index 2 and 3 = moderate effort, and Software Risk Index 4 and 5 = minimum effort. However, if the Software Risk Index is 2, consider whether it is a "high" 2 (closer to level 1 – more risk). A high 2 should follow the full safety effort, or somewhere between full and moderate. Also, if the Software Risk Index is a high 4, then the safety effort falls into the moderate category.

Note that category IV software, which does not participate in any hazardous functions, may still require a minimum software safety effort. Normally, no safety effort would be needed for such software. However, with catastrophic and critical hazards, non-safety-critical software should be evaluated for possible failures and unexpected behavior that could lead to the hazard or to the compromise of a hazard control or mitigation.

Further explanation of **Full**, **Moderate**, and **Minimum** software safety effort is found in Section 3.2.

Table 3-5 Required Software Safety Effort

Software Category	Hazard Severity Level from Table 2-2			
See Table 3-3	Catastrophic	Critical	Moderate	Negligible / Marginal
IA (Software Risk Index 1)	Full	Full	Moderate	Minimum
IIA & IIB (Software Risk Index 2/3)	Full	Moderate	Minimum	Minimum
IIIA & IIIB (Software Risk Index 4/5)	Moderate	Moderate	Minimum	None
IV Software does not directly control hazardous operations.	Minimum	Minimum	None	None

> **WARNING: Requirements are subject to change as the system design progresses!** Often items that were assigned to hardware are determined to be better (or more cheaply) developed in software. Some of those items may be safety-critical. As system elements are redistributed, it is **vital** to revisit the software safety effort determination. If the new requirements lead to software controlling hazardous hardware, then more effort needs to be applied to the software safety program.

3.1.3.2 Oversight Required

The level of software quality assurance and independent oversight required for safety assurance depends on the system risk index as follows:

Table 3-6 Degree of Oversight vs. System Risk

Software Risk Index	System Risk Index	Degree of Oversight
	1	Not applicable (Prohibited)
1	2	Fully independent IV & V[1] organization, as well as in-house SA
2	3	In house SA organization; Possible software IA[1]
3	4	In house SA organization
4,5	5-7	Minimal in house Software Assurance (SA)

---

[1] NASA NPG 8730.x (draft) "Software Independent Verification and Validation (IV&V) Management" details the criteria for determining if a project requires IV&V or Independent Assessment (IA). This NPG should be followed by all NASA projects when establishing the level of IV&V or IA required.

The level of oversight indicated in the preceding table is for safety purposes, not for mission success. The oversight required for a project would be the greater of that required for either mission success or safety purposes.

A full-scale software safety development effort is typically performed on a safety-critical flight system, (e.g., a human space flight vehicle, or high value one-of-a-kind spacecraft or aircraft, critical ground control systems, critical facilities, critical ground support equipment, payloads on expendable vehicles.). Other types of aerospace systems, such as non-critical ground control systems, facilities, and ground support equipment, or unmanned payloads on expendable vehicles, often use less rigorous development programs. In these cases, subsets of the software safety development and analysis tasks can be used.

3.2   Tailoring the Software Safety Effort

Once the scope of the software safety effort has been determined, it is time to tailor it to a given project or program. The safety activities should be sufficient to match the software development effort and yet ensure that the overall system will be safe.

The scope of the software development and software safety effort is dependent on risk. Software safety tasks related to lifecycle phases are listed within the development phase chapters (Chapters 5 through 10) of this guidebook. A recommendation[2] is given for each technique or analysis and each software safety effort level (full, moderate, and minimum). Software developers may employ several techniques for each development phase, based on a project's level of software safety effort. At the very minimum, a project must review all pertinent specifications, designs, implementations, tests, engineering change requests, and problem/failure reports to determine if any hazards have been inadvertently introduced. Software assurance activities should always verify that all safety requirements can be traced to specific design features, to specific program sets or code elements, and to specific tests conducted to exercise safety control functions of software (See Section 6.6.1 *Software Safety Requirements Flow-down Analysis*).

 Each NASA project, regardless of its level of safety-criticality, must perform an IV&V evaluation at the beginning of the project, and whenever the project changes significantly. NPD 8730.4 describes the process and responsibilities of all parties. IV&V provides for independent evaluation of the project software, including additional analyses and tests performed by the IV&V personnel. This is in addition to any analyses and tests performed by the project Software Assurance.

If your system will include off-the-shelf software (COTS, GOTS), reused software from another project, or software developed by a contractor, refer to Chapter 12 *Software Acquisition*.

2

Recommendation Codes			
★	Mandatory	✓✓	Highly Recommended
✓	Recommended	⊘	Not Recommended

"Not Recommended" are expensive relative to the required level of effort and the expected benefits. "Recommended" techniques may be performed if extra assurance of safety or mission success is desired. "Highly Recommended" entries should receive serious consideration for inclusion in system development. If not included, it should be shown that safety is not compromised. "Mandatory" are required.

Additional analyses and tests may need to be performed, depending on the criticality of the acquired software and the level of knowledge you have about how it was developed and tested. The level of safety effort may be higher if the COTS/reused/contracted software is safety-critical itself or interacts with the safety-critical software.

Sections 3.2.1 through 3.2.4 below help determine the appropriate methods for software quality assurance, software development, and software safety for full, moderate, and minimum safety efforts. Ultimately, the categorization of a project's software and the range of selected activities must be negotiated and approved by project management, software development, software quality assurance, and software systems safety personnel together.

Other techniques, which are not listed in this guidebook, may be used if they can be shown to produce comparable results. Ultimately, the range of selected techniques must be negotiated and approved by project management, software development, software quality assurance, and software systems safety.

The following software activities can be tailored:

Development	The use of safety features such as firewalls, arm-fire commanding, etc. depends on where it is best applied and needed. The degree to which each of these activities is performed is related to the software risk. Software Safety features should be reflected in the requirements.
Analysis	There are many types of analyses that can be completed during software development. Every phase of the lifecycle can be affected by increased analysis as a result of safety considerations. The analyses can range from Requirements Criticality Analysis to Software Fault Tree Analysis of the design to Formal Methods.
Inspections	Inspections can take place in a number of settings and with varying products (requirements to test plans). The number of inspections and products is dependent on the risk related to the system.
Reviews	The number of formal reviews and the setting up of delta reviews can be used to give the organization more places to look at the products as they are being developed.

Verification and Validation Activities	Verification checks that the system is being "built right" by determining whether the products of a given phase of software development fulfill the requirements established during the previous phase. Verification methods include analysis, review, inspection, testing, and auditing. Validation checks that the "right product" is being built, with testing as the usual primary method.
	The number of tests, amount of code subjected to detailed testing, and the level of test coverage can be tailored. The frequency of Software Assurance and Safety audits of development processes and products, as well as the number of products to be audited, can also be tailored. Analyses, inspections, and reviews are discussed in the paragraphs above.

3.2.1 "Full" Software Safety Effort

Systems and subsystems that have severe hazards which can escalate to major failures in a very short period of time require the greatest level of software safety effort. Some examples of these types of systems include life support, fire detection and control, propulsion/pressure systems, power generation and conditioning systems, and pyrotechnics or ordnance systems. These systems may require a formal, rigorous program of quality and safety assurance to ensure complete coverage and analysis of all requirements, design, code, and tests. Safety analyses, software development analyses, safety design features, and Software Assurance (SA) oversight are highly recommended. In addition, IV&V activities may be required.

3.2.2 "Moderate" Software Safety Effort

Systems and subsystems which fall into this category typically have either 1) a limited hazard potential or 2) the response time for initiating hazard controls to prevent failures is long enough to allow for human operators to respond to the hazardous situation. Examples of these types of systems include microwave antennas, low power lasers, and shuttle cabin heaters. These systems require a rigorous program for safety assurance of software identified as safety-critical. Non-safety-critical software must be regularly monitored to ensure that it cannot compromise safety controls or functions. Some analyses are required to assure there are no "undiscovered" safety-critical areas that may need software safety features. Some level of Software Assurance oversight is still needed to assure late design changes do not affect the safety criticality.

 A project of this level may require IV&V. However, it is more likely to require a software Independent Assessment (IA).

Software independent assessment (IA) is defined as a review of and analysis of the program/project's system software development lifecycle and products. The IA differs in scope from a full IV&V program in that IV&V is applied over the lifecycle of the system whereas an IA is usually a one time review of the existing products and plans. In many ways, IA is an outside audit of the project's development process and products (documentation, code, test results, and others).

3.2.3 "Minimum" Software Safety Effort

For systems in this category, either the inherent hazard potential of a system is very low or control of the hazard is accomplished by non-software means. Failures of these types of systems are primarily reliability concerns. This category may include such things as scan platforms and systems employing hardware interlocks and inhibits. Software development in these types of systems must be monitored on a regular basis to ensure that safety is not inadvertently compromised or that features and functions are added which make the software safety-critical. A formal program of software safety is not usually necessary. Of course, good development practices and SA are always necessary. The development activities and analyses in described in Chapters 5 through 10 can provide increased reliability as well as safety, and for a minimal effort.

3.2.4 Projects with Mixed Levels of Effort

Not all projects fall into neat categories for classification. Some projects may be large and complex, but with a small portion of safety-critical, low risk software. Other projects may be small, but a significant portion of the software is safety-critical and high risk.

Not all the software within a project needs to be treated in an identical way. Safety-critical software components can have different levels of software safety effort applied to them. High-risk safety-critical software components may undergo a "full" safety effort, while low risk safety-critical components may only undergo the "minimum" safety effort tasks and analyses.

 Too often smaller projects argue that they have no safety-critical software out of concern that the label will lead to massive amounts of work. This is not the case. Partitioning the safety-critical software from code that is not safety-critical allows the safety effort to be applied only to that safety-critical portion. Further tailoring of the software safety program to match the risk from the safety-critical portion may lead to a reduced, or at least more focused, safety effort. The extent of the software safety effort can be negotiated between the project manager, software developers, software assurance engineers, and system or software safety engineers.

Chapter 4   Safety-Critical Software Development

> **The cardinal rules for safety are:**
>
> ♦ No single event or action shall be allowed to initiate a potentially hazardous event.
>
> ♦ When an unsafe condition or command is detected, the system shall
>
>   o Inhibit the potentially hazardous event sequence.
>
>   o Initiate procedures or functions to bring the system to a predetermined "safe" state.

 We all want systems with software products that work reliably, provide required functionality, and are safe. The software we create must not allow hazardous events to occur, and must be capable of returning the system to a safe state when it has veered into dangerous territory. Software designers must be aware of the safety implications of their design, and software engineers must implement that design with care. Safety must be in the forefront of everyone's mind.

> **A structured development environment and an organization using state of the art methods are prerequisites to developing dependable safety-critical software.**

Safe software does not just "happen". It is crafted by a team of software engineers and designers from well-understood requirements. The software products are analyzed by the developer, software assurance engineers, and software safety engineers. The final code is tested, either by the developer, assurance personnel, or a separate test organization. The whole process is overseen by a manager cognizant of the entire project. All disciplines contribute to the production of safer software.

This chapter provides an overview of a safety-oriented software development process. System safety engineers unfamiliar with software development, and software developers unfamiliar with safety-critical systems, are the intended audience.

4.1   Crafting Safer Software

> **Five Rules for Creating Safer Software**
>
> 1. **Communicate**
>
> 2. **Have and Follow Good Software Engineering Practices and Procedures**
>
> 3. **Perform Safety and Development Analyses**
>
> 4. **Incorporate Appropriate Software Development Methodologies, Techniques & Design Features**
>
> 5. **Caveat Emptor**

4.1.1 Communication

Communication is an intangible process that can greatly improve the safety of the software and the system being created. Communication is more than just verbal exchange. It includes documentation, notes, email, video, and any other form of communication. It is important that all team members communicate regularly. Some goals of communication are to:

- **Prevent misunderstandings.** Everyone on the team makes assumptions as part of their work, but the assumptions are not always the same. For example, the electronic design engineer may order the bits high-to-low, but the software engineer may interpret them low-to-high. Communication – verbal or written – prevents this type of problem.

- **Identify risks before they become problems.** Communication is the center of the Risk Management paradigm (see NPR 8000.4, Risk Management Procedures and Guidelines). Brainstorming is often used to identify project risks. People from varying backgrounds and points-of-view see different risks. A diverse team, skilled in communication, will usually find better solutions to the problems.

- **Provide insight into the reasoning behind design decisions.** Knowing the reasons why a design decision was made can prevent problems when the design is changed down the road in response to a requirements change, or when "fixes" are introduced into the system.

- **Make team members aware of anomalies, problems, or other issues.** Prior to established baselines, anomaly or problem tracking is often minimal or non-existent. Regular communication provides an informal tracking system. It also promotes a cross-disciplinary approach to problems. For example, if the operators make similar mistakes, perhaps the graphical display needs to be made more user friendly.

- **Provide management with a qualitative insight into the state of the project.** Besides giving a feel for the progress, communication allows management to spot some problems early. Grumbling among the developers may indicate personality problems, management problems, or the effects of too much schedule pressure, for example. An informal communication channel between software safety and management may allow resolution of safety concerns before the problem gets out of hand.

- **Help engineers grow in knowledge and experience.** The quality of the team members has a direct effect on the safety and reliability of the software. Communication helps junior engineers learn from the experiences of more senior engineers.

Communication is one aspect of human factors in safety-critical systems. Human factors are discussed in more detail in section 11.9.

4.1.2 Good Software Engineering Practices and Procedures

Before beginning software development, processes and methodologies need to be selected from those available. **No one process or methodology is a "silver bullet."** Intelligent selection needs to be done, matching the process with the needs, resources, and talents of the software development team. "Cutting edge" techniques or processes may not be the best choice, unless time and budget exist to allow extensive training of the development and assurance teams. Staying with a well understood process often produces better (i.e. safer and more reliable) software than following the process-of-the-year.

This guidebook cannot go into great detail on how to craft good software. Several important elements of a good development process are discussed in the following sections. The references below are just a few examples, and are provided to give a starting point for those interested in learning more about software engineering.

- *Software Engineering: A Practitioner's Approach* by Roger Pressman, 5th Edition (2001)

- *Software Engineering* 5th Edition, by I. Sommerville (1996)

- *Software Systems Engineering* by Andrew Sage and James D. Palmer.

- *Software Engineering: The Production of Quality Software* by Shari Pfleeger, 2nd Edition (1991)

- *Classic and Object-Oriented Software Engineering*, 3rd Edition, by Stephen R. Schach (1996)

- *Code Complete: A Practical Handbook of Software Construction*, by S. McConnell (1993)

- *Object-Oriented Software Engineering: A Use-Case Driven Approach*, by I. Jacobson (1997)

4.1.3 Perform Safety and Development Analyses

Well-crafted software is not the only prerequisite for safe software. Safety analyses are used to verify that the software properly addresses the safety issues. As designs change, or the design is implemented in code, analyses verify that no new hazards were introduced. Software development analyses are used to confirm that the design or code does what is needed, especially within the safety-critical areas.

Safety and development analyses are discussed in Chapters 5 through 10, coordinated with the phase of the software development. For each phase, tailoring information is provided to select the most appropriate analyses for the project.

4.1.4 Incorporate Appropriate Methodologies, Techniques, and Design Features

There are many development methodologies, techniques, and design features that can help create safer software. This guidebook does not provide an exhaustive list of all such areas. However, the following sections detail some of the development and design techniques and methodologies for crafting safer software:

Section 4.2.1	Software Lifecycles
Section 4.2.2	Design Methodologies
Section 4.2.2.3	Formal Methods
Section 4.2.2.5	Design patterns
Section 4.3.8	Software Development Capability Frameworks
Section 4.5	Software Configuration Management
Section 4.6	Programming for Safety
Section 6.5.2	Fault and Failure Tolerance
Section 6.5.5	Formal Inspections
Sections 7.4.4 and 11.1	Language selections
Sections 7.4.4 11.2, 11.3 and 11.4	Tool and Operating System selections
Sections 7.4.5 and 8.4.1	Coding Checklists, Standards, and Language restrictions
Section 7.4.6	Defensive Programming
Section 8.4.3	Refactoring
Section 11.9.3	Interface Design/Human Factors
Section 12.1.2	Integrating COTS software

4.1.5   Caveat Emptor

"Buyer Beware." COTS software and hardware are extremely common in most systems. Even if the software is developed in-house, the tools used (e.g., compiler, editor, debugger) are usually purchased. Operating systems are rarely created by the development team, but are usually procured from a commercial vendor or selected from those freely available.

 Safety is usually not on anyone's mind when they select a compiler, editor, or other tool, but it should be. **All** software must be considered potentially flawed. This isn't a cause for panic, however. Understanding how the software tool, library, operating system, or other element **could** fail is important in guarding against such a failure. Knowing that a potential failure could impact the safety of the system is the most important aspect. Don't become complacent when safety is involved!

Chapter 12 discusses issues and concerns with off-the-shelf, reused, and contracted software in more detail.

4.2 The Software Development Process

Software engineering, like mechanical, electrical, civil, or structural engineering, requires a disciplined process. No one would consider building a bridge, or a spacecraft, without using the rules for development that have become second nature to developers of hardware. With software being so flexible and "easy" to alter, it is even more important to have a disciplined and planned approach for software.

Creating *any* software involves more than just coding. For safety-critical software, having and following an appropriate development methodology that includes requirements analysis, design, and verification is essential.

A thorough software development process helps assure that:

- **All** the requirements are understood, well documented, and incorporated in the software

- The needed functionality is indeed incorporated into the system and all elements work together without conflict

- Analysis and testing have assured the viability of the product under less than friendly conditions.

The steps to a good software development process are:

- Choose a Process
  - Lifecycle (Section 4.2.1)
  - Design Methodology (Section 4.2.2)
- Manage the process (Section 4.3)
  - Metrics
  - Tasks
  - Products
  - Tools & Methods
- Tailor the process in a plan (Section 4.4)

> **At the very minimum, a project team must review all pertinent specifications, designs, implementations, tests, engineering change requests, and problem/failure reports to determine if any hazards have been introduced.**

In the software development process, software engineers ideally perform the following functions:

- Work with systems engineers, safety engineers, and assurance engineers to help formulate the software functionality and determine the role of software in this project/product. Most of this will be done at the project concept stage, though hardware and software functions may be redistributed during the system design phase. During the concept phase, when everything is flexible, is the time to propose possible technical innovations and approaches. It is also the time to begin to formulate the management plans and development plans for the software.

- Complete software management and development plans. A software management plan will include schedules, deliverables, reviews, and other details. The development plan will contain the lifecycle, methodology, language, standards, and techniques to be used to specify, design, test, manage configuration, and deliver the software. The level of detail in these documents can be tailored to match the complexity and criticality of the software.

- Analyze requirements and create the software specification. The system requirements that pertain to software must be specified and included in a software requirements document (also called a software specification). Any additional requirements (including safety requirements), standards and guidelines chosen must also be included. Analysis of those requirements assures that all requirements are included and that they are achievable and verifiable.

- Create a design that implements the requirements. Analyses assure that the design will be able to meet the functional and performance requirements.

- Implement the design (code) and perform unit testing.

- Test the software. Tests include integration, functional, stress, load, and other varieties of system tests. Final acceptance testing is performed when the system is ready to be delivered.

While the software engineers are creating the software, software safety engineers perform their own set of tasks. These activities include:

- Perform analyses, or verify the analyses of others. Provide inputs to hazard reports, tracking matrices, and safety checklists. The analysis work will stretch out over the life of the software development activity and into the operations or maintenance phase. For highly safety-critical software, many analyses will be performed by the safety engineer.

- Implement the tasks that "fall out" of the analyses. This includes making sure that a missed safety requirement is actually included in the software requirements and flows down to the current development phase. Tracking requirements and maintaining traceability or verification matrices are also implementation activities.

- Verify the changes. After the problem was fixed, the software safety engineer needs to verify that the problem was corrected (usually via inspection or test) and change its tracking status to "closed." The engineer also makes sure that the fix does not have a negative effect on any other portions of the system.

- Suggest changes to the software development and verification activities to increase safety. Examples include Formal Inspections of safety-critical code and enhanced safety testing to verify the software does not have undesired effects.

> **A good software development process, understood and followed, greatly increase the odds of developing safer, more reliable software.**

4.2.1   Software Lifecycles

Lifecycle models describe the interrelationship between software development phases. Software development tasks are usually broken down into the following activities:

   a.   Identification of Requirements

   b.   Design

   c.   Implementation (Coding)

   d.   Testing and Verification

These are not usually linear, sequential tasks. There may be much overlap, depending on the lifecycle chosen. The tasks may be performed sequentially, but in small increments, until the software is completed.

 Selecting a software lifecycle is one of the first decisions that will need to be made. The lifecycle chosen will have a strong impact on how the software is developed and what products (such as documentation) will be produced. Time spent researching the options, and especially the types of systems the model works best with, directly benefits the project as a whole.

As with any important project decision, choosing the appropriate lifecycle should not be done in a vacuum. Besides the Software Lead Engineer, knowledgeable software, systems, and safety engineers can, and should, have an impact on these choices.

The lifecycle models discussed in the following sections are not an exhaustive list. New models are being developed and older models are modified, as software engineering research struggles to find the best model (or more likely, the best *set* of models) for software development. The models included in this guidebook are well-established models that are commonly used for software development projects.

Any lifecycle model can be used with any design methodology, but some fit better than others. Because most of the lifecycle models were developed before object-oriented design was popular, they can all be used easily with structured development. If your project will use object-oriented design, consider how well the lifecycle method will work together with the design methodology.

This guidebook makes no recommendation for a specific lifecycle model. Each has its strengths and weaknesses, and no one model is best for all situations. It is important to intelligently evaluate the potential lifecycles and select one that best matches the product you are producing. Standards or organizational policy may dictate a particular lifecycle model. Also, keep in mind that the familiar may be the best choice, because of reduced uncertainty in how to implement the process.

4.2.1.1 Waterfall Model

The first publicly documented software development model is the classic Waterfall model. It was developed to help cope with the increasing complexity of aerospace products. The Waterfall model is documentation driven and linear (sequential). It is probably the best known of the lifecycle models.

The Waterfall model is characterized by a strict (more or less) one-way flow structure. It consists of up to seven phases, each with products and activities. The usual phases are: Concept, Requirements (Analysis), Design, Implementation (Code), Testing, and Operation (Maintenance). The Design phase is sometimes broken up into Architectural (high-level) and Detailed design phases.

Figure 4-1 Waterfall Lifecycle Model

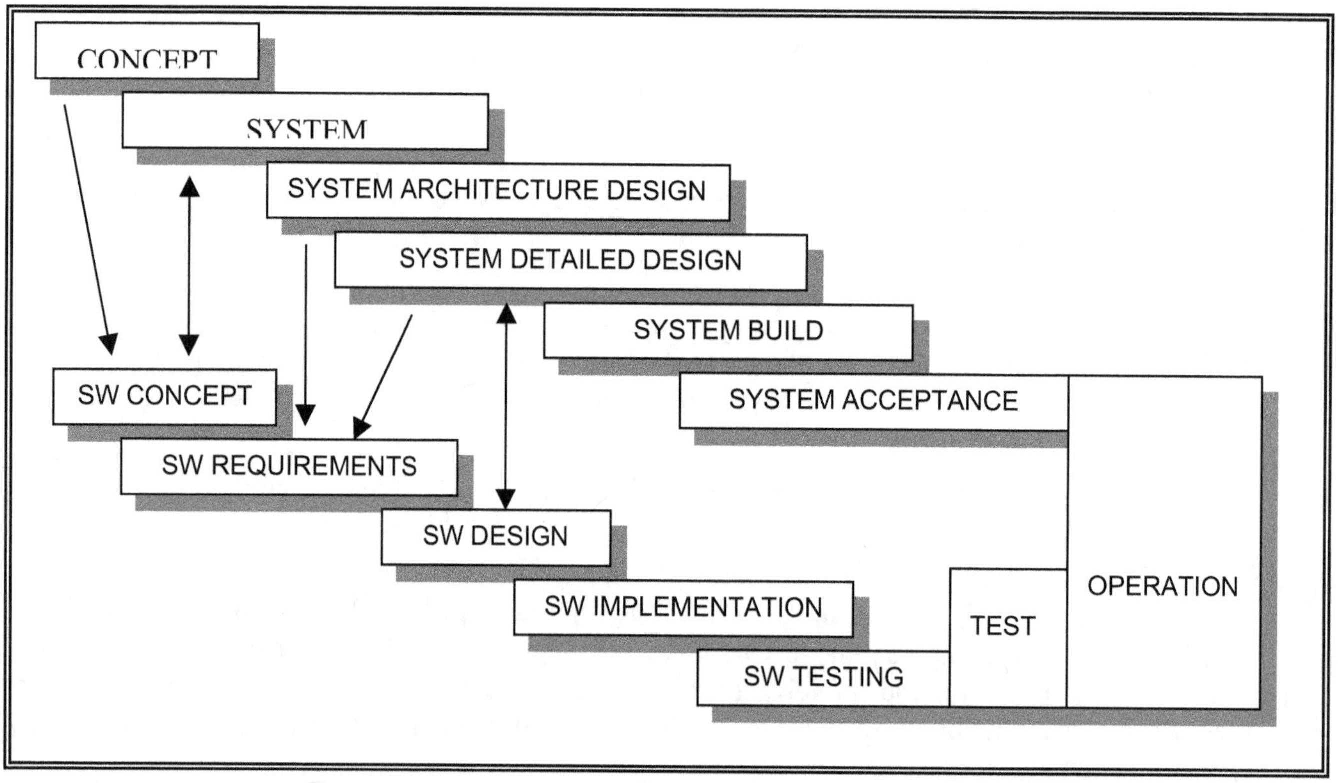

The overall system can have a top level Waterfall and the software, hardware, testing, and operations organizations, groups, or teams may each have their own lifecycle that feeds into and fits within the overall system lifecycle. Specified activities and deliverables are called out for each phase and must be approved prior to moving into the next phase.

Notice that there are clear delineations between the phases of the waterfall lifecycle. All phases start with deliverable(s) from a previous phase. New deliverables are created and reviewed to determine if the current phase of the product is properly prepared to move to the next stage. The product, as its current phase deliverables define it, is usually formally reviewed in either a system phase review (Systems Requirements Review, System Design Review, Preship Review) or may have lower level, internal phased reviews in place of, or in addition to, system reviews.

This model is the most widely used and modified because it is graphically, and intellectually, easy to grasp. The Waterfall lifecycle came from industry where the products are usually similar, the requirements are known upfront, and the products are created the same way time after time. The model is seldom, if ever, followed exactly, especially in Research and Development (R&D) work. Some **problems** with the waterfall model include:

- Assumption that requirements can be specified up front.
- Assumption that requirements and design do not change significantly (or often).
- No products (other than documentation) delivered until late in the development cycle.
- Team members "blocked" waiting for others to complete dependent tasks.

Variations of the individual phases of the waterfall model are used in most of the other lifecycle models. Even the deliverables are similar. The main difference is that instead of one monolithic process, an iterative or repetitive approach is used.

4.2.1.2 Rapid Prototyping

A prototype is a model of a product or system, in part or in whole. Depending on the purpose of the prototype, and the nature of the product, the prototype will demonstrate various aspects of the product, such as its interfaces, functionality, and so on. It is used as "Proof of Concept" and as a means to undergo concept development when no clear approach is immediately evident.

Usually, a portion of a system is prototyped up front (rapidly, with little strict development discipline) to prove out a possible design feature or technique. Examples include testing out the feasibility of using web-based interfaces or read/write CD memory instead floppies, getting user feedback on a graphical interface design, or determining if planned hardware (or a software algorithm) can produce the required timing.

Rapid prototyping is used in large extent to quickly see if something will work. It is also used at times to quickly model the basics of an entire system to allow the user to see early on what the system will be like, what it will do, and how it will operate.

In general the prototype should be built with the "20/80" rule in mind, such that it is usually the case that 20% of the functions in a system provide 80% of what the user wants. The prototype should concentrate on these functions, allowing the user to get their specification tied down as soon as possible. It is possible for the prototype to be a "full" working model, in which case it can be used in a live situation to see how the software performs, and what real users think of it. Once the concepts are all worked out and chosen, the final product is specified, designed, built, tested, and formally released using the information gained from the prototyping stage(s).

Figure 4-2 Rapid Prototyping

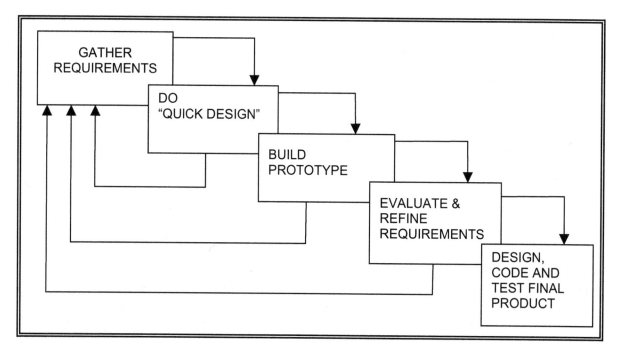

Problems and pitfalls with this model include:

- **Customers misunderstand the quality of the prototype.** The customer may see what appears to be a working system, and balk when informed that the system must be completely rewritten. Explaining the concepts behind rapid prototyping to the customer up front can help prevent this problem.

- **Developer or management desire to not "recreate the wheel" leads to the prototype being used as the basis of the complete system.** Sometimes, the prototype appears to perform so well that it is felt there is no need to build the "real" system. If this happens, some development organizations will just go ahead and add on the remaining 80% of the functions without implementing a **thorough** development process.

- **Choices made for the prototype may not be applicable for the complete system.** Operating systems, languages, or tools may be chosen to get the prototype done quickly, but these choices may not be the best for the final system. Evaluation may not be done to determine what is best, and the original choices may be used without question.

Rapid prototyping is a valuable lifecycle method and should be considered when there is uncertainty about the best approach, equipment, or interaction. What is learned from rapid prototyping should be feed into a thorough development process that provides the discipline of documentation, review, analysis, and thorough testing for a safer, more maintainable, robust finished product.

4.2.1.3 Spiral Model

The spiral model combines the idea of iterative development (prototyping) with the systematic, controlled aspects of the waterfall model. It allows for incremental releases of the product, or incremental refinement through each time around the spiral. The spiral model also explicitly includes risk management within software development. Identifying major risks, both technical and managerial, and determining how to lessen the risk helps keep the software development process under control.

The spiral model is based on continuous refinement of key products for requirements definition and analysis, system and software design, and implementation (the code). At each iteration around the cycle, the products are extensions of an earlier product. This model uses many of the same phases as the waterfall model, in essentially the same order, separated by planning, risk assessment, and the building of prototypes and simulations.

Documents are produced when they are required, and the content reflects the information necessary at that point in the process. All documents will not be created at the beginning of the process, nor all at the end (hopefully). Like the product they define, the documents are works in progress. The idea is to have a continuous stream of products produced and available for user review.

Figure 4-3 Spiral Lifecycle Model

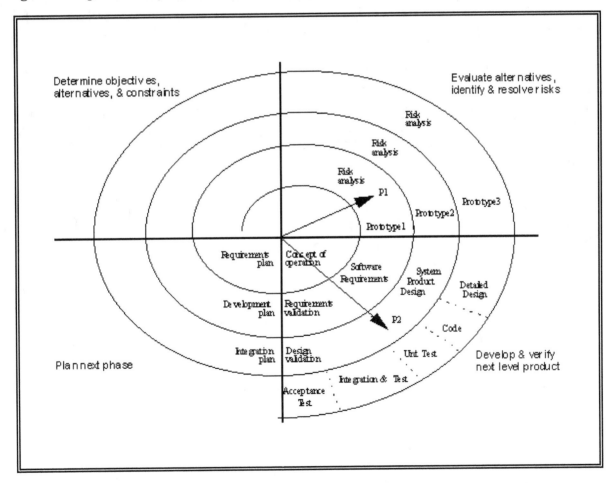

The spiral lifecycle model allows for elements of the product to be added in when they become available or known. This assures that there is no conflict with previous requirements and design. This method is consistent with approaches that have multiple software builds and releases and allows for making an orderly transition to a maintenance activity. Another positive aspect is that the spiral model forces early user involvement in the system development effort. For projects with heavy user interfacing, such as user application programs or instrument interface applications, such involvement is helpful.

Starting at the center, each turn around the spiral goes through several task regions:

- Determine the objectives, alternatives, and constraints on the new iteration.

- Evaluate alternatives and identify and resolve risk issues.

- Develop and verify the product for this iteration.

- Plan the next iteration.

Note that the requirements activity takes place in multiple sections and in multiple iterations, just as planning and risk analysis occur in multiple places. Final design, implementation, integration, and test occur in iteration 4. The spiral can be repeated multiple times for multiple builds.

Using this method of development, some functionality can be delivered to the user faster than the waterfall method. The spiral method also helps manage risk and uncertainty by allowing multiple decision points and by explicitly admitting that all of *anything* cannot be known before the subsequent activity starts.

4.2.1.4 Incremental Development - Single Delivery

The incremental development - single delivery model is effective for early development of some of the features of the software. This model enables you to get those efforts that are risky started, and the concepts tested and accepted, early in the development process. The increments are developed separately but integrated and delivered as a single system. Figure 4-4 shows the lifecycle phases of this model.

Note that the model uses the same phases as those in the waterfall model.

4.2.1.5 Incremental Development - Incremental Delivery

Where the Incremental Development – Single Delivery model produced only one deliverable product (the final version), the Incremental Development – Incremental Delivery model produces products in stages. This means that the system will have limited but partial functionality for some period of time. An example would be an application with a Beta release, a Version 1, Version 2, and so on. This lifecycle may be used if the customer wants some functions delivered early and can wait for other functions and refinements until later. Figure 4-5 shows the lifecycle phases of this model.

Note again that this model uses the phases from the waterfall model.

Figure 4-4 Incremental Development Lifecycle – Single Delivery

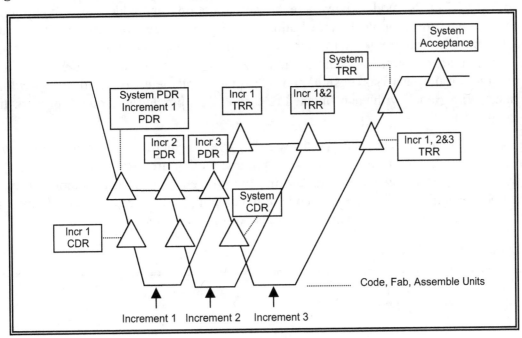

Figure 4-5 Incremental Development Lifecycle – Incremental Delivery

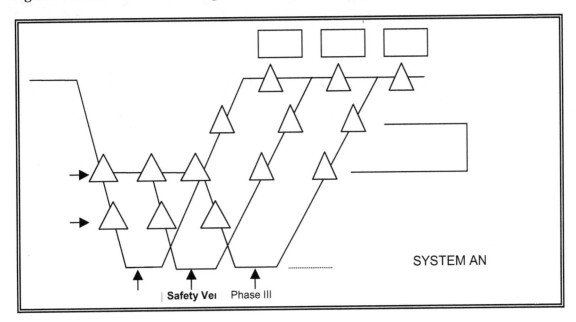

The emphasis with an incremental delivery life cycle is that you can **plan** to release incrementally. This allows the project to focus the resources and efforts accordingly. All too often a single grand release is planned, but then the schedule slips, resources are not available, technical difficulties arise, or other problems occur. The project may just ship whatever it has at the due date, promising a future update to complete the application or fix remaining problems. Using Incremental Development-Incremental Delivery can help avoid these problems.

4.2.1.6 Evolutionary Development

In the evolutionary lifecycle model, new or enhanced functions are added to a functioning system iteratively. Each development cycle builds on the experience from earlier increments, defining and refining the requirements for subsequent increments. Increments are developed sequentially, rather than in parallel. Within each incremental development cycle, there is a normal progression through analysis, design, code, test and implement, followed by operations and maintenance. Experience with each finished release is incorporated in requirements for the next development cycle.

From the customers' point of view, the system will "evolve" as increments are delivered over time. From the developers' point of view, those requirements that are clear at the beginning of the project will dictate the initial increment, and the requirements for each development cycle there after will be clarified through the experience of developing prior increments. Care must be taken to ensure that the evolving system architecture is both efficient and maintainable.

Figure 4-6 Evolutionary Lifecycle Model

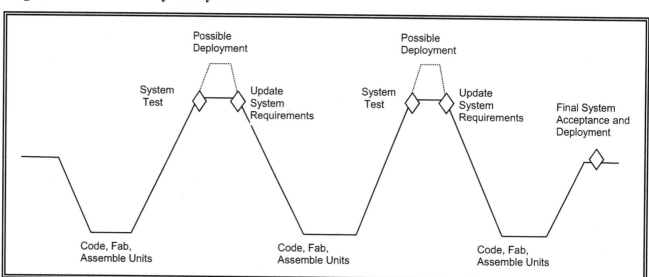

The **benefits** from using the evolutionary model are:

- Early deliveries of portions of the system, even though some of the requirements are not yet decided.

- Use of early releases as tools for requirements elicitation.

Limitations of the evolutionary lifecycle model include:

- It may be difficult to estimate costs and schedule at the start of the project when scope and requirements have not been established.

- The overall elapsed time for the project may be longer than if the scope and requirements are established before any increments are developed.

- Time apparently gained on the front end of a project because of early releases may be lost later because of the need for rework resulting from evolving requirements.

- Additional time must also be planned for integration and regression testing as increments are developed and added to the system.

4.2.2 Design Methodologies

A design is a meaningful engineering representation of something that is to be built. It is a higher-level interpretation of what will actually be implemented in the source code. Designs should be traceable back to a customer's requirements. They should also be assessed for quality against a set of predefined criteria for a good design.

Analysis and design methods for software have been evolving over the years, each with its approach to modeling the needed worldview into software. The following methodologies are most commonly used. Specific methodologies under the main categories are just a sample of available methodologies.

- Structured Analysis and Structured Design (SA/SD). SA/SD methods were among the first to be developed. They provided means to create and evaluate a "good" design. Prior to the introduction of SA/SD processes, "code and debug" was the normal way to go from requirements to source code. Even in this "object-oriented" time, SA/SD is still used by many.

  - Functional Decomposition

  - Data Flow (also called Structured Analysis)

  - Information Modeling

- Object Oriented Analysis and Object Oriented Design (OOA/OOD). OOA/OOD breaks the world into abstract entities called objects, which can contain information (data) and have associated behavior. OOA/OOD has been around for nearly 30 years. In the last decade the majority of development projects have shifted to this collection of methodologies. Object-orientation has brought real benefits to software development, but it is not a silver bullet.

  - Object-Oriented Analysis and Design (OOA/OOD) method (Coad & Yourdon)

  - Object Modeling Technique (OMT) (Rumbaugh et. al.)

  - Object-Oriented Analysis and Design with Applications (OOADA) (Booch)

  - Object-Oriented Software Engineering (OOSE) (Jacobson et. al.)

  - UML

- Formal Methods (FM) and Model-based Development. FM is a set of techniques and tools based on mathematical modeling and formal logic that are used to specify and verify requirements and designs for computer systems and software. FM is also a process that allows the logical properties of a computer system (primarily software) to be predicted (in a process similar to numerical calculation) from a mathematical model of the system by means of a logical calculation.

  - Formal Specification

  - Formal Verification

  - Software models (with automatic code generation)

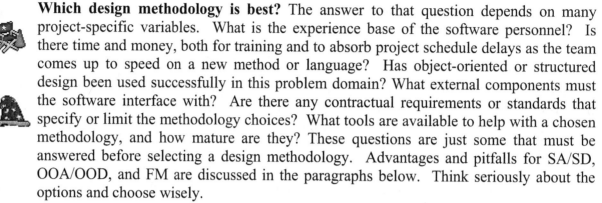**Which design methodology is best?** The answer to that question depends on many project-specific variables. What is the experience base of the software personnel? Is there time and money, both for training and to absorb project schedule delays as the team comes up to speed on a new method or language? Has object-oriented or structured design been used successfully in this problem domain? What external components must the software interface with? Are there any contractual requirements or standards that specify or limit the methodology choices? What tools are available to help with a chosen methodology, and how mature are they? These questions are just some that must be answered before selecting a design methodology. Advantages and pitfalls for SA/SD, OOA/OOD, and FM are discussed in the paragraphs below. Think seriously about the options and choose wisely.

4.2.2.1 SA/SD

Structured software development is a phrase with multiple meanings. In a general sense, it applies to all methodologies for creating software in a disciplined, structured manner. In the context of this section, however, "structured" refers to the various analysis and design methods that are not object-oriented.

In the following discussion, "analysis" is defined as a process for evaluating a problem space (a concept or proposed system) and rendering it into requirements that reflect the needs of the customer. "Design" is the process of taking those requirements and creating the desired system.

Among the structured methods used, the most popular have been Functional Decomposition, Data Flow (or Structured Analysis), and Information Modeling.

Functional Decomposition focuses on what functions and sub-functions the system needs to perform and the interfaces between those functions. It is a technique for developing a program in which the problem is divided into more easily handled sub-problems, the solutions of which create a solution to the overall problem. Functional decomposition is a "top-down" development methodology.

Functional decomposition begins with the abstract (the functions the software must perform) and works toward the particular (algorithmic steps that can be translated directly into code). The process begins by breaking the functionality into a series of major steps. Each step is then further decomposed, until a level is reached where a step cannot be reasonably subdivided. The result is usually a collection of "units" or components that perform a single sub-step of the process. The relationship between the components is hierarchical.

The general complaints with this method are that:

- The functional capability is what most often changes during the design lifecycle and is thus very volatile.

- It is often hard to see the connection between the proposed system as a whole and the functions determined to create that system.

- Data plays a secondary role in support of actions to be performed.

Structured Analysis (DeMarco [16], Yourdon [15]) became popular in the 1980's and is still used by many. The analysis consists of interpreting the system concept (or real world) into data and control terminology, graphically displayed as data flow diagrams. Data dictionaries describe the data, including where and how it is used. A process specification captures the transaction and transformation information.

The steps to performing a structured analysis are:

- Start with the Data Flow Diagram.
- Determine major flow from input to output.
- Partition into input, central transform, and output processes.
- Convert to high level structure chart.
- Refine.
- Validate using coupling and cohesion.

This methodology has some problems in practical usage. The flow of data and control from bubble (i.e. processes) to data store to bubble can be very hard to track. Also, the number of bubbles can get to be extremely large. One approach to avoiding this problem is to first define events from the outside world that require the system to react, then assign a bubble to that event. Bubbles that need to interact are then connected until the system is defined. This can be rather overwhelming, so the bubbles are usually grouped into higher-level bubbles.

The main difficulties in using this method have been:

1. Choosing bubbles appropriately.
2. Partitioning those bubbles in a meaningful and mutually agreed upon manner.
3. The size of the documentation needed to understand the Data Flows.
4. This method is still strongly functional in nature and thus subject to frequent change.
5. Though "data" flow is emphasized, "data" modeling is not. There is little understanding of just what the subject matter of the system is about.
6. It is hard for the customer to follow how the concept is mapped into these data flows and bubbles. It is also very hard for the designers who must shift the data flow diagram organization into a format that can be implemented.

Information Modeling, using entity-relationship diagrams, is really a forerunner for OOA. The analysis first finds objects in the problem space, describes them with attributes, adds relationships, refines them into super and sub-types and then defines associative objects. Some normalization then generally occurs. Information modeling is thought to fall short of true OOA in that, according to Peter Coad & Edward Yourdon [17],

1. Services or processing requirements for each object are not addressed.
2. Inheritance is not specifically identified.
3. Poor interface structures (messaging) exist between objects.
4. Classification and assembly of the structures are not used as the predominate method for determining the system's objects.

Modern structured analysis often combines elements from all three analysis methodologies (functional decomposition, structured analysis, and information modeling).

4.2.2.2 OOA/OOD

Object Oriented Analysis and Design (OOA/OOD) represents the new paradigm for creating software. OOA/OOD is viewed by many as the best solution to most problems. Like the older SA/SD, OOA/OOD provides a way to model the real world in a defined, disciplined manner. OOA actually incorporates structured analysis techniques at a lower level, once the system is cast into objects or classes with attributes and methods (i.e. functions).

The Object-oriented (OO) paradigm says:

1. **Look** at your problem in terms of individual, independent objects.

2. **Decompose** your domain into objects. Each object has some certain properties and a certain behavior or set of actions particular to each object.

3. **Organize** your objects so that:

   a. They interact among each other by sending messages that may trigger actions on the object to which they arrive.

   b. They are defined in a hierarchical way so that objects in lower levels inherit automatically all properties and behavior of the objects in upper levels.

   c. Objects in lower levels may add or modify the properties or behavior that they have inherited.

Modeling the real world into objects can have some advantages. This methodology tends to follow a more natural human thinking process. Also, objects, if properly chosen, are the most stable perspective of the real world problem space and can be more resilient to change as the functions/services, data, and commands/messages are isolated and hidden from the overall system.

 For example, while over the course of the development lifecycle the number, as well as types, of functions (e.g., turn camera 1 on, download sensor data, ignite starter, fire engine 3) may change. The basic objects (e.g., cameras, sensors, starter, engines, operator) needed to create a system usually are constant. That is, while there may now be three cameras instead of two, the new Camera-3 is just an instance of the basic object 'camera'. OOA/OOD should not be confused with OO programming languages. While an OO language is usually chosen to implement the design, it is not required. A procedural language can be used to implement OOD.

OOA incorporates the principles of <u>abstraction</u>, <u>information hiding</u>, and <u>inheritance</u>, which are the three most "human" means of classification. These combined principles, if properly applied, establish a more modular, bounded, stable, and understandable software system. These aspects of OOA should make a system created under this method more robust and less susceptible to changes--properties that help create a safer software system design.

<u>Abstraction</u> refers to concentrating on only certain aspects of a complex problem, system, idea, or situation in order to better comprehend that portion. The perspective of the analyst focuses on similar characteristics of the system objects that are most important to them. Later, the analyst can address other objects and their desired attributes or examine the details of an object and deal with each in more depth. An object is defined by the attributes it has and the functions it performs on those attributes. An abstraction can be viewed as a simplified description of a

system that emphasizes some of the system's details or properties while suppressing others. A good abstraction is one that emphasizes details that are significant to the reader or user and suppresses details that are, at least for the moment, immaterial or diversionary.

Information hiding also helps manage complexity in that it allows encapsulation of requirements that might be subject to change. In addition, it helps to isolate the rest of the system from some object specific design decisions. Thus, the rest of the software system sees only what is absolutely necessary for the inner workings of any object.

Inheritance "defines a relationship among classes [objects], wherein one class shares the structure or behavior defined in one or more classes. Inheritance thus represents a hierarchy of abstractions, in which a subclass [object] inherits from one or more superclasses [ancestor objects]. Typically, a subclass augments or redefines the existing structure and behavior of its superclasses" [19].

Classification theory states that humans normally organize their thinking by:

- Looking at an object and comparing its attributes to those experienced before (e.g. looking at a cat, humans tend to think of its size, color, temperament, or other attributes in relation to past experience with cats)

- Distinguishing between an entire object and its component parts (e.g., a rose bush versus its roots, flowers, leaves, thorns, andstems.)

- Classification of objects as distinct and separate groups (e.g., trees, grass, cows, cats, politicians)

In OOA, the first step is to take the problem space and render it into objects and their attributes (abstraction). The second step is classifying an object into Assembly Structures, where an object and its parts are considered. The third step includes organizing the problem space into Classification Structures. This involves examining the problem space for generalized and specialized instances of objects (inheritance). The purpose of all this classification is to partition the system into well-defined boundaries that can be individually and independently understood, designed, and revised. However, despite "classification theory," choosing what objects represent a system is not always that straightforward. In addition, each analyst or designer will have their own abstraction, or view, of the system which must be resolved. Shlaer and Mellor [87], Jacobson [88], Booch [19], and Coad and Yourdon [17] each offer a different look at candidate object classes, as well as other aspects of OOA/OOD. These are all excellent sources for further introduction (or induction) into OOA and OOD. OOA/OOD provides a structured approach to software system design and can be very useful in helping to bring about a safer, more reliable system.

 While there is a growing number of OO "gurus" with years of practical experience, many OO projects are implemented by those with book-knowledge and little direct experience. Remember that everything written in the OOA/OOD books are not the only correct way to do things. Adaptation of standard methods may be important in your environment. As an example, a team of software designers who worked on the Mars Pathfinder mission [89] decided to use Object Oriented Design, though their developers had only book-knowledge of the methodology. Attempting to follow the design methodologies verbatim led to a rapidly increasingly complex set of objects. The team eventually modified the design methodology by combining the "bottom up" approach they had been using with a more "top down" division into subsystems. The AIPS team [18] found that it took 6 months for structured (procedural) developers to be productive in an object-oriented environment. Once OO gurus were on the project, new developers progressed more quickly.

Reference [101] provides a "cookbook," or design guide, to creating software based on *use cases*, while stressing software requirements, traceability, and testing. Reference [102] describes the Dynamic Systems Development Method of software development. DSDM provides a framework of controls and best practices for Rapid Application Development.

OOA/OOD is not a silver bullet for software development. Besides the steep learning curve for those unfamiliar with the methodology, other problems or pitfalls exist. Many software development organizations have shown a significant increase in productivity when OO techniques were adopted. However, it is not clear that all the benefits resulted strictly from the object-oriented philosophy. In some cases, the extra focus on design provided most of the gain. Also, not all of the promised advantages have come about in practice. Code reuse, touted as a major benefit of OO methodologies, has not been implemented to the extent originally expected.

Other examples of problems or concerns are:

- **Not every problem domain is a candidate for OOD.** Real-time or embedded systems, distributed computing, and rapidly evolving systems, among others, should evaluate whether OO is the right methodology for the domain.

- **It is difficult to determine "objects" for abstract entities.** Is wind an object, or the behavior of an air object?

- **Weakness in large-scale reuse and integration.** With its focus on small-scale objects, OOD does not provide sufficient mechanisms to achieve large-scale reuse or integration of off-the-shelf system components without significant prior planning.

- **Weakness in system decomposition.** Decomposing the real world into objects or classes is useful for modeling data-centric aspects of a system. Other decompositions (e.g., by-feature; by-function) are better for modeling other aspects. Without them, maintainability, comprehensibility, and reusability suffer.

- **Weakness in multi-team and decentralized development.** OOD leads to contention over shared, centralized classes. It forces all developers to agree on a single domain model, rather than using models more appropriate to their tasks.

- **OO Testing methods are still an evolving science.** At the system level, testing an OO and structured system is identical. "Unit testing" and "integration testing" for OO systems differs in some ways from structured or procedural software. The best ways to test OO software is not well understood yet.

- **Changing the OO model for evolving systems is not as easy as claimed.** Lubars et al [21] showed that for one system, the object model was simple to change as the system evolved, but the behavioral model was much more complex.

Shah et al [20] describes additional pitfalls, both technical and managerial, when moving to OOD.

Unified Modeling Language (UML)

UML is a language and methodology for specifying, visualizing, and documenting the development artifacts (design) of an object-oriented system. The UML represents the unification of the Booch, Objectory, and OMT (spell) methods and is their direct and upwardly compatible successor. It also incorporates ideas from many other methodologists, including Coad, Gamma, Mellor, Shlaer, and Yourdon.

UML uses a variety of diagrams and charts to show the structure and relationships of an object-oriented design. Class diagrams show the individual classes and how they relate to each other, e.g. subclass, superclass, or contained within another class. Each class box can contain some or all of the attributes (data) and operations (methods) of the class.

Relationships among classes come from the following set:

- **Associations** between classes means that they communicate via messages (calling each other's methods).
- **Aggregations** are a specialized association, where one class "owns" the other.
- **Compositions** show that one class is included within another class.
- **Generalizations** represent an inheritance relationship between the classes.
- **Dependencies** are similar to associations, but while one class depends on another, it does not contain a pointer or reference to the other class.
- **Realizations** are relationships where one modeling element is the implementation (realization) of another.

Features of UML	Types of diagrams
Use cases and scenarios	Use-case diagrams
Object and class models	Class diagrams
State charts and other behavioral specifications	State-machine diagrams
Large-scale structuring	Message-trace diagrams
Design patterns	Object-message diagrams
Extensibility mechanisms	Process diagrams
	Module diagrams
	Platform diagram

UML is quickly becoming the standard OO modeling language. Tools already incorporate it, and some can even generate code directly from the UML diagrams. UML has been adapted for real-time systems. Many books now exist for learning UML, as well as on applying UML to specific environments or integrating it with other design methodologies.

4.2.2.3 Formal Methods (FM)

The NASA Formal Methods Guidebook [22] states: "Formal Methods (FM) consists of a set of techniques and tools based on mathematical modeling and formal logic that are used to specify and verify requirements and designs for computer systems and software." Formal Methods therefore has two parts – formal specification and formal verification.

Software and system requirements are usually written in "human-readable" language. This can lead to ambiguity, when a statement that is clear to one person is interpreted differently by another. To avoid this ambiguity, requirements can be written in a formal, mathematical language. This formal specification is the first step in applying FM.

Formal verification provides the proof that the result (software) meets the formal specification. Verification is a progressive activity. At each stage, the new product is formally verified to be consistent with the previous product. For example, the detailed design is verified against the preliminary design, which was verified against the desired properties such as safety or security.

In the production of safety-critical systems or systems that require high assurance, FM provides a methodology that gives the highest degree of assurance for a trustworthy software system. FM has been used with success on NASA, military, and commercial systems that were considered safety-critical applications. The benefits from the application of the methodology accrue to both safety and non-safety areas. FM does not guarantee a precise quantifiable level of reliability. At present, FM is only acknowledged as producing systems that provide a high level of assurance.

FM is used in several ways:

   a. As a way to assure the software after-the-fact
   b. As a way to assure the software in parallel.
   c. As a way to develop the software.

"After the fact" software verification can increase the confidence in a safety-critical system. When the regular software development is <u>completed</u>, then the formal specification and verification begin. The Software Assurance, Safety, or IV&V engineer converts the "human readable" requirements into a formal specification and proves properties about the specification. The code that implements the system may also be formally verified to be consistent with the formal specification. With this approach, two separate development activities occur, increasing cost and schedule. In addition, problems found at this late stage are costly to fix.

"In parallel" software verification still uses two separate teams (software development and FM verification), but they operate in parallel during the whole process. The development team uses the regular practices of good software development. At the same time the FM team writes formal specifications for the system and verifies them. While still costly, this method of assuring the software allows for quicker development. Software errors are found earlier in the development cycle when they are less expensive to correct. However, communication between the two teams is vital for this approach to work.

Rather than two teams working in parallel, the software can be developed using FM exclusively. This is an integrated approach. Requirements and design are written in a formal language. The design is formally verified *before* code is generated. This method is the least costly of the three, though the developers must be trained in FM for it to work.

 FM has not gained a wide acceptance among all industries, mostly due to the difficulty of the formal proofs. A considerable learning curve must be surmounted for newcomers, which can be expensive. Once this hurdle is surmounted successfully, some users find that it can reduce overall development lifecycle cost by eliminating many costly defects prior to coding. In addition, many tools are now available to aid in using FM. Also, the process of creating a formal specification, even without the mathematical proofs, can be invaluable. Removing ambiguity and uncertainty from the specification helps to prevent future errors when that specification is implemented.

Lutz and Ampo [23] described their successful experience using formal specification and verification at the requirements level. As a result of the Formal Specification, 37 issues were found in the requirements, including undocumented assumptions, inadequate off-nominal or boundary case behavior, traceability and inconsistency, imprecise terminology and logic errors. The project being used as a test subject was following an Object-oriented (OO) development process. FM worked well with the OO approach.

A new approach to "light" formal methods is the SpecTRM modeling language [109]. This language is human-readable and supports a safety-driven design process. "Under the hood" of the modeling language is a formal (mathematical) basis that supports formal and even automated analysis. In addition, the models can be executed, allowing dynamic analysis of the specified system's behavior before any code is written. The design of the formal modeling language emphasizes readability so it can serve as a model and as the specification of the software requirements.

Detailed descriptions of FM are given in the NASA Formal Methods Guidebook [22]. In addition, the following publications are recommended reading as primers in FM: Rushby [24], Miller, et al [25], and Butler, et al [26]. Anthony Hall [27] gives "Seven Myths of Formal Methods," and discusses using formal specification of requirements without formal proofs in a real-world development environment. Richard Kemmerer [28] shows how to integrate FM with the development process.

The NASA Langley Formal Methods Group website (http://atb-www.larc.nasa.gov/fm/index.html) provides good general information on the *what* and *why* of FM. This website also provides links for more information. The NASA FM page is http://eis.jpl.nasa.gov/quality/Formal_Methods/home.html.

A quick search of the Internet produces links to many FM tools. The web-site http://www.afm.sbu.ac.uk has a list of notations and tools, as well as other resources. The FM page produced by Jonathan Bowen (http://www.afm.sbu.ac.uk/) also contains resources and tool information.

The following list contains some of the tools available for FM. Links to these can be found through the above URLs or via a search of the World Wide Web.

- Theorem provers (ACL2, Boyer-Moore, HOL, Isabelle, JAPE, leant, LEGO, Nqthm, Otter, PVS, RRL, and SteP).

- Specification languages and formal notations (Z, SDL, Algebraic Design Language (ADL), Calculus of Communicating Systems (CCS), Estelle, Esterel, Larch, LUSTRE, Murphi, OBJ and TAM.

- Methods and Systems (B-Method, Circal, Evolving Algebras, KIV, LOTOS, Penelope, Refinement Calculus, RESOLVE, and VDM).

- Others (ASLAN, Binary Decision Diagrams, NP-Tools, Nuprl, PVS, Specware, HyTech for embedded systems, LAMBDA for hardware/software co-design, Maintainer's Assistant for re-engineering code, UNITY for parallel and distributed programs, and Trio, Kronos, TTM/RTTL, and UPPAAL for real-time systems).

4.2.2.4 Model-based Software Development

Model-based software development focuses on creating a complete (and possibly formal) model of the software system. Models are an abstract and high level description of the system, expressed as statements in some modeling language or as elements in a modeling tool. Unlike standard design documents, models can be executable (able to simulate the process flow within the system).

The standard "requirements→design→code→unit, integration, and system test" development cycle becomes "requirements→model→verify (test) and debug→generate code→system test". Unit and software integration testing is pushed up in the life cycle to the modeling phase. In theory, the model-driven approach allows developers to construct, test, and analyze their designs before they write any code.

When the model is formally defined, it becomes "formal methods" (section 4.2.2.3). Another growing trend in software engineering is to use the Unified Modeling Language (UML, section 4.2.2.2) to describe the system. In many cases, tools can take the developed model and automatically generate the source code.

One advantage of model-based development is moving some of the testing activities earlier in the life cycle. If major problems are found, they can be resolved with less impact on the budget or schedule of the project. Disadvantages include a reliance on the automatically generated source code (which may not be generated correctly) and the difficulty of knowing how well the model conforms to reality. Interactions between parts of the system may not be evident until the system is operational. Testing on the model should not replace thorough system testing.

4.2.2.5 Design Patterns

In software engineering, the wheel is reinvented on a regular basis. Creating reusable software components is one way to avoid that reinvention process. Design patterns are another. Unlike reusable software, however, design patterns are not *things* (software components) but *ideas*. They are proven solutions to recurring problems in software engineering.

The idea of software patterns derives from several sources: an architectural design movement conceived by Christopher Alexander, the literate programming[3] concepts, and the documentation of best practices and lessons learned in all vocations. Software engineering solutions to a problem are usually specific to the context of a particular system. A pattern is a generalization from the specific solutions that captures the essential insight into the problem solution, as well as the context-specific elements. Or, more succinctly, "a pattern is a named nugget of insight that conveys the essence of a proven solution to a recurring problem within a certain context amidst competing concerns". [95]

Software patterns are given names, which then become part of the vocabulary of software engineering. One of the software patterns community's goals is to create a body of literature to help software developers resolve recurring problems encountered throughout all of software development. Patterns provide a shared language for communicating insight and experience about these problems and their solutions. Formally codifying these solutions and their relationships captures this body of knowledge. The primary focus of the patterns community is

---

[3] *Literate programming* is a phrase coined by Donald Knuth to describe the approach of developing computer programs from the perspective of a report or prose. Literate programming is the combination of documentation and source together in a fashion suited for reading by human beings. [91]

not so much on technology as it is on creating a culture to document and support sound engineering architecture and design.

Patterns have been used for many different domains, including organizations, processes, teaching and architecture. At present, the software engineering community is using patterns largely for software architecture and design, and (more recently) software development processes and organizations.

Software patterns have four basic elements:

1. **Pattern name.**

2. **Problem description.** This explains the problem and its context, conditions that must be met, and when to apply the pattern.

3. **Solution.** This describes the elements that make up the design, their relationships, responsibilities, and collaborations.

4. **Consequences.** The results and trade-offs of applying the pattern, often program space and execution time trade-offs.

Patterns provide proven solutions to specific problems where the solution is usually not obvious. The best patterns *generate* a solution to a problem indirectly. Patterns describe deeper system structures and mechanisms, rather than modules. Good patterns do more than just identify a solution; they also explain why the solution is needed.

Resources for software patterns include:

- **Design Patterns: Elements of Reusable Object-Oriented Software** by Erich Gamma, Richard Helm, Ralph Johnson, and John Vlissides, October 1994, ISBN 0-201-63361-2.

- **Pattern-Oriented Software Architecture: A System of Patterns** by Frank Buschmann, Regine Meunier, Hans Rohnert, Peter Sommerlad, and Michael Stal, 1996, ISBN 0-471-95869-7.

- **Pattern Languages of Program Design** (and follow-on volumes) contain selected papers from the conference on Patterns Languages of Program Design. Addison-Wesley published the first volume in 1995.

- Patterns home page, http://www.hillside.net/patterns/patterns.htm.

- Portland Pattern Repository, http://c2.com/ppr/index.html.

4.3   *Managing the Process*

All software development must be managed if it is to be successful. The degree of management and documentation varies with the complexity and size of the project. A large, software-intensive project may require a full-fledged, formal program whose details are found in a specific Software Management Plan. A Software Management Plan describes the necessary software tasks, processes, methodologies, reviews, configuration management approach, reporting, documentation, and other elements of software management. A small software project, without much criticality, will have a tailored process that does not overburden the project. The software processes for a small project will usually be described inside a System Management Plan, rather than in separate documents.

Categorizing the project's software and selecting the range of activities to perform **must be negotiated** early in the system development. Project management, software developers, software assurance engineers, and software and/or systems safety engineers will be involved in the negotiations.

First and foremost, everyone needs to agree on the degree of safety-criticality of the software. The level is based on several factors ranging from control over hazardous hardware to visibility of the system (and therefore a failure) to the outside world. Chapter 3 describes how to determine the safety-criticality of the software.

Starting a project with varying understandings of the criticality of the software system will usually lead to problems down the road. The project manager does not want to have this issue raised repeatedly throughout the development period, as developers and software assurance continue to argue over the criticality of individual sections or the software as a whole.

Along with the criticality level, the development and safety activities need to be negotiated. Tailoring the activities to the criticality level (risk index) is discussed in section 3.2. Further tailoring information is provided in the "Tailoring Guidelines" sections of Chapters 5 through 10.

Determining *who* will perform an activity is as important as *what* tasks will be implemented. This is another area for negotiation, especially when there is no designated software safety engineer. Team members may wear different "hats" at various times. The project manager should distribute the tasks according to the expertise and talents of the team members, keeping in mind that some activities may require a certain amount of independence from the development team.

Part of managing a safety-critical project includes selecting the right team. Experience and successful past performance with similar efforts are prerequisites to developing dependable safety-critical software.

NASA's Software Engineering Initiative Implementation Plan, from the Office of the Chief Engineer, sets out four strategies to improve software engineering practices, especially in cost and schedule predictability, reliability, quality, and cost. This plan (and NPG 2820 (pending) require all NASA Centers to implement software process improvement that will bring the software development up to (or equivalent to) SW-CMM (Software Capability Maturity Mode) or CMMI level 3. Section 4.3.8 discusses the SW-CMM and other process improvement frameworks.

4.3.1 Project Management Best Practices

The focus of this guidebook is on producing safe software. The project manager is one of those responsible for making sure the software produced is safe, and meets all the other requirements. As Section 11.9 points out, the human element is important in meeting the goal of safety.

While a treatise on all aspects of project management is outside the scope of this guidebook, the following list gives an overview of important practices. The list is found on the Software Program Managers Network website (http://www.spmn.com/16CSP.html).

The Airlie Software Council identified nine Principal Best Practices observed in industry and deemed essential for nearly all DoD software development projects. (This list has now been updated to 16 software practices, and is available through the link above.)

- **Formal Risk Management.** Risk management is vital to the success of any software effort. A formal risk management process requires that risks be identified and accepted (with whatever mitigations are determined to be necessary or prudent), and necessary resources be committed to the project. Formal processes for identifying, monitoring, and managing risk must be used.

- **Agreement on Interfaces.** To deal with the chronic problem of vague, inaccurate, and untestable specifications, the Council proposed that a baseline user interface must be agreed upon before the beginning of implementation activities and be included as an integral part of the system specification. For those projects developing both hardware and software, a separate software specification must be written with an explicit and complete interface description.

- **Formal Inspections.** Inspections should be conducted on requirements, architecture, designs at all levels (particularly detailed design), on code prior to unit test, and on test plans.

- **Metric-based Scheduling and Management.** Statistical quality control and schedules should be maintained. This requires early calculation of size metrics, projection of costs and schedules from empirical patterns, and tracking of project status through the use of metrics. Use of a parametric analyzer or other automated projection tool is also recommended.

- **Binary Quality Gates at the Inch-Pebble Level.** Completion of each task in the lowest-level activity network needs to be defined by an objective binary indication. These completion events should be in the form of gates that assess either the quality of the products produced, or the adequacy and completeness of the finished process. Gates may take the form of technical reviews, completion of a specific set of tests which integrate or qualify software components, demonstrations, or project audits.

- **Program-wide Visibility of Progress vs. Plan.** The core indicators of project health or dysfunction should be made readily available to all project participants. Anonymous channel feedback should be encouraged to enable unfavorable news to move freely up and down the project hierarchy.

- **Defect Tracking Against Quality Targets.** Defects should be tracked formally at each project phase or activity. Configuration management (CM), or a form of Problem Reporting or Defect Management, allows each defect to be recorded and traced through to removal.

- **Configuration Management** (CM). The discipline of CM is vital to the success of any software effort. CM is an integrated process for identifying, documenting, monitoring, evaluating, controlling, and approving all changes made during the life-cycle of the program for information that is shared by more than one individual or organization.

- **People-aware Management Accountability.** Management must be accountable for staffing qualified people (those with domain knowledge and similar experience in previously successful projects) as well as for fostering an environment conducive to high morale and low voluntary staff turnover.

More information on project management can be found in the NASA Software Management Guide [13]. Additional information on project management can be found at:

- Project Management Institute – http://www.pmi.org

- Project manager http://www.project-manager.com/

- ALLPM - The Project Manager's Homepage http://www.allpm.com

- Center for Project Excellence – http://projectexcellence.com

- Michael Greer's Project Management Resources – http://www.michaelgreer.com

4.3.2 Requirements

Requirements solicitation, analysis, and management are key elements of a successful and safe software development process. Many of the costly and critical system failures that are attributed to software can ultimately be traced back to missing, incorrect, misunderstood, or incompatible requirements.

Figure 4-7 Sources of Software Requirements

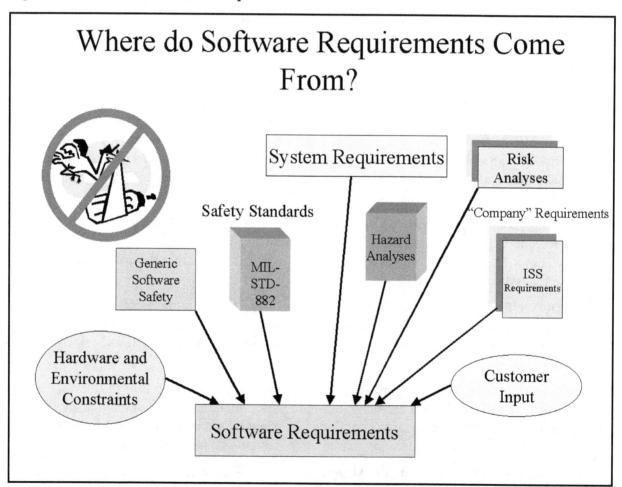

Software requirements are not delivered by the stork, but flow down from many sources, including:

- System Requirements (Specification)
- Safety and Security Standards
- Hazard and Risk Analyses
- System Constraints
- Customer Input
- Software Safety "Best Practices"

Analyses described in Chapter 6 describe methods for assuring that all these requirements, especially safety requirements, are in the software specification (requirements document).

 Most people will think to look for requirements among the system specification, safety standards, and the potential hazards or risks. What may be overlooked are system constraints, such as activities the hardware must not do or limitations in sensor precision. These constraints need to be identified and verified as early as possible. When constraints are found to be more limiting as the system is built (such as motor speed being less than expected), software will usually be asked to compensate. It is in the software developer's best interest to determine what items might constrain the software, and at least make sure the issues are being tracked.

Another overlooked area is **security**. With more systems able to access a network, or be controlled over one, making sure that only authorized users can affect the system is a requirement. Command authentication schemes may be necessary for network-controlled systems. Access to the system may be inadvertent or malicious, but either needs to be prevented or, in worst case, contained.

Software safety "best practices" (also sometimes called generic requirements) should also be considered when deriving the software requirements. Building in error handling, fault or failure detection and recovery, or having the program terminate in a safe state is an obvious "best practice.". Other examples are:

- Notifying controller when automated safety-critical process is executed.
- Requiring hazardous commands to involve multiple, independent steps to execute.
- Requiring hazardous commands or data to differ from non-hazardous commands by multiple bits.
- Making the current state of all inhibits available to controller (human or executive program).
- Ensuring unused code cannot cause a hazard if executed.

All requirements must be specified and analyzed to insure **completeness** (to the extent possible), **clarity**, and **verifiability** of the desired functions and performance. In addition, the software system must be evaluated to determine if any of it is safety-critical or has safety-critical characteristics. Top-down analyses, such as Software Fault Tree Analysis, are often used to identify safety-critical software. Any safety-critical characteristics found during the requirements analyses should be written into the software and system requirements.

Requirements must be **managed.** They must be traced all the way through the development process into the final test cases. The process of requirements management is described in Section 6.4.

Once the requirements are known, it is possible to create the system and acceptance test plans. Even if the plans are not completed at this stage (depending on the lifecycle chosen), beginning the process may help identify ambiguous or confusing requirements. In addition, special safety tests may need to be conducted as part of the safety verification process. These can be separate tests or be included as one of the system tests.

Chapter 6 discusses requirements development and analysis in more detail.

4.3.3 Design

The process of design provides the structure for converting the requirements into the final code. Where the requirements state *what* must be done, the design provides *how* it will be done. Many requirements may be implemented in multiple ways. Design selects just one approach.

The process for designing software for safety-critical systems includes:

- **Identify design features and methods.** The design process identifies design features and methods (object/class choice, data hiding, functional distribution, etc.), including safety features (e.g., inhibits, traps, interlocks, and assertions) that will be used throughout the software to implement the software requirements.

- **Allocate all software requirements to the software design.** Each requirement is implemented in a portion of the design, though design features may include more than one requirement.

- **Identify safety-critical computer software components.** Any component of the software that implements a safety-critical requirement is flagged as safety-critical.

- **Perform design analyses to assure feasibility and functionality.** Analyses should be performed as early as possible to verify that the design can meet its requirements.

- **Perform a safety analysis of the design.** Safety analyses identify potential hazards. Bottom-up analyses, such as Software Failure Modes and Effects Analysis, are often used. They may be combined with top-down analyses for a thorough look at the software system. Each safety-critical component is analyzed to verify that it does not cause or contribute to a hazard. All components must be reviewed to verify that a non-critical component cannot affect safety-critical components. Data, sequencing, timing constraints, and other means of influencing safety-critical components should not be overlooked.

- **Develop and review software integration test plans; update system and acceptance test plans.** Integration testing deals with how the software components will be incorporated into the final software system and what will be tested at each integration step. When developing these plans, it is important to think about how the safety features can be tested. Some may be able to be verified at a high level (system testing), others at a low level (unit testing), and some during a particular stage of the integration.

The Design phase may be divided into architectural and detailed design phases. Architectural design is the high level design, where many components are undeveloped black boxes. The Detailed Design phase fills in the blanks. The level of analysis possible will vary with the details available. Some analyses can be started early and then updated as more detail is added. Others cannot begin until the design is nearly complete.

During Design, the operating system and development language are usually chosen. Tools such as compilers and editors are chosen. These decisions can have a significant impact on the safety of the software. Sections 11.1 and 11.2 discuss issues to consider when selecting these elements in a safety-critical system.

Chapter 7 discusses design development and analysis in more detail.

4.3.4 Implementation

Implementation (coding) is the process of taking the design and translating it into a specific programming language. For a detailed design, the act of implementation is usually very straightforward. When working from a higher-level design, implementation will involve non-structured design steps, often performed in the mind of the programmer. Leaving key design decisions to a lower-level programmer is not recommended for safety-critical software. Safety-critical components must be well designed before being created in code.

It is during software implementation that software controls of safety hazards are actually implemented. All the requirements should have been passed down through the design(s) to the coding level. Managers and software designers must communicate **all** issues relating to the program and components they assign to programmers. Safety-critical designs and coding assignments should be clearly identified. Programmers must recognize not only the explicit safety-related design elements but should also be cognizant of the types of errors that can be introduced into non-safety-critical code that can compromise safety controls. Coding checklists should be provided to alert for these common errors.

Unit level testing begins during the software implementation phase. Each unit is tested individually to verify correct functionality. The amount of unit testing is one of the negotiable elements in a safety program. Remember, however, that units often cannot be thoroughly tested during integration because individual component level inputs and outputs are no longer accessible. Unit level testing can identify implementation problems that require changes to the software. For these reasons, unit level testing must be mostly completed prior to software integration.

Chapter 8 discusses implementation and code analysis in more detail.

4.3.5 Testing

Testing is the operational execution of a software component in a real or simulated environment. Testing serves several purposes: to find defects, to validate the system or an element of the system, and to verify functionality, performance, and safety requirements. The focus of testing is often on the verification and validation aspects. However, defect detection is probably the most important aspect of testing. While you cannot test quality into the software, you can certainly work to remove as many defects as possible.

Various types of testing can be done. Unit testing exercises individual components in isolation. Integration testing occurs while the system is being assembled and focuses on interface verification and component interaction. System testing comprises a range of tests that are performed when the software is completely integrated. Functionality, performance, load, stress, safety, and acceptance testing are just a few of the kinds of system tests.

Some basic principles of testing are:

- All tests should be traceable to the requirements and all requirements should be tested.

- Tests should be planned before testing begins. Test planning can occur as soon as the relevant stage has been completed. System test planning can start when the requirements document is complete.

- The "80/20" principle applies to software testing. In general, 80 percent of errors can be traced back to 20 percent of the components. Anything you can do ahead of time to identify components likely to fall in that 20 percent (e.g. high risk, complex, many interfaces, demanding timing constraints) will help focus the testing effort for better results.

- Start small and then integrate into larger system. Finding defects deep in the code is difficult to do at the system level. Such defects are easier to uncover at the unit level.

- You can't test everything. Exhaustive testing cannot be done except for the most trivial of systems. However, a well-planned testing effort can test all parts of the system. Missing logic paths or branches may mean missing important defects, so test coverage should be determined.

- Testing by an independent party is most effective. It is hard for developers to see their own bugs. While unit tests are usually written and run by the developer, it is a good idea to have a fellow team member review the tests. A separate testing group will usually perform the other tests. An independent viewpoint helps find defects, which is the goal of testing.

Scheduling testing phases is always an art, and depends on the expected quality of the software product. Relatively defect free software passes through testing within a minimal time frame. An inordinate amount of resources can be expended testing buggy software. Previous history, either of the development team or similar projects, can help determine how long testing will take. Some methods (such as error seeding and Halstead's defect metric) exist for estimating defect density (number of defects per unit of code) when historical information is not available.

Chapter 9 discusses testing and test analysis in more detail.

4.3.6   Products from the Development Process

 A collection of products will be produced as a result of the software development process. Products include plans, diagrams, reports, procedures, code, and other items. The exact complement of products will be determined during the tailoring process early in the project. Tailoring will not only select the products to be produced, but the level of detail that must be contained in the document or other artifacts. The size and criticality of the software project will determine what documents need to be created. For smaller projects, many of the documents can be combined, or the software sections can be part of a system-wide document.

 Documentation is quite often the last thing on the software developer's mind. On many projects, the documentation follows the completion of the code instead of preceding it. On others, the documents are produced and then promptly ignored. These management problems need to be addressed. Having a tailored document set is a start. Making sure that *usability* is a prime factor within the documents will also help.

Products that may be created during the software development process include:

- **Requirements**, including specifications, traceability matrices, and use case diagrams.

- **Design**, usually including a written document, but also diagrams (such as UML) and notes. It is important to document *why* a particular approach was taken, to guard against problems if the designer leaves, new requirements force design changes, or if maintenance or upgrades lead to a change many years down the road.

- **Code**. Well commented source code, as well as any files required to build the system.

- **Milestone Reviews**. Many projects have major reviews at predefined milestones. One beneficial outcome is making sure required documentation is completed by the review. The reviews also allow others from different disciplines within the team to see what is being considered. In addition, outside experts may also be present to point out problems or suggest areas for further work.

- **Inspection Reports** from formal inspections.

- **Analyses Reports** from various development and safety analyses performed. Analyses are performed by the software developer, software assurance engineer, and software safety engineer throughout the development process. The following describes some of the analyses that may be performed:

    o **Software Requirements Analysis** verifies that all requirements for the software were properly flowed down, and that they are correct, consistent, complete, unambiguous, and verifiable.

    o **Design Analyses** look at feasibility, timing, interfaces, interdependence of components, and other areas of concern. Chapter 7 describes many of the analyses performed at this stage of development.

    o **Code Analysis** verifies that the coded program correctly implements the verified design and does not violate safety requirements. Traceability from the code back to the requirements will be verified by analysis.

    o **Test Analysis** includes two types of analyses: 1) analyses before the fact to ensure validity of the tests, and 2) analyses of the test results.

- **Plans**. Some plans that will be developed for all safety-critical systems are:

    o **System Safety Plan.** This plan should include software as a subsystem and identify tasks associated with developing and assuring the safety-critical software.

    o **Software Concepts Document.** This document identifies technically challenging areas and any safety-critical processes.

o **Software Management Plan.** This plan documents what management processes will be used to oversee the software development. Items to be included are work breakdown structure, budget, schedule, and resource allocation. Coordination of development with systems or software safety tasks should also be addressed here. How requirements, especially safety-critical requirements, will be managed may be addressed here or in the Software Development Plan.

o **Software Configuration Management Plan.** All software products, which includes far more than just code, must be configuration managed. Old files in a software build are a notorious problem, as are lost updates and other problems with changed files. This plan specifies what will be under configuration management (CM), what CM system will be used, and the process for moving an item into or out of the CM system.

o **Software Development Plan.** This plan defines the process and activities used by the developers in the creation of the software. Lifecycle, methodology, use of prototypes, products to be produced, integration strategy, reviews to perform, and baselines or increment descriptions are some of the items to include. The required support environment for development or integration is also described in this plan.

o **Software Security Plan.** The plan addresses the security of safety-critical software as well as other security issues.

o **Software Assurance Plan.** Also called a Software Quality Assurance Plan. This plan describes how the software products will be assured and what the Software Assurance engineer's tasks will be. Areas to address include support to software safety, verification of software safety requirements, and safety and software assurance engineer participation in software reviews and inspections.

- **Management Reports**, such as work breakdown structure, schedule, or budget.

- **Software Assurance Records**, including process audit reports, document review notes, and Functional Configuration and Physical Configuration Audit reports.

- **Test Verification Reports** detailing the results of testing (unit, integration, system, acceptance, or safety).

- **Problem or Anomaly Reports** describing unexpected behavior of the software or system, the analysis performed to determine the cause, and what was done to correct the problem. Projects usually have a formal system for problem reports after the software has reached a level of maturity. However, defects or problems that occur before this time are also important. Tracking these problems, or at least reviewing them to make sure no major defect slips through, is recommended in safety-critical systems.

- **Metrics**, such as number of defects found by an inspection or percent of design complete.

- **Other Documents** as negotiated during the tailoring process.

4.3.7   Managing Object-Oriented Projects

While most of the tasks of project management are divorced from the type of software development, object-oriented (OO) software development does add some twists to the process. Some of the differences are listed below.

Lifecycle. OO software development is recursive and parallel in nature. The definition of systems, subsystems, and objects can occur in parallel, rather than sequentially. This does not map well to the waterfall lifecycle model. Also, a common idea in OO development is a short interactive cycle of "analyze, design, implement, and test" until the software is complete. This type of development fits well with lifecycles such as the spiral, incremental development, and evolutionary development.

Requirements. Some OO methodologies use iterative methods by which the system's requirements are discovered, captured, documented, and communicated. Each "turn around the spiral," for instance, may start with an update to the requirements based on what was learned in the last iteration. It should be noted, however, that many OOD methods are non-iterative as well.

Planning. A significant difference between object-oriented and traditional software projects is the regularly repeated delivery (through the point of actual coding and testing) of a portion of the end-product's functionality. Plans for object-oriented projects may have to reflect multiple iterations, with the quantity varying based on size and complexity of the project. A suggested limitation to the number of iterations per lifecycle phase is three. [106]

Reusability. As one of the principal goals of OO software development is reusability, project managers may find it useful to identify a separate timeline for identifying reusable components. Furthermore, project plans for object-oriented projects may be treated as a reusable set of artifacts, which should have schedule and staffing templates that can be adapted to many different projects.

Estimating. Estimating schedules is often difficult, especially if your organization or project manager has little experience with OO projects. One of the aspects to consider when defining the schedule is the number of iterations an object will require. Simple objects can be designed, implemented, and tested in one iteration. Complex and critical objects will require several iterations to fully define them.

Risk Management. The iterative style of object-oriented projects mitigates several risks, such as clarifying user requirements up front and pre-testing project feasibility. Regardless, a proactive approach to risk management needs to be practiced. Risks of using OO include new technology, new tools, tools that have many defects, and software developer inexperience.

Measuring Progress. Appropriate measures may include the number of key classes, support classes, and classes per subsystem; number of interface operations, message sends, and nesting levels; and classes per developer. A particularly useful measure illustrative of object-oriented engineering is the number of classes reused in a project, determined by counting classes at the outset of a project and at the end.

Team roles. For an object-oriented software development project team, new professional roles may be necessary. Some roles to consider are librarians to manage class libraries, library-class programmers (at the foundation and application levels), application programmers and prototypers, requirements analysts, implementation designers, modeling experts, and gurus.

Tools. Project management tools (software or "paper and pencil") are geared toward the waterfall lifecycle. It is much harder to represent an alternative lifecycle within these tools. One way to deal with this is to plan multiple iterations of the same set of activities. As each iteration occurs, less and less time is required for the iteration. This adds an order of magnitude of complexity to managing an OO project from a project management tool perspective. For a large project, managing this additional complexity can be a significant cost. Because project management tools have not yet evolved to meet the requirements of OO project management; project managers need to be careful to not let the limitations of the project management tool control the actual management of the project.

Project Deliverables. OO project design documentation will typically include:

- Object and class specifications.
- Reusable component information (including past-use and testing information).
- Class hierarchy and interaction information.
- Class interface information (what is visible outside the class).
- Use-cases and UML diagrams.

4.3.8   Software Development Capability Frameworks

Several standardized frameworks exist that measure a software development organization's process maturity. ISO 9000 and the Software Capability Maturity Model (SW-CMM) are two of the best known. The concept behind process maturity measurement is that if you follow a well-structured process in developing your software, that software is more likely to be a quality product. While this is not always true, such process measurements can provide a way to compare development organizations (such as for contracts). They also provide a way for an individual organization to measure improvements within software development.

While process maturity is important, the actual practices the software developer follows are also essential. Having a well defined but inadequate process may slip by the assessors or auditors, but it is unlikely to produce good software. It also does no good to have a process that no one follows because it is too unwieldy, too inflexible, or designed for projects much larger or smaller than the current one.

Frameworks fall into several types:

- **Standards and Guidelines used for contractual purposes.** Standards and Guidelines can be tailored and are often used as recommendations of good practices, if not imposed as standards.
    - o MIL-STD-498
    - o ISO 9000
    - o DO-178B (aviation safety)
    - o IEEE 1228
- **Process Improvement Models and Internal Appraisal Methods.** These frameworks define characteristics of good process, but not specific implementations. They provide a roadmap from the current process to the improved process.
    - o CMM family (SW-CMM, CMMI (integrated SW/Systems Engineering), etc.)
    - o Systems Engineering Capability Assessment Model (SECAM), International Council on Systems Engineering

- **Contractor Selection Vehicles.** Assessment methods that can be used by an outsider (e.g. software acquirer) to evaluate a companies software development process. Aids in selection of software development company, minimizes risk.
  - CMM-Based Appraisal for Internal Process Improvement (CBA IPI), associated with the SW-CMM
  - Software Capability Evaluation, an external SW-CMM evaluation
  - Software Development Capability Evaluation (SDCE), US Air Force
  - Standard CMMI Assessment Method for Process Improvement (SCAMPI)
  - ISO/IEC TR 15504 (originally Software Process Improvement Capability dEtermination, or SPICE). Technical report describing assessment method.
- **Quality Awards.** Awards given to companies with a high focus on quality. Strict selection criteria.
  - Malcolm Baldrige National Quality Award
  - European Quality Award
- **Software Engineering Lifecycle Models.** Standards that specify elements of a software development process. Focused more on the "how" of software creation than process improvement models.
  - MIL-STD-498
  - IEEE 12207
- **Systems Engineering Models.** Software is a major element of a system, but it is not the whole system. Many problems develop when the pieces (hardware, software, operators, etc.) do not fit together will.
  - MIL-STD-499B (Systems Engineering)
  - Systems Engineering CMM (SE-CMM) and CMMI (integrated software and systems CMM)
  - SECAM
  - IEEE 1220
  - Systems Engineering Capability Model (EIA/IS 731)

Understanding how these frameworks fit together is a complicated issue. The Software Productivity Consortium maintains a website dedicated to showing the relationships among the quagmire of various frameworks (http://www.software.org/quagmire). The interrelationships are shown in Figure 4-8, reprinted with permission from the Software Productivity Consortium.

The Capability Maturity Model for Software (SW-CMM) is the most common standard used to measure a software development organization's software process capabilities. The SW-CMM was developed by the Software Engineering Institute at Carnegie Mellon University. Their work on the SW-CMM was initiated by the US Government's need to solve a basic problem of software acquisition -- "Why do all these software projects not work, come in late, and/or cost too much?"

Figure 4-8 Development Frameworks Quagmire

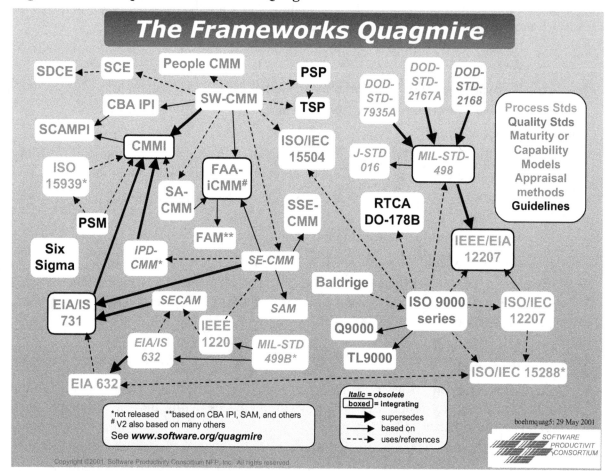

The Software CMM describes the principles and practices underlying software process maturity. It is intended to help software organizations understand where they are now, and to improve the maturity of their software processes. The SW-CMM provides an evolutionary path from ad hoc, chaotic processes to mature, disciplined software processes.

The SW-CMM is organized into five maturity levels:

1. **Initial.** The software process is characterized as ad hoc, and occasionally even chaotic. Few processes are defined, and success depends on individual effort and heroics. Software products may be quite good (especially with a knowledgeable team), but quality will vary between teams or products.

2. **Repeatable.** Basic project management processes are established to track cost, schedule, and functionality. The necessary processes are in place to repeat earlier successes on projects with similar applications.

3. **Defined.** The software process for both management and engineering activities is documented, standardized, and integrated into a standard software process for the organization. All projects use an approved, tailored version of the organization's standard software process for developing and maintaining software.

4. **Managed.** Detailed measures of the software process and product quality are collected. Both the software process and products are quantitatively understood and controlled.

5. **Optimizing.** Continuous process improvement is enabled by quantitative feedback from the process and from piloting innovative ideas and technologies.

Figure 4-9 Software Capability Maturity Model

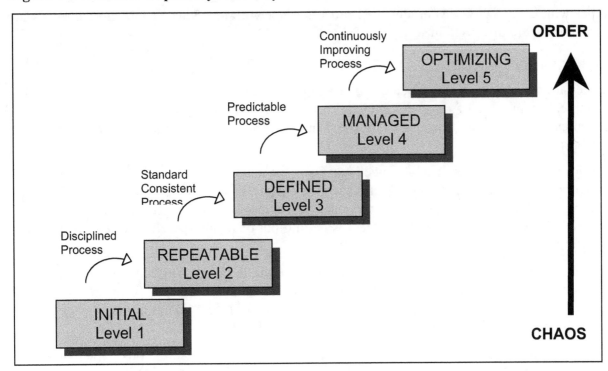

For each level (except Level 1), <u>key process areas</u> specify where an organization should focus to improve its software process.

The key process areas (KPA's) at Level 2 focus on establishing basic project management controls. They are Requirements Management, Software Project Planning, Software Project Tracking and Oversight, Software Subcontract Management, Software Quality Assurance, and Software Configuration Management.

Level 3 addresses both project and organizational issues, as the organization establishes an infrastructure that institutionalizes effective software engineering and management processes across all projects. The KPA's are Organization Process Focus, Organization Process Definition, Training Program, Integrated Software Management, Software Product Engineering, Inter-group Coordination, and Peer Reviews.

Level 4 focuses on establishing a quantitative understanding of both the software process and the software work products being built. The KPA's are Quantitative Process Management and Software Quality Management.

The KPA's at Level 5 cover the issues that both the organization and the projects must address to implement continual, measurable software process improvement. They are Defect Prevention, Technology Change Management, and Process Change Management.

The SW-CMM is an especially important framework. Within NASA, many contracts are now specifying that the software development company must be CMM level 3. NASA itself is moving toward implementing a process improvement strategy that will help the Agency achieve at least the equivalent of CMM level 3. Other organizations are mandating some level of SW-CMM or CMMI (Integrated Capability Maturity Model), which merges the SW-CMM with the Systems CMM.

Issues with using SW-CMM or any other process framework to evaluate contractors for software development are discussed in section 12.2.1.

4.3.9 Metrics

A measurement is the empirical, objective assignment of a value to a specific attribute. For example, the number of days to complete a task is a measurement. A metric is a series of measurements that yield insight into the state of processes or products, and that drives appropriate action.

Metrics are used to understand a project's status, a piece of software, or the process of creating the software, among other things. Metrics can be defined to measure project status and product quality. They provide insight and patterns that allow the project manager to better manage the process. They can show when the project is getting out of hand, as well as when everything is going smoothly.

The first step in good metrics collection is understanding the goal. Do you want to reduce risk by maintaining the software complexity below a specific threshold? Do you want to keep the development schedule to within 10% of the desired schedule? Determining the goals will determine what metrics to use.

A metrics plan should be created to document the goals and associated metrics. The plan should also detail how the metrics will be used, and what decisions might depend on the metrics. Having a clear purpose will help reduce the number of measurements collected that are not actually used.

Collecting metrics is not a "free" activity. In general, collection should be as unobtrusive as possible and directed toward achieving your goal. Too much data is as problematic as too little data. [107]

Specific data snapshots have curiosity value, but the real power comes from collecting and analyzing metrics over time. The goal of analysis is the identification of patterns. Patterns in the software development for a specific project may point to the need for more training, more developers, or more time for a particular phase. Patterns outside a specific project may point to organizational factors that influence projects, for better or for worse.

Once you have analyzed the metric, an action needs to be taken. The action needs to be visible and congruent, and it must close the feedback loop to the suppliers of the information. Consider an OO project where many of the developers are new to the OO world. The metrics may show that the software design is taking more time than expected. They may also show that the developers with the least OO experience are the slowest. From this pattern, an action must be generated. Perhaps OO gurus are hired (or moved from another project) to help the developers who are new to come up to speed.

For a metrics program to succeed, it is necessary to establish trust, value, communication, and understanding. Those providing the measurements must agree that the metrics have value. As a worst-case example, team members who do not understand why the measurements are being collected and who feel that the data collection is a waste of time may not accurately collect the measurements, or may even go so far as to "fake" them after the fact.

As a project continues, the metrics plan should be reviewed. [108] Are the metrics used in decision making? Metrics that are never looked at or that never result in an action should be discontinued. Are the metrics providing enough information? If not, perhaps additional measurements need to be added (or new measurements defined to replace those that are currently collected but not used).

What metrics to measure are determined by what you want to accomplish. The project management resources listed in section 4.3.1 contain pointers to more information on metrics. Many of the software engineering websites listed in Appendix A.2 also contain information on project and software development metrics.

4.4 *Tailoring your process*

Tailoring the safety effort was discussed in section 3.2. This section looks at tailoring the software development process. The goal is to do all the necessary work, but only what is necessary.

There are quite a few elements of software development that can be tailored. In some cases, tailoring will involve selecting the choice that best suits the project. In others, items will be added to or subtracted from a particular process.

Before beginning a tailoring exercise, the software developer must consider the scope of the software under development. The larger, more complex, more critical, and riskier the software is, the more thorough the development process must be.

Factors that affect the tailoring include:

- Safety and mission criticality.

- Size and complexity.

- Required standards, such as IEEE 12207.

- Cost and schedule risks.

- Innovation and technical risks.

Depending on the software development process chosen, you may need to tailor down (from "heavyweight" processes) or tailor up (from "lightweight" or agile processes). Processes include such items as documentation required (or suggested), inspections or reviews, tests to be conducted, and methods of handling change.

"Development process" and "amount of documentation" are often considered synonymous. While not strictly true, the development process chosen will often determine the amount of documentation required and the level of detail necessary.

Lightweight or agile processes, such as Extreme Programming, the Crystal family, Adaptive Software Development, and SCRUM, were developed partly because the heavyweight processes did not fit in an environment with short time-to-market or constantly changing requirements. Within each methodology are valuable ideas. However, there is a tendency among some developers to use these processes as an excuse for ad hoc programming and no documentation. Because of their newness and low rigor, this guidebook does not recommend using agile processes for the safety-critical elements of your software.

Other issues to consider when tailoring the software development process include:

- **Reviews**. What reviews (requirements, design, code, or other) and types of reviews (formal inspections, code walkthroughs, informal design reviews, etc) will be conducted? Will the reviews be formal, informal, or a combination? What products are subject to wider review (outside of the development team)?

- **Design methodology** (structured, OO, FM, or other). What is the history of the project (e.g. brand new or drawing on a previous project)? Will components be reused from other projects? If so, how were they developed? Will COTS software be included, and does it have any impact on the design methodology? What is the expertise of the team members? Are resources available to train the team in a new methodology? Is the team comfortable with, or does it have significant experience with, a particular methodology?

- **Lifecycle.** What lifecycle best fits the project? Does the lifecycle need to be modified?

- **Testing.** When should testing start? Who will do the testing? What specific tests need to be conducted? Many possible tests are listed in Chapter 9.

- **Tools**. What tools should be used to aid the project? Will CASE (Computer Aided Software Engineering) tools be used? Simulators? Automatic code generators?

- **Organization.** Are the team members assigned to tasks according to their expertise? Do senior members of the team handle flowdown of requirements and safety issues? What should be done to maintain a good working relationship among the team members?

All of the above issues combine to create a tailored process. Each element must work well for the specific aspect for which it was chosen (client, development organization, schedule, technology) and work well with each of the other elements of development (the tools, the organization, lifecycle, method).

"Process Tailoring for Software Project Plans" [29] provides more detail on a tailoring method that meets the Software Capability Maturity Model (SW-CMM) Level 3 process tailoring and project planning activities.

4.5 *Software Configuration Management*

Software Configuration Management (SCM) is often considered a part of project management and not software development or testing. It is a vital part of the development process, however, that should not be overlooked. It is very unlikely that you can produce "safe" software without it. You certainly cannot convince the quality, assurance, or safety personnel that the software is safe if you have not implemented SCM.

SCM is much more than just version control of source code. It is a process to maintain and monitor the software development process as well. SCM includes:

- Identification. Identifying the structure and kinds of components, making them unique and accessible in some form by giving each component a name, version identification, and configuration identification.

- Control. Controlling the release of a product and changes to it throughout the lifecycle by having controls in place that ensure consistent software via the creation of a baseline product.

- Status Accounting. Recording and reporting the status of components and change requests, and gathering vital statistics about components in the product.

- Audit and review. Validating the completeness of a product and maintaining consistency among the components by ensuring that components are in an appropriate state throughout the entire project life cycle and that the product is a well defined collection of components.

Be aware of potential problems if you split control of software configuration management (e.g. having software documents is maintained by a project or company configuration management group, and the source code version control handled by the programmers). It may be difficult to keep the documents (e.g. design) synchronized with the code. Someone with configuration management experience should be "in charge" of the source code, to enforce change control and comprehensive documentation of changes.

Software Configuration Management is usually performed using a tool (program). However, a file or folder should be maintained, to collect information that is not in electronic form. This information could include the design notes scribbled on a napkin or a fax that only exists in hardcopy. The point is to collect all pertinent information in one place. It is a good idea to catalog all the hardcopy information in the electronic SCM system, so that it can be found again when needed.

4.5.1   Change Control

Change control is an important part of developing safe software. Arbitrary changes should be avoided. Once a piece of software has reached a level of maturity, it should be subject to a formal change control process. What that level of maturity is will vary by group. It could be when the component compiles, when the CSCI (which may contain several components) is completed, or when the whole program is at its first baseline.

Formal change control usually includes a form to request a change (Software Change Request, Engineering Change Request, or other). The form is filled out by the developer, the customer, or someone else involved in the project. The form should include both what should be changed and why. A Change Control Board (CCB), also called an Engineering Review Board, and by other names, is convened to evaluate the change request. The board consists of several people, including a representative from the software quality assurance group. When safety is an issue, someone from safety or risk management should also be included on the board. The requestor may be at the CCB meeting, or the board may just evaluate the submitted form. The board may approve the change, reject it, combine it with other requests, or suggest a modification.

Another way software changes occur is through a problem reporting/corrective action (PRACA) process. A PRACA is issued during the operation of the software, usually during testing. If the software is not operating as it should, a PRACA is written. The problem report goes to the developers, who must find out what the problem is. If the fix to the problem involves a change to the software, it must go through the CCB.

All the paperwork from the change control process should be archived in the configuration management system. This includes software requests, PRACA's, notes from CCB meetings, and any other pertinent information. The configuration management system provides a repository for storing this data for later retrieval.

In addition, a cross-index should be created between software changes, requirements, code component versions, and tests. This could be a database, a spreadsheet, or some other format. Being able to know what components a software change impacts determines what tests need to be run. The change may also indicate that a requirement changed, and that the software requirements document needs to be updated.

4.5.2   Versioning

Versioning is the part of software configuration management that most people think of first. It involves archiving the source code, keeping previous versions when a new version is added to the SCM tool. Sometimes a complete previous version is kept; other tools use a "delta" (difference) from the previous version to the new version.

Each component will have a version number associated with it. A "release" will consist of all the components and their associated version numbers. Some SCM tools allow branching, where a release will go down two or more paths (perhaps a "freeware" version and a commercial enhanced version, for example). Versioning keeps the changes straight and allows "roll back" to previous versions if a bug is found down the road.

Most SCM tools also have a check-in/check-out policy to prevent changes by multiple programmers on the same component. Some will allow only one programmer to work on the component at one time. Other SCM tools will do a "merge" when multiple developers check in the same component.

One weakness of many SCM tools is that the programmer can get away without good documentation on what changes were made and why. The tool keeps the changes, but the reasoning behind it usually is added as a comment upon check-in of the component. (Some tools force the developer to say *something*, but not necessarily something useful.) At a minimum, when a component is changed the following should be done:

- Clearly identify the area of code that is changed (within the source code). Use a comment with some character string (such as *****) that is easy to spot when flipping through the source code. Identify the end of the changed area the same way.

- Have a header at the top of the altered code that includes why the change occurred (change request, problem report, or other reason), what was changed (in English, not code-ese), when it was changed, and by whom.

- Include the what/when/why/who information in the component check-in comment. This information can be extracted for status accounting (see below).

4.5.3 Status Accounting

According to MIL-STD-482A, configuration status accounting is the "recording and reporting of the information that is needed to manage configuration effectively, including a listing of the approved configuration identification, the status of proposed changes to configuration, and the implementation status of approved changes."

Status accounting answers the question "how complete is the software?" Decide what stages of incompleteness, correctness, and obsoleteness need to be known about each item and to what audience, give each stage a status name (e.g. draft, under review, ready for integration/delivery, operational, superseded), and collect the status of each item. Collate the information into a human-understandable format.

Part of status accounting is the ability to create reports that show the status of each document (version, whether it is checked-out, when it was last updated, who made the changes, and what was changed). The status of change requests and problem reports are also included in status accounting.

While the status information can be compiled by hand, it can be a tedious process. Many tools exist that provide an integrated configuration management system for all kinds of documents, including source code, and that can generate the status reports when requested. Some of these tools are free or low-priced.

The configuration management system needs to be audited occasionally. The audit can be a formal affair, or an informal look at the system by someone other than the configuration manager, such as a software assurance engineer or a software quality assurance engineer. The purpose of the audit is to verify that what the status accounting says about the project is actually true, and to look for holes in the process that can lead to problems in the future.

4.5.4 Defect Tracking

Defect (bug) tracking is sometimes handled outside of SCM. However, integrating defect tracking with the SCM process facilitates control of information. (When it is the middle of the night and you're trying to find information on a bug you thought you had killed a week ago, you'll appreciate a well-ordered system.)

Defect tracking has several purposes. One is to record all the defects for future reference. This can be simply for historical purposes, or to have something to reference to compare defects found before. Having defect information from previous projects can be a big plus when debugging the next project.

Recording the defects allows metrics to be determined. One of the easiest ways to judge whether a program is ready for serious safety testing is to measure its defect density—the number of defects per line of code. If testing has found the majority of defects, then the software is likely to be stable. Safety testing then puts software through its paces, usually by generating error conditions and verifying graceful behavior by the program.

To determine the defects per lines of code, you need to know two pieces of information, both of which can be extracted from a good configuration management system: lines of code and number of defects. You also need a "history" from other projects on defects/lines of code (from your projects, or general industry numbers). If the average defects/thousand lines of code (KLOC) is 6, and the software is 10,000 lines of code (LOC), then about 60 defects exist in the software. If testing has only found 10, a lot more tests need to be done. The software in the example has a high risk, because many more defects linger in the code.

 One question in defect tracking is whether to use bugs found during unit testing by developers. It would be best if those defects were documented. The developer can see if he has a tendency to a certain kind of bug. Other programmers can learn from the experience of the developer and avoid similar defects.

4.5.5 Metrics from your SCM system

Monitoring the various elements of your software development project can show when the project is getting into trouble (cost, schedule, cannot meet delivery date) and can aid in planning future projects. Items to track, if possible, are:

* Lines of code (LOC)[4] for the project (total).

* LOC per component, average component size, distribution of sizes.

* Complexity per component, average complexity, distribution of complexities

* Estimated and actual time to complete development for a change request or problem report.

* Estimated and actual time to code a component.

* Estimated and actual time to unit test a component.

* Estimated and actual time for integration tests (black box) and system tests.

* Number of defects found per test type. Defects can be categorized for further breakdown.

From these raw inputs, other determinations can be made. For example:

* Number of defects per LOC for the team or organization.

* How good estimations are for completion of a software change.

* How much time it takes to unit testing. Correlated with the defects/LOC to see if more or less time should be spent on unit testing.

* How much time to estimate for the various development phases (design, coding, testing) for the next project.

* How much time it will take to update the software for a future change request.

* Where to put extra resources in testing. If the majority of the defects are found in system testing, more time in unit and integration testing may find the defects earlier.

* If there was a software development process change, the numbers may show how much of an improvement the change made.

4.5.6 What to include in the SCM system

* Documents and plans (specifications, formal design documents, verification matrix, presentation packages).

---

[4] Function points can be substituted for Lines of Code, or both numbers can be collected.

- Design information (data flow charts, UML or OOD products, inputs to automatic code generation programs, and any miscellaneous related information).

- Interface information (Interface Control Documents, flow charts, message formats, data formats).

- Source code.

- Test cases/scenarios.

- Test scripts, for manual or automated testing.

- Test reports.

- Defect lists (or defect database).

- Change requests.

- Problem reports/corrective actions

- Information for metrics, such as lines of code, number of defects, estimated and actual start or completion dates, and estimated/actual time to complete a change.

4.6   Good Programming Practices for Safety

A good software development process provides a solid foundation for creating safety-critical software. However, there are many practices that can be incorporated into the design or implementation that also increase the safety of the software. Some of these are listed below. The practices come from various sources, which are referenced. In addition, they are summarized in a checklist in Appendix H.

The following list of good software safety development practices is from "Solving the Software Safety Paradox" by Doug Brown [30].

- **CPU self test.** If the CPU becomes partially crippled, it is important for the software to know this. Cosmic Radiation, EMI, electrical discharge, shock, or other effects could have damaged the CPU. A CPU self-test, usually run at boot time, can verify correct operations of the processor. If the test fails, then the CPU is faulty, and the software can go to a safe state.

- **Guarding against illegal jumps**. Filling ROM or RAM with a known pattern, particularly a halt or illegal instruction, can prevent the program from operating after it jumps accidentally to unknown memory. On processors that provide traps for illegal instructions (or a similar exception mechanism), the trap vector could point to a process to put the system into a safe state.

- **ROM tests**. Prior to executing the software stored in ROM (EEPROM, Flash disk), it is important to verify its integrity. This is usually done at power-up, after the CPU self test, and before the software is loaded. However, if the system has the ability to alter its own programming (EEPROMS or flash memory), then the tests should be run periodically.

- **Watchdog Timers.** Usually implemented in hardware, a watchdog timer resets (reboots) the CPU if it is not "tickled" within a set period of time. Usually, in a process implemented as an infinite loop, the watchdog is written to once per loop. In multitasking operating systems, using a watchdog is more difficult. Do NOT use an interrupt to tickle the watchdog. This defeats the purpose of having one, since the interrupt could still be working while all the real processes are blocked!

- **Guard against Variable Corruption.** Storing multiple copies of critical variables, especially on different storage media or physically separate memory, is a simple method for verifying the variables. A comparison is done when the variable is used, using two-out-of-three voting if they do not agree, or using a default value if no two agree. Also, critical variables can be grouped, and a CRC used to verify they are not corrupted.

- **Stack Checks.** Checking the stack guards against stack overflow or corruption. By initializing the stack to a known pattern, a stack monitor function can be used to watch the amount of available stack space. When the stack margin shrinks to some predetermined limit, an error processing routine can be called that fixes the problem or puts the system into a safe state.

- **Program Calculation Checks.** Simple checks can be used to give confidence in the results from calculations.

"30 Pitfalls for Real-Time Software Developers," by David B. Stewart [31][32] discusses problems faced by real-time developers. Of the problems he considers, the following are especially applicable to safety and reliability:

- **Delays implemented as empty loops.** This can create problems (and timing difficulties) if the code is run on faster or slower machines, or even if recompiled with a newer, optimizing compiler.

- **Interactive and incomplete test programs.** Tests should be planned and scripted. This prevents tests from being missed. Also, functional tests should be run after a change, to make sure that the software change did not indirectly impact other code.

- **Reusing code not designed for reuse.** If the code was not designed for reuse, it may have interdependencies with other components. Usually, it will not use abstract data types (if object-oriented) or have a well-defined interface.

- **One big loop.** A single large loop forces all parts of the software to operate at the same rate. This is usually not desirable.

- **No analysis of hardware peculiarities before starting software design.** Different processors have peculiarities that can affect the time a calculation can take, or how long it takes to access an area of memory, for instance. Understanding the hardware before designing the software will decrease the number of "gotchas" at integration time.

- **Fine-grain optimizing during first implementation.** "Some programmers foresee anomalies (some are real, some are mythical). An example of a mythical anomaly is that multiplication takes much longer than addition."

- **Too many inter-component dependencies.** To maximize software reusability, components should not depend on each other in a complex way.

- **Only a single design diagram.** "Most software systems are designed such that the entire system is defined by a single diagram (or, even worse, none!). When designing software, getting the entire design on paper is essential."

* **Error detection and handling are an afterthought and implemented through trial and error.** Design in the error detection and handling mechanisms *from the start*. Tailor the effort to the level of the code – do not put it everywhere! Look at critical locations where data needs to be right or areas where the software or hardware is especially vulnerable to bad input or output.

* **No memory analysis.** Check how much memory your system uses. Estimate it from your design, so that you can adjust the design if the system is bumping up against its limits. When trying to decide between two different implementations of the same concept, knowing the memory usage of each will help in making a decision.

* **Documentation was written after implementation.** Write what you need, and use what you write. Do not make unnecessarily verbose or lengthy documentation, unless contractually required. It is better to have short documents that the developers will actually read and use.

* **Indiscriminate use of interrupts. Use of interrupts can cause priority inversion in real-time systems if not implemented carefully.** This can lead to timing problems and the failure to meet necessary deadlines.

* **No measurements of execution time.** "Many programmers who design real-time systems have no idea of the execution time of any part of their code."

Bill Wood, in "Software Risk Management for Medical Devices," Table III [33], gives a list of mitigation mechanisms for various possible failures. Some of the practices that are not duplicated in the lists above are summarized below (and expanded upon):

* **Check variables for reasonableness before use.** If the value is out of range, there is a problem – memory corruption, incorrect calculation, hardware problems (if sensor), or other problem.

* **Use execution logging, with independent checking, to find software runaway, illegal functions, or out-of-sequence execution.** If the software must follow a known path through the components, a check log will uncover problems shortly after they occur.

* **Come-from checks.** For safety-critical components, make sure that the correct previous component called it, and that it was not called accidentally by a malfunctioning component.

* **Test for memory leakage.** Instrument the code and run it under load and stress tests. See how the memory usage changes, and check it against the predicted usage.

* **Use read-backs to check values.** When a value is written to memory, the display, or hardware, another function should read it back and verify that the correct value was written.

In addition to the suggestions above, consider doing the following to enhance the software safety:

* **Use a simulator or ICE (In-circuit Emulator)** system for debugging in embedded systems. These tools allow the programmer/tester to find some subtle problems more easily. Combined with some of the techniques described above, they can find memory access problems and trace back to the statement that generated the error.

- **Reduce complexity.** Calculate a complexity metric. Look at components that are very complex and reduce them if possible. Complexity metrics can be very simple. One way to calculate McCabe's Cyclomatic Complexity is to add the number of decisions and subtract one. An "if" is a 1. A case/switch statement with 3 cases is 2. Add these up and subtract one. If the complexity is over 10, look at simplifying the routine.

- **Design for weak coupling** between components (modules, classes, etc.). The more independent the components are, the fewer undesired side effects there will be later in the process. "Fixes" when an error is found in testing may create problems because of misunderstood dependencies between components.

- **Consider the stability of the requirements.** If the requirements are likely to change, design as much flexibility as possible into the system.

- **Consider compiler optimization carefully.** Debuggers may not work well with optimized code. It is hard to trace from the source code to the optimized object code. Optimization may change the way the programmer expected the code to operate (removing "unused" features that are actually used!).

- **Be careful if using multi-threaded programs.** Developing multi-threaded programs is notoriously difficult. Subtle program errors can result from unforeseen interactions among multiple threads. In addition, these errors can be very hard to reproduce since they often depend on the non-deterministic behavior of the scheduler and the environment.

- **A dependency graph** is a valuable software engineering aid. Given such a diagram, it is easy to identify what parts of the software can be reused, create a strategy for incremental testing of components, and develop a method to limit error propagation through the entire system.

- **Follow the two person rule**. At least two people should be thoroughly familiar with the design, code, testing and operation of each software component of the system. If one person leaves the project, someone else understands what is going on.

- **Prohibit program patches.** During development, patching a program is a bad idea. Make the changes in the code and recompile instead. During operations, patching may be a necessity, but the pitfalls should still be carefully considered.

- **Keep Interface Control Documents up to date.** Out-of-date information usually leads to one programmer creating a component or unit that will not interface correctly with another unit. The problem isn't found until late in the testing phase, when it is expensive to fix. Besides keeping the documentation up to date, use an agreed-upon method to inform everyone of the change.

- **Create a list of possible hardware failures that may impact the software**, if they are not spelled out in the software requirements document. Have the hardware and systems engineers review the list. The software must respond properly to these failures. The list will be invaluable when testing the error handling capabilities of the software. Having a list also makes explicit what the software can and cannot handle, and unvoiced assumptions will usually be discovered as the list is reviewed.

The following programming suggestions are derived from SSP 50038, Computer-Based Control System Safety Requirements for the International Space Station Program:

- Provide **separate authorization and separate control functions** to initiate a critical or hazardous function. This includes separate "arm" and "fire" commands for critical capabilities.

- **Do not use input/output ports for both critical and non-critical functions**.

- Provide **sufficient difference in addresses** between critical I/O ports and non-critical I/O ports, such that a single address bit failure does not allow access to critical functions or ports.

- Make sure all **interrupt priorities** and responses are defined. All interrupts should be initialized to a return, if not used by the software.

- Provide for an **orderly shutdown** (or other acceptable response) upon the detection of **unsafe conditions**. The system can revert to a known, predictable, and safe condition upon detection of an anomaly.

- Provide for an **orderly system shutdown** as the result of a **command shutdown**, power interruptions, or other failures. Depending on the hazard, battery (or capacitor) backup may be required to implement the shutdown when there is a power failure.

- Protect against **out-of-sequence transmission** of safety-critical function messages by detecting any deviation from the normal sequence of transmission. Revert to a known safe state when out-of-sequence messages are detected.

- Initialize all **unused memory** locations to a pattern that, if executed as an instruction, will cause the system to revert to a known safe state.

- **Hazardous sequences should not be initiated by a single keyboard entry**.

- Prevent **inadvertent entry into a critical routine**. Detect such entry if it occurs, and revert to a known safe state.

- **Don't use a stop or halt instruction**. The CPU should be always executing, whether idling or actively processing.

- **When possible, put safety-critical operational software instructions in nonvolatile read-only memory.**

- **Don't use scratch files** for storing or transferring safety-critical information between computers or tasks within a computer.

- When **safety interlocks** are removed or bypassed for a test, the software should verify the reinstatement of the interlocks at the completion of the testing.

- **Critical data** communicated from one CPU to another should be verified prior to operational use.

- Set a **dedicated status flag** that is updated between each step of a hazardous operation. This provides positive feedback of the step within the operation, and confirmation that the previous steps have been correctly executed.

- **Verify critical commands** prior to transmission, and upon reception. It never hurts to check twice!

- **Make sure all flags used are unique and single purpose.**

- Put the majority of **safety-critical decisions and algorithms** in a single (or few) software development component(s).

- **Decision logic** using data from hardware or other software components should not be based on values of all ones or all zeros. Use specific binary patterns to reduce the likelihood of malfunctioning hardware/software satisfying the decision logic.

- **Safety-critical components should have only one entry and one exit point.**

- **Perform reasonableness checks on all safety-critical inputs**.

- Perform a **status check** of critical system elements prior to executing a potentially hazardous sequence.

- Always **initialize the software into a known safe state.** This implies making sure all variables are set to an initial value, and not the previous value prior to reset.

- **Don't allow the operator to change safety-critical time limits in decision logic**.

- When the system is safed, usually in response to an anomalous condition or problem, provide the **current system configuration** to the operator.

- Safety-critical routines should include **"come from" checks** to verify that they are being called from a valid program, task, or routine.

Chapter 5   System and Software Concept Stage

Safety must be an integral part of the system and software from the very start.

Two basic types of activities are performed by the software organizations during the concept stage: system review and planning. While the system is being defined, the software and safety teams have an opportunity to help ensure that a safe and functional system is created. For the purposes of this guidebook, the concept phase includes all activities that occur prior to the development of software requirements. Developing the high-level system concept, project planning, and determining system level requirements are all included.

The distribution of functionality from hardware to software is one area where software and safety engineers should be involved. Because software is flexible (i.e., easy to change, especially at a later date), it is tempting to implement functions in software rather than hardware. This may not always be the best choice.

The questions below are meant to help the system engineer consider the consequences of implementing functions in hardware or software. These questions should be considered a starting point for deciding which requirements to allocate to software and which to hardware.

- For each requirement or function, where is the best place in the system to perform this activity, and why? Should the functionality be in hardware, software, or a combination? What are the benefits of the approach? What problems may occur as a result of the approach?

- What will happen if a hardware or software safety component fails? What are the backups, options, and plans for dealing with the failure? Does the outcome of a possible failure indicate that any additional resources (hardware or software) are required?

- How confident are you in the estimates on time/budget to complete the task? For most organizations, software estimates are usually inaccurate, as most projects come in late and over budget.

- How much are things likely to change – that is, how much flexibility is needed by the system?

- Is there adequate hardware to support the software? Will the software have all the information it needs to perform a safety-critical function? Sometimes extra hardware (sensors, backup systems) is required for the software to do its job safely.

During the system concept phase, the software team is involved in the initial planning of the software development effort. Several plans are produced, or at least started, at this stage. This is the time to think about how you will be doing your job in the months ahead. Some plans typically developed in the concept stage include:

- Software Management Plan
- Software Development Plan
- Software Assurance Plan
- Software Safety Plan

- Software Verification and Validation Plan
- Software Acquisition Plan
- Software Configuration Management Plan.

 A good plan has practical details on the process to be followed. Information will include not just *what* will be done, but *how* it will be done. External procedures that give the explicit steps may be referenced, or the steps may be given in the plan.

 When developing the plans, think about issues that may affect safety, both now and in the future. Consider the reliability of the system and software, and how that reliability may be verified. Look at what can be done to improve the maintainability of the created software, so that changes down the road will not create problems. Be creative. Up-front planning can help prevent larger problems in the future. However, keep in mind that not everything can be thought of at any one time. The project will evolve, so flexibility must also be "planned in."

5.1   Tasks and Analyses

Although most project work during this phase is concentrated on the system level, software developers and safety engineers have several tasks that must be initiated. These include the creation of software documents and plans that will determine how, what, and when important software products will be produced or activities will be conducted.

Table 5-1 System Concept Phase Tasks

Software Engineering Tasks	System and Software Safety Tasks	Software Assurance or IV&V Tasks
Provide input to project concept and software concept documents.	Create the Software Safety Plan, including planning and tailoring the safety effort. The plan can be an independent document or part of the system Safety Plan.	Review project and software concept documents.
Provide input to Software Safety Plan.	Conduct Preliminary Hazard Analysis (PHA) [Section 2.3.1].	Review Software Safety Plan.
Plan the software management and development processes [Chapter 4].	Set up hazards tracking and problem resolution process	Review Software Management and Development Plan.
Plan the configuration management system [Section 4.5].	Prepare hazard verification matrix.	Review Software Configuration Management Plan.
Plan the verification and validation process.	Review PHA for safety-critical software.	Review the Software Verification and Validation Plan.
Participate in "make or buy" decisions for software. Review software acquisition (including COTS) [Section 12.1]. Provide input to contracts for acquiring software [Section 12.2].	Participate in "make or buy" decisions for software. Review software acquisition (including COTS) [Section 12.1]. Provide input to contracts for acquiring software [Section 12.2].	Participate in "make or buy" decisions for software. Review software acquisition (including COTS) [Section 12.1]. Provide input to contracts for acquiring software [Section 12.2].
	Develop safety-critical software tracking process.	Plan the software assurance process.
	Conduct Software Subsystem Hazard Analysis [Section 2.3.4].	

5.2   Documentation and Milestones

The exact documents that a project will produce, and when they will be produced, are determined during this Concept phase. Documentation should reflect the project size, complexity, and criticality. Contractual obligations or required standards may also influence the amount of documentation produced.

The following table lists documents that are commonly produced for the concept phase of development:

Table 5-2 Project/Software Conception Documentation

Document	Software Safety Section
System Safety Plan	Include software as a subsystem. Identify tasks (e.g. analyses, requirements tracing) and personnel.
Software Concepts Document	Identify safety-critical processes.
Software Management Plan	Discuss coordination with systems safety tasks, flow-down incorporation of safety requirements and applicability to safety-critical software.
Software Security Plan	Determine security of safety-critical software.
Risk Management Plan	Identify software risks, especially those related to safety and reliability.
Software Configuration Management Plan	Identification and handling of safety-critical components.
Software Verification and Validation Plan	Discuss verification and validation of safety-critical components.
Software Quality Assurance Plan	Identify quality assurance support to software safety function, verification of software safety requirements, and safety participation in software reviews and inspections.

Milestones that will usually occur during the concept phase include:

- Software Concept Review (SCR)
- Software Management Plan Review

At the end of a lifecycle activity or phase, it is important to **verify** that
- ❖ All system safety requirements have been satisfied by this lifecycle phase.
- ❖ No additional hazards have been introduced by the work done during this lifecycle phase.

IEEE 1228-1994

5.3 Tailoring Guidelines

Section 3.2 *Tailoring the Effort* describes how to determine the software safety effort required (full, moderate, or minimal).

Table 5-3 Software Safety Effort for Conception Phase

Technique or Analysis	Safety Effort Level		
	MIN	MOD	FULL
2.3.1 Preliminary Hazard Analysis (PHA)	☆	☆	☆
2.3.4 Software Subsystem Hazard Analysis	☆	☆	☆
6.5 Software Safety Requirements	☆	☆	☆
6.5.7 Checklists and cross references	✓✓	✓✓	☆

Recommendation Codes			
☆	Mandatory	✓✓	Highly Recommended
✓	Recommended	⃠	Not Recommended

5.4 Independent Verification and Validation

For high value systems with high-risk software, an IV&V organization is usually involved to oversee the software development. Verification & Validation (V&V) is a system engineering process employing a variety of software engineering methods, techniques, and tools for evaluating the correctness and quality of a software product throughout its life cycle. IV&V is performed by an organization that is technically, managerially, and financially independent of the development organization.

IV&V should supplement, not supersede, the in-house software quality/product assurance efforts. Software QA and safety engineers should still be involved with the project from the start, reviewing documents, offering advice and suggestions, and monitoring the software development process. Depending on what is negotiated with the project manager, the IV&V personnel may be a second set of eyes, shadowing the software QA engineers, conducting independent audits, witnessing testing, or otherwise assisting the project team. This requires the IV&V team to be stationed with the project, or to visit frequently. A more remote form of IV&V involves reviewing the software products (plans, designs, code, test results, code review reports, etc.), with a few in-person audits to verify the software development process. IV&V analysts usually conduct the more in-depth analyses and verifications of the software, rather than software QA engineers.

When IV&V is used within a project, the exact functions and roles should be negotiated among all the parties. Currently, the relationship of IV&V activities and personnel to project software assurance activities and personnel within NASA is not clearly defined in software policy. However, IV&V does not take the place of software QA, but rather should be an integrated addition. IV&V does not replace the software safety role, either. The IV&V team may perform some software safety activities, such as specific safety analyses. Even some software engineering functions, such as requirements management, may be performed by the IV&V team.

The decision to use IV&V, and the level of IV&V required, should be made during the Concept phase. IV&V may be required by your organization for all safety-critical software, or based on the size and complexity of the project. For NASA, NPD 8730.4 provides the IV&V policy, and

NPG 8730.x (draft) provides the criteria under which a project must use Independent Verification and Validation or Independent Assessment.

 The NASA IV&V Facility in Fairmont, West Virginia (http://www.ivv.nasa.gov), is an excellent resource for all NASA projects. The IV&V Facility provides tailored technical, program management, and financial analyses for NASA programs, industry, and other Government agencies, by applying software engineering "best practices" to evaluate the correctness and quality of critical and complex software systems throughout the system development life cycle.

5.5   Safety Analyses

Safety is an integral part of the software life-cycle, from the specification of safety-related requirements, through inspection of the software controls, and into verification testing for hazards. Within each life cycle phase, the safety engineer performs various analysis tasks. If problems are found, they are fed back through the system until they are corrected or mitigated. While finding unsafe elements of the system is often the focus of the analyses, a "negative" analysis (no hazards or major problems) can give the project assurance that they are on the right path to a safe system.

Analysis techniques fall into two categories:

1. Top down system hazards and failure analyses, which look at possible hazards or faults and trace down into the design to find out what can cause them.

2. Bottom up review of design products to identify failure modes not predicted by top down analysis. This analysis ensures the validity of assumptions of top down analysis, and verifies conformance to requirements.

Typically, both types of analyses are used in a software safety analysis activity, though the specific techniques used are tailored for the project. Results of software safety analysis are reported back to the system safety organization for integration in the system safety plan.

As the software becomes more defined within the software life cycle, individual program sets, modules, or units are identified that are safety-critical. The analyses used vary with the phase of development, building on previous analyses or using the new level of software definition to refine the safety analysis.

Chapters 6-10 describe various techniques that have been useful in NASA activities and within industry. Tailoring by safety effort level is provided in the X.3 sections (X = the chapter number). In addition, a benefit and cost rating is given for most techniques, to assist in the planning of software safety activities. The ratings are subjective and meant to be only one consideration when choosing analysis techniques.

Chapter 6 Software Requirements

The cost of correcting software faults and errors escalates dramatically as the development life cycle progresses, making it important to correct errors and implement correct software requirements from the very beginning. Unfortunately, it is generally impossible to eliminate all errors.

Software developers must therefore work toward two goals:

1. To develop complete and correct requirements and correct code.

2. To develop fault-tolerant designs, which will detect and compensate for software faults.

Note that (2) is required because (1) is usually impossible.

This chapter of the guidebook describes developing and analyzing safety requirements for software. The software safety requirements can be top-down (flowed down from system requirements), bottom-up (derived from hazards analyses), or a combination of both. In some organizations, top-down flow is the only permitted route for requirements into software. In those cases, newly derived bottom-up safety requirements must be flowed back into the system specification first.

The requirements of software components are typically expressed as functions with corresponding inputs, processes, and outputs, plus additional requirements on interfaces, limits, ranges, precision, accuracy, and performance. There may also be requirements on the data of the program set, its attributes, relationships, and persistence, among others. The term "functions," in this case, does not mean software components, but a more general set of "things the software system must do." Management of requirements is a vital function and is discussed in Section 6.4.

Software safety requirements are derived from the system and subsystem safety requirements, which were developed to mitigate hazards identified in the Preliminary, System, and Subsystems Hazard Analyses (see *Section 2.3.1 PHA* and *Section 2.3.4 Software Subsystem Hazard Analysis*). Additional requirements may be imposed by standards, organizational requirements, and other sources. Good software safety techniques may be written into the requirements to make sure the software development process includes these techniques or practices.

The software safety requirements should be included in the following documents:

- Software Requirements Document (SRD) or Software Specification (SS)

- Software Interface Specification (SIS) or Interface Control Document (ICD)

Safety-related requirements must be clearly identified in the SRD. This can be in a separate section, or mixed with other requirements organized by function, system element, or other approach. Safety requirements should also be clearly identified in the requirements and interface documents, as well as any requirements traceability matrix.

An interface specification identifies, defines, and documents interface requirements internal to the [sub]system in which software resides, and between system (including hardware and operator interfaces), subsystem, and program set components and operation procedures. Note that the interface information is sometimes effectively contained in the SRD, or within an Interface Control

Document (ICD) which defines all system interfaces, including hardware to hardware, hardware to software, and software to software.

6.1 Tasks and Analyses

Table 6-1 Software Requirements Tasks

Software Engineering Tasks	System and Software Safety Tasks	Software Assurance or IV&V Tasks
Software requirements development [Sections 6.4.2 and 6.5]	Development of software safety requirements [Section 6.5]	Formal methods for verification [Sections 4.2.2.3 and 6.6.4]
Requirements management [Section 6.4]	Safety Requirements Flow-down Analysis [Section 6.6.1]	Model checking [Section 6.6.5]
Formal methods for specification [Sections 4.2.2.3 and 6.6.4]	Requirements Criticality Analysis [Section 6.6.2]	Formal inspections of software requirements [Section 6.5.5]
Formal inspections of software requirements [Section 6.5.5]	Specification Analysis of Safety-critical Requirements [Section 6.6.3]	Specification analysis [Section 6.6.3]
System test planning [Section 6.5.6]	Software Fault Tree Analysis [Section 6.6.7 and Appendix C]	Timing, throughput and sizing analysis [Section 6.6.6]
Timing, throughput and sizing considerations [Section 6.5.4]	Software Failure Modes and Effects Analysis [Section 6.6.8 and Appendix D]	
	Formal inspections of Software requirements [Section 6.5.5]	
	Develop Safety Package for Phase 0/1 Safety Review or other external safety review.	

6.2 Documentation and Milestones

Table 6-2 Software Requirements Documentation

Document	Software Safety Section
Software Requirements Document	Identification of all safety-critical software requirements
Software Interface Specification	Identification of any interfaces that are part of safety-critical elements
Formal Inspection of Requirements Report	Identification of any safety-critical requirements defects that are considered major (must be fixed).
Requirements Traceability Matrix	Special identification given to safety-critical requirements
Analysis Reports	Identification of any safety-related aspects or safety concerns.
Acceptance Test Plan	This is the customer acceptance test. Includes all safety testing necessary to assure the customer that the system is safe.
System Test Plan	Includes stress, load, disaster, stability, and other tests, as well as functional testing. Verifies that the system cannot go into an unsafe mode under adverse conditions.

Milestones that will usually occur during this phase include:

- Software Requirements Review (SRR)
- Phase 0/1 Safety Review or other carrier- or program-specific safety review

6.3   Tailoring Guidelines

See Section 3.2 *Tailoring the Effort* for how to determine the software safety effort required (full, moderate, or minimal).

Table 6-3 Software Safety Effort for Requirements Phase

Technique or Analysis	Safety Effort Level		
	MIN	MOD	FULL
2.3.1 Preliminary Hazard Analysis (PHA) (if not previously performed)	☆	☆	☆
2.3.4 Software Subsystem Hazard Analysis (if not previously performed)	☆	☆	☆
Software safety requirements development 6.5.1 Generic requirements 6.5.2 Fault and Failure Tolerance 6.5.3 Hazardous Commands	✓ ✓ ☆	✓✓ ✓✓ ☆	✓✓ ☆ ☆
6.4 Requirements Management	☆	☆	☆
6.5.5 Formal Inspections	✓	☆	☆
6.6.1 Software Safety Requirements Flow-down Analysis	✓✓	☆	☆
6.6.2 Requirements Criticality Analysis	✓	✓✓	☆
6.6.3 Specification Analysis	⊘	✓	✓✓
4.2.2.3 and 6.6.4 Formal Methods	⊘	✓✓ (Specification)	✓✓ (Specification & Verification)
6.6.5 Model Checking	⊘	✓✓	✓✓
Timing, Throughput, and Sizing 6.5.4 Development Considerations 6.6.6 Analysis	✓✓ ✓✓	☆ ☆	☆ ☆
6.6.7 Software Fault Tree Analysis	✓	✓✓	☆
6.6.8 Software Failure Modes and Effects Analysis	⊘	✓	✓✓

Recommendation Codes			
☆	Mandatory	✓✓	Highly Recommended
✓	Recommended	⊘	Not Recommended

6.4 Requirements Management

Requirements management is the process of eliciting, documenting, organizing, communicating, and tracking requirements. Management of requirements is one of the most important activities you can do to assure a safe system. Deficient requirements are the single largest cause of software project failure, and usually are the root cause of the worst software defects.

Requirements management is also referred to as requirements engineering. It is a set of processes relating to requirements, from gathering them to assuring that that they have all been verified. The aspects of gathering and documenting requirements is outside the scope of this guidebook. The process of specifying software safety requirements is covered in *Sections 6.5.1 through 6.5.3*. The process of verifying that all appropriate safety requirements have been identified is described in Section 6.6.1.

The advantages of following a requirements management process include:

- **Improve understanding and communications.** During the process of requirements elicitation, and the refinement into a specification, software development team members obtain a clearer understanding of the system to be delivered. The software development team should involve the customers in the process, so that the final system will meet the customers' needs. A central repository of information obtained through the process provides a common knowledge base for the user community, management, analysts, developers, and test personnel.

- **Prevention of requirements creep or scope change**. Requirements management works to prevent (or at least expose to management attention) requirements creep and scope changes by identifying and tracking changes to the requirements. Trending analyses can also be performed to look for project areas subject to frequent or critical requirements changes. Control of these issues can be through the project's risk management system or through another designated process.

- **Improved quality and end-user satisfaction.** Higher quality results when customers, developers, analysts, and assurance personnel have a common understanding of what must be delivered.

- **Reduced project costs and delays.** Research shows that requirements errors are pervasive and expensive to fix. Reducing the number of these errors early in the development cycle lowers the total number of errors, lowers project costs, and maintains the projected schedule.

- **Compliance with standards or contracts.** Requirements management is a "best practice." Following this process can help meet regulatory or contractual obligations, such as obtaining a specific Software CMM level (see section 4.3.8). Managing the project requirements will also help if you must present a "safety case" to a regulatory body. (A safety case is a documented body of evidence that provides a demonstrable and valid argument that a system is adequately safe for a given application and environment over its lifetime. Safety cases are required by the FAA.)

6.4.1 Requirements Specification

Determining what your project's requirements are is not necessarily an easy process. The first step is to realize that there are different types of requirements.

Some basic types of requirements are:

- **Business requirements.** These describe why the product is being built and identify the benefits that both customers and the business will reap. [98]

- **User requirements.** These detail the tasks a user will be able to perform with the product and are often captured in the form of use cases. [98]

- **Functional requirements.** These identify the specific system behaviors that must be implemented. The functional requirements are the traditional "shall" statements found in a software requirements specification. [98]

- **Quality requirements.** Performance, efficiency, system availability, reliability, robustness, usability, flexibility, maintainability, portability, and reusability are all quality areas that should be considered.

- **Safety requirements.** Safety requirements development is discussed in section 6.5.

6.4.1.1 Requirements Elicitation

Requirements elicitation involves querying the customer, potential users or operators, domain experts, and others (i.e. the stakeholders) to determine a set of features, functions, or activities that must be included in the system. This is the time to be broad and inclusive. Requirements can be combined or removed later in the process. Requirements elicitation is the most difficult of the requirements management activities because you are creating something from nothing.

Some techniques that can be used include: [97]

- **Structured interviews.** These can be highly effective in collecting requirements from experts and prospective users.

- **Brainstorming.** This is a structured yet creative technique for eliciting ideas, capturing them, and then subjecting them to objective criteria for evaluation.

- **Domain environment.** Placing engineers and designers in the environment where the device will be used, even for a day, is a quick way to learn about potential problems and issues.

- **Structured workshops.** Workshops are managed by trained facilitators and include as many stakeholders as possible. Joint Application Development (JAD) [99] is a structured process that uses workshops to elicit requirements.

One necessary step in the elicitation process is to record the requirements. This can be done in a word processor, spreadsheet, or other office tool. It can also be done in a requirements management tool. A list of requirements management tools is given in Table 6-4.

6.4.1.2 Requirements Refinement

The mass of requirements that result from the elicitation needs to be refined into a manageable set. Some requirements will be deemed unnecessary, others may be combined, and many more will need to be clarified. Priorities should be applied to the requirements at this stage, to separate the "must have" requirements from those that are desired.

Requirements often start as an abstraction, such as "The spacecraft will have a color camera." As the process continues, the requirements become more specific, diverge, recombine in new ways, and eventually emerge as a set of detailed requirements such as, "The camera will weigh less than 12 ounces," and "The camera will be able to take 30 pictures a second with a frame size of 800 by 600 pixels." [97]

Good requirements have the following attributes:

- **Unambiguous.** If a requirement has multiple interpretations, what is built may not match what the user wanted.

- **Complete**. It is impossible to know all of a system's future requirements, but all of the known ones should be specified.

- **Consistent.** Requirements must not conflict with each other.

- **Traceable.** The source of each requirement should be identified.

- **Verifiable.** Each requirement must be able to be verified, usually by test, analysis, inspection, or demonstration.

Requirements can be very detailed, as long as they address external behaviors (as viewed by users or by interfacing systems). They become design information, however, once they specify the existence of particular subcomponents or algorithms.

Requirements specifications can include auxiliary information that is not a requirement. Such information may include introductory text, summary statements, tables, and glossaries. The real requirements should be clearly identified.

"Any project with resource limitations must establish the relative priorities of the requested features, use cases, or functional requirements. Prioritization helps the project manager plan for staged releases, make trade-off decisions, and respond to requests for adding more functionality. It can also help you avoid the traumatic 'rapid descoping phase' late in the project, when you start throwing features overboard to get a product out the door on time." [98]

6.4.1.3 Requirements Documentation

The final result of the elicitation and refinement activities is a software requirements specification or similar document. This document defines not only the complete external behaviors of the software system to be built, but also its non-behavioral requirements. The format of the document may be defined by a standard or company template. The SRS is most often written in natural language, perhaps augmented by appropriate analysis models. It can also be written in a formal specification language (see Section 4.2.2.3).

Requirements must have a way to be verified. This verification method should be included in the software requirements document, either when the requirement is stated or in a separate verification matrix at the end of the document. Verification methods include test (exercising the software), inspection (software review or formal inspection), analysis, or demonstration (simply running the software). Test is usually the preferred verification, but other methods may be much easier for some requirements or testing may not be feasible. Software assurance engineers and software safety engineers should concur with the verification method.

The software requirements need to be reviewed by all stakeholders and other interested parties. Reviews help find ambiguous, conflicting, or incomplete requirements. They also bring the team "up to speed" on the system and the software subsystem. Reviews can be formal inspections, informal assessments, or formal project reviews. Formal inspection (Section 6.5.5) is a valuable tool in finding requirements defects (e.g., ambiguity, conflicting requirements, missing requirements) and is highly recommended.

Requirements management tools (Table 6-4) store the project requirements and related information in a multi-user database. These products let you manipulate the database contents, import and export requirements, and connect requirements to objects stored in testing, design, and project management tools. You can define attributes for each requirement, such as its version number, author, status, origin or rationale, allocated release, and priority. Traceability links between individual requirements and other system elements help you evaluate the impact of changing or deleting a requirement. Web access permits real-time sharing of database updates with members of geographically distributed teams.

Table 6-4 Requirements Management Tools

Tool	Vendor
Caliber-RM	Borland http://www.borland.com/caliber/
DOORS	Telelogic http://www.telelogic.com/
RequisitePro	Rational Software Corporation; http://www.rational.com/
RTM Workshop	Integrated Chipware, Inc.; http://www.chipware.com/
Vital Link	Compliance Automation, Inc. http://www.complianceautomation.com/

6.4.2 Requirements Traceability and Verification

Traceability is a link or definable relationship between two entities. Requirements are linked from their more general form (e.g., the system specification) to their more concrete form (e.g., subsystem specifications). They are also linked forward to the design, source code, and test cases. This is important for all requirements, especially those that are safety-critical. Knowing what part of the code implements the safety function, or what test verifies that function, is a vital part of creating a safe system.

The key benefits of tracing requirements include:

- Verification that all user needs are implemented and adequately tested. Full requirements test coverage is virtually impossible without some form of requirements traceability.

- Verification that there are no "extra" system behaviors that cannot be traced to a user requirement.

- Improved understanding of the impact of changing requirements.

Requirements verification involves evaluating the correctness and completeness of the requirements, to ensure that a system built to those requirements will satisfy the users' needs and expectations. The goal of verification is to ensure that the requirements provide an adequate basis to proceed with design, construction, and testing. As mentioned in 6.4.1.3, formal inspection is an excellent way to verify the requirements. Analyses may also be used, such as those described in section 6.6.

A traceability matrix is one tool that can help detail how the requirements trace through the design, source code, and test products. The matrix can be manually created and maintained, or may be a by-product of a requirements management tool. The manual method can be tedious and difficult to maintain.

6.4.3 Requirements Change Management

Requirements traceability provides a methodical and controlled process for managing changes that inevitably occur as a system is developed and deployed. "Without traceability, every change would require project team members to review all documents on an ad hoc basis in order to determine what other elements of the project, if any, require updating. Because such a process would make it difficult to establish whether all affected components have been identified over time, changes to the system would tend to decrease its reliability and safety." [1] With traceability, when a change occurs the affected products (documentation, source code, test cases) can be quickly identified.

The actual process of making changes should be a structured, defined process. This process should describe how a proposed change is submitted, evaluated, decided upon, and incorporated into the requirements baseline. Usually a change control board, consisting of people from various disciplines and perspectives, will review potential changes and either approve or reject them. A requirements management tool can help manage the changes made to many individual requirements, maintain revision histories, and communicate changes to those affected by them.

Part of the change management process should be an evaluation of the impact the change will have on the system and other requirements. Traceability information is an important tool in this evaluation. Further information on analysis that can be done to determine the impact of software changes can be found in Section 10.5.2.

6.5   Development of Software Safety Requirements

Software safety requirements are obtained from various sources (see Figure 4-7), and are usually sorted into two categories: generic and specific.

The generic software safety requirements are derived from sets of requirements that can be used in different programs and environments to solve common software safety problems. Examples of generic software safety requirements and their sources are given in Section 6.5.1 *Generic Software Safety Requirements*. Specific software safety requirements are system-unique functional capabilities or constraints that are identified in the following three ways. For complete identification of all software safety requirements, all three methods should be used.

Method 1	Through top- down analysis of system design requirements and specifications:
	The system requirements may identify system hazards upfront and specify which system functions are safety-critical, or a Fault Tree Analysis may be completed to identify safety-critical functions. The software safety organization participates or leads the mapping of these requirements to software.
Method 2	From the Preliminary Hazard Analysis (PHA):
	PHA looks down into the system from the point of view of system hazards. Preliminary hazard causes are mapped to, or interact with, software. Software hazard control features are identified and specified as requirements.
Method 3	Through bottom-up analysis of design data, (e.g., flow diagrams, Failure Mode Effects and Criticality Analysis (FMECA)).
	Design implementations allowed but not anticipated by the system requirements are analyzed and new hazard causes or contributors are identified. Software hazard controls are specified via requirements when the hazard causes are linked to or interact with software.

6.5.1   Generic Software Safety Requirements

Similar processors, platforms, and/or software can suffer from similar or identical problems. Generic software safety requirements are derived from sets of requirements and best practices used in different programs and environments to solve common software safety problems. Generic software safety requirements capture these lessons learned and provide a valuable resource for developers.

Generic requirements prevent costly duplication of effort by taking advantage of existing proven techniques and lessons learned rather than reinventing techniques or repeating mistakes. Most development programs should be able to make use of some generic requirements. However, these requirements should be used with care and may have to be tailored from project to project.

As technology evolves, or as new applications are implemented, new "generic" requirements will likely arise, and other sources of generic requirements might become available. A partial listing of sources for generic requirement is shown below:

    1. NSTS 19943, Command Requirements and Guidelines for NSTS Customers.

2. STANAG 4404 (Draft), NATO Standardization Agreement (STANAG) Safety Design Requirements and Guidelines for Munition Related Safety-Critical Computing Systems.

3. EWRR 127-1, Range Safety Requirements - Western Space and Missile Center, Attachment-3, Software System Design Requirements. See Section 3.16 Safety-Critical Computing System Software Design Requirements.

4. AFISC SSH 1-1, System Safety Handbook - Software System Safety, Headquarters Air Force Inspection and Safety Center.

5. EIA Bulletin SEB6, A System Safety Engineering in Software Development (Electrical Industries Association).

6. Underwriters Laboratory - UL 1998, Standard for Safety - Safety-Related Software, January 4th, 1994.

7. NUREG/CR-6263 MTR 94W0000114, High Integrity Software for Nuclear Power Plants, The MITRE Corporation, for the U.S. Nuclear Regulatory Commission.

Appendix H has a checklist of generic software safety requirements developed by the Marshall Space Flight Center.

Benefit Rating for Use of Generic Requirements:	HIGH

6.5.2 Fault and Failure Tolerance

Most NASA space systems employ failure tolerance (as opposed to fault tolerance) to achieve an acceptable degree of safety. This is primarily achieved via hardware, but software is also important, because improper software design can defeat the hardware failure tolerance and vice versa. While the actual implementation of fault or failure tolerance is a design issue, the question of whether it is necessary, or to what extent it is necessary, must be captured in software requirements.

While not all faults lead to a failure, every failure results from one or more faults. A fault is an error that does not affect the functionality of the system, such as bad data from either input, calculations, or output, an unknown command, or a command or data coming at an unknown time. If properly designed, the software, or system, can respond to errors by detecting and correcting them intelligently. This would include checking input and output data by doing limit checking and setting the value to a known safe value, or requesting and/or waiting for the next data point.

Occasional bad I/O, data, or commands should not be considered failures, unless there are too many of them and the system cannot handle them. One or more intelligent fault collection routines should be part of the program to track, and possibly log, the number and type of errors. These collection routines can then either handle the caution, warning, and/or recovery for the software system, or raise a flag to a higher level of control when the number of faults over time or the combination of fault types indicates that a system failure is imminent. With faults, the system should continue to operate normally.

A failure tolerant design detects a failure and puts the software and/or system into a changed operating state, either by switching to backup software or hardware (e.g., alternate software routine or program, backup CPU, secondary sensor input, or valve cut-off) or by reducing the functionality of the system while it continues to operate.

 It is important to decide early in the project whether the system will be fault tolerant, failure tolerant, or both. Fault tolerant systems are built to handle most probable, and some less probable but hazardous, faults. Taking care of the faults will usually help prevent the software, or the system, from going into failure. The down-side to fault tolerance is that it requires multiple checks and monitoring at very low levels. If a system is failure tolerant, it will ignore most faults and only respond to higher-level failures. A presumption is that it requires less work and is simpler to detect, isolate, stop, or recover from the failures. A project must weigh the costs and benefits of each approach and determine what will provide the most safety for the least cost and effort.

For safety-critical systems, it is best to require some level of both fault and failure tolerance. The fault tolerance keeps most of the minor errors from propagating into failures. Failures must still be detected and dealt with, whether as a result of fault collection/monitoring routines or by direct failure detection routines and/or hardware. In this guidebook, both fault and failure tolerance are discussed. The proper blending of both to meet the requirements of your particular system must be determined by the system engineers, software designers, and the safety engineers.

If too many faults or very serious failures occur, it may be necessary for the system to shut itself down in an orderly, safe manner. This is a good time to consider if the system will have the required capabilities to perform the orderly shut down (such as battery backup). For example, if a system has to close a valve before power down, a backup power supply is required to allow the system to perform this action in the event of a power failure.

Software responses to off-nominal scenarios should address safety considerations, and be appropriate to the situation. Complete system shutdown may not be appropriate in many cases.

Designing for safety is discussed in Sections 7.4.1 and 7.4.2 .

6.5.3   Hazardous Commands

A hazardous command is one whose execution (including inadvertent, out-of-sequence, or incorrect execution) could lead to an identified critical or catastrophic hazard, or a command whose execution can lead to a reduction in the control of a hazard (including reduction in failure tolerance against a hazard or the elimination of an inhibit against a hazard). Commands can be internal to a software set (e.g., from one component to another) or external, crossing an interface to/from hardware or a human operator. Longer command paths increase the probability of an undesired or incorrect command response due to noise on the communications channel, link outages, equipment malfunctions, or (especially) human error.

Reference [34] NSTS 1700.7B section 218 defines "hazardous command" as "...those that can remove an inhibit to a hazardous function, or activate an unpowered payload system". It continues to say "Failure modes associated with payload flight and ground operations including hardware, software, and procedures used in commanding from Payload Operations Control Centers (POCC's) and other ground equipment must be considered in the safety assessment to determine compliance with the (failure tolerance) requirements. NSTS 19943 treats the subject of hazardous commanding and presents the guidelines by which it will be assessed."

NSTS 1700.7B section 218 focuses on remote commanding of hazardous functions, but the principles can and should be generally applied. Both NSTS 19943 and EWRR 127-1 (Paragraphs 3.16.2.7 c and d) recommend and require respectively, two-step commanding. EWRR 127-1 states "Two or more unique operator actions shall be required to initiate any potentially hazardous function or sequence of functions. The actions shall be designed to minimize the potential for inadvertent actuation". Note that two-step commanding is in addition to any hardware (or software) failure tolerance requirements, and is neither necessary nor sufficient to meet failure tolerance requirements. A two-step command does not constitute an inhibit.

Software interlocks or preconditions can be used to disable certain commands during particular mission phases or operational modes. However, provision should be made to provide access to (i.e. enable) all commands in the event of unexpected emergencies. Flight crews generally require emergency command access. For example, when Apollo 13 experienced major problems, the nominal Lunar Module power up sequence timeline could not be completed before the Command Module battery power expired. A different (shorter) sequence was improvised.

Benefit Rating: HIGH	Cost Rating: LOW

6.5.4 Timing, Sizing and Throughput Considerations

System design should properly consider real-world parameters and constraints, including human operator and control system response times, and flow these down to software. Adequate margins of capacity should be provided for all these critical resources. As software requirements are generated for these areas, the system design should be evaluated for appropriate capability.

This section provides guidance for developers in specifying software requirements to meet the safety objectives. Subsequent analysis of software for these factors is discussed in Section 6.6.6 *Timing, Sizing and Throughput Analysis*.

- **Time to Criticality**

  Safety-critical systems sometimes have a characteristic "time to criticality", which is the time interval between a fault occurring and the system reaching an unsafe state. This interval represents a time window in which automatic or manual recovery and/or safing actions can be performed, either by software, hardware, or by a human operator. The design of safing and recovery actions should fully consider the real-world conditions and the corresponding time to criticality. Automatic safing can only be a valid hazard control if there is ample margin between worst-case (long) response time and worst-case (short) time to criticality.

- **Automatic safing**

  Automatic safing is often required if the time to criticality is shorter than the realistic human operator response time, or if there is no human in the loop. This can be performed by either hardware or software or a combination depending on the best system design to achieve safing.

- **Control system design**

  Control system design can define timing requirements. The design is based on the established body of classical and modern dynamic control theory, such as dynamic control system design, and multivariable design in the s-domain (Laplace transforms) for analog continuous processes. Systems engineers are responsible for overall control system design. Computerized control systems use sampled data (versus continuous data). Sampled analog processes should make use of Z-transforms to develop difference equations to implement the control laws. This will also make most efficient use of real-time computing resources. [35]

- **Sampling rates**

  Sampling rates should be selected with consideration for noise levels and expected variations of control system and physical parameters. For measuring signals that are not critical, the sample rate should be at least twice the maximum expected signal frequency to avoid aliasing. For critical signals, and parameters used for closed loop control, it is generally accepted that the sampling rate must be much higher. A factor of at least ten above the system characteristic frequency is customary. [35]

- **Dynamic memory allocation**

  Dynamic memory allocation requires several varieties of resources be available and adequate. The amount of actual memory (RAM) available, whether virtual memory (disk space) is used, how much memory the software (programs and operating system) uses statically, and how much is dynamically allocated are all factors in whether a dynamic allocation will fail or succeed. Several factors may not be known in detail, and worst-case values should be used.

  How the software will deal with failed dynamic allocation should be specified. Allowing a default similar to the MS-DOS "abort, retry, fail" is a very bad idea for safety-critical software.

  Protecting critical memory blocks from inadvertent corruption or deletion should be a requirement.

- **Memory Checking**

  Testing of random access memory (RAM) can be a part of BIT/self-test and is usually done on power up of a system to verify that all memory addresses are available, and that the RAM is functioning properly. Periodic verification of memory functionality may be required, especially in environments where memory problems are likely to occur, due to a single event upset or hardware (RAM) problems.

6.5.5 Formal Inspections of Software Requirements

Formal Inspections[5] are structured technical reviews of a "product" of the software development life cycle, conducted for the purpose of finding and eliminating defects. The product can be any documentation, including requirements, design notes, test plans, or the actual source code.

---

[5] Formal inspections are also known as Fagan Inspections, named after John Fagan of IBM who devised the method.

Formal Inspections differ from informal reviews or walkthroughs in that there are specified steps to be taken, and roles are assigned to individual reviewers.

Formal inspections are not formal methods! Formal inspections are a structured way to find defects in some software product, from a requirements document to the actual code. Formal methods are a mathematical way of specifying and verifying a software system. The two methods can be used together or separately.

NASA has published a standard and guidebook for implementing the Formal Inspection (FI) process, Software Formal Inspections Standard (NASA-STD-2202-93) [37] and Software Formal Inspections Guidebook (NASA-GB-A302) [22]. FI's should be performed within every major step of the software development process, including requirements specification, design, coding, and testing.

Formal Inspections have the most impact when applied *early* in the life of a project, especially the requirements specification and definition stages of a project. Impact means that the defects are found earlier, when it's cheaper to fix them. Studies have shown that the majority of all faults and failures, including those that impinge on safety, come from missing or misunderstood requirements. Formal Inspection greatly improves the communication within a project and enhances understanding of the system while scrubbing out many of the major errors and defects.

For the FI of software requirements, the inspection team should include representatives from Systems Engineering, Operations, Software Design and Code, Software Product Assurance, Safety, and any other system function that software will control or monitor. It is very important that software safety be involved in the FI's. Each individual may review the requirements from a generic viewpoint, or they may be assigned a specific point of view (tester, programmer, designer, user, safety) from which to review the document.

It is also very helpful to have inspection checklists for each phase of development that reflect both generic and project specific criteria. A special safety checklist may also be used when reviewing the requirements. The requirements discussed in this section and in Robyn R. Lutz's paper "Targeting Safety-Related Errors During Software Requirements Analysis" [6] will greatly aid in establishing this checklist. Also, the checklists provided in the NASA Software Formal Inspections Guidebook are helpful.

The method of reporting findings from FI's is described in references [22] and [37]. After the inspection, the safety representative should review the official findings of the inspection and translate any that require safety follow-up on to a worksheet such as that in *Table 6-5 Subsystem Criticality Analysis Report Form*. This form can then serve in any subsequent inspections or reviews as part of the checklist. It will also allow the safety personnel to track to closure safety specific issues that arise during the course of the inspection.

Benefit Rating:	HIGH	Cost Rating: MODERATE

Table 6-5 Example Subsystem Criticality Analysis Report Form

Document Number: CL-SPEC- 2001				
Document Title: Software Requirements Specification - Cosmolab Program				
Paragraph Number / Title	Requirements(s) text excerpt	Problem /Hazard Description	Recommendations	Hazard Report Reference Number
3.3 Limit Checking	Parameters listed in Table 3.3 shall be subjected to limit checking at a rate of 1 Hz.	Table only gives one set of limits for each parameter, but expected values for parameters will change from mode to mode.	During certain modes, false alarms would result because proper parameter values will exceed preset limit check values. Implement table driven limit values which can be changed during transitions from mode to mode.	CL-1;9

6.5.6   Test Planning

At the end of the software specification phase, the system and acceptance test plans can be written. System tests can be defined that verify the functional aspects of the software under nominal conditions, as well as performance, load, stress, and other tests that verify acceptable behavior in non-standard situations.

Safety tests of the system should also be designed at this time and documented in a software safety test plan. These tests should demonstrate how the software and system meets the safety requirements in the Software Requirements Document. The test plan should specify pass/fail criteria for each test. Any special procedures, constraints, and dependencies for implementing and running safety tests should also be included. The review and reporting process for safety-critical components, including problem and non-conformance reporting, should also be part of this plan.

6.5.7   Checklists and cross references

Checklists are a tool for making sure you haven't forgotten anything important, while doing an analysis or reviewing a document. They are a way to put the collective experience of those who created and reviewed the checklist to work on your project. They are a starting point, and should be reviewed for relevance for each project. A collection of checklists is provided in Appendix H. For the requirements phase, they include a safety checklist that contains standard hazards to look for when reviewing the requirements specification.

 Cross-references are matrices that list related items. A matrix that shows the software-related hazards and hazard controls and their corresponding safety requirements should be created and maintained. This should be a living document, reviewed and updated periodically. Refreshing your mind on the hazards that software must control while working on the software design, for example, increases the likelihood that the hazard controls will be designed in correctly. Another cross-reference matrix would list each requirement and the technique that will verify it (analysis, test, etc.).

You should develop a systematic checklist of software safety requirements and hazard controls, ensuring they correctly and completely include (and cross-reference) the appropriate specifications, hazard analyses, test and design documents. This should include both generic and specific safety requirements as discussed in Section 6.5 *Development of Software Safety Requirements*. Section 6.5.5 *Formal Inspections* lists some sources for starting a safety checklist.

Also, develop a hazard requirements flow-down matrix that maps safety requirements and hazard controls to system and software functions and, from there, to software components. Where components are not yet defined, flow to the lowest level possible and tag for future flow-down.

6.6 Software Safety Requirements Analysis

The Requirements Analysis activities verify that safety requirements for the software were properly flowed down from the system safety requirements, and that they are correct, consistent and complete. They also look for new hazards, software functions that can impact hazard controls, and ways the software can behave that are unexpected. These are primarily top down analyses.

Bottom up analysis of software requirements, such as Requirements Criticality Analysis, are performed to identify possible hazardous conditions. This results in another iteration of the PHA (or Software Subsystem Hazard Analysis) that may generate new software requirements. Specification analysis is also performed to ensure consistency of requirements.

Analyses related to the Software Requirements are:

- Software Safety Requirements Flow-down Analysis
- Requirements Criticality Analysis
- Specification Analysis
- Formal Methods
- Timing, Throughput And Sizing Analysis
- Preliminary Software Fault Tree Analysis
- Preliminary Software Failure Modes and Effects Analysis

6.6.1 Software Safety Requirements Flow-down Analysis

Generic safety requirements are established "a priori" and placed into the system specification and overall project design specifications. From there they are flowed into the subsystem specifications, such as the software subsystem requirements.

Other safety requirements, derived from bottom-up analysis, are flowed up from subsystems and components to the system level requirements. These new system level requirements are then flowed back down across all affected subsystems. During the software requirements phase, software components may not be well defined. In this case, bottom-up analysis (such as a Software Failure Modes and Effects Analysis) might not be possible until sometime in the design phase.

Problems in the flow-down process can be caused by incomplete analysis, inconsistent analysis of highly complex systems, or use of ad hoc techniques by biased or inexperienced analysts. The following references are a good starting point for anyone who falls into the "inexperienced" category :

* MIL-STD-882C System Safety Program Requirements (the 'C' version, not the current 'D', has some description on how to verify flow down of requirements)

* NSTS-22254 Methodology for Conduct of Space Shuttle Program Hazard Analyses

* "Safeware : System Safety and Computers" (Book), Nancy Leveson, April 1995

* "Safety-Critical Computer Systems" (Book), Neil Storey, August 1996

* "Software Assessment: Reliability, Safety, Testability" (Book), Michael A. Friedman and Jeffrey M. Voas(Contributor), August 16, 1995

* "Discovering System Requirements", A. Terry Bahill and Frank F. Dean, http://tide.it.bond.edu.au/inft390/002/Resources/sysreq.htm

The most rigorous (and most expensive) method of addressing this concern is adoption of formal methods for requirements analysis and flow-down. This was described previously in Section 4.2.2.3 *Formal Methods*. Less rigorous and less expensive ways include checklists and a standardized structured approach to software safety as discussed below and throughout this guidebook.

Benefit Rating:	HIGH	Cost Rating: LOW to HIGH (Formal Methods)

6.6.2   Requirements Criticality Analysis

Criticality analysis identifies program requirements that have safety implications. A method of applying criticality analysis is to analyze the hazards of the software/hardware system and identify those that could present catastrophic or critical hazards. This approach evaluates each program requirement in terms of the safety objectives derived for the software component.

The evaluation will determine whether the requirement has safety implications and, if so, the requirement is designated "safety-critical". It is then placed into a tracking system to ensure traceability of software safety requirements throughout the software development cycle from the highest level specification all the way to the code and test documentation.

The system safety organization coordinates with the project system engineering organization to review and agree on the criticality designations. Software safety engineers and software development engineers should be included in this discussion. Software is a vital component in the whole system, and the "software viewpoint" must be part of any systems engineering activity. Requirements can be consolidated to reduce the number of critical requirements. In addition, they can be flagged for special attention during design, to reduce the criticality level.

Keep in mind that not all "safety-critical" requirements are created equal. Later in the process, the concept of *risk* is used to prioritize which requirements or components are more critical than others. For now, it's best to look at everything that can cause a safety problem, even a trivial one. It's easier, and cheaper, to remove or reduce requirements later than it is to add them in.

It is probable that software components or subsystems will not be defined during the requirements phase, so those portions of the Criticality Analysis would be deferred to the design phase. In any case, the Criticality Analysis will be updated during the design phase to reflect the more detailed definition of software components.

You perform the Requirements Criticality Analysis by doing the following:

- All software requirements are analyzed to identify additional potential system hazards that the system PHA did not reveal. A checklist of PHA hazards is a good thing to have while reviewing the software requirements. The checklist makes it easier to identify PHA-designated hazards that are not reflected in the software requirements, and new hazards missed by the PHA. In addition, look for areas where system requirements were not correctly flowed to the software. Once potential hazards have been identified, they are added to the system requirements and then flowed down to subsystems (hardware, software and operations) as appropriate.

- Review the *system* requirements to identify hardware or software functions that receive, pass, or initiate critical signals or hazardous commands.

- Review the *software* requirements to verify that the functions from the system requirements are included. In addition, look for any new software functions or objects that receive/pass/initiate critical signals or hazardous commands.

- Look through the *software* requirements for conditions that may lead to unsafe situations. Consider conditions such as out-of-sequence, wrong event, inappropriate magnitude, incorrect polarity, inadvertent command, adverse environment, deadlocking, and failure-to-command modes.

The software safety requirements analysis also looks at characteristics of the software system. Not all characteristics of the software are governed by requirements. Some characteristics are a result of the design, which may fulfill the requirements in a variety of ways. It is important that safety-critical characteristics are identified and explicitly included in the requirements. "Forgotten" safety requirements often come back to bite you late in the design or coding stages.

All characteristics of safety-critical software must be evaluated to determine if they are safety-critical. Safety-critical characteristics should be controlled by requirements that receive rigorous quality control in conjunction with rigorous analysis and test. Often all characteristics of safety-critical software are themselves safety-critical.

Characteristics to be considered include at a minimum:

- ✓ Specific limit ranges
- ✓ Out of sequence event protection requirements
- ✓ Timing
- ✓ Relationship logic for limits. Allowable limits for parameters might vary depending on operational mode or mission phase. For example, the temperature may be more constrained during an experiment run than when the system is idle.
- ✓ Voting logic
- ✓ Hazardous command processing requirements (see Section 6.5.3 *Hazardous Commands*)
- ✓ Fault response

✓ Fault detection, isolation, and recovery

✓ Redundancy management/switchover logic. What components to switch, and under what circumstances, should be defined for any hazard control that requires redundancy. For example, equipment which has lost control of a safety-critical function should be switched to a good spare before the time to criticality has expired. Hot standby units (as opposed to cold standby) should be provided where a cold start time would exceed time to criticality.

This list is not exhaustive and often varies depending on the system architecture and environment.

The following resources are available for the Requirements Criticality Analysis:

Software Development Activities Plan [Software Development Plan] Software Assurance Plan [None], Software Configuration Management Plan [Same] and Risk Management Plan [Software Development Plan]

System and Subsystem Requirements [System/Segment Specification (SSS), System/Segment Design Document]

Requirements Document [Software Requirements Specifications]

External Interface Requirements Document [Interface Requirements Specifications] and other interface documents

Functional Flow Diagrams and related data

Background information relating to safety requirements associated with the contemplated testing, manufacturing, storage, repair, installation, use, and final disposition of the system

Storage and timing analyses and allocations

Program structure documents

Information from the system PHA concerning system energy, toxic, and other hazardous event sources, especially ones that may be controlled directly or indirectly by software

Historical data such as lessons learned from other systems and problem reports

Note: documents in [parentheses] correspond to terminology from DOD-STD-2167 [38]. Other document names correspond to NASA-STD-2100.91.

Output products from this analysis are:

- Table 6-6 Subsystem Criticality Matrix

- Updated Safety Requirements Checklist

- Definition of Safety-critical Requirements

The results and findings of the Criticality Analyses should be fed back to the System Requirements and System Safety Analyses. For all discrepancies identified, either the system requirements should be changed because they are incomplete or incorrect, or else the software requirements must be altered to match the system requirements. The Criticality Analysis identifies additional hazards that the system analysis did not include, and identifies areas where system or interface requirements were not correctly assigned to the software.

The results of the criticality analysis may be used to develop Formal Inspection (FI) checklists for performing the FI process described in Section 6.5.5 *Formal Inspections of Software Requirements.*

Table 6-6 Example Subsystem Criticality Matrix

Mission Operational Control Functions	Hazards		
	IMI	CA	ICD
Communication	X	X	X
Guidance		X	
Navigation		X	
Camera Operations			X
Attitude Reference	X	X	X
Control	X	X	
Pointing		X	
Special Execution			
Redundancy Management	X		
Mission Sequencing	X		
Mode Control	X	X	

Key

IMI	Inadvertent Motor Ignition
CA	Collision Avoidance
ICD	Inadvertent Component Deployment

The above matrix is an example output of a software Requirements Criticality Analysis. Each functional subsystem is mapped against system hazards identified by the PHA. In this example, three hazards are addressed.

This matrix is an essential tool to define the criticality level of the software. Each hazard should have a risk index as described in Section 2.3.2 *Risk Levels* of this guidebook. The risk index is a means of prioritizing the effort required in developing and analyzing respective pieces of software.

Benefit Rating:	**HIGH**	Cost Rating: LOW

6.6.3 Specification Analysis

Specification analysis evaluates the completeness, correctness, consistency, and testability of software requirements. Well-defined requirements are strong standards by which to evaluate a software component. Specification analysis should evaluate requirements individually and as an integrated set. Techniques used to perform specification analysis are:

- reading analysis
- traceability analysis
- control-flow analysis,
- information-flow analysis
- functional simulation

These techniques are described in detail (plus background and theory) within a large, well established body of literature. Look in books on software testing and software engineering for further information on these techniques. A brief description of each technique will be given so that the analyst can determine if further study is warranted.

The safety organization should ensure the software requirements appropriately influence the software design and the development of the operator, user, and diagnostic manuals. The safety representative should review the following documents and/or data:

System/segment specification and subsystem specifications

Storage allocation and program structure documents

Software requirements specifications

Background information relating to safety requirements

Interface requirements specifications and all other interface documents

Information concerning system energy, toxic and other hazardous event sources, especially those that may be controlled directly or indirectly by software

Functional flow diagrams and related data

Software Development Plan, Software Quality Evaluation Plan, and Software Configuration Management Plan and Historical data

6.6.3.1 Reading Analysis and Traceability Analysis

Reading analysis examines the requirements specification to uncover inconsistencies, conflicts, and ambiguous or missing requirements. The analysis is usually manual, involving a review of the specification and supporting documents. A Formal Inspection (6.5.5) of the specification can be used as a reading analysis.

The Automated Requirement Measurement (ARM) Tool was developed by the Software Assurance Technology Center (SATC) at the NASA Goddard Space Flight Center. This tool was designed to assess requirements that are specified in natural language. The objective of the ARM tool is to provide measures that can be used by project managers to assess the quality of a requirements specification document. The tool is not intended to evaluate the correctness of the specified requirements. Information on the tool and a free download can be found at http://satc.gsfc.nasa.gov/tools/arm/index.html.

Traceability Analysis involves tracing the requirements throughout the various software products. Section 6.6.1 discusses the flow-down (tracing) of various requirements into the software specification. It is focused on safety requirements, but the technique applies to all other requirements as well. Section 7.5.9 discusses tracing the requirements into the design, and eventually into the code and test cases.

Benefit Rating:	HIGH	Cost Rating: LOW

6.6.3.2 Control-flow analysis

Control-flow analysis examines the order in which software functions will be performed. It identifies missing and inconsistently specified functions. Control-flow examines which processes are performed in series, and which in parallel (e.g., multitasking), and which tasks are prerequisites or dependent upon other tasks.

Benefit Rating:	HIGH	Cost Rating: MODERATE

6.6.3.3 Information-flow analysis

Information-flow analysis examines the relationship between functions and data. Incorrect, missing, and inconsistent input/output specifications are identified. Data flow diagrams are commonly used to report the results of this activity. This technique can be effective for understanding the basic data and command flow.

Benefit Rating:	HIGH	Cost Rating: MODERATE

6.6.3.4 Functional simulation models

Simulators are useful development tools for evaluating system performance and human interactions. You can examine the characteristics of a software component to predict performance, check human understanding of system characteristics, and assess feasibility. Simulators have limitations in that they are representational models and sometimes do not accurately reflect the real design, or make environmental assumptions which can differ from conditions in the field.

Benefit Rating:	MEDIUM	Cost Rating: MODERATE

6.6.4 Formal Methods - Specification Development

Among the most successful applications of Formal Methods is Formal Specification. This is the process of writing the requirements (specification) in a formal, mathematical language. Even if Formal Verification is not used (to verify that the specification, and later the design and code), the act of creating a Formal Specification often catches many errors.

 Formal Specification removes ambiguity and uncertainty. It allows errors of omission to be discovered, including undocumented assumptions and inadequate off-nominal behavior. Conflicting requirements and logic errors are also uncovered. When defects are found and corrected early in the lifecycle, they are much less costly to fix.

More information on Formal Methods can be found in Section 4.2.2.3.

Benefit Rating:	HIGH	Cost Rating: MODERATE to HIGH

6.6.5   Model Checking

Model checking is a form of Formal Methods that verifies finite-state systems. Over the last 5 years, model checking has taken on a life of its own, apart from the rest of the Formal Methods arena. Many projects that might not consider the full Formal Methods are using Model Checking as an analysis and verification technique.

Model checking is an "automatic" method, and tools exist to provide that automation (for instance: SPIN and SMV). Model checking can be applied to more than just software, and has been used to formally verify industrial systems.

The technique is especially aimed at the verification of reactive, embedded systems, i.e. systems that are in constant interaction with the environment. Model checking can be applied relatively easily at any stage of the existing software process without causing major disruptions. It has been extended to work with at least some infinite-state systems and also with real-time systems. Model checking can verify simple properties like reachability (does as system ever reach a certain state) or lack-of-deadlock (is deadlock avoided in the system), or more complex properties like safety (nothing bad ever happens) or liveness (something good eventually happens).

Benefit Rating: HIGH	Cost Rating: MODERATE

6.6.5.1   *How Model Checking Works*

The first step in model checking is to describe the system in a state-based, formal way. Each model checker uses a different language for system description.

The second step is to express program flow using propositional temporal logic. This logic deals with transitions from one state to another (stepping through the program), and what may or may not be true in each state. For instance, you can express a formula (property) that is true in some future state (eventually) or in all future states (always).

Once the system is modeled and the temporal logic is determined, algorithms are used to traverse the model defined by the system and check if the specification holds or not. Very large state-spaces can often be traversed in minutes. The technique has been applied to several complex industrial systems, ranging from hardware to communication protocols to safety-critical plants and procedures.

For more details, the book "Model Checking" [39] describes the technique in detail. The website http://www.abo.fi/%7Ejolilius/mclinks.htm contains references to current model checking research, people, tools, and projects.

6.6.5.2   *Tools*

Among the automated tools, the primary ones are SMV and SPIN. SMV is a symbolic model checker specialized on the verification of synchronous and asynchronous systems. SPIN is an on-the-fly model checker specialized on the verification of asynchronous systems.

Spin (http://netlib.bell-labs.com/netlib/spin/whatispin.html) is designed to test the specifications of concurrent (distributed) systems - specifically communications protocols, though it applies to any concurrent system. It will find deadlocks, busy cycles, conditions that violate assertions, and race conditions. The software was developed at Bell Labs in the formal methods and verification group starting in 1980. Spin targets efficient software verification, not hardware verification. It uses a high level language to specify systems descriptions (PROMELA - PROcess MEta LAnguage). Spin has been used to trace logical design errors in distributed systems design, such as operating systems, data communications protocols, switching systems, concurrent algorithms, railway signaling protocols, etc. The tool checks the logical consistency of a specification. Spin also reports on deadlocks, unspecified receptions, flags incompleteness, race conditions, and unwarranted assumptions about the relative speeds of processes. It uses an "on-the-fly" approach where not all of the model must be in memory at once.

SMV (Symbolic Model Verifier) (http://www.cs.cmu.edu/~modelcheck/smv.html) comes from Carnegie Mellon University. The SMV system requires specifications to be written in the temporal logic CTL, and uses Kripke diagrams. The input language of SMV is designed to allow the description of finite state systems that range from completely synchronous to completely asynchronous, and from the detailed to the abstract. The language provides for modular hierarchical descriptions, and for the definition of reusable components. Since it is intended to describe finite state machines, the only data types in the language are finite ones - Booleans, scalars and fixed arrays. The logic CTL allows safety, liveness, fairness, and deadlock freedom to be specified syntactically.

In addition, other "academic" systems include:

- HyTech (http://www-cad.EECS.Berkeley.EDU/~tah/HyTech/)
- Kronos (http://www-verimag.imag.fr//TEMPORISE/kronos/index-english.html)
- MONA (http://www.brics.dk/mona/)
- Murphi (http://sprout.stanford.edu/dill/murphi.html)
- TREAT (http://www.cis.upenn.edu/~lee/inhye/treat.html)
- TVS (http://tvs.twi.tudelft.nl/)
- UPPAAL (http://www.docs.uu.se/docs/rtmv/uppaal/index.html)
- Verus (http://www.cs.cmu.edu/~modelcheck/verus.html)
- Vis (http://www-cad.eecs.berkeley.edu/~vis/)

Commercial programs include:

- Time Rover (http://www.time-rover.com/TRindex.html)

6.6.5.3   *Challenges*

The main challenge in model checking is the state explosion problem - the fact that the number of states in the model is frequently so large that model checkers exceed the available memory and/or the available time. Several techniques are used to cope with this problem.

One type of technique is to build only a part of the state-space of the program, while still maintaining the ability to check the properties of interest. These are "partial-order techniques" (interleaving) and "abstraction techniques" (simpler system).

The "symbolic approach" is another way to overcome the problem. The idea is to *implicitly* represent the states and transitions of the system, rather than *explicitly*. Binary Decision Diagrams (BDDs) are an efficient encoding of Boolean formulas. The BDD is used with the temporal formulas for the model checking. Therefore, the size of the BDD representation is the limiting factor and not the size of the explicit state representation.

"On-the-fly" techniques analyze portions of the model as it goes along, so that not all of it must be in memory at any one time.

6.6.6 Timing, Throughput And Sizing Analysis

Timing, throughput and sizing analysis for safety-critical functions evaluates software requirements that relate to execution time, I/O data rates and memory/storage allocation. This analysis focuses on program constraints. Typical constraint requirements are maximum execution time, maximum memory usage, maximum storage size for program, and I/O data rates the program must support. The safety organization should evaluate the adequacy and feasibility of safety-critical timing, throughput and sizing requirements. These analyses also evaluate whether adequate resources have been allocated in each case, under worst case scenarios. For example, will I/O channels be overloaded by many error messages, preventing safety-critical features from operating?

Quantifying timing/sizing resource requirements can be very difficult. Estimates can be based on the actual parameters of similar existing systems.

Items to consider include:

- **Memory usage versus availability.**

  Assessing memory usage can be based on previous experience of software development if there is sufficient confidence. More detailed estimates should evaluate the size of the code to be stored in the memory, and the additional space required for storing data and scratch pad space for storing interim and final results of computations (heap size). As code is developed, particularly prototype or simulation code, the memory estimates should be updated.

  Consider carefully the use of Dynamic Memory Allocation in safety-critical code or software that can impact on the safety-critical portions. Dynamic memory allocation can lead to problems from not freeing allocated memory (memory leak), freeing memory twice (causes exceptions), or buffer overruns that overwrite code or other data areas. When data structures are dynamically allocated, they often cannot be statically analyzed to verify that arrays, strings, etc. do not go past the physical end of the structure.

- **I/O channel usage (Load) versus capacity and availability**

  Look at the amount of input data (science data, housekeeping data, control sensors) and the amount of output data (communications) generated. "I/O channel" should include internal hardware (sensors), interprocess communications (messages), and external communications (data output, command and telemetry interfaces). Check for resource conflicts between science data collection and safety-critical data availability. During failure events, I/O channels can be overloaded by error messages and these important messages can be lost or overwritten (e.g. the British "Piper Alpha" offshore oil platform disaster). Possible solutions includes adding components to capture, correlate and manage lower level error messages or passing error codes through the calling routines to a level that can handle the problem. This allows only passing on critical faults or combinations of faults that may lead to a failure.

- **Execution times versus CPU load and availability**

  Investigate the time variations of CPU load and determine the circumstances that generate peak load. Is the execution time under high load conditions acceptable? Consider the timing effects from multitasking, such as message passing delays or the inability to access a needed resource because another task has it. Note that excessive multitasking can result in system instability leading to "crashes". Also consider whether the code will execute from RAM or from ROM, which is often slower to access.

- **Sampling rates versus rates of change of physical parameters**

  Design criteria for this is discussed in Section 6.5.4 *Timing, Sizing and Throughput Considerations*. Analysis should address the validity of the system performance models used, together with simulation and test data, if available.

- **Program storage space versus executable code size**

  Estimate the size of the executable software in the device it is stored in (EPROM, flash disk, etc.). This is may be less than the memory footprint, as only static or global variables take up space. However, if not all components will be in memory at the same time, then the executable size may be larger. The program size includes the operating system as well as the application software.

- **Amount of data to store versus available capacity**

  Consider how much science, housekeeping, or other data will be generated and the amount of storage space available (RAM, disk, etc.). If the data will be sent to the ground and then deleted from the storage media, then some analysis should be done to determine how often, if ever, the "disk" will be full. Under some conditions, being unable to save data or overwriting previous data that has not been downlinked could be a safety related problem.

Benefit Rating:	HIGH	Cost Rating: LOW

6.6.7 Software Fault Tree Analysis

It is possible for a system to meet requirements for a correct state and still be unsafe. Complex systems increase the chance that unsafe modes will not be caught until the system is in the field. Fault Tree Analysis (FTA) is one method that focuses on how errors, or even normal functioning of the system, can lead to hazards. Software Fault Tree Analysis (SFTA) is an extension of the hardware FTA into the software arena.

The requirements phase is the time to perform a preliminary software fault tree analysis (SFTA). This is a "top down" analysis, looking for the causes of presupposed hazards. The top of the "tree" (the hazards) must be known before this analysis is applied. The Preliminary Hazard Analysis (PHA) or Software Subsystem Hazard Analysis is the primary source for hazards, along with the Requirements Criticality Analysis and other analyses described above.

The result of a fault tree analysis is a list of contributing causes (e.g., states or events), or combination of such contributing causes, that can lead to a hazard. Some of those failures will be in software. At this top level, the failures will be very general (e.g., "computer fails to raise alarm"). When this analysis is updated in later phases (as more detail is available), the failures can be assigned to specific functions or components.

FTA was originally developed in the 1960's for safety analysis of the Minuteman missile system. It has become one of the most widely used hazard analysis techniques. In some cases, FTA techniques may be mandated by civil or military authorities.

The quality of the analysis depends on the analyst's experience and capability. An inexperienced analyst may miss possible hazards or hazard causes. Even with experienced people, it is important that input from all project areas be included. Software is more of a symbiotic system (working as part of the whole) than a subsystem. It has influence into many areas, especially hardware and system operations. Separating out the "software only" aspects is difficult, if not impossible.

Software Fault Tree Analysis (SFTA) works well in conjunction with the Software Failure Modes and Effects Analysis (SFMEA) (section 6.6.8). While the SFTA is "top down", working from the hazard to possible causes, the SFMEA starts with individual components and works from the bottom (component) up to a hazard. When used in combination, these two analyses are very good at finding all the possible failure modes or areas of concern. However, they can be time-consuming, and therefore expensive. On smaller projects, usually only one analysis is performed. Because the experience of the analyst affects the quality of the analysis, analysts may choose to use the analysis they are most familiar with (SFTA or SFMEA). Conversely, they may choose to perform the analysis they are least familiar with, to force a new perspective on the system.

Much of the information presented in this section is extracted from Leveson et al. [41,42].

SFTA is a complex subject, and is described further in Appendix C.

Benefit Rating:	HIGH	Cost Rating: MODERATE

6.6.8   Software Failure Modes and Effects Analysis

A "bottom up" analysis technique is the FMEA (Failure Modes and Effects Analysis). It looks at how each component could fail, how the failure propagates through the system, and whether it can lead to a hazard. This technique requires a fairly detailed design of the system. At early stages in the software development, such as requirements or early design, only a preliminary analysis can be performed.

A Software FMEA uses the methods of a standard (hardware) FMEA, substituting software components for hardware components in each case. A widely used FMEA procedure is MIL-STD-1629, which is based on the following steps:

1. Define the system to be analyzed.
2. Construct functional block diagrams.
3. Identify all potential item and interface failure modes.
4. Evaluate each failure mode in terms of the worst potential consequences.
5. Identify failure detection methods and compensating provisions.
6. Identify corrective design or other actions to eliminate / control failure.
7. Identify impacts of the corrective change.
8. Document the analysis and summarize the problems which could not be corrected.

Software Fault Tree Analysis (SFTA) (section 6.6.7) works well in conjunction with the Software Failure Modes and Effects Analysis (SFMEA). While the SFTA is "top down", working from the hazard to possible causes, the SFMEA starts with individual components and works from the bottom (component) up to a hazard. When used in combination, these two analyses are very good at finding all the possible failure modes or areas of concern. This bi-directional analysis can provide limited but essential assurances that the software design has been systematically examined and complies with requirements for software safety. [90]

Performing both analyses, while very useful, can be time-consuming and therefore expensive. On smaller projects, usually only one analysis is chosen. Because the experience of the analyst affects the quality of the analysis, analysts may choose to use the analysis they are most familiar with (SFTA or SFMEA). Conversely, they may choose to perform the analysis they are least familiar with, to force a new perspective on the system.

More detailed information on SFMEA (Software Failure Modes and Effects Analysis) can be found in Appendix D.

Benefit Rating:	HIGH	Cost Rating:	HIGH

Chapter 7   Software Design

The design of a program set represents the static and dynamic characteristics of the software that will meet the requirements specified in the governing Software Requirements Document (SRD). Projects developing large amounts of software may elect to separate design development into multiple phases, such as preliminary (architectural) and detailed (critical). Those with relatively small software packages will usually have only a single design phase.

For most lifecycles other than the waterfall, the various phases are broken up over time. Instead of one monumental "design" phase, there will be several iterative requirements-design-code-test phases. In some lifecycles, the initial design may be equivalent to the architectural design in the waterfall, with subsequent design activities adding detail or functionality to the initial design.

7.1   Tasks and Analyses

Table 7-1 Software Design Tasks

Software Engineering Tasks	System and Software Safety Tasks	Software Assurance or IV&V Tasks
Create Design from Requirements, incorporating safety requirements and features	Trace safety-critical requirements into the design Design Traceability Analysis [Section 7.5.9]	Review selection of language, OS, and tools. Pass any safety concerns to Software Safety.
Formal Inspection of Design Products [Section 7.5.4]	Update Criticality Analysis [Section 7.5.1.1]	Review COTS and reused software. Pass any safety concerns to Software Safety.
Design for reliability and maintainability [Section 7.4.9]	Formal Inspection of Design Products [Section 7.5.4]	Review coding standards and checklists for inclusion of good practices and exclusion of unsafe functions or practices.
Select language, operating system and tools [Section 7.4.4]	Hazard Risk Assessment [Section 7.5.1.2]	Review complexity measurements. Work with developer if too high.
Select COTS and reusable components (7.4.3 and 12.1)	Design Safety Analysis [Section 7.5.2]	Review reliability and maintainability metrics. [Section 7.4.9]
Develop language restrictions and coding standards (7.4.5)	Software Element Analysis [Section 7.5.10]	Formal Inspection of Design Products [Section 7.5.4]

Software Engineering Tasks	System and Software Safety Tasks	Software Assurance or IV&V Tasks
Evaluate complexity of software design and individual components. [Section 7.4.8]	Review previous analyses and update with new information. (PHA moves to Sub-system Hazard Analysis [SSHA] and Systems Hazard Analysis [SHA])	Formal Methods and Model Checking [Section 7.5.5]
	Review coding standards and checklists for inclusion of good practices and exclusion of unsafe functions or practices.	Independence Analysis [Section 7.5.3]
	Review Analyses from Software Assurance for any safety implications.	Design Logic Analysis [Section 7.5.6]
	Update Safety Data Package for Phase II Safety Review or other carrier- or program-specific safety review.	Design Data Analysis [Section 7.5.7]
		Design Interface Analysis [Section 7.5.8]
		Design Traceability Analysis [Section 7.5.9]
		Dynamic Flowgraph Analysis [Section 7.5.12]
		Rate Monotonic Analysis [Section 7.5.11]
		Markov Modeling [Section 7.5.13]
		Requirements State Machines Section 7.5.14, Appendix E
		Review previous analyses and update with new information.

7.2   Documentation and Milestones

The following table lists documents that are commonly produced for this phase of development:

Table 7-2 Software Design Documentation

Document	Software Safety Section
Software Design Specification and other design documents	Identify the safety-critical units, data, and interfaces throughout the design. Identify non-critical units that can interact with safety-critical ones.
Integration Test Plan	Specify the order of unit integration such that safety-critical units can be fully tested. Include tests that verify non-critical components cannot influence critical components.
Formal Inspection Reports	Any safety-critical design defects should be considered major (must be fixed).
Coding Standards	Include language restrictions, functions to avoid, and unacceptable programming practices.
Analysis Reports	Identification of any safety-related aspects or safety concerns.
Traceability Matrix	Identify Design components that incorporate safety-critical requirements

Milestones that will usually occur during this phase include:

- Software Preliminary Design Review (PDR)
- Software Critical Design Review (CDR)
- Phase II Safety Review or other carrier- or program-specific system safety review

7.3 Tailoring Guidelines

See Section 3.2 *Tailoring the Effort* for how to determine the software safety effort required (full, moderate, or minimal).

Table 7-3 Software Design Safety Effort

Technique or Analysis	Safety Effort Level		
	MIN	MOD	FULL
7.4.5 Language Restrictions and Coding Standards	☆	☆	☆
7.4.6 Defensive Programming	✓✓	☆	☆
7.5.1.1 Criticality Analysis 7.5.1.2 Hazard Risk Assessment	✓✓	☆	☆
7.5.2 Design Safety Analysis	✓✓	☆	☆
7.5.3 Independence Analysis	✓	✓✓	☆
7.5.4 Formal Inspections of Design Products	✓	✓✓	☆
7.5.5 Formal Methods and Model Checking	⊘	✓	✓✓
7.5.6 Data Logic Analysis	⊘	✓	☆
7.5.7 Design Data Analysis	✓	✓✓	☆
7.5.8 Design Interface Analysis	✓	✓✓	☆
7.5.9 Design Traceability Analysis	☆	☆	☆
7.5.10 Software Element Analysis	✓	✓✓	☆
7.5.11 Rate Monotonic Analysis	⊘	✓	✓✓
7.5.12 Dynamic Flowgraph Analysis	⊘	⊘	✓
7.5.13 Markov Modeling	⊘	✓	✓✓
7.5.14 Requirements State Machines	⊘	✓	✓✓

Recommendation Codes			
☆	Mandatory	✓✓	Highly Recommended
✓	Recommended	⊘	Not Recommended

7.4 Design of Safety-Critical Software

7.4.1 Designing for Safety

Creating a good design is an art as well as a science. This guidebook will not deal with the process of creating a design or ensuring that it is a "good" design. Many books exist that teach design methods. Section 4.2.2 discusses several design methodologies.

What this section will do, however, is list some concepts that should at least be considered for a safety-critical design. Questions will be posed for the designer to answer. Specific activities will be mentioned that support the process of creating a safe design. The intent of this section is for the designer to *think* about the design from a safety perspective.

One of the most important aspects of a software design for a safety-critical system is designing for minimum risk. This "minimum risk" includes hazard risk (likelihood and severity), risk of software defects, risk of human operator errors, and other types of risk (such as programmatic, cost, schedule, etc.). When possible, eliminate identified hazards or reduce associated risk through design. Some ways to reduce the risk include:

- Reduce complexity of software and interfaces.

- Design for user-safety instead of user-friendly (though keep operator usage patterns in mind). Section 11.9 discusses human factors for software safety.

- Design for testability during development and integration.

- Give more design "resources" (time, effort, etc.) to higher-risk aspects (hazard controls, etc.)

SSP 50038, Computer-Based Control System Safety Requirements [42], provides a checklist of design criteria for minimum risk. Items include: Separation of Commands/Functions/Files/Ports, Interrupts, Shutdown/Recovery/Safing, Monitoring/Detection, and other design considerations.

Tasks, ideas, and questions for the design phase include:

- **Functional Allocation**

  o Determine what modules, classes, etc. will implement the safety-critical requirements. Isolate these components from the non-critical components as much as possible.

  o Minimize the number of safety-critical components. Interfaces between critical components should also be designed for minimum interaction (low coupling).

  o Categorize the components as safety-critical or not. Software Safety should review this determination for concurrence.

  o Document the positions and functions of safety-critical components in the design hierarchy.

  o Document how each safety-critical component can be traced back to original safety requirements and how the requirement is implemented.

  o Specify safety-related design and implementation constraints.

o   Document execution control, interrupt characteristics, initialization, synchronization, and control of the components. Include any finite state machines. For high risk systems, interrupts should be avoided as they may interfere with software safety controls. Any interrupts used should be priority based.

- **Program Interfaces**

    o   Define the functional interfaces between all components. For safety-critical components, limit their interaction with other components as much as possible.

    o   Identify shared data within the software. The design should segregate safety-critical data from other data. Non-critical components should not have access to safety-critical data. How will the safety-critical data be protected from inadvertent use or changes by non-safety-critical components?

    o   Document the databases and data files which contain safety-critical data and all the components that access them, whether they are safety-critical or not.

    o   For each interface specify a design that meets the safety requirements in the ICD, SIS document of equivalent.

    o   Identify safety-critical data used in interfaces.

- **Fault Detection. Recovery and Safing**

    o   Specify any error detection or recovery schemes for safety-critical components.

    o   Include response to language generated exceptions and to unexpected external inputs, e.g. inappropriate commands or out-of-limit measurements.

    o   Consider hazardous operations scenarios. How can the design prevent human errors from occurring? How can the design recognize faults before they become failures? What can be added to the design to reduce the risk of the hazard occurring?

    o   Will memory testing during operation be required? When will the tests be run? Can the tests ever impact safety-critical functions?

    o   Consider using memory utilization checks to give advance warning of imminent saturation of memory.

    o   The design of safing and recovery actions should fully consider the real-world conditions and the corresponding time to criticality. Automatic safing can only be a valid hazard control if there is ample margin between worst-case (long) response time and worst-case (short) time to criticality.

    o   Automatic safing is often required if the time to criticality is shorter than the realistic human operator response time, or if there is no human in the loop. This can be performed by either hardware or software or a combination depending on the best system design to achieve safing.

    o   How will critical memory blocks be protected from inadvertent corruption or deletion? Processors with Memory Management Units (MMU) provide one mechanism for protection. Checking the address range returned by the dynamic allocation routine against the critical memory addresses will work in systems that use physical (RAM) addresses or logical memory addresses. Care must be taken that logical and physical addresses are not compared to each other. CRC values or error-correcting codes are software ways to detect and/or correct critical data that may be accidentally corrupted

o What levels of fault and failure tolerance must be implemented, and how will this be done? Will independent versions of software functionality be used? How will the independence be assured? Section 6.5.2 discusses fault and failure tolerance. Section 7.4.2 provides more details on how to achieve it.

- **Inherited or Reused Software and COTS** (see Chapter 12)

  o Were any hazard analyses performed on COTS, inherited or reused software? What information and documentation exists on the analysis, testing, or other verification of the software?

  o How well understood is this software? What functionality is it missing? What extra functionality does it contain?

  o Document where this software is used and its relationship to safety-critical components.

- **Design Feasibility, Performance, and Margins**

  o Show how the design of safety-critical components is responsive to safety requirements. Include information from any analyses of prototypes or simulations. Define design margins of these components.

  o Sampling rates should be selected with consideration for noise levels and expected variations of control system and physical parameters. For measuring signals that are not critical, the sample rate should be at least twice the maximum expected signal frequency to avoid aliasing. For critical signals, and parameters used for closed loop control, it is generally accepted that the sampling rate must be much higher. A factor of at least ten above the system characteristic frequency is customary. [35]

  o Digitized systems should select word lengths long enough to reduce the effects of quantization noise to ensure stability of the system [36]. Selection of word lengths and floating point coefficients should be appropriate with regard to the parameters being processed in the context of the overall control system. Too short word lengths can result in system instability and misleading readouts. Too long word lengths result in excessively complex software and heavy demand on CPU resources, scheduling and timing conflicts etc.

  o Computers take a finite time to read data and to calculate and output results, so some control parameters will always be out of date. Controls systems must accommodate this. Also, check timing clock reference datum, synchronization and accuracy (jitter). Analyze task scheduling (e.g., with Rate Monotonic Analysis (RMA) – section 7.5.11).

- **Traceability**

  o For each component, identify traceability to software requirements, especially software safety requirements.

  o All requirements must be flowed down into the design. Maintaining a traceability matrix or other document helps to verify this.

  o Identify test and/or verification methods for each safety-critical design feature.

- **Testing**

  o Design for testability. Include ways that internals of a component can be adequately tested to verify that they are working properly.

  o Results of preliminary tests of prototype code should be evaluated and documented in the Software Development Folders (SDFs).

  o Any safety-critical findings should be reported to the Safety Engineer to help work out viable solutions.

7.4.2 Designing around Faults and Failures

The main safety objective of the design phase is to define the strategy for achieving the required level of failure tolerance in the various parts of the system. The degree of failure tolerance required can be inversely related to the degree of fault reduction used (e.g. Formal Methods). However, even the most rigorous level of fault reduction will not prevent all faults, and some degree of failure tolerance is generally required.

Fault Propagation is a cascading of a software (or hardware or human) error from one component to another. To prevent fault propagation within software, safety-critical components must be fully independent of non-safety-critical components. They must also be able to both detect an error within themselves and not allow it to be passed on. Alternately, the receiving component can catch and contain the error.

- **Must Work Functions (MWF)**[6]

  MWF's achieve failure tolerance through independent parallel redundancy. For parallel redundancy to be truly independent there must be dissimilar software in each parallel path. Software can sometimes be considered "dissimilar" if N-Version programming (section 7.4.2.1) is properly applied, though true independence is very difficult to achieve.

  For two parallel strings to be independent, no single failure may disable both strings. For three parallel strings, no two failures may disable all three strings.

---

[6] Must Work and Must Not Work functions are discussed in Section F.2, along with examples.

- **Must Not Work Functions (MNWF)**[6]

  MNWF's achieve failure tolerance through independent multiple series inhibits. For series inhibits to be considered independent, they must be (generally) controlled by different processors containing dissimilar software.

  For two in-series inhibits to be independent, no single failure, human mistake, event or environment may activate both inhibits. For three series inhibits to be independent, no two failures, human mistakes, events or environments (or any combination of two single items) may activate all three inhibits. Generally this means that each inhibit must be controlled by a different processor with different software (e.g. N-Version programming, see section 7.4.2.1).

- **Fault/Failure Detection, Isolation and Recovery (FDIR)**

  FDIR is a problematic area, where improper design can result in system false alarms, "bogus" system failures, or failure to detect important safety-critical system failures. Consider the possible consequences as well as the benefits when determining FDIR design.

Fault-tolerant design techniques include:

- **Shadowing (Convergence testing).** For non-discrete continuously varying parameters that are safety-critical, a useful redundancy technique is convergence testing or "shadowing". A higher level process emulates lower level process(es) to predict expected performance and decide if failures have occurred in the lower level processes. The higher-level process implements appropriate redundancy switching when it detects a discrepancy. Alternatively, the higher-level process can switch to a subset or degraded functional set to perform minimal functions when insufficient redundancy remains to keep the system fully operational.

- **Built-in Test(BIT):** Sometimes FDIR can be based on self-test (BIT) of lower tier processors where lower level units test themselves, and report their good/bad status to a higher processor. The higher processor switches out units reporting a failed or bad status.

- **Majority voting.** Some redundancy schemes are based on majority voting. This technique is especially useful when the criteria for diagnosing failures are complicated. (e.g. when an unsafe condition is defined by exceeding an analog value rather than simply a binary value). Majority voting requires more redundancy to achieve a given level of failure tolerance, as follows: 2 of 3 achieves single failure tolerance; 3 of 5 achieves two failure tolerance. An odd number of parallel units are required to achieve majority voting.

- **N-Version programming.** See section 7.4.2.1.

- **Fault containment regions.** See section 7.4.2.2.

- **Redundant Architecture.** See section 7.4.2.3.

- **Recovery blocks** use multiple software versions to find and recover from faults. The output from a block is checked against an acceptance test. If it fails, then another version computes the output and the process continues. Each successive version is more reliable but less efficient. If the last version fails, the program must determine some way to fail safe.

- **Resourcefulness.** Resourcefulness concentrates on achieving system goals through multiple methods. For example, if the goal is to point a scan platform at a particular target, the exact movement scenario is not specified. Whether it moves +10 degrees or – 350 degrees, it points at the same location. This approach allows the system to compensate for problems. It requires systems that are functionally rich, to provide the options necessary to fulfill the goal.

- **Abbott-Neuman Components.** Components must be self-protecting and self-checking. A self-protecting component does not allow other components to crash it; rather it returns an error indication to the calling component. A self-checking component detects its own errors and attempts to recover from them.

- **Self-checks** are a type of dynamic fault-detection that is used by other techniques (e.g. N-Version programming and recovery blocks). Varieties of self-checks include replication (copies that must be identical if the data is to be considered correct), reasonableness (is the data reasonable, based on other data in the system), and structural (are components manipulating complex data structures correctly).

7.4.2.1 N-Version Programming

N-Version Programming is one method that can be used to implement failure tolerant behavior. Multiple, independent versions of the software execute simultaneously. If the answers all agree, then the process continues. If there is disagreement, then a voting method is used to determine which of the answers is correct.

In the past, some NASA policy documents have essentially stipulated the use of N-Version programming in any attempt to achieve failure tolerance. Reference [42] discusses in more detail the JSC position on N-Version programming. They recognize that the technique has limitations. Many professionals regard N-Version programming as ineffective, or even counter productive.

Efforts to implement N-Version programming should be carefully planned and managed to ensure that valid independence is achieved. In practice, applications of N-Version programming on NSTS payloads are limited to small simple functions. However, the NSTS power up of the engines has N-Version programming as well.

Note that, by the NSTS 1700.7B stipulation, two processors running the same operating system are neither independent nor failure-tolerant of each other, regardless of the degree of N-Version programming used in writing the applications.

In recent years, increasing controversy has surrounded the use of N-Version programming. In particular, Knight and Leveson [43] have jointly reported results of experiments with N-Version programming, claiming the technique is largely ineffective. Within NASA, Butler and Finelli [44] have also questioned the validity of N-Version programming, even calling it "counter productive". Though it has worked very effectively on some occasions, it should be evaluated carefully before being implemented.

One major problem with N-Version programming is that it increases complexity, which has a direct relationship with the number of errors. In one NASA study of an experimental aircraft, all of the software problems found during testing were the result of the errors in the redundancy management system. The control software operated flawlessly! Another difficulty with N-Version programming is that achieving true independence is very difficult. Even if separate teams develop the software, studies have shown that the software is still often not truly independent.

Reference [45] gives some useful background for N-Version programming.

7.4.2.2 Fault Containment Regions

One approach is to establish Fault Containment Regions (FCRs) to prevent propagation of software faults. This attempts to prevent fault propagation such as from non-critical software to safey-critical components; from one redundant software unit to another, or from one safety-critical component to another. Techniques such as firewalling or "come from" checks should be used to provide sufficient isolation of FCRs to prevent hazardous fault propagation.

FCRs are best partitioned or firewalled by hardware. Leveson [9] states that "logical" firewalls can be used to isolate software components, such as isolating an application from an operating system. To some extent this can be done using defensive programming techniques and internal software redundancy (e.g., using authorization codes or cryptographic keys). However, within NASA this is normally regarded as hazard mitigation, but not hazard control, because such software/logical safeguards can be defeated by hardware failures or EMI/Radiation effects.

A typical method of obtaining independence between FCRs is to host them on different and independent hardware processors. Sometimes it is acceptable to have independent FCRs hosted on the same processor depending on the specific hardware configuration (e.g. the FCRs are stored in separate memory chips and they are not simultaneously or concurrently multitasked in the same Central Processing Unit (CPU)).

Methods of achieving independence are discussed in more detail in Reference [35], "The Computer Control of Hazardous Payloads", NASA/JSC/FDSD, 24 July 1991. FCRs are defined in reference [42], SSP 50038 "Computer Based Control System Safety Requirements - International Space Station Alpha".

7.4.2.3 Redundant Architecture

Redundant architecture refers to having two versions of the operational code. Unlike N-Version programming, the two versions do not need to operate identically. The primary software is the high-performance version. This is the "regular" software you want to run – it meets all the required functionality and performance requirements.

However, if problems should develop in the high-performance software, particularly problems or failures that impact safety, then a "high-assurance" kernel (also called a safety kernel) is given control. The high-assurance kernel may have the same functionality as the high-performance software, or may have a more limited scope. The primary aspect is that it is *safe*. The high-assurance kernel will almost certainly be less optimized (slower, stressed more easily, lower limits on the load it can handle, etc.).

The Carnegie Mellon Software Engineering Institute (SEI) Simplex Architecture [46] is an example of a redundant architecture. This architecture includes the high-performance/high-assurance kernels, address-space protection mechanisms, real-time scheduling algorithms, and methods for dynamic communication among components. This process requires using analytic redundancy to separate major functions into high-assurance kernels and high-performance subsystems.

7.4.3 Selection of COTS and Reusing Components

Early in the design phase, and sometimes even during requirements definition, decisions are made to select Off-The-Shelf (OTS) items (software, hardware, or both) that are available "as is" from a commercial source (Commercial Off-The-Shelf (COTS)) or to reuse applications developed from other similar projects (i.e., Government Off-The-Shelf (GOTS) items). Any modifications of these items place them in another category – Modified Off-the-Shelf (MOTS) items.

OTS items commonly used include operating systems, processor and device microcode, and libraries of functions. It is becoming prohibitively expensive to custom develop software for these applications. In addition, the desire to not "reinvent the wheel" is strong, especially when faced with budget and schedule constraints. There is also a trend in government to use commercial products instead of custom developing similar but much more expensive products.

Section 12.1 *Off-the-Shelf Software* covers the pros and cons of OTS and reused software in more detail. Many issues need to be considered before making the decision to use OTS software, or to reuse software from a previous project. While OTS software may appear cost-effective, the additional analyses, tests, glueware code development, and other activities may make it more expensive than developing the software in-house. The section also provides recommendations for additional analyses and tests for OTS software in safety-critical systems.

Section 12.2 *Contractor-developed Software* discusses issues relating to having custom software created by a contractor, rather than in-house.

7.4.4 Selection of language, development tools and operating systems

It is during the design phase that the language used to develop the software, the tools used in the creation of software, as well as the operating system (OS) it will run on, are often selected. The choice of language, tools, and OS can have an impact on the safety of the software. Some operating systems have more "safety" features than others. Some tools make finding errors easier.

When choosing a programming language, many factors are important. For example, consider the variations of memory size (footprint) and execution speed of an algorithm between candidate languages. The existence of tools (compiler, integrated development environment, etc.) that support the language for the specified processor and on the development platform, and the availability of software engineers who have training and experience with the language are also important. When developing safety-critical applications or components, however, the "safeness" of the programming language should be a high priority factor.

A "safe" programming language is one in which the translation from source to object code can be rigorously verified. Compilers that are designed to use safe subsets of a programming language are often certified, guaranteeing that the object code is a correct translation of the source code. In a more general sense, a "safe" language is one that enforces good programming practices, and that finds errors at compile time, rather than at run time. Safe languages have strict data types, bounds checking on arrays, and discourage the use of pointers, among other features.

Section 4.6 *Good Programming Practices for Safety* contains a technical overview of safety-critical coding practices for developers and safety engineers. Many of the coding practices involve restricting the use of certain programming language constructs.

Section 11.1 provides an introduction on the criteria for evaluating the risks associated with the choice of a particular programming language. Some are well suited for safety-critical applications, and therefore engender a lower risk. Others are less "safe" and, if chosen, require additional analysis and testing to assure the safety of the software. Where appropriate, safe subsets of languages will be described. Common errors ("bugs") in software development are also included.

When choosing a language, consider the language "environment" (compiler, Integrated Development Environment (IDE), debugger, etc.) as well. Is the compiler certified? Is there a list of known defects or errors produced by the compiler? Does the code editor help find problems by highlighting or changing the color of language-specific terms? Does the compiler allow you to have warnings issued as errors, to enforce conformance? Is there a debugger that allows you to set break points and look at the source assembly code?

No programming language is guaranteed to produce safe software. The best languages enforce good programming practices, make bugs easier for the compiler to find, and incorporate elements that make the software easier to verify. Even so, the "safeness" and reliability of the software depend on many other factors, including the correctness of the requirements and design. Humans are involved in all aspects of the process, and we are quite capable of subverting even the "safest" of languages. Select a language based on a balance of all factors, including safety.

Suggestions for what to look for when selecting an operating system, programming language, and development tool are included in Chapter 11 *Software Development Issues*.

11.1	Programming Languages
11.2	Compilers, Editors, Debuggers, IDEs and other Tools
11.3	CASE tools and Automatic Code Generation
11.4	Operating Systems

7.4.5 Language Restrictions and Coding Standards

When it comes to safety-critical software, some aspects of various programming languages should be avoided. These aspects may be undefined by the standard (and therefore vary between compilers). They may perform a function or activity that is undesired or detrimental to the system (such as disabling interrupts for too long). Or they may simply be "bad practice" – functions or constructs that are often used improperly or lead to many defects.

It is important that the chosen language is surveyed for such potential problems before the design is actually implemented in code. This can be done as part of the initial language selection process. It is far easier to implement "good practice" early on, than to have to retrain software engineers to avoid certain language constructs when they have been using them for some time.

A Coding Standard is one way to implement such language restrictions. The standard can indicate what software constructs, library functions, and other language-specific information *must* or *must not* be used. As such, it produces, in practice, a "safe" subset of the programming language. Coding standards may be developed by the software designer, based on the software and hardware system to be used, or may be general standards for a "safer" version of a particular language.

The process compilers use internally to convert the higher level language into machine operations may be undefined and is often highly variable between compilers. For example, the implementation method for dynamic memory allocation is not part of most language specifications, and therefore varies between compilers. Even for a specific compiler, information on how such a process is implemented is difficult to obtain. The location of the allocated memory is usually not predictable, and that may not be acceptable for a safety-critical software component. Another example is the order that global items are initialized. Coding standards can be used to make sure that no global item depends on another global item having been already initialized.

It is important that all levels of the project agree to the coding standards, and that they are enforced. If the programmers disagree, they may find ways to circumvent it. Safety requires the cooperation of everyone. Include those who will actually do the programming, as well as software designers and software leads, in any meetings where coding standards will be discussed.

Coding standards may also contain requirements for how the source code is to look, such as indentation patterns and comment formats. However, it is best to separate these requirements into a separate **coding style** document. This avoids the problem of developers shelving the coding standards because they disagree with the coding style. While trivial in many ways, coding style requirements help make the software more readable by other developers. In addition, they make it more difficult for "typical" errors to be inserted in the code, and easier for them to be found during an inspection.

Create a checklist from the agreed-upon coding standard, for use during software formal inspections and informal reviews. Enforce conformance to the standard during the inspections. Do not rate "style" issues as highly as safety issues. In fact, style issues can be ignored, unless they seriously impact on the readability of the code, or the project decides that they must be enforced.

Coding standards can be enforced some development tools. See section 11.2 for details on what to look for when choosing development tools.

Benefit Rating:	HIGH	Cost Rating: LOW

7.4.6   Defensive Programming

Defensive programming is the art of making sure your software can gracefully handle anything thrown at it. In other words, it is a collection of methods, techniques, and algorithms designed to prevent faults from becoming failures. The faults (defects) you want to be concerned about can be in your own software (e.g. incorrect logic), another program in the system (e.g. sends invalid message), hardware faults (e.g. sensor returns bad value), and operator error (e.g. mistyping command). Consider the system to be a hostile environment that might throw anything at you and design your software to handle it gracefully.

A simple example of defensive programming is range checking on an input variable. If the variable is only supposed to be in the range of 1 to 10, check for that before the variable is used. If the input variable is outside that range, the software needs to do something. What that something is should be part of an overall strategy. One option is to stop processing in that function and return with an error code. Another is to replace the out-of-range value with a preset default value. A third option is to throw an exception or use another high-level error handling method. Of course, one option is to just proceed onward, allowing the fault (bad input number) to eventually lead to a failure. This approach is not recommended.

Another example of defensive programming is "come from" checks. Critical routines test whether they should be executing at some particular instant. If the checks are not validated, then the critical routine does not execute, and usually issues an error message. One method of implementing these "come from" checks is for each preceding process to set a bit flag. If all the appropriate bits are set, then the critical routine is authorized to execute.

The strategy for dealing with defects, errors, and faults should be thought-out early in the program. Will each function (routine, method, etc.) check input variables, or will variables be checked before they are passed during a function call? Will faults be handed up to higher-level error handling software? Will certain faults be allowed, and the resulting failure handled when (or if) it occurs? Regardless of the strategy chosen, consistency is important. All functions, methods, modules, units, etc. should use the same strategy, unless there is a very good reason to deviate.

Section 7.4.2 dealt with fault and failure tolerance. Defensive programming is, in many ways, a lower-level part of that strategy. However, it deals more with the actual implementation details, and is language-specific. Defensive programming is discussed here because it needs to be *planned* into the software design, not tacked-on later.

Section 8.4.1 calls for the development of a defensive programming checklist. This checklist will be used by the programmers while developing the code. The defensive programming strategy must be included in this checklist, as well as language-specific problem areas and good practices.

Benefit Rating: HIGH	Cost Rating: LOW

7.4.7 Integration Test Planning

At this development phase, the main components (units) of the software have been defined. This is the time to determine the integration order of the units, and the integration tests that will be run. Consider the hardware development schedule, as some units may require the real hardware to run on. You do not want to hold up integration testing while waiting for a piece of hardware to be completed.

Consider where to integrate the safety-critical components. Integration testing is the time to look for unexpected interactions among the units. Whether safety-critical units are integrated first with non-critical units added later, or the reverse, does not really matter. However, testing for interactions with the safety-critical units as each unit is added is recommended. One advantage of early integration of the safety-critical units is that they will undergo more testing than if they are integrated later in the process. Each additional test opens up the possibility of finding defects. Each defect-free test increases the confidence in the safety-critical unit.

7.4.8 Complexity

The complexity of the software components and interfaces should be evaluated, because the level of complexity can affect the understandability, reliability and maintainability of the code. Highly complex data and command structures are difficult, if not impossible, to test thoroughly. Complex software is difficult to maintain, and updating the software may lead to additional errors. Not all paths can usually be thought out or tested for, and this leaves the potential for the software to perform in an unexpected manner. When highly complex data and command structures are necessary, look at techniques for avoiding a high a level of program interweaving.

Linguistic and structural metrics exist for measuring the complexity of software, and are discussed below. The following references provide a more detailed discussion of and guidance on the techniques.

1. "Software State of the Art: selected papers", Tom DeMarco, Dorset House, NY, 2000.

2. "Black-Box Testing: Techniques for Functional Testing of Software and Systems", Boris Beizer, Wiley, John & Sons Inc., 1995

3. "Applying Software Metrics", Shari Lawrence Pfleeger and Paul Oman, IEEE Press, 1997

4. "A Framework of Software Measurement", Horst Zuse, Walter deGruyter, 1998

5. "Metrics and Models in Software Quality Engineering", Stephen Kan, Addison Wesley, 1995

6. "Object-Oriented Metrics: Measures of Complexity", Brian Henderson-Sellers, Prentice Hall, 1996

7. "Software Metrics: A Rigorous and Practical Approach", Norman E. Fenton, PWS Publishing, 1998

8. "Function Point Analysis: Measurement Practices for Successful Software Projects", David Garmus and David Herron, Addison, 2000

Linguistic measurements assess some property of the text without regard for the contents (e.g., lines of code, function points, number of statements, number and type of operators, total number and type of tokens, etc). Halstead's Metrics is a well-known measure of several of these arguments.

Structural metrics focuses on control-flow and data-flow within the software and can usually be mapped into a graphics representation. Structural relationships such as the number of links and/or calls, number of nodes, nesting depth, etc. are examined to get a measure of complexity. McCabe's Cyclomatic Complexity metric is the most well-known and used metric for this type of complexity evaluation.

Object-oriented software does not always fit easily into the structured complexity metrics. Reference 6 (above) describes complexity metrics for OO software. Such metrics include: Weighted Methods per Class, Depth of Inheritance Tree, Number of Children (subclasses), Degree of Coupling Between Objects, Degree of Cohesion of Objects, and Average Method Complexity.

Resources used by these techniques are the detailed design, high level language description, any source code or pseudocode, and automated complexity measurement tool(s). Outputs from this process are the complexity measurements, predicted error estimates, and areas of high complexity identified for further analysis or consideration for simplification.

Several automated tools are available that provide these metrics. The level and type of complexity can indicate areas where further analysis or testing may be warranted. Do not take the numbers at face value, however! Sometimes a structure considered highly complex (such as a case statement) may actually be a simpler, more straightforward method of programming, thus decreasing the risk of errors during maintenance.

Recommendations:

Apply one or more complexity estimation techniques, such as McCabe or Halstead, to the design products. If an automated tool is available, the software design, pseudo-code, or prototype code can be run through the tool. If there is no automated tool available, examine the critical areas of the detailed design and any preliminary code for areas of deep nesting, large numbers of parameters to be passed, intense and numerous communication paths, etc. The references above give detailed instructions on what to look for when estimating complexity.

Complexity limits may be imposed. Limiting complexity at all stages of software development helps avoid the pitfalls associated with high complexity software. McCabe recommends a Cyclomatic Complexity limit of 10, though limits as high as 15 have been used successfully. "Limits over 10 should be reserved for projects that have several operational advantages over typical projects, for example experienced staff, formal design, a modern programming language, structured programming, code walkthroughs, and a comprehensive test plan. In other words, a development group can pick a complexity limit greater than 10, but only if they make an informed choice based on experience and are willing to devote the additional testing effort required by more complex modules." [93]

Complexity involves more than just individual modules or classes. Complexity of interfaces is another type of complexity that must be considered. As the number of modules increases (perhaps due to limits on individual module complexity), the number of interfaces increases. Other elements of the software may also contribute to its complexity. For example, global data introduces the possibility that virtually any part of the software can interact with any other part through their operations on the same data. This can dramatically increase the complexity, especially for a human reader attempting to understand the program. [92]

Reducing the complexity of software is a complicated task. It involves balancing all the various types of complexity (module, interface, communication, etc.). Often, reducing complexity in one area will increase the complexity of another area. The correct balance will have to be determined by the project team. Limit the complexity in areas that are not well understood, that will not undergo detailed inspections or reviews, or that may not be tested comprehensively. Higher complexity can be tolerated in software that the team has experience in, that are well understood, or that will be subjected to rigorous reviews and testing.

Benefit Rating:	HIGH	Cost Rating: LOW

7.4.8.1 Function Points

The most common size metric used is software lines of code (SLOC). While easy to measure, this metric has some problems. The lines of code it takes to produce a specific function will vary with the language – more lines are needed in assembly language than in C++, for instance. Counting the lines can only be done once the code is available, and pre-coding estimates are often not accurate.

Function Points are an alternative measurement to SLOC that focuses on the end-user, and not on the technical details of the coding. Function Point Analysis was developed by Allan Albrecht of IBM in 1979, and revised in 1983. The FPA technique quantifies the functions contained within software in terms which are meaningful to the software users. The measure relates directly to the requirements which the software is intended to address. It can therefore be readily applied throughout the life of a development project, from early requirements definition to full operational use.

The function point metric is calculated by using a weighted count of the number of the following elements:

- **User inputs** provide application-oriented data to the software.

- **User outputs** provide application-oriented information to the user. This includes reports, screens, error messages, etc. Individual data items within a report are not counted separately.

- **User inquiries** are an on-line input that results in the generation of some immediate software response in the form of an on-line output. Typing a question in a search engine would be an inquiry.

- **Files** include both physical and logical files (groupings of information).

- **External interfaces** are all machine readable interfaces used to transmit information to another system.

The weighting factors are based on the complexity of the software.

"Function Point Analysis: Measurement Practices for Successful Software Projects", by David Garmus and David Herron (reference 8 in section 7.4.8), provides information on calculating and using function points. The International Function Point Users Group (IFPUG, http://www.ifpug.org/) supports and promotes the use of function points.

7.4.8.2 Function Point extensions

Function points are business (database, transaction) oriented. Extensions are needed for systems and engineering software applications, such as real-time, process control, and embedded software.

Feature points are one such extension. This metric takes into account algorithmic complexity. A feature point value is the sum of the weighted function point factors and the weighted algorithm count. Algorithms include such actions as inverting a matrix, decoding a bit string, or handling an interrupt. Feature points were developed in 1986 by Capers Jones.

The "3D function point" was developed by Boeing for real-time and embedded systems. The Boeing approach integrates the data, functional, and control dimensions of a software system.

The data dimension is essentially the standard function point. The functional dimension counts the transformations, which are the number of internal operations to transform the input data into output data. The control dimension is measured by counting the number of transitions between states.

7.4.9 Design for Maintainability and Reliability

To build maintainable software, numerous metrics can be collected to evaluate the quality of the design from a maintainability point of view. Metrics developed prior to object-oriented software include cyclomatic complexity, lines of code, and comment percentage. Object-oriented metrics include weighted methods per class, response for a class, lack of cohesion of methods, coupling between objects, depth of inheritance tree, and number of children. A Maintainability Index was developed by the Software Engineering Institute (SEI), and is calculated using a combination of widely used and commonly available measures [103].

Basically, what these metrics do is evaluate a design for qualities that enhance the software's ability to be maintained over a long period of time. A lot of the metrics provide a way for evaluating parts of the design and giving it a numerical value. For instance, cohesion is the degree to which methods within a class are related to one another and work together to provide well-bounded behavior. A high cohesion value indicates good class subdivision. Lack of cohesion or low cohesion indicates more complexity and a higher likelihood of errors occurring.

In addition to the metrics, a project should also set itself up to build maintainable software by doing the following:

- Plan early - anticipating what and how software might be modified
- Modular design - define subsets; simplify functionality (1 function/module)
- Object-oriented design
- Uniform conventions
- Naming conventions
- Coding standards
- Documentation standards
- Common tool sets
- Configuration Management

The Maintenance Phase (section 10.5) is also critical. JSC estimates that in a large system, software life cycle costs typically exceeds hardware, with 80-90% of the total system cost going into software maintenance. If this phase is not properly planned for, the extra effort that was put into the development phase will be wasted. It is critical that the Maintenance Phase be planned for early so that maintainability is built into the software.

The Maintenance Phase, including the transition from development to maintenance, needs to be planned in order to make the change without disrupting the system. Planning needs to include how maintenance will be carried out, what types of changes will be covered, who is responsible for each aspect of maintenance, what is the process by which maintenance changes will be made, what resources will be needed, etc.

Building reliable software also depends on collecting the right metrics and analyzing them properly, along with having good processes in place. The IEEE Standard 982.2-1988 lists 39 metrics which can be used to determine software reliability. The IEEE standard does not recommend to collect them all, but to do a determination of which ones will apply to your system. It also recommends that different metrics be collected in the different life cycle phases and has a table that cross-references metrics and phases. The standard also provides practical advice for building reliable software:

- Do it right first - get skilled, competent personnel; early user involvement; use modern methods, languages and tools.

- Detect it early; fix it as soon as possible - detect faults early through reviews, inspections, prototyping, simulation, etc.; reliability cannot be tested into a product

- Monitor it - collect metrics; state objective of how a metric will be used, otherwise don't use it.

AIAA/ANSI R-013-1992 has an 11 step generic procedure for estimating software reliability:

- Identify application
- Define the requirement
- Allocate the requirement
- Define failure
- Characterize the operational environment
- Select tests
- Select modes
- Collect data
- Estimate parameters
- Validate the model
- Perform analysis

The document also provides details of analysis procedures for some common engineering or management activities that can be aided by software reliability engineering technology. Section 6 of the document provides many software reliability estimation models.

The IEEE Technical Council on Software Engineering (TCSE) Committee on Software Reliability Engineering has a web site with more information. It is http://www.tcse.org/sre.

A software reliability case can be written to provide justification of the approach taken and document evidence that verifies that the software meets reliability requirements. The reliability case should be a living document that records what has been done in the various phases of software development pertaining to reliability.

Resources for more information:

- IEEE Std 1219-1998 IEEE Standard For Software Maintenance

- "Realities of Software Sustainment vs. Maintenance", Crosstalk magazine, May 1997

- Review of "Practical Software Maintenance", Journal of Software Maintenance and Practice, May 2000

- "A JPL Software Reliability Study and a Windows-based Software Reliability Tool" by Allen P. Nikora/JPL

- "The Prediction of Faulty Classes Using Object-Oriented Design Metrics" by Emam and Melo, November 1999, National Research Council Canada

- "A Practical Software-Reliability Measurement Framework Based on Failure Data" by Minyan, Yunfeng and Min, IEEE 2000 Proceedings Annual Reliability and Maintainability Symposium

- "Software Quality Metrics for Object Oriented System Environments", http://ourworld.compuserve.com/homepages/qualazur/$swmesu2.htm

- "Software Reliability Cases: The Bridge Between Hardware, Software and System Safety and Reliability", IEEE 1999 Proceedings Annual Reliability and Maintainability Symposium

- "Maintainability Index Technique for Measuring Program Maintainability", http://www.sei.cmu.edu/activities/str/descriptions/mitmpm.html

- "Software Design For Maintainability" from JSC

- IEEE Std 982.2-1988 IEEE Guide for the Use of IEEE Standard Dictionary of Measures to Produce Reliable Software

- AIAA/ANSI R-013-1992 Recommended Practice for Software Reliability

7.5 Design Analysis

The software preliminary (architectural) design process develops the high level design that will implement the software requirements. All software safety requirements developed in Section 6.5 are incorporated into the high-level software design as part of this process. The design process includes identification of safety design features and methods (e.g., inhibits, traps, interlocks and assertions) that will be used throughout the software to implement the software safety requirements.

As part of the architectural design process, the software requirements are allocated to software subsystems and various software layers (operating system, device driver, application, API, etc.). These higher-level components generally correspond to Computer Software Configuration Items (CSCIs). Individual Computer Software Components (CSCs) are then identified within these higher level components.

Some of the CSCs will implement safety-critical requirements or features, or work with other safety-critical CSCs. These CSCs are designated as safety-critical. These components implement the safety features, can potentially impact the safety features, or can potentially impact any other safety-critical component. A software component that can write to a safety-critical data area, even if it does not do so during normal operations, is safety-critical. Malfunctioning of that component will affect the safety of the system.

Safety analyses are performed on the design to identify potential hazards and to define and analyze safety-critical components. Early test plans are reviewed to verify incorporation of safety-related testing. Software safety analyses begun earlier are updated as more detail becomes available.

During the detailed (critical) design phase, the software artifacts (design documents) are greatly enhanced. This additional detail now permits rigorous analyses to be performed. Detailed design analyses can make use of products such as detailed design specifications, emulators and Pseudo-Code Program Description Language products (PDL). Preliminary code produced by code generators within CASE tools should be evaluated.

Many techniques to be used on the final code can be "dry run" on these design products. In fact, it is recommended that all analyses planned on the final code should undergo their first iteration on the code-like products of the detailed design. This will catch many errors before they reach the final code where they are more expensive to correct.

7.5.1 Update Previous Analyses

At this stage of development, the software functions begin to be allocated to components. Software for a system, while often subjected to a single development program, actually consists of a set of multipurpose, multifunction entities. The software functions need to be subdivided into many components and further broken down to modules.

A software safety checklist should have been produced during the requirements phase that lists all safety-related software requirements. This checklist can be used to help verify that all safety requirements are incorporated into the design, and ultimately into the software code.

Many previous analyses could only be started, as the necessary detail was lacking. During the design process, these analyses should be revisited and updated.

Table 7-4 Previous Software Safety Analyses

Analysis	Guidebook Section
Preliminary Hazard Analysis (PHA)	2.3.1
Software Subsystem Hazard Analysis	2.3.4
Software Safety Requirements Flow-down Analysis	6.6.1
Requirements Criticality Analysis	6.6.2
Timing, Sizing, and Throughput	6.6.6
Software Fault Tree Analysis	6.6.7
Software Failure Modes and Effects Analysis	6.6.8
Control-flow and Information-flow Analyses	6.6.3.2, 6.6.3.3

7.5.1.1 Criticality Analysis

Some of the software components will be safety-critical, and some will not. Each component that implements a safety-critical requirement must now be assigned a criticality index, based on the criticality analysis (See Section 6.6.2 *Requirements Criticality Analysis*). The safety activity during the design phase is to relate the identified hazards to the Computer Software Components (CSCs) that may affect or control the hazards.

Develop a matrix that lists all safety-critical Computer Software Components and the safety requirements they relate to. Include any components that can affect the safety-critical components as well. This would include components that write to data in memory shared with the safety-critical components, or that provide information to the safety-critical components. The safety-critical designation should be applied to any component (class, module, subroutine or other software entity) identified by this analysis.

7.5.1.2 Software Component Risk Assessment

Once safety-critical Computer Software Components (CSCs) have been identified, they need to be prioritized based on risk. Not all safety-critical components warrant further analysis beyond the design level, nor do all warrant the same depth of analysis. Several factors determine how risky an individual safety-critical component is, including:

- System risk index (Table 2-3)

- Degree of software control of hazard or influence over other controls or mitigations

- Amount of redundant control (e.g. hardware control as backup for software)

- Complexity of the component

- Timing criticality of the system

While Sections 6.6.2 *Requirements Criticality Analysis* and 7.5.1.1 *Criticality Analysis* simply assign a "Yes" or "No" to whether each component is safety-critical, the Risk Assessment process takes this further. Each safety-critical component is prioritized for degree of development effort, analysis and verification activities according to the five levels of ranking given previously in *Table 3-3 Software Risk Matrix*.

 The purpose of this activity is to identify safety-critical components that require extra attention (above that determined by the software safety effort (Table 3-5)) or less effort. While many of the techniques and analyses apply to the software as a whole, some can be applied to individual components at varying levels. For example, Formal Inspections of safety-critical design or code elements should be performed. Within that broad activity, the number of inspections for each component can be tailored. High risk components may be inspected at all stages of design and coding. Low risk components may only have a code inspection.

Determination of the severity and the probability of failure for the software components is sometimes a source of contention between the safety group and the project. It is best to sit down and work out any disagreements at an early stage. Getting the software development group's "buy in" on what is truly safety-critical is vital. Software developers may give less attention to what they do not see as important. Getting everybody on one "side" early prevents the problem of having to force the project to add safety code or testing later in the development cycle.

7.5.1.3 Software FTA and Software FMEA

The preliminary Software Fault Tree generated in the requirements phase can now be expanded. Broad functions can be specified down to some component, at least at a high level. In addition, the system is now understood in greater depth. Failures that were credible during the requirements phase may no longer be possible. Additional causes for the top hazard may be added to the tree.

The individual components have now been specified, at least to some degree. The Software Failure Modes and Effects Analysis (SFMEA) can be updated to reflect the improved understanding of the system. The SFMEA will improve throughout the design phase, as more detail becomes available. Be especially aware of the interactions of non-critical components with those that are safety-critical. A non-critical component that can influence the safety-critical components becomes safety-critical itself.

7.5.2 Design Safety Analysis

Okay, you've got your list of SCCSCs that will be further analyzed. Next you analyze the design of those components to ensure all safety requirements are specified correctly and completely. In addition, review the design, looking for places and conditions that lead to unacceptable hazards. This is done by postulating credible faults or failures and evaluating their effects on the system.

Consider the following types of events and failures:

- input/output timing
- multiple event
- out-of-sequence event
- failure of event
- wrong event
- inappropriate magnitude
- incorrect polarity
- adverse environment
- deadlocking in a multitasking system
- hardware failures

Formal Inspections (see 6.5.5 Formal Inspections of Software Requirements) or design reviews can be used to augment this process. As a design is reviewed, asking the "what if" questions with a diverse group of reviewers may lead to identification of weaknesses (or strengths) within the software. Prototype, animation or simulation of aspects of the design may also show where the software can fail.

7.5.2.1 Design Reviews

Design reviews are conducted to verify that the design meets the requirements. Often the reviews are formal (e.g. Preliminary Design Review (PDR) and Critical Design Review (CDR)) and for the whole system. Separate software PDRs and CDRs may be held, or the software may be a part of the system review.

At all reviews, software safety must be addressed. Does the design meet all the applicable software safety requirements? Does the design use "best practices" to reduce potential errors? Are safety-critical components properly separated from the rest of the software? This is the time to make design changes, if necessary, to fulfill the safety requirements.

Applicability matrices, compliance matrices, and compliance checklists are resources which can be used to assist in completing this task. Output products from the reviews are engineering change requests, hazard reports (to capture design decisions affecting hazard controls and verification) and action items.

7.5.2.2 Prototype and Simulation

Some aspects of the safety system may require certain constraints to be met, such as response time or data conversion speed. Creating a prototype or simulation early in the project may answer the question of whether the software (and system) will be able to meet that constraint.

Prototypes are usually "quick and dirty" and used only for determining if the system can do what it needs to do. Prototypes may also be used to get the customer's input into a user interface. They can show if the user interface is confusing, especially regarding the safety-critical information or commands. Different ways to present data to the operator can be prototyped, and the best way selected. The operator can try hazardous commanding sequences, and either the interface or procedures can be "tweaked" if the process is not as anticipated.

Simulations of all or part of the software and system can be used to test out some of the constraints, such as timing or throughput. Full simulations can be used to "try out" various failure scenarios to see how the system will respond. They can provide preliminary verification of the safety features designed into the system, or can show areas where more safety-related work will need to be done.

Documented test results can confirm expected behavior or reveal unexpected behavior. Keep in mind, however, that the tests are of a prototype or simulation. The behavior of the real software may differ. If the prototype or simulation shows that a requirement can not be met, then the requirement must be modified as appropriate.

7.5.3 Independence Analysis

The safety-critical Computer Software Components (CSCs) should be independent of non-critical functions. Independence Analysis is a way to verify that.. Those CSCs that are found to affect the output of safety-critical CSCs are designated as safety-critical themselves. Areas where FCR (Fault Containment Region) integrity is compromised are identified. As a side result, the interdependence between safety-critical components and other software components will also be identified.

To perform this analysis, map the safety-critical functions to the software components, and then map the software components to the hardware hosts and FCRs. All the input and output of each safety-critical component should be inspected. Consider global or shared variables, as well as the directly passed parameters. Consider "side effects" that may be included when a component is run. If a non-critical CSC modifies a safety-critical one, either directly, by violation of an FCR or indirectly through shared memory, then it becomes safety-critical itself.

The exact definition of a component will vary with the type of software development. Structured or procedural development will use functions and modules as components. Higher-level components may be files (a collection of functions) or applications. Dependence is determined by the calling structure (what module calls what module) and by access to global or shared data. Object-oriented development will use classes as the primary component. Packages are one example of higher-level components. Interactions among classes are determined by inheritance, composition (one class is a component of another), method calling sequences, and access to any shared data.

Resources used in this analysis are the definition of safety-critical functions (MWF and MNWF) that need to be independent (from Section 6.5.3 *Hazardous Commands*), design descriptions, and control flow and data diagrams.

Design changes to achieve valid FCRs and corrections to safety-critical components may be necessary.

Benefit Rating: HIGH	Cost Rating: MODERATE

7.5.4 Formal Inspections of Design Products

The process of Formal Inspection begun in previous requirements phase (e.g. Section 6.5.5 *Formal Inspections*) should continue during the design phase. At the preliminary (architectural) design phase, Formal Inspection should focus on the major breakdown of software components, verifying the modularity and independence of all safety-critical components. At the detailed level, pseudo-code or prototype code may be available for inspection.

For the design inspections, create new checklists that are appropriate to the design products. Include "lessons learned" from the requirements phase and any previous inspections.

 While inspecting all design products would be best, projects may choose to inspect only the design aspects that deal with the safety-critical components. Be aware, however, that unexpected interactions between non-critical and critical code may not be detected under these circumstances.

Benefit Rating: HIGH	Cost Rating: LOW to MODERATE

7.5.5 Formal Methods and Model Checking

Formal methods (sections 4.2.2.3 and 6.6.4) may be used only to create the software specification. If this is the case, then the work was completed during the requirements phase. Otherwise, the formal specification may be "fleshed out" with increasing detail during as the software design progresses.

The formal method "design" or model may be the complete architectural design, or it may be created in parallel with a "normal" design process. If using the parallel approach (normal software development life cycle and formal methods on separate tracks, usually with separate teams), it is important to verify that the designs created by the development team match those of the formal methods team.

Model checking (section 6.6.5) may be used to verify the design still meets the required properties.

7.5.6 Design Logic Analysis (DLA)

Design Logic Analysis (DLA) evaluates the equations, algorithms, and control logic of the software design. Logic analysis examines the safety-critical areas of a software component. A technique for identifying safety-critical areas is to examine each function performed by the software component. If it responds to, or has the potential to violate one of the safety requirements, it should be considered critical and undergo logic analysis. A technique for performing logic analysis is to compare design descriptions and logic flows and note discrepancies.

The ultimate, fully rigorous DLA uses the application of Formal Methods (FM). Where FM is inappropriate, because of its high cost versus software of low cost or low criticality, simpler DLA can be used. Less formal DLA involves a human inspector reviewing a relatively small quantity of critical software products (e.g. PDL, prototype code), and manually tracing the logic. Safety-critical logic to be inspected can include failure detection and diagnosis, redundancy management, variable alarm limits, and command inhibit logical preconditions.

Commercial automatic software source analyzers can be used to augment this activity, but should not be relied upon absolutely since they may suffer from deficiencies and errors, a common concern of COTS tools and COTS in general.

Benefit Rating: HIGH	Cost Rating: MODERATE to HIGH

7.5.7 Design Data Analysis

Design data analysis evaluates the description and intended use of each data item in the software design. Data analysis ensures that the structure and intended use of data will not violate a safety requirement. A technique used in performing design data analysis is to compare description to use of each data item in the design logic.

Interrupts and their effect on data must receive special attention in safety-critical areas. Analysis should verify that interrupts and interrupt handling routines do not alter critical data items used by other routines.

The integrity of each data item should be evaluated with respect to its environment and host. Shared memory and dynamic memory allocation can affect data integrity. Data items should also be protected from being overwritten by unauthorized applications. Considerations of EMI and radiation affects on memory should be reviewed in conjunction with system safety.

Benefit Rating: HIGH	Cost Rating: MODERATE

7.5.8 Design Interface Analysis

Design interface analysis verifies the proper design of a software component's interfaces with other components of the system. The interfaces can be with other software components, with hardware, or with human operators. This analysis will verify that the software component's interfaces, especially the control and data linkages, have been properly designed. Interface requirements specifications (which may be part of the requirements or design documents, or a separate document) are the sources against which the interfaces are evaluated.

Interface characteristics to be addressed should include interprocess communication methods, data encoding, error checking and synchronization.

The analysis should consider the validity and effectiveness of checksums, CRCs, and error correcting code. The sophistication of error checking or correction that is implemented should be appropriate for the predicted bit error rate of the interface. An overall system error rate should be defined, and budgeted to each interface.

Examples of interface problems:

- Sender sends eight bit word with bit 7 as parity, but recipient believes bit 0 is parity.

- Sender transmits updates at 10 Hz, but receiver only updates at 1 Hz.

- Message used by sender to indicate its current state is not understood by the receiving process.

- Interface deadlock prevents data transfer (e.g., receiver ignores or cannot recognize "Ready To Send").

- User reads data from wrong address.

- Data put in shared memory by one process is in "big endian" order, while the process that will use it is expecting "little endian".

- In a language such as C, where data typing is not strict, sender may use different data types than receiver expects. (Where there is strong data typing, the compilers will catch this).

Benefit Rating: HIGH	Cost Rating: MODERATE

7.5.9 Design Traceability Analysis

This analysis ensures that each safety-critical software requirement is covered and that an appropriate criticality level is assigned to each software element. Tracing the safety requirements throughout the design (and eventually into the source code and test cases) is vital to making sure that no requirements are lost, that safety is "designed in", that extra care is taken during the coding phase, and that all safety requirements are tested. A safety requirement traceability matrix is one way to implement this analysis. See section 6.4.2 *Requirements Traceability and Verification* for more information.

Some of the requirements will deal with system constraints or restrictions. They should include real world and environmental limitations. Part of the traceability analysis should verify that the proposed design solution meets these constraints. If new constraints are uncovered as part of this analysis, they should be flowed back up to the requirements.

The design materials should describe all known or anticipated restrictions on a software component. These design constraints must be clear to those who will develop the source code.

Restrictions or constraints to consider include:

- Update timing, throughput and sizing constraints as per Section 6.6.6 *Timing, Throughput And Sizing Analysis*

- Equations and algorithms limitations

- Input and output data limitations (e.g., range, resolution, accuracy)

- Design solution limitations

- Sensor and actuator accuracy and calibration

- Noise, EMI

- Digital word length (quantization/roundoff noise/errors)

- Actuator power or energy capability (motors, heaters, pumps, mechanisms, rockets, valves, etc.)

- Capability of energy storage devices (e.g., batteries, propellant supplies)

- Human factors, human capabilities and limitations [47]

- Physical time constraints and response times

- Off nominal environments (fail safe response)

- Friction, inertia, backlash in mechanical systems

- Validity of models and control laws versus actual system behavior

- Accommodations for changes of system behavior over time: wear-in, hardware wear-out, end of life performance versus beginning of life performance, degraded system behavior and performance.

Benefit Rating: HIGH	Cost Rating: LOW

7.5.10 Software Element Analysis

Each software element that is **not** safety-critical is examined to assure that it cannot cause or contribute to a hazard. When examining a software element, consider, at a minimum, the following ideas:

- Does the element interface with hardware that can cause a hazard?

- Does the element interface with safety-critical software elements?

- Can the software element tie up resources required by any safety-critical components?

- Can the software element enter an infinite loop?

- Does the software element use the same memory as safety-critical data, such that an error in addressing could lead to overwriting the safety-critical information?

- Is priority inversion or deadlocking a possibility, and can it impact a safety-critical task?

- Can the software element affect the system performance or timing in a way that would affect a safety-critical component?

* Does the software element call any functions also called by a safety-critical component? Can it change any aspect of that function, such that the safety-critical component will be affected?

* Is the software element on the same platform and in the same partition as a safety-critical component?

Benefit Rating: MEDIUM	Cost Rating: MODERATE

7.5.11 Rate Monotonic Analysis

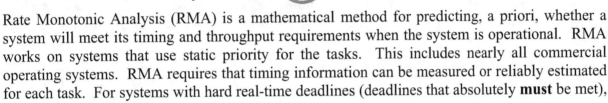

Rate Monotonic Analysis (RMA) is a mathematical method for predicting, a priori, whether a system will meet its timing and throughput requirements when the system is operational. RMA works on systems that use static priority for the tasks. This includes nearly all commercial operating systems. RMA requires that timing information can be measured or reliably estimated for each task. For systems with hard real-time deadlines (deadlines that absolutely **must** be met), RMA is a valuable tool.

For further details on this technique, refer to publications by Sha and Goodenough, References [48] and [49]. A case study using RMA when integrating an intelligent, autonomous software system with Flight software, as part of the NASA New Millennium project, is discussed in reference [50].

Benefit Rating: MEDIUM	Cost Rating: HIGH

7.5.12 Dynamic Flowgraph Analysis

Dynamic Flowgraph Analysis is a relatively new technique that is not yet widely used and still in the experimental phase of evaluation. It does appear to offer some promise, building on the benefits of conventional 6.6.7 *Software Fault Tree Analysis (SFTA)*.

The Dynamic Flowgraph Methodology (DFM) is an integrated, methodical approach to modeling and analyzing the behavior of software-driven embedded systems for the purpose of dependability assessment and verification. The methodology has two fundamental goals: 1) to identify how events can occur in a system; and 2) identify an appropriate testing strategy based on an analysis of system functional behavior. To achieve these goals, the methodology employs a modeling framework in which models expressing the logic of the system being analyzed are developed in terms of causal relationships between physical variables and temporal characteristics of the execution of software components.

Further description of this method is given in the paper by Garrett, Yau, Guarro and Apostolakais [51].

Benefit Rating: LOW	Cost Rating: HIGH

7.5.13 Markov Modeling

Markov Modeling techniques were developed for complex systems and some analysts have adapted these techniques for software intensive systems. They can provide reliability, availability and maintainability data. They model probabilistic behavior of a set of equipment as a continuous time, homogeneous, discrete state Markov Process. The statistical probability of the system being in a particular macro state can be computed. These statistics can be translated into a measure of system reliability and availability for different mission phases.

However, attempting to apply these types of reliability modeling techniques to software is questionable because, unlike hardware, software does not exhibit meaningful (random) failure statistics. Also, unlike hardware component failures, software failures are often not independent. Software errors depend on indeterminate human factors, such as alertness or programmer skill level.

Benefit Rating: LOW	Cost Rating: HIGH

7.5.14 Requirements State Machines

Requirements State Machines (RSM) are sometimes called Finite State Machines (FSM). An RSM is a model or depiction of a system or subsystem, showing states and the transitions between the states. Its goal is to identify and describe ALL possible states and their transitions.

RSM analysis can be used on its own, or as a part of a structured design environment, (e.g., Object Oriented Design (4.2.2.2) and Formal Methods (4.2.2.3)).

Whether or not Formal Methods are used to develop a system, a high level RSM can be used to provide a view into the architecture of an implementation without being engulfed by all the accompanying detail. Semantic analysis criteria can be applied to this representation and to lower level models to verify the behavior of the RSM and determine that its behavior is acceptable.

Details on using Requirements State Machines are given in Appendix E.

Benefit Rating: LOW	Cost Rating: HIGH

Chapter 8   Implementation

It is during software implementation (coding) that software controls of safety hazards are actually realized. Safety requirements have been passed down through the designs to the coding level. Managers and designers must communicate all safety issues relating to the program sets and code components they assign to programmers. Safety-critical designs and coding assignments should be clearly identified. Programmers must recognize not only the explicit safety-related design elements but should also be cognizant of the types of errors which can be introduced into non-safety-critical code which can compromise safety controls. Coding checklists should be provided to alert for these common errors.

Code analysis verifies that the software correctly implements the verified design and does not violate safety requirements. Having the source code permits real measurements of size, complexity and resource usage of the software. These quantities could only be estimated during the design phase, and the estimates were often just educated guesses. The results of code analyses may lead to significant redesign if the analyses show that the "guesses" were wildly incorrect. However, the main purpose is to verify that the code meets the requirements (traceable through the design) and that it produces a safe system.

Which analyses will be performed, and who will perform them, was part of the early project negotiations. A tailored set of plans (software development, software assurance, and safety) should contain this information. Table 8-3 lists the various safety-related techniques and analyses and provides broad tailoring suggestions (by safety effort).

Some of the code analysis techniques mirror those used in design analysis. However, the results of the analysis techniques might be significantly different than during earlier development phases, because the final code may differ substantially from what was expected or predicted. Many of these analyses will be undergoing their second iteration, since they were applied previously to the code-like products of the detailed design.

There are some commercial tools available which perform one or more of these analyses in a single package. These tools can be evaluated for their validity in performing these tasks, such as logic analyzers and path analyzers. However, unvalidated COTS tools, in themselves, cannot generally be considered valid methods for formal safety analysis. COTS tools are often useful to reveal previously unknown defects.

Note that the definitive formal code analysis is that performed on the final version of the code. A great deal of the code analysis is done on earlier versions of code, but a complete check on the final version is essential. For safety purposes it is desirable that the final version has no "instrumentation" (i.e., extra code) added to detect problems, such as erroneous jumps. The code may need to be run on an instruction set emulator which can monitor the code from the outside, without adding the instrumentation, if such problems are suspected.

8.1   Tasks and Analyses

Table 8-1 Software Implementation Tasks

Software Engineering Tasks	System and Software Safety Tasks	Software Assurance or IV&V Tasks
Create source code that implements the design, including safety features.	Participate in Source code Formal Inspections of safety-critical code.	Participate in Source code Formal Inspections
Perform unit testing on individual source units. Prepare and follow test procedures for safety-critical units.	Review Analyses from Software Assurance for any safety implications.	Verify unit tests adequately test the software and are actually performed.
Maintain source code within a Configuration Management system, with adequate documentation of changes. [Section 4.5]	Verify that safety-critical software is designated as such, and that it will receive special treatment by the programmers.	Witness any formal unit testing.
Follow coding standards and checklists. [Section 8.4.1]	Review unit test plans and results for safety-critical units.	Review previous analyses and update with new information.
Participate in Formal Inspections and informal code reviews. [Section 8.5.7]	Review previous analyses and update with new information.	Audit software configuration management system to verify proper usage.
Follow formal change process for changes to baselined system. [Section 4.5.1]	Program Slicing for safety-critical variables or data. [Section 8.4.4]	Audit software development to verify processes followed and coding standards used.
Program Slicing for debugging. [Section 8.4.4]	Safety Data Package for Phase III Safety Review	Participate in formal change process (change control board)
Test Coverage Analysis [Section 8.5.6]		Audit software change process.
		Code Logic Analysis [Section 8.5.1]
		Code Data Analysis [Section 8.5.2]
		Code Interface Analysis [Section 8.5.3]
		Unused Code Analysis [Section 8.5.4]
		Program Slicing [Section 8.4.4]
		Interrupt Analysis [Section 8.5.5]

8.2 Documentation and Milestones

The following table lists documents that are commonly produced or updated for this phase of development:

Table 8-2 Software Implementation Documentation

Document	Software Safety
Source Code	Safety-critical software should be so designated (via comment block or other mechanism). Traceability from safety requirements to the source code that implements them should be clear.
Unit Test Plans and Procedures	Safety-critical software units should have formal Unit Test Plans and Procedures. Unit tests for non-critical units may be informally documented, e.g. in a lab notebook.
Unit Test Reports	Formal reports should be written for safety-critical unit tests. Reports for other unit tests may be informally documented (e.g. notes in a log book).
Formal Inspection Reports	All defects in safety-critical software should be tracked through correction and testing.
Analysis Reports	Identification of any safety-related aspects or safety concerns.
Traceability Matrix	Add traceability to software components (modules, classes, methods, etc.) and unit test cases.

Milestones that will usually occur during this phase include:

- Software Code reviews or Formal Inspections
- Phase III Safety Review or other carrier- or program-specific safety review

8.3 Tailoring Guidelines

See Section 3.2 *Tailoring the Effort* for how to determine the software safety effort required (full, moderate, or minimal).

Table 8-3 Software Safety Effort for Implementation Phase

Technique or Analysis	Software Safety Effort Level		
	MIN	MOD	FULL
8.4.1 Coding Checklists and Standards	☆	☆	☆
8.4.2 Unit Testing (Mandatory for safety-critical units) 8.5.8 Safety-critical Unit Test Plans	✓✓	✓✓	☆
8.4.4 Program Slicing of Safety-critical Data	✓	✓	✓✓
8.5.1 Code Logic Analysis	⊘	⊘	✓
8.5.2 Code Data Analysis	✓	✓✓	☆
8.5.3 Code Interface Analysis	✓	✓✓	☆
8.5.4 Unused Code Analysis	✓	✓✓	☆
8.5.5 Interrupt Analysis	✓	✓✓	☆
8.5.6 Test Coverage Analysis	✓	☆	☆
8.5.7 Formal Inspections of Source Code	✓✓	☆	☆
8.5.9 Final Timing, Throughput, and Sizing Analysis	✓✓	☆	☆

Recommendation Codes			
☆	Mandatory	✓✓	Highly Recommended
✓	Recommended	⊘	Not Recommended

Table 9-4 lists various tests that might be performed during unit (or integration) testing and provides tailoring guidance.

8.4   Software Development Techniques

8.4.1   Coding Checklists and Standards

Software developers should use coding checklists in software coding and implementation. The coding checklists should be an on-going activity, beginning in the requirements phase. As more knowledge is gained about the system (e.g. as the design progresses) the checklists can be updated with the subset of information relevant to the software implementation. Checklists should contain questions that can serve as reminders to programmers to look for common defects.

Coding standards are best used to identify unsafe functions or procedures that the software developer should avoid. They may also contain programming style information, naming and commenting formats, and other aspects necessary to create consistency among the various components. Coding standards should have been specified during the design phase (or earlier), and used throughout the coding (implementation) phase.

Additional checklists that might be used include:

- **Safety Checklists.** A software safety checklist will list all software safety requirements for the project. Use this checklist as a "reminder", so that all safety features and requirements will be incorporated into the software code. A software safety traceability matrix will also be helpful. This matrix should map the requirements into the design elements, and ultimately into the source code components.

- **Defensive Programming Checklist.** This checklist should detail the chosen techniques to implement defensive programming. The checklist should include both generic and language-specific techniques and practices. Practices may be positive ("Always declare the C++ class destructor to be virtual") or negative ("Do not use the *memcpy* library routine"). Coding standards, Appendix H.14 (Safety Programming), Appendix H.5 (Generic practices) and Appendices H.6 though H.12 (language-specific practices) are good starting places to develop this checklist. Lessons learned from other projects, personal experience of the software developers, and other resources should also be included in the checklist.

- **Code Review Checklists.** These checklists are for use by the developer, when reviewing her own code or the code of a fellow developer. The checklist should be derived from a "master" list that includes common errors as well as the project coding standards. Personalize the checklist to include individual "common" errors, such as forgetting to end a comment block. This serves as a means to find those errors, and as reminder not to make the same mistakes. Additional, more formal checklists should be used during Formal Inspections (see section 8.5.7). These will emphasize the coding standards and the most common errors. Common errors may be gleaned from the individual developers, from this guidebook, or from other sources such as textbooks and articles.

- **Requirements checklist.** Often during this development phase, missing requirements are identified, or new system requirements are added and flowed down to software, such as fault detection and recovery. It may become apparent that various capabilities were assumed but not explicitly required, so were not implemented. Checklists can help identify these missing requirements. Once missing requirements are identified, they must be incorporated by "back-filling" (updating) the requirements specifications prior to implementation in order to maintain proper configuration control. This is less likely to be necessary if Formal Methods or Formal Inspections are used, at least during the requirements phase.

- **Automated tools** that aid in enforcing coding standards, such as style checkers, context-sensitive editors, lint, and profilers are discussed in section 11.2.

8.4.2 Unit Level Testing

The unit level tests were *planned* during the detailed design phase, when the functions within a unit were defined. These tests are *executed* once the code compiles. Since the code is likely to contain defects, these tests will be re-executed with each new iteration of the unit. This testing is usually performed by the developer, though another developer in the group may perform the unit testing. A basic entry criterion for unit testing is that the unit compile without errors.

Unit level testing is important because it can access levels of the software that might not be reachable once the units are integrated. Testing the possible inputs to a unit may not be feasible once the unit is integrated into the system. Unit level testing can also identify implementation problems or performance issues requiring changes to the software. The earlier these issues are identified, the less costly they are to fix.

Special safety tests should be designed for any safety-critical units, if this level of code access is required. These tests should demonstrate coverage of the safety test requirements (see Section 9.4.7 *Software Safety Testing*). Each safety test should have pass/fail criteria. The test plan or software management plan should describe the review and reporting process for safety-critical components, including how to report problems discovered in unit test. A test report should be written for unit tests of safety-critical items.

The formality of the testing will vary with the software safety effort level (full, moderate, or minimum) and any extra tailoring. Safety-critical units should always be formally tested (written test plan, witnessed testing, written test report) at least once, before they are integrated into the system. For a full software safety effort, all unit tests may be formal. For moderate, all units that may interact with the safety-critical unit should be considered for formal unit testing.

Informal unit testing does not mean ad-hoc testing. The tests should still be well thought out and documented. Documentation could be in a lab notebook, in a Software Development Folder, or even as comments within the test code. The point is to provide evidence both that the test was performed and that the test was thorough.

Unit level tests come in two varieties: white-box and black-box. White-box tests include all those where you must know something about the innards of the component. Black-box tests check the inputs/outputs of the component only, and are not concerned about what happens inside. White-box tests include those that check the path and branch coverage, loop implementation and statement execution. Black-box tests look at the input domain (values), output ranges, and error handling.

Unit tests for object-oriented software consists of testing the class methods in the same way that procedures and functions are tested in structured programs. Construction, destruction, and copying of the class should also be tested.

Automated testing programs are available for many operating systems and languages. When a test will be run more than a few times, such automated testing will usually save time and effort. Automated testing also removes the possibility of human error when a test procedure is followed. This removes the random error component, but does leave open the possibility of systematic error (i.e. the automated test makes the same error every time it is run).

It is good practice for the developer to keep a list of bugs found while unit testing. This list is a learning tool for the developer to discover what his common errors are. Feed those errors back into the code review checklist, so they are found earlier (at review, rather than test) in the development cycle. In a team where the developers are not penalized for the defects they find, sharing the bug list with other developers and the QA department can help in education and process improvement. Developers can learn from the mistakes of others, and the metrics derived from them can help identify areas to focus on when trying to improve the software development process.

Test coverage analysis verifies that an adequate number of tests have been performed. See Section 8.5.6 *Test Coverage Analysis* for more details.

Benefit Rating: HIGH	Cost Rating: LOW to MODERATE

8.4.3 Refactoring

Refactoring is a technique to restructure object-oriented code in a disciplined way. It is the process of taking an object design and rearranging it in various ways to make the design more flexible and/or reusable. There are several reasons you might want to do this, efficiency and maintainability being probably the most important. Refactoring is included here because the technique is becoming more widely used, and it may have implications for safety-critical software.

The term "refactoring" comes from mathematics, where you factor an expression into an equivalence. The factors are cleaner ways of expressing the same statement. In software refactoring, there must also be equivalence. The beginning and end products must be functionally identical.

Practically, refactoring means making code clearer, cleaner, simpler and elegant. Refactoring is a good thing, in general, because complex expressions are typically built from simpler, more easily understood components. Refactoring either exposes those simpler components or reduces them to the more efficient complex expression (depending on which way you are going).

Some of the benefits of refactoring are:

- Unify duplicate code
- Make the code read better (typically introducing more "why")
- Remove unused indirection
- Isolate existing logic from a needed change
- Replace one algorithm with another
- Make the program run faster

Be careful if using refactoring for safety-critical code, however. Regression tests should show if the refactored unit is functionally identical to the original. If it is not, then the code has been broken by the refactoring, or was broken originally and is now corrected. Either way, you now have a problem that needs to be fixed.

Too much refactoring may also invalidate code inspections that were done on the original code. Refactoring safety-critical units should be avoided. If performed, a re-inspection of the code is necessary, preferably by the original Formal Inspection team.

8.4.4 Program Slicing

When you get a wrong answer from your software, program slicing can help. It is a technique to trace back through the program and show you all, and only, the statements that affect the variable you are interested in. In a large, complex program, slicing can focus in on the statements of interest.

Slicing has been mainly used in debugging (finding the source of an error) and reengineering (pulling out part of a program to create a new program). It can also be used to check the "lineage" of any safety-critical data. Using a slicing tool to pull out all the statements that affect the safety-critical variable, and then examining the results, may point to errors or unexpected interactions with other, non-critical data. You may even wish to do a Formal Inspection on the sliced code.

Slicing comes in two forms: static and dynamic. Static slicing, introduced in 1982, is done on the source code (compile-time). Originally, it had to be an executable subset of the program, though that is not always necessary now. Static slicing shows every statement that may impact the variable of interest. Dynamic slicing first appeared around 1988, and works on programs as they operate (run-time). While static slicing shows all the statements that *may* affect the variable of interest, dynamic slicing shows only those that *do* affect the variable as the software is exercised.

Program slicing by hand would be a tedious job. Tools are beginning to be available for a variety of languages.

Program slicing to determine what statements can (or do) affect **safety-critical data** may find defective code that can unintentionally impact that data. It can also be used as a verification that non-critical code does not interact with the safety-critical data.

Benefit Rating: MEDIUM	Cost Rating: MODERATE

8.5   Code Analyses

8.5.1   Code Logic Analysis

Code logic analysis evaluates the sequence of operations represented by the coded program. Code logic analysis will detect logic errors in the coded software. This analysis is conducted by performing logic reconstruction, equation reconstruction and memory decoding. For complex software, this analysis is applied only to safety-critical components. Other software components may be analyzed if they are deemed important to the system functionality.

- Logic reconstruction entails the preparation of flow charts from the code and comparing them to the design material descriptions and flow charts.

- Equation reconstruction is accomplished by comparing the equations in the code to the ones provided with the design materials.

- Memory decoding identifies critical instruction sequences even when they may be disguised as data. The analyst should determine whether each instruction is valid and if the conditions under which it can be executed are valid. Memory decoding should be done on the final un-instrumented code.

This analysis is tedious if done by hand, and automatic tools are sparse. Implementation errors, from the design into the code, are possible, but are not the primary source of problems. Other methods, such as Formal Inspections, will usually find many of the same errors as this analysis.

Benefit Rating: LOW	Cost Rating: HIGH

8.5.2 Code Data Analysis

Code data analysis concentrates on data structure and usage in the coded software. Data analysis focuses on how data items are defined and organized. Ensuring that these data items are defined and used properly is the objective of code data analysis. This is accomplished by comparing the usage and value of all data items in the code with the descriptions provided in the design materials.

Of particular concern to safety is ensuring the integrity of safety-critical data against being inadvertently altered or overwritten. For example, check to see if interrupt processing is interfering with safety-critical data. Also, check the "typing" of safety-critical declared variables.

Benefit Rating: MEDIUM	Cost Rating: MODERATE

8.5.3 Code Interface Analysis

Code interface analysis verifies the compatibility of internal and external interfaces of a software component. A software component is composed of a number of code segments working together to perform required tasks. These code segments must communicate with each other, with hardware, other software components, and human operators to accomplish their tasks.

Each of these interfaces is a source of potential problems. Code interface analysis is intended to verify that the interfaces have been implemented properly. Check that parameters are properly passed across interfaces. Verify that data size, measurement unit, byte sequence, and bit order within bytes are the same on all sides of the interface.

Benefit Rating: HIGH	Cost Rating: MODERATE

8.5.4 Unused Code Analysis

A common real world coding error is generation of code which is logically excluded from execution; that is, preconditions for the execution of this code will never be satisfied. Such code is undesirable for three reasons:

1. It is potentially symptomatic of a major error in implementing the software design.

2. It introduces unnecessary complexity and occupies memory or mass storage which is often a limited resource.

3. The unused code might contain routines which would be hazardous if they were inadvertently executed (e.g., by a hardware failure or by a Single Event Upset. SEU is a state transition caused by a high speed subatomic particle passing through a semiconductor - common in nuclear or space environments).

There is no particular analysis technique for identifying unused code. However, unused code is often identified during the course of performing other types of code analysis. Unused code can be found during Formal Inspections, Code Logic Analysis, or during unit testing with code coverage analyzer tools.

Care should be taken to ensure that every part of the code is eventually exercised (tested) at some time, within all possible operating modes of the system.

Benefit Rating: MEDIUM	Cost Rating: MODERATE

8.5.5 Interrupt Analysis

Interrupt Analysis looks at how interrupts are used by the software. The effect of interrupts on program flow and data corruption is the primary focus of this analysis. Can interrupts lead to priority inversion or prevent a high priority or safety-critical task from completing? If interrupts are locked out for a period of time, can the system stack incoming interrupts to prevent their loss? Can a low-priority process interrupt a high-priority process and change critical data?

When performing interrupt analysis, consider the following areas of the code:

- **Program segments/components where interrupts are inhibited (locked out).** Look at how long the interrupts are inhibited and whether the system can buffer interrupts for this period of time. The expected and maximum interrupt rates would be needed to check for buffering capacity. Identify impacts from lost interrupts. Look for possible infinite loops.

- **Re-entrant code.** Re-entrant code is designed to be interrupted without loss of state information. Check that re-entrant components have sufficient data saved for each interruption, and that the data and system state are correctly restored. Make sure that components that need to be re-entrant are implemented as such.

- **Interruptible code segments/components.** Make sure that timing-critical areas are protected from interrupts, if a delay would be unacceptable. Check for sequences of instructions that should not be interrupted.

- **Priorities.** Look over the process priorities of the real-time tasks. Verify that time-critical events will be assured of execution. Also consider the operator interface. Will the interface update with important or critical information in a timely fashion?

- **Undefined interrupts.** What happens when an undefined interrupt is received? Is it ignored? Is any error processing required?

Benefit Rating: HIGH	Cost Rating: LOW

8.5.6 Test Coverage Analysis

Test coverage analysis (also called code coverage analysis) is the process of:

- Identifying areas of a program not exercised by a set of test cases.

- Identifying redundant test cases that do not increase coverage.

- Providing a quantitative measure of code coverage.

Various types of "coverage" can be measured. Each has advantages and disadvantages. Ideally, all varieties of test coverage would be used. In reality, usually only a subset is used. For safety-critical code, Table 9-4 recommends what types of coverage to verify, depending on the software safety effort for the project.

There is a strong connection between software complexity and amount of testing required. For example, "numerous studies and general industry experience have shown that the cyclomatic complexity measure correlates with errors in software modules. Other factors being equal, the more complex a module is, the more likely it is to contain errors." [93] Since complex components are more likely to have errors, testing should focus on these components, though not to the exclusion of all others.

The types of Test Coverage include:

- **Statement Coverage** verifies that each executable statement is executed. The chief disadvantage of statement coverage is that it is insensitive to some control structures, such as loops, logical operators, and switch statements. Also, test cases generally correlate more to decisions than to statements.

- **Decision Coverage** verifies that Boolean expressions tested in control structures (such as *if* and *while*) evaluated to both true and false. Additionally, this measure includes coverage of switch-statement cases, exception handlers, and interrupt handlers. A disadvantage is that this measure ignores branches within Boolean expressions which occur due to short-circuit operators.

- **Condition Coverage** is similar to decision coverage. It verifies the true or false outcome of each Boolean sub-expression, separated by logical-and and logical-or if they occur. Condition coverage measures the sub-expressions independently of each other.

- **Multiple Condition Coverage** reports whether every possible combination of Boolean sub-expressions occurs. As with condition coverage, the sub-expressions are separated by logical-and and logical-or, when present. A disadvantage of this measure is that it can

be tedious to determine the minimum set of test cases required, especially for very complex Boolean expressions.

- **Path Coverage** verifies that each of the possible paths in each function has been followed. A path is a unique sequence of branches from the function entry to the exit. Since loops introduce an unbounded number of paths, this measure considers only a limited number of looping possibilities. Path coverage has the advantage of requiring very thorough testing. Path coverage has two severe disadvantages: 1) the number of paths is exponential to the number of branches and 2) many paths are impossible to exercise due to relationships of data.

- **Function Coverage** reports whether each function or procedure was invoked. It is useful during preliminary testing to assure at least some coverage in all areas of the software.

- **Call Coverage** verifies that each function call has been executed.

- **Loop Coverage** reports whether each loop body was executed zero times, exactly once, and more than once (consecutively). This measure determines whether while-loops and for-loops execute more than once.

- **Race Coverage** reports whether multiple threads execute the same code at the same time. It helps detect failure to synchronize access to resources.

- **Relational Operator Coverage** reports whether boundary situations occur with relational operators (<, <=, >, >=). The hypothesis is that boundary test cases find off-by-one errors and mistaken uses of wrong relational operators such as < instead of <=.

Many tools are available to provide the test coverage analysis. They are often bound with, or can be integrated with, automated testing tools. Testing tools will be operating system and language dependent. The coverage tools often require instrumentation (adding extra code) of the source code. Section 9.5.1 provides a list (sample) of available tools.

8.5.7 Formal Inspections of Source Code

Formal Inspections, introduced in Section 6.5.5 *Formal Inspections*, should be performed on the safety-critical software components, at a minimum. Consider doing Formal Inspections on other complex or critical software components. Formal Inspections are one of the best methodologies available to evaluate the quality of code components and program sets. Having multiple eyes and minds review the code, in a formal way, makes errors and omissions easier to find.

Checklists should be developed for use during formal inspections to facilitate inspection of the code. They should include:

- requirements information for components under review

- design details for components under review

- coding standards (subset/most important)

- language-independent programming errors

- language-specific programming errors

<u>Appendix H</u> contains a sample checklists of common errors, both independent of language and language specific.

Benefit Rating: HIGH	Cost Rating: MODERATE

8.5.8 Safety-Critical Unit Test Plans

Because unit tests are usually in the hands of the software developers, they are often not reviewed by software assurance or safety. However, safety-critical units must be treated more formally. Written test plans should be produced and reviewed by Software Assurance and Software Safety. Ideally, the plans should be Formally Inspected.

Software Assurance and Software Safety should witness tests of safety-critical units. Formal test reports should be written for these tests, and the test results reviewed by Software Assurance and Software Safety.

The goal of this formal activity is not to create more useless paperwork. The earlier problems are found, the less costly they are to fix. Also, some aspects of the safety-critical code may not be accessible once it is integrated. These tests may be the only time certain safety-critical components can be thoroughly tested. Documentation is required to prove adequate safety testing of the software.

8.5.9 Final Timing, Throughput, and Sizing Analysis

With the completion of the coding phase, the timing, throughput, and sizing parameters can be measured. The size of the executable component (storage size) is easily measured, as is the amount of memory space used by the running software. Special tests may need to be run to determine the maximum memory used, as well as timing and throughput parameters. Some of these tests may be delayed until the testing phase, where they may be formally included in functional or load/stress tests. However, simple tests should be run as soon as the appropriate code is stable, to allow verification of the timing, throughput, and sizing requirements. The earlier a problem is discovered, the easier and cheaper it is to fix.

Benefit Rating: HIGH	Cost Rating: LOW

8.5.10 Update Previous Analyses
Software Fault Tree Analysis and Software Failure Modes and Effects Analysis

Review any changes to the design that developed during the coding phase. Often creating the actual code will point out problems with the design, or elements that are missing. If the design was modified during this phase, review the Software FMEA and FTA and make any updates as necessary.

Complexity Measurement

Now that code exists, the complexity metrics can be recalculated. Complex code should be evaluated by a human. Some logic structures (such as case statements) may be flagged as complicated, when they really improve the comprehensibility of the software.

Complex software increases the number of errors, while making it difficult to find them. This makes the software more likely to be unstable, or suffer from unpredictable behavior. Reducing complexity is generally a good idea, whenever possible. Modularity is a useful technique to reduce complexity. Encapsulation can also be used, to hide data and functions from the "user" (the rest of the software), and prevent their unanticipated execution.

Software flagged as complex should be analyzed in more depth, even if it is not safety-critical. These components are prime candidates for formal inspections and the logic/data/constraint analyses.

Design Traceability Analysis

The criteria for design constraints applied to the detailed design in Section 7.5.9 *Design Traceability Analysis*, can be updated using the final code. At the code phase, real testing can be performed to characterize the actual software behavior and performance in addition to analysis.

The physical limitations of the processing hardware platform should be addressed. Timing, sizing and throughput analyses should also be repeated as part of this process (see section 8.5.9) to ensure that computing resources and memory available are adequate for safety-critical functions and processes.

Underflows or overflows in certain languages (e.g., Ada) give rise to "exceptions" or error messages generated by the software. These conditions should be eliminated by design if possible. If they cannot be precluded, then error handling routines in the application must provide appropriate responses, such as automatic recovery, querying the user (retry, etc.), or putting the system into a safe state.

Chapter 9 Testing

Testing is the operational execution of a software component in a real or simulated environment. Software testing verifies analysis results, investigates program behavior, and confirms that the program complies with safety requirements. Software testing beyond the unit level (integration and system testing) is usually performed by someone other than the developer, except in the smallest of teams.

Normally, software testing ensures that the software performs all required functions correctly, and can exhibit graceful behavior under anomalous conditions. Safety testing focuses on locating program weaknesses and identifying extreme or unexpected situations that could cause the software to fail in ways that would violate safety requirements. Safety testing complements rather than duplicates developer testing.

One example of a special safety testing technique is software fault injection. It has been successfully used to test safety-critical software (e.g. BART in San Francisco), and also for security testing and COTS verification. Faults are inserted into code before starting a test and the response is observed. In addition, all boundary and performance requirements should be tested at, below and above the stated limits. It is necessary to see how the software system performs, or fails, outside of supposed operational limits.

The safety testing effort should be encompass those software requirements classed as safety-critical items, but is not necessarily limited to just those items. If the safety-critical components are separated from the others via a partition or firewall, the integrity of the partitioning must be tested. In addition, testing should be performed to verify that non-safety-critical software cannot adversely impact the safety-critical software. Remember that any software that impacts or helps fulfill a safety-critical function is safety-critical as well. Safety testing must verify that all safety requirements have been correctly implemented. The actual safety tests can be performed independently or as an integral part of the developer's test effort.

Integration testing is often done in a simulated environment, and system testing is usually done on the actual hardware. However, hazardous commands or operations should be tested in a simulated environment first. You don't want to start the rocket engines or set off the ordnance by accident!

Any problems discovered during testing should be analyzed and documented in discrepancy reports and summarized in test reports. Discrepancy reports contain a description of the problems encountered, recommended solutions, and the final disposition of the problem. These reports are normally generated after the software has reached a level of maturity (e.g. is baselined or in beta version). Changes that result from identified problems usually go through a software Change Control Board for discussion and approval or rejection. These problem reports need to be tracked, and management needs to have visibility into the past and current software problems.

As software is being developed, defect information may be kept in a defect tracking database. Such a database not only allows tracking of problems for a particular project, but can serve as a source for "lessons learned" and improvement for subsequent projects. When the software "moves up" into the formal system, some defects should be written up as problem reports for continued tracking. In particular, defects that may indicate system problems (e.g. problems when running on incomplete flight hardware that could not be reproduced) or fixes that had far-reaching impacts (e.g. many components or an interface affected) should be considered for "formal" problem reports.

9.1   Tasks and Analyses

Table 9-1 System Testing Tasks

Software Engineering Tasks	System and Software Safety Tasks	Software Assurance or IV&V Tasks
Integrate individual software units into a complete software system. Test throughout the process.	Participate in Test Plan and Procedures Formal Inspections when safety-critical functions are to be tested. [Section 9.5.2]	Participate in Formal Inspections of test plans and procedures. [Section 9.5.2]
Integrate the software with the hardware system and perform testing throughout the process.	Review Analyses from Software Assurance for any safety implications.	Analyze test reports for completeness and requirements coverage. [Section 9.5.4]
Create and follow written test procedures for integration and system testing.*	Verify all safety requirements have been adequately tested (Safety Verification Matrix).	Verify all requirements have been adequately tested. [Section 9.5.1]
Perform regression testing after each change to the system.*	Witness testing of safety-critical software and special safety tests. [Section 9.4.8]	Review problem reports
Participate in Formal Inspections of test plans and procedures. [Section 9.5.2]	Review problem reports for safety implications.	Witness all integration tests, or at least those involving safety-critical units. [Section 9.4.8]
Prepare Test Report upon completion of a test.	Reliability Modeling [Section 9.5.3]	Witness all system tests. [Section 9.4.8]
Verify COTS software operates as expected.	Review previous analyses and update with new information.	Review previous analyses and update with new information.
Use formal Configuration Management system for source code , executables, test plans and procedures, and test data. [Section 4.5]	Safety Verification Tracking Log Closeout	
Follow problem reporting and corrective action procedures when defects are detected.		

* Testing may be performed by a separate Test group

9.2 Documentation and Milestones

The following table lists documents that are commonly produced for this phase of development:

Table 9-2 Software Testing Documentation

Document	Software Safety Section
Integration Test Plan	Testing should exercise the connections between safety-critical units and non-critical units or systems.
System Test Plan	Extreme, but possible, environments should be tested (heavy load, other stressors) to verify the system continues to function safely within all plausible environments.
Test Reports	Verify test was completed as planned and all safety-critical elements were properly tested. Report results of testing safety-critical interfaces versus the requirements outlined in the Software Test Plan. Any safety-critical findings should be used to update the hazard reports.
Configuration Management Audit Report	Verify that configuration management system is properly used, especially for safety-critical elements.
Formal Inspections Report	All defects related to safety-critical elements should be considered major (must fix).
Analysis Reports	Identification of any safety-related aspects or safety concerns.
Problem or Failure Reports (with Corrective Action)	Problem or Failure reports should be reviewed for any safety implications. Any corrective action should be verified to not cause an additional hazard, or to adversely impact any other safety-critical software or hardware.
Traceability Matrix	Verify that requirements are traceable all the way into the test cases. Verify that all safety requirements have been adequately tested.

Milestones that will usually occur during this phase include:

- Test Readiness Review
- Safety Verification Tracking Log Closeout (post Phase III)

9.3 Tailoring Guidelines

See Section 3.2 *Tailoring the Effort* for how to determine the software safety effort required (full, moderate, or minimal). .

Table 9-3 Software Safety Effort for Testing Phase

Technique or Analysis	Safety Effort Level		
	MIN	MOD	FULL
9.4.3 Integration Testing	✓	✓✓	☆
9.4.5 System & Functional Testing (Number of tests is tailorable)	☆	☆	☆
9.4.6 Regression Testing (amount of testing is tailorable)	☆	☆	☆
9.4.7 Software Safety Testing	☆	☆	☆
12.1.4 OTS Analyses and Test	✓	✓✓	☆
9.5.1 Test Coverage Analysis	✓	✓✓	☆
9.5.2 Formal Inspections of Test Plan and Procedures	✓	✓✓	☆
9.5.3 Reliability Modeling	⊘	✓	✓✓
9.5.4 Test Results Analysis	☆	☆	☆

Recommendation Codes			
☆	Mandatory	✓✓	Highly Recommended
✓	Recommended	⊘	Not Recommended

The tables below list various tests that might be performed. Recommendations are based on a balance of the benefits to the cost. What tests are actually performed should be determined by project-specific factors. The availability of automated tools or analysis software, the cost of such tools or analysis software, number of team members and their level of knowledge, and schedule are some factors that will influence the number of tests performed. Use the tailoring recommendations in the following tables as a starting point for further tailoring.

Table 9-4 Dynamic Testing (Unit or Integration Level)

Technique	Safety Effort Level		
	MIN	MOD	FULL
Typical sets of sensor inputs	✓✓	☆	☆
Test specific functions	✓✓	☆	☆
Volumetric and statistical tests	⊘	✓	✓✓
Test extreme values of inputs	✓✓	☆	☆
Test all modes of each sensor	✓✓	☆	☆
Every statement executed once	✓✓	☆	☆

Technique	Safety Effort Level		
Every branch tested at least once	✓✓	★	★
Every predicate term tested	✓	✓✓	★
Every loop executed 0, 1, many, max-1, max, max+1 times	✓✓	★	★
Every path executed	✓	✓✓	★
Every assignment to memory tested	⊘	✓	✓✓
Every reference to memory tested	⊘	✓	✓✓
All mappings from inputs checked	⊘	✓	✓✓
All timing constraints verified	✓	✓✓	★
Test worst case interrupt sequences	✓	✓✓	★
Test significant chains of interrupts	✓	✓✓	★
Test Positioning of data in I/O space	✓	✓✓	★
Check accuracy of arithmetic	⊘	✓	✓✓
All components executed at least once	★	★	★
All invocations of components tested	✓✓	★	★

Table 9-5 Software System Testing

Technique	Safety Effort Level		
	MIN	MOD	FULL
Simulation (Test Environment)	✓	✓✓	★
Load Testing [9.4.5]	✓✓	★	★
Stress Testing [9.4.5]	✓✓	★	★
Boundary Value Tests	✓	✓✓	★
Test Coverage Analysis [9.5.1]	✓	✓✓	★
Functional Testing [9.4.5]	★	★	★
Performance Monitoring	✓	✓✓	★
Disaster Testing [9.4.5]	✓	✓✓	✓✓
Resistance to Failure Testing [9.4.5]	✓	✓✓	★
"Red Team" Testing [9.4.5]	⊘	✓	✓✓
Regression Testing [9.4.6] (Tailored to the level of original testing)	★	★	★

9.4   *Software Integration and Test*

Various tests that can be performed include:

- Integration Testing
  - *   Unit integration and testing
  - *   Integration of the software with the hardware
- System Testing
  - *   Functional testing
  - *   Performance testing
  - *   Load testing
  - *   Stress testing
  - *   Disaster testing
  - *   Stability testing
  - *   Acceptance testing
  - *   "Red Team" testing

Note that the "system test" is not a single test, but a collection of possible tests to perform. These tests are done using the full system (hardware and software), though a simulator may be used under certain circumstances. The point of the system tests is to exercise the system in such a way that all functionality is tested, its limits are known, and its ability to survive faults and failures is well understood.

 A very useful tool for testers, developers, and project management is a high level view of all test activities for a system (including subsystems and software). This information may be displayed in a large table (often as a wall chart) listing all the various levels of testing in the column headers. Pertinent data that differentiates each level of testing (e.g., who is responsible, when will it occur, what is the objective of the test, what is the characteristic of the test data, what environment is used to execute the tests, what products are produced, and what is the entry and exit criteria) is placed in the table rows.

9.4.1   Testing Techniques and Considerations

This section provides an introduction to software testing for those unfamiliar with it. The section includes descriptions of various tests, how to write test cases, what to do when a defect is found, and suggestions for dealing with a tight testing schedule. If you are familiar with software testing, you may wish to skip to section 9.4.2 which continues the safety-specific information.

All of this section is taken, with permission, from the Frequently Asked Questions (FAQ) created by Rick Hower, © 1996-2000. The website is "Software QA and Testing Frequently-Asked-Questions", http://www.softwareqatest.com/, and is an excellent introduction to software testing.

9.4.1.1 What kinds of testing should be considered?

* Black box testing - not based on any knowledge of internal design or code. Tests are based on requirements and functionality.

* White box testing - based on knowledge of the internal logic of an application's code. Tests are based on coverage of code statements, branches, paths, and conditions.

* unit testing - the most 'micro' scale of testing; to test particular functions or code components. Typically done by the programmer and not by testers, as it requires detailed knowledge of the internal program design and code. Not always easily done unless the application has a well-designed architecture with tight code; may require developing test driver modules or test harnesses.

* incremental integration testing - continuous testing of an application as new functionality is added; requires that various aspects of an application's functionality be independent enough to work separately before all parts of the program are completed, or that test drivers be developed as needed; done by programmers or by testers.

* integration testing - testing of combined parts of an application to determine if they function together correctly. The 'parts' can be code components, individual applications, client and server applications on a network, etc. This type of testing is especially relevant to client/server and distributed systems.

* functional testing - black-box type testing geared to functional requirements of an application; this type of testing should be done by testers. This doesn't mean that the programmers shouldn't check that their code works before releasing it (which of course applies to any stage of testing.)

* system testing - black-box type testing that is based on overall requirements specifications; covers all combined parts of a system.

* end-to-end testing - similar to system testing; the 'macro' end of the test scale; involves testing of a complete application environment in a situation that mimics real-world use, such as interacting with a database, using network communications, or interacting with other hardware, applications, or systems if appropriate.

* sanity testing - typically an initial testing effort to determine if a new software version is performing well enough to accept it for a major testing effort. For example, if the new software is crashing systems every 5 minutes, bogging down systems to a crawl, or destroying databases, the software may not be in a 'sane' enough condition to warrant further testing in its current state.

* regression testing - re-testing after fixes or modifications of the software or its environment. It can be difficult to determine how much re-testing is needed, especially near the end of the development cycle. Automated testing tools can be especially useful for this type of testing.

* acceptance testing - final testing based on specifications of the end-user or customer, or based on use by end-users/customers over some limited period of time.

* load testing - testing an application under heavy loads, such as testing of a web site under a range of loads to determine at what point the system's response time degrades or fails.

* stress testing - term often used interchangeably with 'load' and 'performance' testing. Also used to describe such tests as system functional testing while under unusually heavy loads, heavy repetition of certain actions or inputs, input of large numerical values, large complex queries to a database system, etc.

* performance testing - term often used interchangeably with 'stress' and 'load' testing. Ideally 'performance' testing (and any other 'type' of testing) is defined in requirements documentation or QA or Test Plans.

* usability testing - testing for 'user-friendliness'. Clearly this is subjective, and will depend on the targeted end-user or customer. User interviews, surveys, video recording of user sessions, and other techniques can be used. Programmers and testers are usually not appropriate as usability testers.

* install/uninstall testing - testing of full, partial, or upgrade install/uninstall processes.

* recovery testing - testing how well a system recovers from crashes, hardware failures, or other catastrophic problems.

* security testing - testing how well the system protects against unauthorized internal or external access, willful damage, etc; may require sophisticated testing techniques.

* compatibility testing - testing how well software performs in a particular hardware/software/operating system/network/etc. environment.

* user acceptance testing - determining if software is satisfactory to an end-user or customer.

* comparison testing - comparing software weaknesses and strengths to competing products.

* alpha testing - testing of an application when development is nearing completion; minor design changes may still be made as a result of such testing. Typically done by end-users or others, not by programmers or testers.

* beta testing - testing when development and testing are essentially completed and final bugs and problems need to be found before final release. Typically done by end-users or others, not by programmers or testers.

9.4.1.2 What steps are needed to develop and run software tests?

The following are some of the steps to consider:

* Obtain requirements, functional design, and internal design specifications and other necessary documents

* Obtain budget and schedule requirements

* Determine project-related personnel and their responsibilities, reporting requirements, required standards and processes (such as release processes, change processes, etc.)

* Identify application's higher-risk aspects, set priorities, and determine scope and limitations of tests

* Determine test approaches and methods - unit, integration, functional, system, load, usability tests, etc.

* Determine test environment requirements (hardware, software, communications, etc.)

* Determine testware requirements (record/playback tools, coverage analyzers, test tracking, problem/bug tracking, etc.)

* Determine test input data requirements

* Identify tasks, those responsible for tasks, and labor requirements

* Set schedule estimates, timelines, milestones

* Determine input equivalence classes, boundary value analyses, error classes

* Prepare test plan document and have needed reviews/approvals

* Write test cases

* Have needed reviews/inspections/approvals of test cases

* Prepare test environment and testware, obtain needed user manuals/reference documents/configuration guides/installation guides, set up test tracking processes, set up logging and archiving processes, set up or obtain test input data

* Obtain and install software releases

* Perform tests

* Evaluate and report results

* Track problems/bugs and fixes

* Retest as needed

* Maintain and update test plans, test cases, test environment, and testware through life cycle

9.4.1.3 What's a 'test case'?

A test case is a document that describes an input, action, or event and an expected response, to determine if a feature of an application is working correctly. A test case should contain particulars such as test case identifier, test case name, objective, test conditions/setup, input data requirements, steps, and expected results.

Note that the process of developing test cases can help find problems in the requirements or design of an application, since it requires completely thinking through the operation of the application. For this reason, it's useful to prepare test cases early in the development cycle if possible.

9.4.1.4 What should be done after a bug is found?

The bug needs to be communicated and assigned to developers that can fix it. After the problem is resolved, fixes should be re-tested, and determinations made regarding requirements for regression testing to check that fixes didn't create problems elsewhere. If a problem-tracking system is in place, it should encapsulate these processes. A variety of commercial problem-tracking/management software tools are available (see the 'Tools' section for web resources with listings of such tools). The following are items to consider in the tracking process:

* Complete information such that developers can understand the bug, get an idea of its severity, and reproduce it if necessary.

* Bug identifier (number, ID, etc.)

* Current bug status (e.g., 'Released for Retest', 'New', etc.)

* The application name or identifier and version

* The function, component, feature, object, screen, etc. where the bug occurred

* Environment specifics, system, platform, relevant hardware specifics

* Test case name/number/identifier

* One-line bug description

* Full bug description

* Description of steps needed to reproduce the bug if not covered by a test case or if the developer doesn't have easy access to the test case/test script/test tool

* Names and/or descriptions of file/data/messages/etc. used in test

* File excerpts/error messages/log file excerpts/screen shots/test tool logs that would be helpful in finding the cause of the problem

* Severity estimate (a 5-level range such as 1-5 or 'critical'-to-'low' is common)

* Was the bug reproducible?

* Tester name

* Test date

* Bug reporting date

* Name of developer/group/organization the problem is assigned to

* Description of problem cause

* Description of fix

* Code section/file/component/class/method that was fixed

* Date of fix

* Application version that contains the fix

* Tester responsible for retest

* Retest date

* Retest results

* Regression testing requirements

* Tester responsible for regression tests

* Regression testing results

A reporting or tracking process should enable notification of appropriate personnel at various stages. For instance, testers need to know when retesting is needed, developers need to know when bugs are found and how to get the needed information, and reporting/summary capabilities are needed for managers.

9.4.1.5 What if there isn't enough time for thorough testing?

Use risk analysis to determine where testing should be focused. Since it's rarely possible to test every possible aspect of an application, every possible combination of events, every dependency, or everything that could go wrong, risk analysis is appropriate to most software development projects. This requires judgment skills, common sense, and experience. (If warranted, formal methods are also available.)

Considerations can include:

* Which functionality is most important to the project's intended purpose?
* Which functionality is most visible to the user?
* Which functionality has the largest safety impact?
* Which functionality has the largest financial impact on users?
* Which aspects of the application are most important to the customer?
* Which aspects of the application can be tested early in the development cycle?
* Which parts of the code are most complex, and thus most subject to errors?
* Which parts of the application were developed in rush or panic mode?
* Which aspects of similar/related previous projects caused problems?
* Which aspects of similar/related previous projects had large maintenance expenses?
* Which parts of the requirements and design are unclear or poorly thought out?
* What do the developers think are the highest-risk aspects of the application?
* What kinds of problems would cause the worst publicity?
* What kinds of problems would cause the most customer service complaints?
* What kinds of tests could easily cover multiple functionalities?
* Which tests will have the best high-risk-coverage to time-required ratio?

9.4.2 Test Environment

Testing should be performed either in a controlled environment in which execution follows a structured test procedure and the results are monitored, or in a demonstration environment where the software is exercised without interference.

Controlled testing executes the software on a real or a simulated computer using special techniques to influence behavior. This is the usual mode of testing, where a test procedure (script) is developed and followed, and the results are noted. Automatic testing is also included in this category. All of the integration and system tests that will be discussed in the following sections are controlled tests.

When using a simulator, rather than the real system, the fidelity of the simulators should be carefully assessed. How close is the simulator to the "real thing"? How accurate is the simulator? Has the simulator itself been verified to operate correctly?

Demonstration testing executes the software on a computer and in an environment identical to the operational computer and environment. Demonstrations may be used in the acceptance test, to show the user how the system works. Autonomous systems, where the internal operation is completely under the control of the software, would also be demonstrated, especially for the acceptance test.

Safety testing must be performed on the final system, both hardware and software. These tests verify that all the hazard controls or mitigations work properly. In addition, software safety testing may exercise the system under extreme or unexpected conditions, to show that other elements of the software cannot interfere with the software hazard controls or mitigations.

Configuration Management should act as the sole distributor of media and documentation for all system tests and for delivery to [sub]system integration and testing. Pulling the latest program off the developer's machine is not a good idea. One aspect of system testing is *repeatability*, which can only be assured if the software under test comes from a known, and fixed, source.

9.4.3 Integration Testing

Integration is the process of piecing together the "puzzle", where each piece is a software unit. The end result is a complete system, and the final integration test is essentially the first system functional test.

The order of integration of the units should be decided at the end of the architectural design, when the units are identified. Various schemes can be used, such as creating a backbone (minimal functionality) and adding to it, or doing the most difficult components first. Keep in mind the hardware schedule when deciding the order of integration. Late hardware may hold up software integration, if the software that needs it is integrated early in the cycle.

Stubs and drivers are used to "simulate" the rest of the system, outside of the integrated section. Stubs represent units below (called by) the integrated section. Drivers represent the part of the software that calls the integrated section.

Integration tests are black-box tests that verify the functionality of the integrated unit. They are "higher level" black-box unit tests, where the "unit" is the new, integrated whole.

Special safety tests may be run as safety-critical units are integrated. These tests should exercise functionality that may be unavailable once the system is completely integrated. Also, some safety tests may be run early, so that any problems can be corrected before development is completed.

9.4.4 Integrating Object-Oriented Software

Object-oriented software requires some changes in the integration test strategy. Once the software is fully integrated, it doesn't matter what the underlying software design is - a system is a system. However, when the system is integrated, whole classes are added at a time. Besides the normal "functional" tests that are performed during integration testing, consider the following tests as well:

- Object A creates Object B, invoking B's constructor

- A deletes B, invoking B's destructor. Check for memory leaks here!

- A sends a "message" to B (invokes a method of B). Check for situations where B is not present (not created or already destroyed). How does the error handling system deal with that situation?

As each class is integrated into the system, it is the *interfaces* with other classes that must be tested.

Object-oriented testing methods have not reached the maturity of more traditional testing. The best way to test OO software is highly debated. The following resources provide some useful insights or links regarding OO testing:

- "Testing Object-Oriented Software" (book), by David C. Kung, Pei Hsia, and Jerry Gao, October 1998. ISBN 0-8186-8520-4

- Cetus links on Object-Oriented Testing: http://www.cetus-links.org/

- State of the art in 1995: http://www.stsc.hill.af.mil/crosstalk/1995/04/index.html

9.4.5 System Testing

System testing begins when the software is completely integrated. Several types of tests are usually run. Not every test is useful for every system, and the software developer should choose those that test specific requirements or that may show problems with the system.

- **Functional Testing** consists of running the system in a nominal manner. The system is verified to perform all the functions specified in the requirements, and to not perform functions that are designated "must not work". A complete, end-to-end functional test is often designated as the System Test, though system testing actually encompasses many more types of tests. A scaled-down version of the functional test is often used as the acceptance test. **Mandatory Test**

- **Stress tests** are designed to see how much the system can handle before it breaks down. While a capacity test (performance) may test that the system can store the required number of files, a stress test will see just how many files can be stored before the disk runs out of room. Aspects of the system that might be stressed are CPU usage, I/O response time, paging frequency, memory utilization, amount of available memory, and network utilization. The closer a system's peak usage is to the breakdown point, the more likely it is that the system will fail under usage. Give yourself adequate margin, if at all possible. **Highly Recommended for safety-critical components**

- **Stability tests** look for sensitivity to event sequences, intermittent bad data, memory leakage, and other problems that may surface when the system is operated for an extended period of time. **Highly Recommended for Systems that must operate for long periods of time or where user access is limited.**

- **Resistance to Failure** tests how gracefully the software responds to errors. Errors should be detected and handled locally. Erroneous user input should be handled appropriately (e.g. ignored with an error message), as well as bad input from sensors or other devices.

Fault injection tests fit in this category. **Highly Recommended for safety-critical components**

- **Compatibility tests** verify that the software can work with the hardware and other software systems it was designed to interface with. **Mandatory Test**

- **Performance testing** verifies the "CARAT" parameters – Capacity, Accuracy, Response time, Availability, and Throughput. Capacity is the number of records, users, disk space, etc. Accuracy is the verification of algorithm results and precision. Response time is often important in real-time systems, and will be included in the specifications. Availability is how long the system can be used (based on how often it fails, and how long to repair it when it does fail). Throughput is the peak or average number of events per unit time that the system can handle. **Load tests** are a form of performance testing. **Mandatory Test for Performance, others are highly recommended, especially when resources are limited.**

- **Disaster testing** checks the software's response to physical hardware failure. Pulling the power plug while the software is running is one example. Disaster tests point to areas where the software needs fixing, or where additional hardware is needed (such as a backup battery, to allow the software to shut down gracefully). **Recommended for safety-critical components**

- **Hot and warm backup testing** involves making sure that the "hot" or "warm" backup systems come on-line when necessary. This usually involves causing the primary system to fail (pull the plug, etc.) and verifying that the necessary backup actually comes on-line. **Recommended for systems that require hot or warm backup systems.**

- **Installation** test shows that the software can be installed successfully. **Recommended for systems that must be installed by end users.**

- **Parallel Operations** testing is necessary when a currently operational system with near zero down time requirements will be replaced with a newer system. The new, replacement system needs to run in parallel with the operational system while it is being verified. One method to do this is to split the operational input data streams to both systems. The test system output data should be stored in a test database or file, and not mixed with the operational system's output data. **Recommended for systems with zero down time requirements.**

- **"Red Team" testing** is a totally unscripted, "break the code" type of testing. It is only performed after all other testing is completed, and in an environment where a true safety problem cannot develop (such as on a simulator). The testers do whatever they want to the software except actually break the hardware it runs on (or related hardware). This is a random test. Successful completion suggests that the program is robust. Failure indicates that something needs to be changed, either in the software or in the operating procedures. **Recommended if time permits or the testing team needs to have some fun.**

Whenever changes are made to the system after it is baselined (first release), a regression test must be run to verify that previous functionality is not affected and that no new errors have been added. This is vitally important! **"Fixed" code may well add its own set of errors to the code.** If the system is close to some capacity limit, the corrected code may push it over the edge. Performance issues, race conditions, or other problems that were not evident before may be there now.

If time permits, the entire suite of system and safety tests would be rerun as the complete regression test. However, for even moderately complex systems, such testing is likely to be too costly in time and money. Usually, a subset of the system tests makes up the regression test suite. Picking the proper subset, however, is an art and not a science.

Minimization is one approach to regression test selection. The goal is to create a regression test suite with the minimal number of tests that will cover the code change and modified blocks. The criteria for this approach is coverage – what statements are executed by the test. In particular, every statement in the changed code must be executed, and every modified block must have at least one test.

Coverage approaches are based on coverage criteria, like the minimization approach, but they are not concerned about minimizing the number of tests. Instead, all system tests that exercise the changed or affected program component(s) are used.

Safe approaches place less emphasis on coverage criteria, and attempt instead to select every test that will cause the modified program to produce different output than the original program. Safe regression test selection techniques select subsets that, under certain well-defined conditions, exclude no tests (from the original test suite) that if executed would reveal faults in the modified software.

Program slicing can be a helpful technique for determining what tests to run. Slicing finds all the statements that can affect a variable, or all statements that a variable is involved with. Depending on the changes, slicing may be able to show what components may be affected by the modification.

The requirements management program (section 6.4) is a useful tool in determining what tests need to be run. When changes impact a specific requirement, especially a safety requirement, all test cases that test that requirement should be run. Knowing what test cases test what requirements is one aspect of requirements traceability.

Whatever strategy is used to select the regression tests, it should be a well thought out process. Balance the risks of missing an error with the time and money spent on regression testing. Very minor code changes usually require less regression testing, unless they are in a very critical area of the software. Also consider including in the regression suite tests that previously found errors, tests that stress the system, and performance tests. You want the system to run at least as well *after* the change as it did *before* the change! For safety-critical code, or software that resides on the same platform as safety-critical code, the **software safety tests must be repeated**, even for minor changes.

> **Regression testing should include functional, performance, stress, and safety testing of the altered code and all modules it interacts with.**

9.4.7 Software Safety Testing

The project must perform software safety testing to ensure that hazards have been eliminated or controlled to an acceptable level of risk. This includes documenting and reviewing safety-related test descriptions, procedures, test cases, and the associated qualifications criteria. Implementation of safety requirements (inhibits, traps, interlocks, assertions, etc.) must be verified. Verify that the software functions safely both within its specified environment (including extremes), and under specified abnormal and stress conditions. For example, a two failure tolerant systems should be exercised in all predicted credible two failure scenarios.

In addition to testing under normal conditions, the software should be tested to show that unsafe states can not be generated by the software as the result of feasible single or multiple erroneous inputs. This should include those outputs which might result from failures associated with the entry into, and execution of, safety-critical computer software components. Negative and No-Go testing should also be employed, and should ensure that the software only performs those functions for which it is intended, and no extraneous functions.

Software safety tests may be included within other tests (unit, integration or system) or may be separate tests. Regardless of where they are performed, it is vital that all safety features be verified and that other elements of the software cannot adversely influence the safety-critical software.

IEEE 1228-1994, Software Safety Plans, calls for the following software safety tests:

- Computer software unit level testing that demonstrates correct execution of critical software elements.

- Interface testing that demonstrates that critical computer software units execute together as specified.

- Computer software configuration item (CSCI) testing that demonstrates the execution of one or more system components.

- System-level testing that demonstrates the software's performance within the overall system.

- Stress testing that demonstrates the software will not cause hazards under abnormal circumstances, such as unexpected input values or overload conditions.

- Regression testing that demonstrates changes made to the software did not introduce conditions for new hazards.

Software Safety, represented by the Software Assurance or System Safety organization, should participate in the testing of safety-critical computer software components at all levels of testing, including informal testing, system integration testing, and Software Acceptance testing.

9.4.8 Test Witnessing

Software Assurance should ensure that tests of safety-critical components are conducted in strict accordance with the approved test plans, descriptions, procedures, scripts and scenarios, and that the results are accurately logged, recorded, documented, analyzed, and reported. Safety personnel should also participate and witness as required or appropriate. Software Assurance should verify that deficiencies and discrepancies are corrected and properly retested.

Witnessing verifies that the software performs properly and safely during all system tests, including integration, stress testing and system acceptance testing. System acceptance testing should be conducted under actual operating conditions or realistic simulations.

The test witness is responsible for being familiar with the test procedure prior to the test. Any questions of a significant nature should be answered prior to the start of testing. Software Safety should note in the test procedure where safety-critical elements are tested.

 Software Assurance (or Software Safety) is responsible for making sure any non-conformances or problems are recorded using the appropriate process. Tracking those non-conformances to completion is an important task. Problems with safety-critical software should be raised to attention of the appropriate level of management.

9.4.9 Use of Computer Models for System Verification

Computer simulations and models, such as finite element analyses programs (e.g. Nastran or Ansys), have become integrated into the system design process and interface directly with CAD programs. These software packages "automatically" perform everything from linear and nonlinear stress analyses, to a variety of steady state and dynamic characteristic analyses, to the modeling of crash tests. These modeling programs are used to examine a variety of things from children's toys to rocket engines. The use of computer modeling for design evaluation will continue to expand since the cost savings potential from limiting or eliminating prototype testing will continue to drive industry.

 The growing dependence on such computer modeling may lead to the potential misuse of these simulations. There is a tendency to assume the software does the analysis correctly and completely. The analyst must do "sanity checks" of the results, as a bare minimum, to verify that the modeling software is functioning correctly. For safety-critical analyses, the modeling tool should be formally verified or tested. In addition, the analyst needs to have knowledge of the proper application of these "virtual design environments". Therefore, users of software simulation programs that analyze safety-critical hardware should be well trained, experienced and certified, if the software vendor provides certification. All program input parameters such as loads, restraints, and materials properties, should be independently verified to assure proper modeling and analysis.

Immersive virtual environment technology (virtual reality) has matured to the point where it is being used for the design and evaluation of safety-critical systems. A virtual environment is a computer-generated environment that allows the user to interact with the virtual word being modeled through multisensory input and output devices. A virtual environment can be used to help understand the limits of safe operation of the system being modeled or to help demonstrate compliance of the modeled system with safety requirements. [100]

9.5   *Test Analysis*

Two sets of analyses should be performed during the testing phase:

1. analyses before the fact to ensure validity and completeness of tests

2. analyses of the test results

Analysis before the fact should, as a minimum, consider test coverage for safety-critical Must-Work-Functions and Must-Not-Work-Functions.

9.5.1   Test Coverage Analysis

For small pieces of code it is sometimes possible to achieve 100% test coverage (i.e., to exercise every possible state and path of the code). However, it is often not possible to achieve 100% test coverage due to the enormous number of permutations of states in a computer program execution, versus the time it would take to exercise all those possible states. Also there is often a large indeterminate number of environmental variables, too many to completely simulate.

For information on the set of possible system tests, refer to Section 9.4.5 *System Testing*. Test coverage analysis should verify adequate coverage for system tests and regression tests (Section 9.4.6)

Some analysis is advisable to assess the optimum test coverage as part of the test planning process. There is a body of theory which attempts to calculate the probability that a system with a certain failure probability will pass a given number of tests. This is discussed in "Evaluation of Safety-critical Software" [52].

Test coverage analysis is best if done prior to the start of testing. At a minimum, analysis should be done to verify that the planned tests cover all paths through the program, that all branches are exercised, and that each statement is executed at least once. Verify that boundary conditions are tested for all inputs, as well as nominal and erroneous input values.

Automated tools are available to aid in the coverage analysis. The list below is not complete and is not an endorsement of any particular tool.

- C++ Test and Jtest, Parasoft, http://www.parasoft.com/
- CodeTEST, Metrowerks, http://www.metrowerks.com/
- Code Warrior Analysis Tools, Metrowerks, http://www.metrowerks.com/
- Cantata, IPL (for C code), http://www.iplbath.com/products/tools/pt200.shtml
- C-Cover, Bullseye; Win32 and Unix; C and C++
- XPEDITER, Compuware; Win32; C, C++, Java and Visual Basic (VB)
- PureCoverage, Rational; Win32 and Unix; C, C++, Java and VB
- TestWorks, Software Research; Win32 and Unix; C, C++, and Java
- LiveCoverage, Paterson Technology; Win32; C, C++, and VB
- DACS™-Object Coverage, DDC-I Inc; Ada; Qualified for FAA verification
- CoverageScope, Real-Time Innovations; VxWorks
- GCOV, GNU; Linux; C and C++

The software development group (or the safety engineer) should create a list of all tests that will be performed. Section 9.4 *Software Integration and Test* discusses the different variety of tests that can be conducted. The test checklist should be maintained by both the development and safety personnel. That provides a cross-check, to make sure no tests are accidentally missed.

Included with this checklist should be an indication of who needs to witness the tests. Software Assurance will usually witness the system tests, but Software Safety may need to witness some as well. Having a list of those involved helps to prevent someone from being forgotten, with the potential of the test having to be run again. In addition, it allows those involved to familiarize themselves with the test procedure prior to witnessing the test.

Benefit Rating: HIGH	Cost Rating: LOW

9.5.2 Formal Inspections of Test Plan and Procedures

Test plans should be created early in the software development lifecycle. Once the requirements are known, a test plan that addresses how the requirements will be verified can be developed. Functional testing, acceptance testing, and off-nominal testing should be included, at a minimum.

Test procedures are the specifics of what is being tested, how to conduct the test, and what the expected results are. The procedures should reference the specific requirements verified by the test. Places to check off the steps should be provided. Important sections, including safety verification steps, have signature blocks for witnesses.

The test plan and test procedures should be reviewed by the safety engineer for a project at the safety minimum level. For higher safety levels, the plan and procedures should undergo formal inspections. (Formal inspections are discussed in Section 6.5.5 *Formal Inspections*.) The goals of the reviews or inspections are to:

- Verify that safety inhibits or controls are not compromised by the test.
- Verify that safety controls or mitigations are adequately tested (when they are included in a test).
- Trace the requirements into the components under test, and determine if the test adequately verifies the requirement.

At the end of testing, all requirements must be verified and all safety features must be tested.

Benefit Rating: HIGH	Cost Rating: LOW to MODERATE

9.5.3 Reliability Modeling

Software reliability contributes to software safety. If the software operates for a long period of time without a failure, then it will be "safe" for that period of time, assuming that an operational (non-failed) mode cannot lead to a hazard.

According to the ANSI standard, software reliability is defined as "the probability of failure-free operation of a computer program for a specified time in a specified environment." Reliability modeling is the process of determining the probability of failure within that specified time. The primary goal of software reliability modeling is to answer the question: Given a system, what is the probability that it will fail in a given time interval, or, what is the expected duration between successive failures?

Software reliability models come in several flavors. **Prediction models** attempt to predict what the reliability of the system will be when it is completed. Prediction models may be developed as early as the requirements phase, or in the design or implementation phase. The questions that a predictive model tries to answer are: Can we reach the reliability goals or requirements? How reliable will the system truly be? Resources that prediction models may use are the failure data of the current system (if it is in test), metrics from the software development process, and failure data from similar systems.

Estimation models evaluate the current software, usually during the test phase. Based on defects found and other factors, the models attempt to estimate how many defects still remain or the time between failures, once the software is in operation. Estimation models include reliability growth models, input domain models, and fault seeding models.

Over 40 varieties of prediction and estimation software reliability models exist. The accuracy of the models varies with the model, the project, and the expertise of the analyst.

Details on reliability modeling, including problems and concerns, are given in the Appendix G.

Benefit Rating: LOW to MEDIUM	Cost Rating: MODERATE to HIGH

9.5.4 Test Results Analysis

Once tests are conducted (and witnessed), a test report is written that describes what was done and how the results match (or differ from) the expected results. The safety engineer uses these test reports, and problem-resolution reports, to verify that all safety requirements have been satisfied. The test results analysis also verifies that all identified hazards have been eliminated or controlled to an acceptable level of risk. The results of the test safety analysis are provided to the ongoing system safety analysis activity.

All test discrepancies of safety-critical software should be evaluated and corrected in an appropriate manner.

9.5.5 Testing Resources

- http://www.chillarege.com/authwork/TestingBestPractice.pdf provides information on the testing, and test development, process.

- Software Testing Hotlist, Resources for Professional Software Testers, http://www.io.com/~wazmo/qa/, is a very good reference site for testing information.

- The Software QA and Testing Resource Center, http://www.softwareqatest.com/, also provides useful information on testing and the QA process.

Chapter 10 Operations and Maintenance

In an ideal world, software development stops when the product is delivered to the customer or placed into operation. In our non-ideal world, defects (faults and failures) are often discovered during operation. Operating software may also be changed to add or alter functionality, work with new hardware, or interface to other software.

Software upgrades, patches, and other maintenance can have unexpected and unwelcome side effects, especially when the system is not well documented. Changes in one part of the software may impact other areas of the software system. Analysis of that impact needs to be performed prior to initiating the change. In a safety-critical system it is vital to make sure that the latest fix or upgrade does not "break" any safety-critical software component.

This section deals with the delivery of the system or software (section 10.4) as well as operations and maintenance tasks (section 10.5).

10.1 Tasks and Analyses

Table 10-1 Operations and Maintenance Tasks

Software Engineering Tasks	System and Software Safety Tasks	Software Assurance or IV&V Tasks
Determine causes of software defects and how to fix them.	Evaluate problem reports for safety impacts.	Help determine causes of software defects.
Propose changes and upgrades to operational software.	Evaluate proposed changes for safety impacts.	Evaluate impact of proposed changes, including COTS. COTS [10.5.1] Change Impact Analysis [10.5.2]
Implement approved changes.	Witness regression testing of safety-critical software.	Witness regression testing.
Perform regression testing after changes implemented.	Evaluate COTS changes for safety impact.	
Maintain COTS software, including patches and upgrades.		

10.2   Documentation and Milestones

The following table lists documents that are commonly produced for this phase of development:

Table 10-2 Operations and Maintenance Documentation

Document	Software Safety Section
Operations or User Manual	Identify any hazardous commands or operations. Include information on how to operate the system safely.
Version Description Document	Safety-critical components should be clearly identified throughout the VDD.
Acceptance Data Package	Traceability Matrix of safety-critical requirements. Verification matrix for all hazard controls.
Software Problem Reports and Change Requests	Problem or Failure reports or software change requests should be reviewed for any safety implications. Any corrective action or software update should be verified to not cause an additional hazard, or to adversely impact any other safety-critical software or hardware.
Traceability Matrix	Update to reflect software after changes implemented.

Milestones that will usually occur during this phase include:

- Software Acceptance Review
- Flight Article Acceptance Review
- Pre-ship Review
- Operations Readiness Review

10.3   Tailoring Guidelines

See Section 3.2 *Tailoring the Effort* for how to determine the software safety effort required (full, moderate, or minimal). Some of these techniques and analyses are provided with a Benefit and Cost rating. The rating is based on engineering judgment, as quantitative evidence is sparse. Use the ratings as a guide only, rather than as an authoritative finding.

Table 10-3 Software Safety Effort for Operations and Maintenance Phase

Technique or Analysis	Safety Effort Level		
	MIN	**MOD**	**FULL**
10.5.2 Software Change Impact Analysis	✓✓	☆	☆

Recommendation Codes			
☆	Mandatory	✓✓	Highly Recommended
✓	Recommended	⊘	Not Recommended

10.4 Software Acceptance and Delivery

Once the software has passed acceptance testing it can be released either as a stand-alone item, or as part of a larger system.

An Acceptance Data Package (ADP) should accompany the release of the software. This package should include the following items for safety-critical software:

- Instructions for installing all safety-critical items.

- Definition of the hardware environment for which the software is certified.

- Identification of all safety-related software liens, such as missing design features or untested features.

- Description of the operational constraints for hazardous activities. List all open, corrected but not tested, or uncorrected safety-related problem reports. Describe environmental limitations of use and the allowable operational envelope.

- Description of all operational procedures and operator interfaces. Include failure diagnosis and recovery procedures.

- Certificate of Conformance to requirements, validated by Quality Assurance organization and the IV & V organization (if applicable).

- List of any waivers of safety requirements, and copies of the waiver forms.

- Acceptance Test Results detailing the results of safety tests.

- List of approved change requests for safety-critical items, and copies of the change requests.

- List of safety-related problem reports, with copies of the reports.

- Version Description Document(s) (VDD) describing the as-built version of the software to be used with this release of the system. Each CSCI may have a separate VDD, or several CSCIs may be grouped together and detailed in a single VDD.

10.5 Software Operations and Maintenance

Maintenance of software differs completely from hardware maintenance. Unlike hardware, software does not degrade or wear out over time[7], so the reasons for software maintenance are different. The main purposes for software maintenance are as follows:

- to correct defects (previously known or discovered during operation)

- to add or remove features and capabilities (as requested by customer, user or operator)

- to compensate or adapt for hardware changes, wear out or failures.

- to compensate for changes in other software components, such as COTS patches or upgrades

---

[7] While software does not "wear out", continuously operating software may degrade due to memory leaks, program errors, or other effects. Such software often requires a restart to clear the problem. It is important to check for and eliminate such problems in systems that must operate for long periods of time.

Proposed changes must go through a change control board and be approved before they are implemented. The changes can be a result of a problem or a request for new features. The safety analyst must ensure that proposed changes do not disrupt or compromise pre-established hazard controls.

The most common safety problem during this phase is lack of configuration control, resulting in undocumented and poorly understood code. "Patching" is a common method used to "fix" software "on the fly". Software with multiple undocumented patches has resulted in major problems where it has become completely impossible to understand how the software really functions, and how it responds to its inputs.

When maintainability was not designed in, the problem of maintaining "clean" code becomes more difficult. The lifetime of the software is often not considered, or not anticipated, when it is designed. Some software will have to operate for years, either in space or on the ground. If the code is not designed for easy change, it will end up looking like spaghetti code once several fixes and upgrades have been applied. Designing for maintainability was discussed in Section 7.4.9.

Sometimes additional software will be added to compensate for unexpected behavior which is not understood. (It is beneficial to determine and correct the root cause of unexpected behavior, otherwise the software can "grow" in size to exceed available resources, or become unmanageable.

After software becomes operational, rigorous configuration control must be enforced. For any proposed software change, it is necessary to repeat all life cycle development and analysis tasks performed previously from requirements (re-) development through code (re-)test. Regression testing should include all safety-critical test cases, a subset of the full system test suite, as well as any additional tests for new features. It is advisable to perform the final verification testing on an identical off-line analog (or simulator) of the operational software system, prior to placing it into service.

Analysis of safety-related anomalies and problem/failure reports during spacecraft flight can help us learn how to make our software safer. This analysis includes the observation, documentation, measurement, and evaluation of post-launch failures and anomalies (including unexpected behavior). From this flight experience we gain insights into how to build, test, and operate safer systems, and how to avoid, detect, and control circumstances that have historically been sources of risk in the systems.

10.5.1 COTS Software

Commercial Off-the-shelf (COTS) software is often a moving target. Fixes, patches, and upgrades are common. For software systems with a short lifetime (less than a year), it is usually possible to use the original COTS software and ignore all upgrades. Sometimes, however, fixes that correct defects in the COTS software are desirable. In addition, software that has a long lifetime will often have to upgrade the COTS software to maintain compatibility with other systems or hardware.

Section 12.1 discusses what to consider when deciding to use COTS software. From the maintenance standpoint, the following are most important:

- How responsive is the vendor to bug-fixes? Does the vendor inform you when a bug-fix patch or new version is available?

- How compatible are upgrades to the software? Has the API changed significantly between upgrades in the past? Will your interface to the OTS software still work, even after an upgrade? Will you have to update your glueware with each iteration?

- Is source code included, or available for purchase at a reasonable price? Will support still be provided if the source code is purchased or if the software is slightly modified?

- Can you communicate with those who developed the software, if serious questions arise? Is the technical support available, adequate, and reachable? Will the vendor talk with you if you modify the product?

- Will the vendor support older versions of the software, if you choose not to upgrade? Many vendors will only support the newest version, or perhaps one or two previous versions.

- Is there a well-defined API (Application Program Interface), ICD (interface control document), or similar documentation that details how the user interacts with the software? Are there "undocumented" API functions?

The first and best choice regarding COTS upgrades is to ignore them. If you do not change that software, nothing in your system needs to be changed. If you are planning to not upgrade, then it is important to purchase the source code of the COTS software, if at all possible. Having the code means that you can make the changes **you** want to the system. It also means that if the company goes out of business a year from now, you can still maintain your system. For the same reasons, the COTS software should be kept under configuration management control. If you need to reconstruct the version of your software system you ran two years ago, you need to have all the necessary pieces. Newer versions of compilers, libraries, and other COTS software are rarely identical to the old versions, and unexpected interactions can occur.

If you must upgrade, then you need to evaluate the change and its impact on your software. Questions to ask yourself include:

- What exactly is being changed and how will it affect your software? How much detail is available on what the change actually affects?

- Has the functionality changed? Has any functionality been added? Has any been removed or deprecated?

- Has the interface (API) changed?

- Will you have to change your glueware when the COTS software is upgraded?

- If you purchased the source code, will you also get the source for the fix or upgrade?

- Is there anything in the COTS upgrade that will not work with your hardware or other software?

- Will you require more capability (memory, storage, etc.) after the upgrade?

- How will the upgrade occur? Can you take your system down long enough for the upgrade to be implemented? What happens if it doesn't work the first time?

- Can you test the upgrade on a simulator or other system, both for initial verification of the change and to make sure safety has not been compromised?

10.5.2 Software Change Impact Analysis

Software change impact analysis determines what parts of the software, documentation, and other software products will be affected if a proposed software change is made. Knowing what will be affected by a change reduces the chance of unanticipated side-effects once the change is implemented. Fixes or upgrades are supposed to improve the software, not break it in a new location.

The information provided by impact analysis can be used for planning changes, implementing the changes, and tracing through the effects of changes. Impact analysis provides visibility into the potential effects of changes before the changes are made.

A major goal of impact analysis is to identify the software work products affected by the proposed changes. Impact analysis starts with the set of software lifecycle objects (SLOs), such as the software specification, design documentation, and source code. These SLOs are then analyzed with respect to the software change. The result is a list of items that should be addressed during the change process. The information from such an analysis can be used to evaluate the consequences of planned changes, as well as the trade-offs among the approaches for implementing the change.

Typical examples of impact analysis techniques include:

- Using cross-referenced listings to see what other parts of a program contain references to a given variable or procedure.

- Using program slicing to determine the program subset that can affect the value of a given variable.

- Browsing a program by opening and closing related files.

- Using traceability relationships to identify software artifacts associated with a change.

- Using configuration management systems to track and find changes.

- Consulting designs and specifications to determine the scope of a change.

Dependency analysis of source code is one type of impact analysis. Basically, the analysis determines "what depends on what" – what objects, modules, variable, etc. depend on other modules. Other analyses that provide information on dependencies include:

- Program slicing. (Section 8.4.4)

- Data flow analysis. (Section 8.5.2)

- Control flow analysis. (Section 8.5.1)

- Test-coverage analysis. (Section 8.5.6)

- Cross-referencing (Section 6.5.7) and Traceability Matrices (Sections 6.4.2 and 7.5.9)

- Browsing (source code and documentation).

Most automated software analysis tools support source code dependencies. Examples of tools include program slicers, cross-referencers, data-flow and control-flow analyzers, source-code comparators, test-coverage analyzers, and interactive debuggers. These tools provide the analyst with automated assistance in identifying the consequences of the proposed change.

Traceability analysis uses the defined relationships among the SLOs to determine the impact. Types of tools used for this analysis include:

- Requirements management tools with traceability. (Section 6.4)

- Database of SLOs with querying capabilities.

- Impact analysis tools.

- Brute-force (manual method using traceability matrix).

The extent of the impact is determined by the number of components affected and how much of each component will be affected if a particular component is changed. Impact determination analyses uses algorithms to identify the impacts.

- Transitive closure algorithms take a graph of objects and relationships as input and determine all objects reachable from any object to any other object through paths of length zero or more. This algorithm finds all components that a particular component could impact.

- Inferencing uses rules to characterize relationships among objects. Inferencing systems usually consist of a database of facts, a way to infer new facts from previous ones, and some executive for managing the search. For example, a database may contain a list of modules and module call information (A calls B, B calls C and D, etc.). Given the calling information, it can be inferred that changes to A will affect B, C, and D – B directly and C and D indirectly.

- Program slicing (Section 8.4.4) provides a mechanism looking only at the parts of the software program (not documentation) that is affected by the change.

Determining the extent of impact also includes evaluating the amount of change, and the risk that imposes. No specific techniques support this aspect of impact analysis. Evaluation is a matter of intelligently looking at the extent of the change, what is changed, and reasoning about the potential consequences (and the likelihood of those consequences).

As a general rule of thumb, the following types of changes are more likely to have unanticipated effects or are generally riskier:

- Changes that impact many modules.

- Changes that impact interfaces, especially low-level interfaces used throughout the system.

- Changes to requirements.

- Changes to low-level modules, classes, or other components used throughout the system.

Much of this section was derived from the book "Software Change Impact Analysis" [104], which is a collection of papers on the topic. Many papers are tutorial or general in nature. Others provide theoretical or experimental approaches.

Chapter 11 Software Development Issues

In this chapter, we'll look at various programming languages, operating systems, tools, and development environments being used to create or as part of safety-critical software. Also included are various new technologies that have particular (and usually unsolved) problems with determining their safety.

Choosing a programming language is a necessity for any project. This chapter examines a subset of the over one hundred available languages. These languages are commonly used in safety-critical or embedded environments. Several languages are included that might be considered because they are popular or new. For each language, any safety-related strengths are discussed, and guidance is given on what aspects to avoid.

This chapter will also look at the environment the software will be developed and run in. Issues with compilers, tools, Integrated Development Environments (IDEs), automatic code generation, and operating systems (especially Real-Time (RTOS)) will be considered.

Software is being used in new environments and new ways. Assuring the safety of these systems is still an area for improved understanding. Distributed computing, artificial intelligence, autonomous systems, programmable logic devices, and embedded web technology are areas considered in this guidebook. The interaction between humans and software systems, in operation or during development, is also a factor in safer software.

Why does software have bugs?[8]

* **miscommunication or no communication** - as to specifics of what an application should or shouldn't do (the application's requirements).

* **software complexity** - the complexity of current software applications can be difficult to comprehend for anyone without experience in modern-day software development. Windows-type interfaces, client-server and distributed applications, data communications, enormous relational databases, and sheer size of applications have all contributed to the exponential growth in software and system complexity. And the use of

---

[8] The list above was taken with permission from the Software QA and Testing Frequently Asked Questions. http://www.softwareqatest.com © 1996-2000 by Rick Hower

object-oriented techniques can complicate instead of simplify a project unless it is well-engineered.

* **programming errors** - programmers, like anyone else, can make mistakes.

* **changing requirements** - the customer may not understand the effects of changes, or may understand and request them anyway - redesign, rescheduling of engineers, effects on other projects, work already completed that may have to be redone or thrown out, hardware requirements that may be affected, etc. If there are many minor changes or any major changes, known and unknown dependencies among parts of the project are likely to interact and cause problems, and the complexity of keeping track of changes may result in errors. Enthusiasm of engineering staff may be affected. In some fast-changing business environments, continuously modified requirements may be a fact of life. In this case, management must understand the resulting risks, and QA and test engineers must adapt and plan for continuous extensive testing to keep the inevitable bugs from running out of control - see 'What can be done if requirements are changing continuously?' in Part 2 of the FAQ.

* **time pressures** - scheduling of software projects is difficult at best, often requiring a lot of guesswork. When deadlines loom and the crunch comes, mistakes will be made.

* **egos** - people prefer to say things like:

> 'no problem'
> 'piece of cake'
> 'I can whip that out in a few hours'
> 'it should be easy to update that old code'

instead of:

> 'that adds a lot of complexity and we could end up making a lot of mistakes'
> 'we have no idea if we can do that; we'll wing it'
> 'I can't estimate how long it will take, until I take a close look at it'
> 'we can't figure out what that old spaghetti code did in the first place'

If there are too many unrealistic 'no problem's, the result is bugs.

* **poorly documented code** - it's tough to maintain and modify code that is badly written or poorly documented; the result is bugs. In many organizations management provides no incentive for programmers to document their code or write clear, understandable code. In fact, it's usually the opposite: they get points mostly for quickly turning out code, and there's job security if nobody else can understand it ('if it was hard to write, it should be hard to read').

* **software development tools** - visual tools, class libraries, compilers, scripting tools, etc. often introduce their own bugs or are poorly documented, resulting in added bugs.

> **Whenever possible, *select for safety*. Otherwise, take steps to mitigate the risks to safety.**

11.1 Programming Languages

The language chosen to convert the design into executable code can have an impact on the safety of the system. Some languages are more prone to certain errors, making rigorous development, review, and testing important. Other languages are designed with safety in mind, though they are not perfect. Determining what language to use is a matter of weighing the risks and benefits of each language.

> Section 11.1.1 discusses subsets of languages that are designed for safety.
>
> Section 11.1.2 mentions some insecurities common to all languages.
>
> Section 11.1.3 provides a method of assessment for choosing a language.
>
> Section 11.1.4 introduces a collection of languages (Ada, Assembly Languages, C, C++, C#, Forth, FORTRAN, Java, LabVIEW, Pascal, Visual Basic)
>
> Section 11.1.5 discusses miscellaneous problems present in most languages.
>
> Section 11.1.6 summarizes this section and provides recommendations.

11.1.1 Safe Subsets of Languages

A safe subset of a language is one that restricts certain features that are error-prone or are undefined or poorly defined. In some cases, a subset may be created by a particular vendor, or may grow out of the user community. In many cases, a standard subset does not exist, but "coding standards" are used to create the subset. Using coding standards means that the compiler will not enforce the subset, however.

There are two primary reasons for restricting a language definition to a subset:

    1) some features are defined in an ambiguous manner

    2) some features are excessively complex or error-prone.

A language is considered suitable for use in a safety-critical application if it provides the necessary functionality, has a precise definition, is logically coherent, and has a manageable size and complexity. The issue of excessive complexity makes it virtually impossible to verify certain language features. Overall, the issues of logical soundness and complexity will be the key toward understanding why a language is restricted to a subset for safety-critical applications.

Compilers for "safer" language subsets are often certified to provide correct translation from the source code to object code. The subset usually undergoes vigorous study and verification before it is accepted by the user community.

Besides formal language subsets, safety specific coding standards are used to stipulate requirements for annotation of safety-critical code and prohibit use of certain language features which can reduce software safety. Avoid including programming style requirements in a coding standard. Put those in a separate coding style document. While you want programmers to use the same style, it is far more important that they follow the safety-critical coding standards. A "style war" can lead to some programmers ignoring the whole document, if style and standards are mixed.

11.1.2 Insecurities Common to All Languages

All programming languages have insecurities either in their definition or their implementation. Newer languages (or updates to existing language standards) try to correct the shortfalls of older generation languages, while adding additional functionality. In reality, they often add new insecurities as well.

Some common problems are:

- **Use of uninitialized variables.** Uninitialized variables are the most common error in practically all programming languages. In particular, uninitialized or improperly initialized pointers (in languages that support them) often cause insidious errors. This mistake is very hard to catch because unit testing will not flag it unless explicitly designed to do so. The typical manifestation of this error is when a program that has been working successfully is run under different environmental conditions and the results are not as expected.

- **Memory management concerns**. Calls to deallocate memory should be examined to make sure that not only is the pointer released but that the memory used by the structure is released. Also, it is important to verify that only one deallocation call is made for a particular memory block. On the other side of the problem, memory that is not deallocated when no longer used will lead to a memory leak, and perhaps to an eventual system crash.

- **Unspecified compiler behavior.** The order in which operands are evaluated is often not defined by the language standard, and is left up to the compiler vendor. Depending on the order of evaluation for certain "side effects" to be carried out is poor programming practice! The order of evaluation may be understood for *this compiler* and *this version* only. If the program is compiled with a different vendor, or a different version, the side effects may well change. Other unspecified behaviors include the order of initialization of global or static variables.

11.1.3 Method of Assessment

When comparing programming languages, we will not deal with differences among vendor implementations. Compiler implementations, by and large, do not differ significantly from the intent of the standard. However, standards are not unambiguous and they are interpreted by the vendor. Be aware that implementations will not adhere 100% to the standard because of the extremely large number of states a compiler can produce. We will present information on the strengths and weaknesses of popular programming languages, and discuss safety related concerns. Common errors specific to the language will be discussed as well.

Safer software can be written in any language. Coding standards can designate how to program in a particular language to produce safer code. But we're human. We make mistakes, we get in a hurry, and the coding standards may not be followed. Languages that are "safer" are those that enforce the standards, that check for common errors, and that do so as early as possible!

When evaluating a language, the following questions should be asked of the language as a minimum:

- Can it be shown that the program cannot jump to an arbitrary location?

- Are there language features that prevent an arbitrary memory location from being overwritten?

- Are the semantics of the language defined sufficiently for static code analysis to be feasible?

- Is there a rigorous model of both integer and floating point arithmetic within the standard?

- Are there procedures for checking that the operational program obeys the model of the arithmetic when running on the target processor?

- Are the means of typing strong enough* to prevent misuse of variables?

- Are there facilities in the language to guard against running out of memory at runtime?

- Does the language provide facilities for separate compilation of modules with type checking across module boundaries?

- Is the language well understood so designers and programmers can write safety-critical software?

- Is there a subset of the language which has the properties of a safe language as evidenced by the answers to the other questions?

*Strong typing implies an explicit data type conversion is required when transforming one type to another

11.1.4 Languages

There are over one hundred programming languages, with more being developed each year. Many are generated within academia as part of a research project. However, the subset of well established languages is more limited. The following languages will be examined in detail, focusing on the strengths and weaknesses each has with regards to producing safe software.

- Ada83, Ada95 and safe subsets
- Assembly Languages
- C
- C++
- C#
- Forth
- FORTRAN
- Java
- LabVIEW
- Pascal
- Visual Basic

11.1.4.1   *Ada83 and Ada95 Languages*

One of the most commonly used languages in military and safety-critical applications is Ada. From the inception of Ada83 until 1997, Ada was mandated by the Department of Defense for all weapons-related and mission critical programs. Though currently not mandated, Ada is still commonly used within military projects. In addition, safety-critical commercial software is being written in Ada. Ada is also the primary language of the International Space Station. The Ada language was designed with safety and reliability in mind. The goal of Ada is to maximize the amount of error detection as early in the development process as possible.

The Ada standard was first released on 17th February 1983 as ANSI/MIL-STD-1815A "Reference Manual for the Ada Programming Language". This original version is now called Ada83. The first major revision of the Ada standard was released on 21 December 1994 via ISO/IEC 8652:1995(E), and is commonly known as Ada95. Ada95 corrects many of the safety deficiencies of Ada83 and adds full object oriented capabilities to the language.

One Ada subset of note is the SPARK language (http://www.sparkada.com/spark.html), which is designed to support the development of software used in applications where correct operation is vital either for reasons of safety or business integrity. A SPARK program has a precise meaning which is unaffected by the choice of Ada compiler and can never be erroneous. SPARK includes Ada constructs regarded as essential for the construction of complex software, such as packages, private types, typed constants, functions with structured values, and the library system. It excludes tasks, exceptions, generic units, access types, use clauses, type aliasing, anonymous types, default values in record declarations, default subprogram parameters, goto statements, and declare statements. SPARK was designed for use in high integrity applications; it is therefore essential that it exhibits logical soundness, simplicity of the formal definition, expressive power, security, verifiability, bounded space and time requirements, and minimal runtime system requirements.

The strengths of Ada95 lie in the following attributes:

- **Object orientation**

  Ada95 supports all the standard elements of object orientation: encapsulation of objects, inheritance, and polymorphism. Encapsulation "hides" information from program elements that do not need to know about it, and therefore decreases the chance of the information being altered unexpectedly. Inheritance and polymorphism contribute to the extensibility of the software.

  Software reuse is one "plus" of object orientation. A previously tested object can be extended, with new functionality, without "breaking" the original object.

- **Strongly typed**

  Ada enforces data typing. This means that you cannot use an integer when a floating point number is expected, unless you explicitly convert it. Nor can you access an integer array through a character pointer. Strong typing finds places where the programmer assumed one thing, but the source code actually lead to another implementation. Forcing conversions helps the programmer think about what she is doing, and why, rather than allowing the compiler to make implicit (and perhaps undefined) conversions.

- **Range checking**

Range checking for arrays, strings, and other dimensioned elements is included in the language. This prevents accidentally overwriting memory outside of the array. The compiler will usually find the error. If not, a Run Time Exception (RTE) will be generated. Also included is checking for references to null.

- **Support for multitasking and threads**

Tasking is built into the language. Support is included to deal with threads and concurrency issues. Protected objects provide a low overhead, data-oriented synchronization mechanism. Asynchronous transfer of control, with "clean up" of the interrupted process, is part of the language.

- **Clarity of source code**

Ada code is closer to "regular" language than most languages, and this makes it easy to read. Often, coming back to code you wrote awhile ago is difficult. Much of the context has been forgotten, and it may be difficult to understand why you did something. When the code is easy to read, those problems are reduced. Also, when the code is reviewed or inspected, others find it easier to understand.

- **Mixed language support**

Ada allows modules written in other languages to be used. Usually, just a "wrapper" must be created before the non-Ada routines can be accessed. This allows well-tested, legacy code to be used with newer Ada code.

- **Real-time system support**

Ada95 has added support for real-time systems. Hard deadlines can be defined. Protected types give a "low overhead" type of semaphore. With dynamic task priorities, the priority of a task can be set at run-time rather than compile-time. Priority inversion, used to prevent deadlock when a high priority task needs a resource being used by a lower priority task, can be bounded. This allows Rate Monotonic Analysis to be used.

- **Distributed systems support**

A "unit" in an Ada95 distributed system is called a partition. A partition is an aggregation of modules that executes in a distributed target environment. Typically, each partition corresponds to a single computer (execution site). Communication among partitions of a distributed system is based upon extending the remote procedure call paradigm.

- **Exception handling**

Exceptions are raised by built-in and standard library functions, when events such as an integer overflow or out-of-bounds check occurs. Exceptions can also be raised by the program specifically, to indicate that the software reached an undesirable state. Exceptions are handled outside of the normal program flow, and are usually used to put the software into a known, safe state. The exception handler, written by the programmer, determines how the software deals with the exception.

- **Support for non-object-oriented (traditional) software development styles**

Though Ada95 supports object-oriented programming, the language can be used with other styles as well. Functional (structural) programming techniques can be used with the language.

Additional safety-related features are

- **Compiler validation**

  All Ada compilers must be validated. This means the compiler is put through a standard set of tests before it is declared a true Ada compiler. This does not mean that the compiler does not have defects, however. When choosing a compiler, ask for the history list of defects.

- **Language restriction ability**

  Ada95 added a restriction pragma that allows features of the language to be "turned off". You can specify a subset of the language, removing features that are not needed or that may be deemed unsafe. If a feature is not included, it does not have to be validated, thus reducing the testing and analysis effort.

- **Validity checking of scalar values**

  Ada95 has added a Valid attribute which allows the user to check whether the bit-pattern for a scalar object is valid with respect to the object's nominal subtype. It can be used to check the *contents* of a scalar object *without formally reading* its value. Using this attribute on an uninitialized object is not an error of any sort, and is guaranteed to either return True or False (and not raise an exception). The results are based on the actual contents of the object and not on what the optimizer might have assumed about the contents of the object based on some declaration.

  Valid can also be used to check data from an unchecked conversion, a value read from I/O, an object for which pragma Import has been specified, and an object that has been assigned a value where checks have been suppressed.

- **Reviewable object code**

  Ada provides mechanisms to aid in reviewing the object code produced by the compiler. Because the compiler will have defects, it is important in safety-critical applications to review the object code itself.

  The pragma Reviewable can be applied to a partition (program) so that the compiler can provide the necessary information. The compiler vender should produce information on the ordering of modules in the object code, what registers are used for an object (and how long is the assignment valid), and what machine code instructions are used. In addition, a way to extract the object code for a particular module, so that other tools can use it, is suggested. Other information should support Initialization Analysis (what is the initialization state of all variables), determining the relationship between Source and Object Code, and Exception Analysis (indicating where compiler-generated run-time checks occur in the object code and which exceptions can be raised by any statement) may also be supported by the compiler vendor.

  An Inspection Point pragma provides a "hook" into the program similar to a hardware test point. At the inspection point(s) in the object code, the values of the specified objects, or all live objects, can be determined.

However, no language is perfect. Ada95 does **not** detect the use of uninitialized variables, though using the "Normalize_Scalars" pragma will help. Some aspects of the language to consider restricting, for a safety-critical application, are:

- The ability to turn off the type checking and other safety features

- Garbage collection…turn it off if timing issues are important.

"Ada Programming Guidelines" are available from Rational Software Corporation.

11.1.4.2   Assembly Languages

Assembly languages are the human-readable version of machine code. They are specific to a processor or processor family. Programming in assembly requires intimate knowledge of the workings of the processor.

Modern assembly languages include macros that allow "higher level" logic flow, such as if…else statements and looping. Variables can be declared and named. Subroutines (procedures) can also be declared and called. All "higher level" constructs improve the readability and maintainability of the assembly program.

Few large programs are written entirely in assembly language. Often, a small section of the software will be rewritten in assembly to increase execution speed or decrease code size. Also, the code used on bootup of a system (that loads the operating system) and BIOS-like utilities are often written in assembly. Interrupt service routines are another place you will find assembly language used. In addition, software that runs on small microcontrollers are often space-limited and therefore assembly coding is a good alternative to a high-level language.

Why use assembly?

- Execution Speed

- Smaller code size

- Ability to do something that higher level languages do not allow.

- Tweaking the compiler's optimization, by editing the assembly output it produces

Problems and safety concerns:

- Can do anything with the processor and access any part of memory

- No notion of data type – a sequence of bytes can be anything you want!

- You can jump anywhere in address space

- All higher level constructs (structures, arrays, etc.) exist only in the programmer's implementation, and not in the language.

- Not portable between processors

Compilers can usually produce assembly source code from the higher level language. This is useful for checking what the compiler does, and verifying its translation to that level. In fact, if the compiler produces correct assembly source code but incorrect object code, creating the assembly source and then using a different assembler to generate the object code could bypass the problem.

More often, the assembly output is used to "tweak" performance in a slow routine. Use a profiling program to find out *where* the slow sections are first. The part of the program that the programmer thinks is likely to be slow is often not the actual problem. Running the program with a profiler will give hard numbers, and point to the truly sluggish sections of code.

11.1.4.3   C Language

The C language is extremely popular because of its flexibility and support environment. C is often used in embedded and real-time environments because hardware access is fairly easy and compact code can be generated. In many ways, C is a higher level assembly language. This gives it great flexibility, and opens a Pandora's box of possible errors. The support environment includes a wide variety of mature and inexpensive development and verification tools. Also, the pool of experienced vendors and personnel is quite large.

However, C's definition lacks the rigor necessary to qualify it as a suitable vehicle for safety-critical applications. There are dozens of dialects of C, raising integrity concerns about code developed on one platform and used on another. Despite its problems, many safety-critical applications have been coded in C and function without serious flaws. If C is chosen, however, the burden is on the developer to provide a thorough verification of code and data sequences, and sufficient testing to verify both functionality and error handling.

One characteristic of C that decreases its reliability is that C is not a strongly typed language. That means that the language doesn't enforce the data typing, and it can be circumvented by representational viewing. (This means that by unintended use of certain language constructs, not by explicit conversion, a datum that represents an integer can be interpreted as a character.) The definition of strong typing implies an explicit conversion process when transforming one data type to another. C allows for implicit conversion of basic types and pointers. One of the features of strong typing is that sub-ranges can be specified for the data. With a judicious choice of data types, a result from an operation can be shown to be within a sub-range. In C it is difficult to show that any integer calculation cannot overflow. Unsigned integer arithmetic is modulo the word length without overflow detection and therefore insecure for safety purposes.

Another feature of C that does not restrict operations is the way C works with pointers. C does not place any restrictions on what addresses a programmer can point to and it allows arithmetic on pointers. While C's flexibility makes it attractive, it also makes it a less reliable programming language. C has other limitations which are mentioned in reference [33].

Restricting the C language to certain constructs would not be feasible because the resulting language would not have the necessary functionality. However, rigorous enforcement of coding standards will decrease certain common errors and provide some assurance that the software will function as expected. Structured design techniques should be used.

Limitations and Problems with the C language:

- **Pointers**

  Pointers in C allow the programmer to access anything in memory, if the operating system does not prevent it. This is good when writing a device driver or accessing memory-mapped I/O. However, a large number of C errors are due to pointer problems. Using a pointer to access an array, and then running past the end of the array, leads to "smash the stack" (see below). Pointer arithmetic can be tricky, and you can easily point outside of the data structure. Use of undefined pointers can trash memory or the stack, and lead the program to wander into undefined territory.

- **Lack of Bounds Checking**

C does not provide any bounds checking on arrays and strings. It is left to the programmer to make sure that the array element is truly in bounds. Since the programmer is fallible, "smash the stack" and "fandango on core" often result. The problem is especially evident when passing an array to a function, which references it via a pointer. The function must know the length of the array, or it may run past the end. Calculations that determine the element to access must also be checked, as a negative or too large value can result, leading to "out of bounds" accesses.

A "wrapper" function can be used when accessing an array or string which checks that the element is within bounds. This adds runtime overhead, but decreases the number of errors.

- **Floating Point Arithmetic**

The ANSI C standard does not mandate any particular implementation for floating point arithmetic. As a result every C compiler implements it differently. The following test calculation can be executed:

$$x = 10^{20}+1$$
$$y = x-10^{20}$$

The resulting value for y will differ greatly from compiler to compiler, and none of them will be correct due to word length round-off.

- **Casting from void***

void* points to data of any type. It is left to the programmer to recast it when the pointer is used. There is no compile time nor run time checking to verify that the pointer is cast to a valid type (based on what the pointer actually points to). This method is inherently tricky and prone to errors.

- **Commenting problems**

The C comment /* ... */ can lead to unexpected problems, by accidentally commenting out working code. Forgetting the end comment marker (*/) can cause the code that follows to be comment out, until another comment end marker is found. A good editor will often show this problem while the code is being developed, if it marks commented text in a different color. Also, compilers should be set up to generate warnings or errors to be generated if an open comment (/*) is found within a comment.

- **Global variables**

Global variables can be considered as input parameters to any function, since a function has full access to them. So a function that takes 2 parameters, in a program with 100 global variables, actually has 102 parameters. This makes verifying the program very difficult. It is best to avoid global variables as much possible. Global variables also cause problems in a multi-threaded program, e.g. when different threads believe they have control of the variable, and both change the global.

- **Common language errors**

    o Confusing = with == (assignment with logical equality)

    o Confusing **&** vs. **&&** (Bitwise AND with logical AND)

    o premature semicolon in control structures

    o fall-through behavior in switch statements when "break" is omitted

    o Comparing signed and unsigned variables. Particularly, testing "unsigned < 0" or "unsigned < negative signed value".

- **Side effects and macros**

    Side effects, such as incrementing a variable with ++, when mixed with macros (including "functions" that are actually implemented as a macro, such as putchar()), may produce unexpected results.

- **"smash the stack"***

    <jargon> In C programming, to corrupt the execution stack by writing past the end of a local array or other data structure. Code that smashes the stack can cause a return from the routine to jump to a random address, resulting in insidious data-dependent bugs.

    Variants include "trash the stack", "scribble the stack", and "mangle the stack".

- **"precedence lossage"***

    /pre's*-dens los'*j/ A C coding error in an expression due to unintended grouping of arithmetic or logical operators. Used especially of certain common coding errors in C due to the nonintuitively low precedence levels of "&", "|", "^", "<<" and ">>". For example, the following C expression, intended to test the least significant bit of x,

      x & 1 == 0

    is parsed as

      x & (1 == 0)

    which the compiler would probably evaluate at compile-time to

      (x & 0)

    and then to 0.

    Precedence lossage can always be avoided by suitable use of parentheses. For this reason, some C programmers deliberately ignore the language's precedence hierarchy and use parentheses defensively.

- **"fandango on core"***

    (Unix/C, from the Mexican dance) In C, a wild pointer that runs out of bounds, causing a core dump, or corrupts the malloc arena in such a way as to cause mysterious failures later on, is sometimes said to have "done a fandango on core". On low-end personal machines without an MMU, this can corrupt the operating system itself, causing massive lossage. Other frenetic dances such as the rumba, cha-cha, or watusi, may be substituted.

- **"overrun screw"***

  A variety of fandango on core produced by a C program scribbling past the end of an array (C implementations typically have no checks for this error). This is relatively benign and easy to spot if the array is static; if it is auto, the result may be to smash the stack - often resulting in heisenbugs of the most diabolical subtlety. The term "overrun screw" is used especially of scribbles beyond the end of arrays allocated with malloc; this typically overwrites the allocation header for the next block in the arena, producing massive lossage within malloc and often a core dump on the next operation to use stdio or malloc itself.

- **"C Programmer's Disease"***

  The tendency of the undisciplined C programmer to set arbitrary but supposedly generous static limits on table sizes (defined, if you're lucky, by constants in header files) rather than taking the trouble to do proper dynamic storage allocation. If an application user later needs to put 68 elements into a table of size 50, the afflicted programmer reasons that he or she can easily reset the table size to 68 (or even as much as 70, to allow for future expansion) and recompile. This gives the programmer the comfortable feeling of having made the effort to satisfy the user's (unreasonable) demands, and often affords the user multiple opportunities to explore the marvelous consequences of fandango on core. In severe cases of the disease, the programmer cannot comprehend why each fix of this kind seems only to further disgruntle the user.

*These quotations were taken from Imperial College, London, UK, world wide web home page "The Free On-Line Dictionary of Computing" Copyright Denis Howe 1993-1999, (http://foldoc.doc.ic.ac.uk/foldoc/index.html). It contains graphic descriptions of common problems with C. The quotations were reproduced by permission of Denis Howe <dbh@doc.ic.ac.uk>.

Reference [54] discusses the important problem of dynamic memory management in C. Note that simply prohibiting dynamic memory management is not necessarily the best course, due to increased risk of exceeding memory limits without warning.

Programming standards for C should include at least the following:

- Use parentheses for precedence of operation, and do not rely on the default precedence. The default may not be what you thought it was, and it will come back to bite you.

- Use parentheses within macros, around the variable name

- Don't use the preprocessor for defining complex macros

- Explicitly cast or convert variables. Do not rely on the implicit conversions.

- Avoid void* pointers when possible.

- Check arrays and strings for "out of bounds" accesses.

- Always use function prototypes. This allows the compiler to find problems with inconsistent types when passing variables to a function.

- Minimize the use of global variables. Each global can be considered a parameter to every function, increasing the chance of accidentally changing the global.

- Always include a *default* clause in a *switch...case* statement.

- Avoid recursion when possible.

- Make extensive use of error handling procedures and status and error logging.

The Ten Commandments for C Programmers
by Henry Spencer

1. Thou shalt run lint frequently and study its pronouncements with care, for verily its perception and judgment oft exceed thine.

2. Thou shalt not follow the NULL pointer, for chaos and madness await thee at its end.

3. Thou shalt cast all function arguments to the expected type if they are not of that type already, even when thou art convinced that this is unnecessary, lest they take cruel vengeance upon thee when thou least expect it.

4. If thy header files fail to declare the return types of thy library functions, thou shalt declare them thyself with the most meticulous care, lest grievous harm befall thy program.

5. Thou shalt check the array bounds of all strings (indeed, all arrays), for surely where thou typest "foo" someone someday shall type "supercalifragilisticexpialidocious".

6. If a function be advertised to return an error code in the event of difficulties, thou shalt check for that code, yea, even though the checks triple the size of thy code and produce aches in thy typing fingers, for if thou thinkest "it cannot happen to me", the gods shall surely punish thee for thy arrogance.

7. Thou shalt study thy libraries and strive not to re-invent them without cause, that thy code may be short and readable and thy days pleasant and productive.

8. Thou shalt make thy program's purpose and structure clear to thy fellow man by using the One True Brace Style, even if thou likest it not, for thy creativity is better used in solving problems than in creating beautiful new impediments to understanding.

9. Thy external identifiers shall be unique in the first six characters, though this harsh discipline be irksome and the years of its necessity stretch before thee seemingly without end, lest thou tear thy hair out and go mad on that fateful day when thou desirest to make thy program run on an old system.

10. Thou shalt foreswear, renounce, and abjure the vile heresy which claimeth that "All the world's a VAX", and have no commerce with the benighted heathens who cling to this barbarous belief, that the days of thy program may be long even though the days of thy current machine be short.

A checklist of Generic and C-specific programming standards is included in Appendix B. Additional guidelines on C programming practices are described in the book "Safer C: Developing Software for High-integrity and Safety-critical Systems" (Reference [55], and also in [56] and [57]). Included in the book are lists of undefined or implementation defined behaviors in the language.

11.1.4.4 C++ Language

The C++ programming language was created by Bjarne Stroustrup as an extension (superset) of the C programming language discussed above (Section 11.1.4.3 C Language). The goal was to add object-oriented features, while maintaining the efficiency of C. The language was standardized in November, 1997 as ISO/IEC 14882. C++ adds Object Orientation (OO) as well as fixing or updating many C features. C++ is also more strongly typed than C. However, C++ suffers from many of the same drawbacks as C.

A standard "safe subset" of C++ does not presently exist.

Strengths of the C++ Language

- **Object Orientation**

  Object orientation allows data abstraction (classes), encapsulation of data and the functions that use the data, and reusable and extensible code.

- **Stronger type checking than C**

  C++ type checking can be subverted, but it is much better than C's. Most of the mechanisms that reduce the type checking were left in to support compatibility with the C language.

- *Const* **to enforce the "invariability" of variables and functions**

  Declaring a function *const* means that the function will not change any passed parameters, even if they are passed by reference. A *const* variable cannot be changed, and replaces the "#define" preprocessor directives. The programmer can get around *const* with a cast.

- **Generic programming (templates).**

  C++ has the ability to use generic containers (such as vectors) without runtime overhead.

- **C++ supports both Object-Oriented and Structural design and programming styles.**

- **The user-defined types (classes) have efficiencies that approach those of built-in types. C++ treats built-in and user-defined types uniformly**

- **Exceptions and error handling**

  Exceptions allow errors to be "caught" and handled, without crashing the program. They may not be the best way to handle errors, and the software does have to be explicitly designed to generate and deal with exceptions. However, exceptions are an improvement over C's *setjmp()* and *longjmp()* means of exception handling.

- **Namespaces**

  Namespaces are most useful for libraries of functions. They prevent function names from conflicting, if they are in different libraries (namespaces). While not primarily a safety feature, namespaces can be used to clearly identify to the reader and the programmers what functions are safety related.

- **References to variables**

  A reference is like a pointer (it points to the variable), but it also simplifies the code and forces the *compiler* to create the pointer, not the programmer. Anything the compiler does is more likely to be error free than what the programmer would do.

- **Inline Functions**

  Inline functions replace #define macros. They are easier to understand, and less likely to hide defects.

Good practices to reduce C++ errors:

- Never use multiple inheritance, only use one to one (single) inheritance. This is because interpretations of how to implement multiple inheritance are inconsistent (Willis and Paddon, [58] 1995. Szyperski supports this view.);

- Minimize the levels of inheritance, to reduce complexity in the program.

- Only rely on fully abstract classes, passing interface but not implementation (suggestion by Szyperski at 1995 Safety through Quality Conference - NASA-KSC [59]).

- Minimize the use of pointers.

- Do not allow aliases.

- No side-effects in expressions or function calls.

- Make the class destructor virtual if the class can be inherited.

- Always define a default constructor, rather than relying on the compiler to do it for you.

- Define a copy constructor. Even if a "bitwise" copy would be acceptable (the default, if the compiler generates it), that may change in the future. If any memory is allocated by the class methods, then a copy constructor is vital. If the class objects should not be copied, make the copy constructor and assignment operator private, and do not define bodies for them.

- Define an assignment operator for the class, or add a comment indicating that the compiler-generated one will be used.

- Use operator overloading sparingly and in a uniform manner. This creates more readable code, which increases the chance of errors being found in inspections, and reduces errors when the code is revisited.

- Use const when possible, especially when a function will not change anything external to the function. If the compiler enforces this, errors will be found at compile time. If not, it will aid in finding errors during formal inspections of the code.

- Don't use the RTTI (Run-Time Type Information). It was added to support object oriented data bases. If you think it's necessary in your program, look again at your design.

- Avoid global variables. Declare them in a structure as static data members.

- Make sure that the destructor removes all memory allocated by the constructor and any member functions, to avoid memory leaks.

- Use templates with care, including the Standard Template Library. The STL is not thread-safe.

- Take special care when using delete for an array. Check that delete[] is used. Also check for deleting (freeing) a pointer that has been changed since it was allocated. For example, the following code will cause problems:
  ```
  p = new int[10];// allocate an array of 10 integers
  p++;                       // change the pointer to point at the second integer
  delete p;        // error, not array delete (delete[]) and  pointer changed
  ```

A review of potential problems in C++ was published by Perara [60]. The headings from that paper are as follows:

- Don't rely on the order of initialization of globals

- Avoid variable-length argument lists

- Don't return non-constant references to private data

- Remember 'The Big Three'

- Make destructors virtual

- Remember to de-allocate arrays correctly

- Avoid type-switching

- Be careful with constructor initialization lists

- Stick to consistent overloading semantics

- Be aware of the lifetimes of temporaries

- Look out for implicit construction

- Avoid old-style casts

- Don't throw caution to the wind exiting a process

- Don't violate the 'Substitution Principle'

- Remember there are exceptions to every rule.

A detailed discussion is provided on each point, in that reference.

11.1.4.5   *C# Language*

C# is a new language created by Microsoft . C# is loosely based on C/C++, and bears a striking similarity to Java in many ways. Microsoft describes C# as follows:

> "C# is a simple, modern, object oriented, and type-safe programming language derived from C and C++. C# (pronounced 'C sharp') is firmly planted in the C and C++ family tree of languages, and will immediately be familiar to C and C++ programmers. C# aims to combine the high productivity of Visual Basic and the raw power of C++."

C# has been created as part of Microsoft's .NET environment, and is primarily designed for it. Any execution environment will have to support aspects that are specific to the Microsoft platform. Since they must support the Win32 API, C# may be restricted to Win32 machines. However, at least one company is considering porting C# to Linux.

C# has the following features:

- Exceptions

- References can be null (not referencing a real object). C# throws an exception if the reference is accessed.

- Garbage collection. You CAN'T delete memory, once it is allocated!

- Array bounds checking (throws an exception)

- Like Java, machine-independent code which runs in a managed execution environment (like the JVM)

- No pointers, except in routines marked **unsafe**

- Multi-dimensioned arrays

- Switch statements do not allow "fall through" to next case.

- Thread support, including locking of shared resources

- No global variables

- All dynamically allocated variables initialized before use.

- The compiler produces warnings if using uninitialized local variable.

- Overflow checking of arithmetic operations (which can be turned off if needed)

- "foreach" loop – simpler way to do a *for* loop on an array or string. This decreases the chance of going out of bounds, because the compiler determines how often to loop, not the programmer.

- Everything is "derived" from the base class (system class). This means that integers, for example, have access to all the methods of the base class. The following code in C# would convert an integer to a string and write it on the console:

  ```
  int i = 5;
  System.Console.WriteLine (i.ToString());
  ```

- Has a goto statement but it may only point anywhere within its scope, which restricts it to the same function or *finally* block, if it is declared within one. It may not jump into a loop statement which it is not within, and it cannot leave a *try* block before the enclosing finally block(s) are executed.

- Pointer arithmetic can be performed in C# within methods marked with the **unsafe** modifier.

- "Internet" oriented (like Java)

The following features are of concern in embedded or safety environments:

- Garbage collection can lead to non-deterministic timing. It is a problem in real-time systems.

- Portability: C# is currently only designed to work on Microsoft Windows systems.

- Speed: C# is an interpreted language, like Java. Unlike Java, there is currently no compiler that will produce native code.

11.1.4.6   *Forth Language*

The Forth language was developed in the 1960's by Charles Moore. He wanted a language that would make his work of controlling telescopes both easier and more productive.

Forth is "stack based" – the language is based on **numbers** and **words**. Numbers are pushed on the stack. Words are "executed" on the stack numbers, and are essentially functions. Words are kept in a Forth dictionary. The programmer can create new words (new functions), usually using existing words.

Forth uses reverse polish notation. The last number pushed on the stack is the first off it. A simple Forth statement to add 3 and 4 is: **3 4 +** (pushes 3, then pushes 4, + pops the top two numbers off the stack and adds them, then pushes the result onto the stack.). In this case, + is a built-in word (function).

Forth has the benefits of "higher level" language (like C), but it is also very efficient (memory and speed-wise). It is used mainly in embedded systems. Forth can be used as the Operating System (OS) as well, and it often is in small embedded microcontrollers.

Forth has no "safety" features. The programmer can do just about anything! It is very similar to C and assembly language this way. The flexibility and speed it gives must be balanced with the need to rigorously enforce coding standards, and to inspect the safety-critical code.

The Forth programmer must know where each parameter or variable is on the stack, and what type it is. This can lead to errors, if the type or location is incorrectly understood.

One positive aspect of Forth, from a safety standpoint, is that it is very easy to unit test. Each "word" is a unit and can be thoroughly tested, prior to integration into larger "words". There is work on applying formal methods to Forth.

The following quote is from Philip J. Koopman Jr.[9] The italics are added to emphasize particular aspects of concern to programming a safe system.

"Good Forth programmers strive to write programs containing very short (often one-line), well-named word definitions and reused factored code segments. The ability to pick just the right name for a word is a prized talent. Factoring is so important that it is common for a Forth program to have more subroutine calls than stack operations. Factoring also simplifies speed optimization via replacing commonly used factors with assembly language definitions….

Forth programmers traditionally value complete understanding and control over the machine and their programming environment. Therefore, what *Forth compilers don't* do reveals something about the language and its use. *Type checking,* macro preprocessing, common subexpression elimination, and other traditional compiler services are feasible, but usually not included in Forth compilers. ….

Forth supports extremely flexible and productive application development while making ultimate control of both the language and hardware easily attainable."

---

[9] Philip J. Koopman Jr. by permission of the Association for Computing Machinery; **A Brief Introduction to Forth**; This description is copyright 1993 by ACM, and was developed for the Second History of Programming Languages Conference (HOPL-II), Boston MA.   koopman@cmu.edu

11.1.4.7   FORTRAN Language

FORTRAN was developed in the 1950's by IBM, and first standardized in the 1960's, as FORTRAN 611. It is primarily a **numerical processing** language, great for number crunching. FORTRAN has gone through several standards since the 1960's. The versions of the language considered here are FORTRAN 77 and Fortran 90.

While not usually used in embedded systems, FORTRAN can still be used in a safety-critical system (or a part of the system), if the numerical results are used in safety decisions.

FORTRAN 77 is a structured, procedural language. It contains all the elements of a high level language (looping, conditionals, arrays, subroutines and functions, globals, independent compilation of modules, and input/output (formatted, unformatted, and file)). In addition, it has complex numbers, which are not part of the other languages considered here. There is **no** dynamic memory (allocate, deallocate) in FORTRAN 77.

Elements of FORTRAN 77 related to safety

- **Weak data typing.** The data type of a variable can be assumed, depending on the first letter of the name, if it is not explicitly defined.

- **GOTO statements**. The programmer can jump anywhere in the program.

- **Fixed-form source input.** This relates to safety only in that it can look OK (in an inspection) and be wrong (incorrect column). However, the compiler should prevent this problem from occurring.

- **Limited size variable names.** The length of the variable name was limited to 8 characters. This prevented using realistic names that described the variable. Programmers often used cryptic names that made understanding and maintaining the program difficult.

- **Lack of dynamic memory.** This prevents the problems related to dynamic memory, though it limits the language for certain applications.

- **The EQUIVALENCE statement** should be avoided, except with the project manager's permission. This statement is responsible for many questionable practices in Fortran giving both reliability and readability problems.[10]

- **Use of the ENTRY statement.** This statement is responsible for unpredictable behavior in a number of compilers. For example, the relationship between dummy arguments specified in the SUBROUTINE or FUNCTION statement and in the ENTRY statements leads to a number of dangerous practices which often defeat even symbolic debuggers.*

- **Use of COMMON blocks.** COMMON is a dangerous statement. It is contrary to modern information hiding techniques and if used freely, can rapidly destroy the maintainability of a package.

- Array bounds checking is not done dynamically (at run time), though compilers may have a switch that allows it at compile time.

---

[10] These elements were extracted from Appendix A of Hatton, L. (1992) "Fortran, C or C++ for geophysical software development", Journal of Seismic Exploration, 1, p77-92.

Fortran 90 is an updated version of FORTRAN 77 that provides rudimentary support for Object Oriented programming, and other features. Fortran 90 includes:

- **Dynamic memory allocation**, specifically allocatable pointers and arrays.

- **Rudimentary support for OOP.** Inheritance is not supported. Constructors simply initialize the data members. There are no destructors. It does have derived types and operator overloading.

- **Rudimentary pointers.** A FORTRAN pointer is more of an alias (reference) than a C-style pointer. It cannot point to arbitrary locations in memory or be used with an incorrect data type. Variables that will be pointed to must declare themselves as TARGETs.

- **Free-style format and longer variable names** (31 characters). These increase readability of the code.

- **Improved array operations**, including operating on a subsection of the array and array notation (e.g. X(1:N)). Statements like A=0 and C=A+B are now valid when A and B are arrays. Also, arrays are actually array objects which contain not only the data itself, but information about their size. There is also a built-in function for matrix multiplication (matmul).

- **Better function declarations (prototyping).**

- **Modern control structures** (SELECT CASE, EXIT, ...)

- **User defined data types (modules).** Like *struct* in C, or *record* in Pascal.

- **Recursive functions** are now a part of the language.

Problems with Fortran 90:

- Order of evaluation in **if** statements (if (a and b)) is undefined. A compiler can evaluate *b* first, or *a* first. So the statement "if (present(a) .and. a)" could cause a problem, if the compiler evaluates '*a*' (right side) first, and '*a*' doesn't exist. Do not rely on order of evaluation in if statements.

- Allocatable arrays open the door to memory leakage (not deallocating when done) and accessing the array after it has been deallocated.

- Implicit variables are still part of the language. Some compilers support the extension of declaring IMPLICIT NONE, which forces the data type to be declared.

11.1.4.8   *Java Language*

Java was created by Sun Microsystems in 1995, with the first development kit (JDK 1.0) released in January, 1996. Since then, Java has become a widespread language, particularly in internet applications. Java is used in embedded web systems as the front end (usually GUI) for other embedded systems, and for data distribution or networking systems, among many other applications.

Java was created to be platform independent. Java programs are not normally compiled down to the machine code level. They compile to "byte code", which can then be run on Java Virtual

Machines (JVM). The JVM's contain the machine-specific coding. When a Java program is run, the JVM interprets the byte code. This interpreted mode is usually slower than traditional program execution. In addition, timing will not be deterministic.

Work is in process to create Java specifications for real-time, embedded systems. In December, 1998, the Java Real-Time Expert Group was formed to create a specification for extensions to Java platforms that add capabilities to support real-time programming in Java and to support the adoption of new methodologies as they enter into practice. The group has focused on new APIs, language, and virtual machine semantics in six key areas (the Java thread model, synchronization, memory management, responding to external stimuli, providing accurate timing, and asynchronous transfer of control). JSR-000001, Real-time Specification for Java, was released in June, 2000.

Compilers for Java programs do exist. They compile the program down to the machine level. This decreases the portability and removes the platform independence, but allows an increase in execution speed and a decrease in program size. Compiled Java programs do not need a Java Virtual Machine (JVM).

Java has the following features:

- Fully Object Oriented. This has the plusses of reusability and encapsulation

- Dynamic loading of new classes, and object and thread creation at runtime.

- No pointers allowed! No pointer arithmetic and other pointer problems common in C. However, objects can be accessed through references.

- Garbage collection to free unused memory. The programmer doesn't have to remember to delete the memory.

- Support for threads, including synchronization primitives.

- Support for distributed systems.

- No goto statement, though labeled break and continue statements are allowed.

- Allows implicit promotion (int to float, etc.), but conversion to lower type needs explicit cast

- Variables initialized to known values (including references)

- Allows recursion

- Checks array bounds and references to null

- Java's document comments (//*) and standard documentation conventions aid in readability.

- Type safe (compile variable and run-time types must match)

- No operator overloading

- Built-in GUI, with support for events

- Built-in security features (language limits uncontrolled system access, bytecode verification is implemented at run-time, distinguishes between trusted and untrusted (foreign) classes, and restricts changing of resources. Packages – downloaded code can be distinguished from local) However, still not secure. Ways to circumvent are found, and "bug fixes" are released

- Java automatically generates specifications (prototypes) (as opposed to using redundant specifications).

Java has these limitations:

- can't interface to hardware; must use native methods of another language to do so.

- Uses a Java Virtual Machine, which must be tested or certified, unless compiled to native code.

- Garbage collection to free unused memory can't be turned off! This affects determinism in real-time systems.

- Selfish threads (those that do not call sleep()), on some OS's, can hog the entire application. Threads can interfere with each other if using the same object. Synchronization makes the thread not be interrupted until done, but deadlock can still occur.

- Doesn't detect "out of range" values (such as integer multiplication leading to an integer value that is too large).

- When passing arguments to functions, all objects, including arrays, are call-by-reference. This means that the function can change them!

- Java is an interpreted language, which is often slower than a compiled language. Compilers are available, however, which will get around this problem.

- Non-deterministic timing. Real-time extensions are being worked on, but they are not standardized yet.

- The Java language has not been standardized by a major standards group. It is in the control of Sun Microsystems.

11.1.4.9 LabVIEW

LabVIEW is a graphical programming language produced by National Instruments. It is used to control instrumentation, usually in a laboratory setting. LabVIEW allows the user to display values from hardware (temperatures, voltages, etc.), to control the hardware, and to do some processing on the data. It is primarily used in "ground stations" that support hardware (such as space flight instruments). The LabVIEW "code" will be considered safety-critical if the "ground station" it supports is safety-critical. In addition, it has been used to support infrastructures (e.g. wind tunnel) that have safety-critical aspects, as well as small flight experiments.

The use of LabVIEW in safety-critical systems is possible, but several factors make it undesirable. The operating system LabVIEW runs on (such as Windows NT) and LabVIEW itself may not be deterministic. There is no "source code" to inspect, so the correct translation from graphical display to executable can only be verified via test. There is no way to partition safety-critical software components from the rest of the LabVIEW program. Testing LabVIEW programs for unexpected interactions among program elements is not a well understood process. For these reasons, LabVIEW should only be used for the non-critical portions of the software, or adequate hardware controls should be in place.

In LabVIEW, the method by which code is constructed and saved is unique. There is no text based code as such, but a diagrammatic view of how the data flows through the program. LabVIEW is a tool of the scientist and engineer (who are not always proficient programmers) who can often visualize data flow, but are unsure of how to convert that into a conventional programming language. Also, LabVIEW's graphical structure allows programs to be built quickly.

Data flow is the fundamental tenet by which LabVIEW code is written. The basic philosophy is that the passage of data through nodes within the program determines the order of execution of the functions of the program. LabVIEW VI's (Virtual Instruments) have inputs, process data and produce outputs. By chaining together VI's that have common inputs and outputs it is possible to arrange the functions in the order by which the programmer wants the data to be manipulated.

LabVIEW development is supported by Windows 9x/2000/NT, Macintosh, PowerMax OS, Solaris, HP-Unix, Sun, Linux, and Pharlap RTOS (Real-Time Operating System). Executables can be compiled under their respective development systems to run on these platforms (native code). Code developed under one platform can be ported to any of the others, recompiled and run.

LabVIEW has rich data structures (For and While loops, Shift registers, Sequencing, and Arrays and clusters). It supports polymorphism and compound arithmetic. Display types include Indicators, Graphs and charts, and Instrument simulation. Strings and file handling are included in LabVIEW. Many debugging techniques, such as breakpoints, single stepping, and probes, are supported.

A real-time version of LabVIEW (LabVIEW-RT) exists for embedded processors.

Though you can't "pop the hood" of LabVIEW and review the source code, formal inspections can be performed on the graphical layout (Virtual Instrument files). Thorough analysis and testing are highly recommended if LabVIEW is used in safety-critical systems.

11.1.4.10   *Pascal Language*

The Pascal language was originally designed in 1971 by Niklaus Wirth, professor at the Polytechnic of Zurich, Switzerland. Pascal was designed as a simplified version for educational purposes of the language Algol, which dates from 1960. The Pascal language was has been used as a tool to teach structured programming. While there is still a strong subset of Pascal advocates, the language is not commonly used anymore.

The original Pascal standard is ISO 7185 : 1990. The Extended Pascal standard was completed in 1989 and is a superset of ISO 7185. The Extended Pascal standard is ANSI/IEEE 770X3.160-1989 and ISO/IEC 10206 : 1991. Object Oriented Pascal was released as a Technical Report by ANSI in 1993. Object Pascal is the language used with the Delphi Rapid Applications Development (RAD) system.

SPADE Pascal[11] is a subset that has undergone the study and verification necessary for safety-critical applications. The major issue with Pascal is that no provision for exception handling is provided. However, if a user employs a good static code analysis tool, the question of overflow in integer arithmetic can be addressed and fixed without needing exception handlers. The SPADE Pascal subset is suited to safety-critical applications.

11.1.4.11 *Visual Basic*

Visual Basic is a Microsoft version of the Basic language for use with Windows operating systems. It is oriented toward GUIs (Graphical User Interfaces), and is proprietary. However, because Visual Basic is easy to use, many programs that will run under Windows use it as the user interface, and some other language for the "meat" of the program. Visual Basic is a Rapid Application Development (RAD) tool, like Delphi (which uses Pascal).

Visual Basic is being used within programs that provide command and control interfaces to hardware instrumentation. For example, the program that an astronaut will run on a standard laptop to control a particular experiment will often be written in Visual Basic. Such software may include safety-critical elements if it can issue hazardous commands or if the displayed values are used in a safety-critical decision.

Features of Visual Basic:

- Strongly typed, if "type checking" is turned on; weakly typed if it is not! Variable types do not have to be declared. The older style of a type suffix on the end of the name (e.g. str$ for a string variable) is still allowed.

- Has a variant data type that can contain data in various formats (numerical, string, etc.). Use of this data type subverts the attempt to enforce strong data typing.

- Component based and not true Object Oriented. A component is a binary package with a polymorphic interface. Other components in the system depend upon nothing but the interface. The underlying implementation can be completely changed, without affecting any other component in the system, and without forcing a re-link of the system. Inheritance is not supported in VB.

- Interpreted environment. The Visual Basic environment checks the syntax of each line of code as you type it in, and highlights these errors as soon as you hit the enter key. Compilers are now available for VB, which speeds up program execution speed.

- Trapping. Visual Basic lets the programmer catch runtime errors. It is possible to recover from these errors and continue program execution.

- The code is hidden from the programmer. This is a strength of Visual Basic, as it makes programming much easier (graphical, drag-and-drop). However, the code is very difficult to inspect, unless the inspectors are intimately knowledgeable about Microsoft Windows and Visual Basic. In many ways, Visual Basic is an automatic code generating program.

---

[11] SPADE PASCAL is a commercially available product and is used here only as an example to illustrate a technical point.

11.1.5 Miscellaneous Problems Present in Most Languages

The following quotations were taken from the Imperial College, London, UK, world wide web home page "The Free On-Line Dictionary of Computing" Copyright Denis Howe 1993-1999, (http://foldoc.doc.ic.ac.uk/foldoc/index.html).[110] It contains graphic descriptions of common problems.

- **aliasing bug**

  <programming> (Or "stale pointer bug") A class of subtle programming errors that can arise in code that does dynamic allocation, especially via malloc or equivalent. If several pointers address (are "aliases for") a given hunk of storage, it may happen that the storage is freed or reallocated (and thus moved) through one alias and then referenced through another, which may lead to subtle (and possibly intermittent) lossage depending on the state and the allocation history of the malloc arena. This bug can be avoided by never creating aliases for allocated memory. Use of a higher-level language, such as Lisp, which employs a garbage collector is an option. However, garbage collection is not generally recommended for real-time systems.

  Though this term is nowadays associated with C programming, it was already in use in a very similar sense in the ALGOL 60 and FORTRAN communities in the 1960s.

- **spam**

  <jargon, programming> To crash a program by overrunning a fixed-size buffer with excessively large input data.

- **heisenbug**

  <jargon> /hi:'zen-buhg/ (From Heisenberg's Uncertainty Principle in quantum physics) A bug that disappears or alters its behaviour when one attempts to probe or isolate it. (This usage is not even particularly fanciful; the use of a debugger sometimes alters a program's operating environment significantly enough that buggy code, such as that which relies on the values of uninitialized memory, behaves quite differently.)

  In C, nine out of ten heisenbugs result from uninitialized auto variables, fandango on core phenomena (especially lossage related to corruption of the malloc arena) or errors that smash the stack.

- **Bohr bug**

  <jargon, programming> /bohr buhg/ (From Quantum physics) A repeatable bug; one that manifests reliably under a possibly unknown but well-defined set of conditions.

- **mandelbug**

  <jargon, programming> /man'del-buhg/ (From the Mandelbrot set) A bug whose underlying causes are so complex and obscure as to make its behaviour appear chaotic or even nondeterministic. This term implies that the speaker thinks it is a Bohr bug, rather than a heisenbug.

- **schroedinbug**

  <jargon, programming> /shroh'din-buhg/ (MIT, from the Schroedinger's Cat thought-experiment in quantum physics). A design or implementation bug in a program that

doesn't manifest until someone reading source or using the program in an unusual way notices that it never should have worked, at which point the program promptly stops working for everybody until fixed. Though (like bit rot) this sounds impossible, it happens; some programs have harboured latent schroedinbugs for years.

- **bit rot**

(Or bit decay). Hypothetical disease the existence of which has been deduced from the observation that unused programs or features will often stop working after sufficient time has passed, even if "nothing has changed". The theory explains that bits decay as if they were radioactive. As time passes, the contents of a file or the code in a program will become increasingly garbled.

There actually are physical processes that produce such effects (alpha particles generated by trace radionuclides in ceramic chip packages, for example, can change the contents of a computer memory unpredictably, and various kinds of subtle media failures can corrupt files in mass storage), but they are quite rare (and computers are built with error-detecting circuitry to compensate for them). The notion long favoured among hackers that cosmic rays are among the causes of such events turns out to be a myth; see the cosmic rays entry for details.

Bit rot is the notional cause of software rot.

- **software rot**

Term used to describe the tendency of software that has not been used in a while to lose; such failure may be semi-humourously ascribed to bit rot. More commonly, "software rot" strikes when a program's assumptions become out of date. If the design was insufficiently robust, this may cause it to fail in mysterious ways.

For example, owing to endemic shortsightedness in the design of COBOL programs, most will succumb to software rot when their 2-digit year counters wrap around at the beginning of the year 2000. Actually, related lossages often afflict centenarians who have to deal with computer software designed by unimaginative clods. One such incident became the focus of a minor public flap in 1990, when a gentleman born in 1889 applied for a driver's licence renewal in Raleigh, North Carolina. The new system refused to issue the card, probably because with 2-digit years the ages 101 and 1 cannot be distinguished.

Historical note: Software rot in an even funnier sense than the mythical one was a real problem on early research computers (eg. the R1). If a program that depended on a peculiar instruction hadn't been run in quite a while, the user might discover that the opcodes no longer did the same things they once did. ("Hey, so-and-so needs an instruction to do such-and-such. We can snarf this opcode, right? No one uses it.")

Another classic example of this sprang from the time an MIT hacker found a simple way to double the speed of the unconditional jump instruction on a PDP-6, so he patched the hardware. Unfortunately, this broke some fragile timing software in a music-playing program, throwing its output out of tune. This was fixed by adding a defensive initialization routine to compare the speed of a timing loop with the real-time clock; in other words, it figured out how fast the PDP-6 was that day, and corrected appropriately.

- **memory leak**

    An error in a program's dynamic store allocation logic that causes it to fail to reclaim discarded memory, leading to eventual collapse due to memory exhaustion. Also (especially at CMU) called core leak. These problems were severe on older machines with small, fixed-size address spaces, and special "leak detection" tools were commonly written to root them out.

    With the advent of virtual memory, it is unfortunately easier to be sloppy about wasting a bit of memory (although when you run out of virtual memory, it means you've got a *real* leak!).

- **memory smash**

    (XEROX PARC) Writing to the location addressed by a dangling pointer.

11.1.6 Programming Languages: Recommendations

The "safest" languages are Ada95 (and Ada83) and the SPARK Ada subset. Ada was specifically created with safety in mind. However, Ada is not the most popular language, and finding and keeping good Ada programmers can be difficult. This is one reason other languages are often chosen.

 Staffing issues and the effects of learning a new language on the project schedule need to be considered, as well as the technical merits of the language. A newly created language, or one that is not familiar to the software developers, will require training and extra development time. Some level of training should be given to Software Assurance and Software Safety, so that oversight of the development process can be adequately accomplished. New developers may need to be hired who have an expertise in the chosen language. The defect rates of developers using a newly-learned language are often higher, and will need to be compensated by extra reviews, inspections and tests. Often staying with a well-understood language is the best choice.

 If choosing a language other than Ada, especially C, assembly language, or Forth, be aware of the limitations. Create and enforce a coding standard. Devote extra time to inspections, analysis and test. Educate the developers on the "best" programming practices for that language, and on the pitfalls of the language chosen. Take a proactive approach to reducing errors up front, then test the stuffing out of the software!

11.2 Compilers, Editors, Debuggers, IDEs and other Tools

The minimal set of tools (programs) that a software developer needs is:

- **Editor** to create the software (source code) with.

- **Compiler** (or cross-compiler) to create object code with, from the source code.

- **Linker** to create an executable application from the object code.

- **Debugger** to find the location of defects in the software.

Often these tools come bundled in an **Integrated Development Environment (IDE)**, where the developer can shift from editing to compiling to linking to debugging, and back to editing, without leaving the programming environment. Many IDE's have additional tools, or have the ability to add in tools from other vendors. How well the tools can be integrated is something the developer should look at when choosing an IDE. In an embedded environment, the IDE can include simulators for the target hardware, the ability to download the software generated into the target hardware, and sophisticated debugging and monitoring capabilities.

 Some IDE's are designed for safety-critical software development. For example, DDC-I, a company that specialized in safety-critical software development and tools, has an IDE called SCORE (Safety-Critical Object-oriented Real-time Embedded). "The SCORE development environment has been designed to address the needs of safety-critical, real-time, embedded systems", according to their website.
http://www.ddci.com/products_SCORoot.shtml

Humans make mistakes, and programmers are only human (despite what some may claim). The goal of a tool is to find as many of the errors as quickly as possible. Some tools help enforce good programming practice. Others make life difficult for the programmer and lead to additional errors, because the programmer is annoyed or is actively subverting the intent of the tool!

In general, look for tools that are:

* Easy to learn.

* Well integrated (if in an IDE) or easy to integrate with other tools. Well integrated means that it is easy to switch between the different tools.

* Default to enforcing standards, rather than relying on the programmer to set the right switches

* Well documented. This includes not only documentation on how to use the tool, but limitations and problems with using the tool. Knowing what the tool *cannot* do is as important as what it *can* do.

A good article on choosing tools for embedded software development is "Choosing The Right Embedded Software Development Tools"[61]

Editors can be a simple text editor (such as Windows NotePad), a text editor designed for programmers (that handles indenting, etc.) or a sophisticated, graphical-interfaced editor. Whatever kind is chosen, look for these features:

✓ Can the "style" (such as indentation) be set to match that chosen for the project?

✓ Does the editor show language keywords and constructs (including comments) in a different way (e.g. various colors), to help the programmer catch errors such as mistyping a keyword or forgetting to close out a multi-line comment?

✓ What kinds of errors can the editor flag?

✓ Can the editor support multiple files and perform search and replace among all of them? Can a variable be tracked across multiple files?

Compilers and linkers usually come together as one piece of software. Cross-compilers run on one system (usually a desktop computer) and produce object code for another processor. When choosing a compiler, consider the following:

- Can warnings (possible problems) be treated as errors? Can this compiler switch be set as the default mode?

- Is there a list of defects (bugs) in the compiler? Is there a list of historical defects, and the versions or patches they were corrected in?

- Can the compiler produce assembly language output? What assembler program is the output targeted to?

- Does the compiler support integration with a debugging tool? Does it include the option of symbolic information, that allows the debugger to reference high-level language source code?

- Does the compiler (or cross-compiler) support the particular processor being used? Does it optimize for that processor? For example, if the software will run on a Pentium II, the compiler should optimize the code for that processor, and not treat it like an 80386.

- Does the compiler offer optimization options that allow you to choose size over speed (or vice versa), or no optimization at all?

- If used in an embedded system, does the compiler support packed bitmaps (mapping high-level structures to the hardware memory map), in-line assembly code, and writing interrupt handlers in the high-level language?

- How optimized is the run-time library that comes with the compiler? Can you use "stubs" to eliminate code you don't need? Is the source code available, so that unneeded code can be stripped out, or for formal verification or inspection?

Debuggers are a vital tool to finding errors, once the defects have reared their ugly little heads. Software debuggers run the defective software within the debugging environment. This can lead to some problems, if the problem is memory violations (out of bounds, etc.), since the debug environment and the normal runtime environment differ. Hardware debuggers (e.g. In-Circuit Emulators) run the code on a simulated processor, with the ability to stop and trace at any instruction.

Debuggers operate by stopping program execution at breakpoints. Breakpoints can be a particular instruction, a variable going to a specific value, or a combination of factors. Once the program is stopped, the environment can be interrogated. You can look at the values of variables, the stack, values in specific memory locations, for example. From the breakpoint, you can single-step through the program, watching what happens in the system, or run until the next breakpoint is triggered.

Debuggers usually need some symbolic information to be included in the object or executable code for them to be able to reference the source code. When debugging, you usually want to be able to see the source code, and not the assembly equivalent. The debugger, the compiler, and the linker must know how to talk to each other for this to happen.

When evaluating debuggers, consider the following:

- How well do the debugger and the compiler get along? Will they talk to each other?

- How much of the system will the debugger let you get at? Can you see memory locations, variable values, and the stack trace? Can you change what's in a memory location or variable?

- Does the debugger allow you to trace back through procedure calls?

- Can you trigger on multiple events simultaneously, such as a variable being set to a value while another variable is at a defined value? Can you stop at a memory location only if the value of a variable matches a preset condition?

- Does the debugger support debugging at the high level language, mixed high level and assembly language, and at the assembly language level?

- Can the debugger display the high-level data structures used?

In addition to "the basics", these tools are very useful in creating good (and safe) code:

* **Lint** – finds problems in the code that compilers might miss. Not everything is a true problem, but should be evaluated. If it's "non standard", treat it as an error!

* **Profiler** – checks speed of program. Good for finding routines that take the most time. Points to areas to where optimization may be useful.

* **Memory check programs** – find memory leaks, writing outside of bounds.

* **Locator** – needed for embedded environments, when you must separate what parts go in ROM (program) and what go in RAM (variables, stack, etc.)

11.3 CASE tools and Automatic Code Generation

11.3.1 Computer-Aided Software Engineering (CASE)

Computer-aided software engineering (CASE) is a collection of automated tools that support the process of software engineering. CASE can include:

- Structured Analysis (SA)
- Structured Design (SD)
- Code Generators
- Documentation Generators
- Defect Tracking
- Requirements Tracing
- Structured Discourse and Collaboration tools
- Integrated Project Support Environments (IPSEs)
- Inter-tool message systems
- Reverse Engineering
- Metric Generators and Analyzers.

Tools such as editors, compilers, debuggers, and Integrated Development Environments may technically be CASE tools, but are usually considered separately. Project management tools (scheduling and tracking) and Configuration Management (Release Management, Change Management (CM)) may also be considered CASE tools.

When CASE was first promoted in the 1980's, the quality of the tools provided was not very good. CASE tools did not cover enough of the software development cycle, did not integrate well with other tools, and were very expensive for what you actually got out of them. While CASE tools are still rather expensive, their quality, reliability, and interoperability have greatly improved. There are even efforts to produce free CASE tool suites.

CASE tools are now classified in three types that describe their functionality and usage. Upper CASE is used during the early phases of software development when initial design, data and process requirements, and the interface design are determined. Requirements analysis and traceability tools, and design tools are included in this classification. Lower CASE tools are primarily those that generate code from the design (output of the Upper CASE tools). These tools can also modify an existing application into a new application with minimal new programming. The third category is integrated CASE (I-CASE), which joins the Upper and Lower CASE tools and helps in the complete software development process.

CASE tools include:

- Analyzers for software plans, requirements and designs
- Methodology support (design, state charts, etc.)
- Model Analysis (consistency checking, behavior analysis, etc.)
- Source code static analyzers (auditors, complexity measurers, cross-referencing tools, size measurers, structure checkers, syntax and semantics analyzers)
- Requirements Tracing
- Design tools (UML modeling, etc.)
- Configuration Management
- System or Prototype simulators
- Requirements-based Test Case Generators
- Test Planning tools
- Test Preparation Tools (data extractors, test data generators)
- Test Execution Tools (dynamic analyzers-assertion analyzers, capture-replay tools, coverage and frequency analyzers, debuggers, emulators, network analyzers, performance and timing analyzers, run-time error checkers, simulators, test execution managers, validation suites)
- Test evaluators (comparators, data reducers and analyzers, defect or change trackers)
- Reengineering tools

11.3.2 Automatic Code Generation

Automatic code generation is one aspect of CASE. It has the advantages of allowing the software to be designed at a higher level then translated, without human error, into source code. The design becomes the "source code".

The downside to automatic code generation is that the tools are only now becoming mature. While human error is eliminated in the translation from design to code, tool error still exists. The correct translation from design to code must be verified for safety-critical software. Keep in mind that in some environments, the source code may not be accessible. In addition, how well the code is optimized may affect performance or size criteria.

Code can be automatically generated in several ways:

- Visual languages, such as LabVIEW, have the developer "design" the program graphically. The underlying source code is not visible (or accessible) to the programmer.

- Visual programming environments (e.g. Visual Basic) provide graphical programming, with access to the source code produced. Wizards automatically generate applications or parts of applications based on feedback about the desired features from the programmer. The wizards automatically generate code based on this feedback.

- Generating code from design models. These models usually use a set of diagrams that depict the structure, communication, and behavior of the system. The model may be supplemented with text-based specifications of system actions, such as computations. Design methodologies that can be used for code generation include the following. Not all tools or approaches will support all design modeling methodologies.

  - Unified Modeling Language (UML)

  - Object Modeling Technique (Rumbaugh)

  - Object-Oriented Software Engineering (Jacobson)

  - Object-Oriented Analysis and Design (Booch)

  - Specification and Description Language (SDL)

  - Real-time Object-Oriented Method (ROOM)

  - Object-Oriented Analysis (OOA – Shlaer and Mellor)

  - Harel's hierarchical statecharts

11.3.2.1   Visual Languages

A visual language is one that uses a visual syntax, such as pictures or forms, to express programs. Text can be part of a visual syntax as well. LabVIEW by National Instruments, VEE by Hewlett Packard, and PowerBuilder (Austin Software Foundry) are examples of visual languages.

Visual languages are wonderful for prototyping applications, especially when the user interface is important. The development can be "participatory", with the users and developers sitting down at a machine and designing the application interface together.

A problem with visual languages in safety-critical applications is the inability to inspect the "code". What happens between the graphical program creation and the operations of the program is a black box. In addition, little formal development is done when visual languages are used. Formal specifications are usually lacking or non-existent. Configuration control is often not considered, and configuration management tools may have problems with the visual representations ("language").

11.3.2.2   *Visual Programming Environments*

A visual programming environment (VPE) uses a visual representation of the software and allows developers to create software through managing and manipulating objects on a visual palette. Examples are Visual Basic (Visual C++, and other "visual" languages) and Delphi (by Borland).

A visual programming environment uses a graphical interface to allow the developer to construct the software. From the visual elements (often the user interface), code is generated in the appropriate language. The developer must hand-code the interactions between elements, and must hand-code all the "guts" of the program. This is very close to traditional programming, with the addition of easily creating graphical user interfaces. In fact, VPE's can be used to create "regular" programs without the fancy user interface, or to hand-code the user interface if desired.

Since VPE's produce source code, it can be formally inspected and analysis tools can be used with it. However, since the code was not generated by the developers, it may not follow the style or coding standards of the development team. The source code may be difficult to follow or understand, and its relationship back to the graphical environment may not always be obvious.

11.3.2.3   *Code Generation from Design Models*

Model-based code generation (see section 4.2.2.4) produces application source code automatically from graphical models (designs) of system behavior or architecture. One advantage of model-based development is to raise the level of abstraction at which developers can work. The design (model) becomes the program, and only the design has to be maintained. "Code Generation from Object Models" [62] discusses the various approaches to code generation for object-oriented systems, and gives some of the plusses and minuses of using each approach.

In many ways, the move to model-based code generation parallels the move from assembly to high-level languages. Each move along the path is a step up the abstraction ladder. Each step frees the developer from some of the gritty details of programming. However, each step also brings with it challenges in verifying that the program is safe!

The methodology and tools go hand in hand. Some tools support multiple design methodologies, some only support one. When choosing a methodology and/or tool, consider:

- The suitability of the modeling language for representing the problem. (How good is the modeling methodology for your particular problem?)

- The sufficiency of modeling constructs for generating code. (How much of the code can it generate, how much will have to be hand coded?)

- The maturity of translators for generating quality code. (Have the translators been used for years, or created yesterday? How much analysis has been done to verify the software that is produced by the translators?)

- Tools for development tasks related to code generation. (Does it integrate with the debugger?)

- Methodologies for employing code generation effectively. (What method does the tool use to translate your design into code?)

- The selection of tools and methods appropriate to the application. (What's the right method for the problem? What's the right tool for the development environment? Do they match (best tool works with best methodology)?)

- The language the tool produces source code in. (Is it Ada? C++?).

For object-oriented systems, there are three approaches to model-based code generation:

- The **Structural** approach is based on state machines. It can create an object framework from the model design. Dynamic behavior and object communication is added by the programmer (hand coded). This includes hard deadlines and interrupt handling. This approach is used with UML and the Rumbaugh, Jacobson, and Booch OO design techniques. Most tool vendors support this approach. The tools usually can be used to reverse engineer can be done on existing code as well.

- The **Behavioral** approach is based on state machines augmented with action specifications. It includes both static and dynamic behavior (state transitions). Specification and Description Language (SDL – a telecommunications standard) and UML, among other methods, support this approach. What needs to be hand coded are event handlers and performance optimizations. Developers must adopt a state-machine view of the system functionality in addition to an object view of the system structure. Because the behavior is fully specified, a simulated model for test and debug can be created prior to code completion.

- The **Translative** approach is based on application and architecture models that are independent of one another. The application model uses Object-Oriented Analysis (OOA) by Shlaer and Mellor. This approach can simulate the system before developing code (same as behavioral). The architecture model is a complete set of translation rules that map OOA constructs onto source code and implementation (run-time) mechanisms.

Some tools support other design methodologies. Structured analysis and design can be used to create code frames for the system structure. The frames have to be fleshed out by the developer, however. Also, data flow diagrams can be used by several tools. One tool can produce code for Digital Signal Processors (DSP). The code generated implements the flow of system. Processing steps are either hand-coded or standard library routines. Data flow diagrams are used in specific application tools for control systems, instruments (e.g. LabVIEW), and parallel data processing.

In an ideal world, the CASE tool would be certified to some standard, and the code generated by it would be accepted without review, in the same way that the object code produced by a compiler is often accepted. However, compilers produce errors in the object code. Automatically generated code is in its infancy. When the code is safety-critical, or resides in an unprotected partition with safety-critical code, the automatically generated code should be subjected to the same rigorous inspection, analysis, and test as hand-generated code.

11.4 Operating Systems

11.4.1 Types of operating systems

Operating Systems (OS) are the software that runs the programmers applications. The OS is loaded when the system boots up. It may automatically load the application program(s), or provide a prompt to the user. Examples of operating systems are MS-DOS, Windows 9x/NT/2000/XP, Macintosh OS X, and VxWorks.

Not all systems use an operating system. Small, embedded systems may load the application program directly. Or a simple "scheduler" program may take the place of the OS, loading the appropriate application (task) and switching between tasks.

The types of operating systems are:

- **No operating system.** Just a boot loader (BIOS) program that loads the application directly and gives it control. The application deals with the computer hardware (processor) as well as any attached hardware, directly. This is sometimes used in small, embedded systems.

- **Simple task scheduler.** Usually written by the software developer. Acts as a mini-OS, switching between different applications (tasks). No other OS services provided.

- **Embedded OS.** This will be a fully-functional operating system, designed with small systems in mind. It will take a minimal amount of storage space (both RAM and disk). It provides task switching, some method for inter-task communications, shared resources, and other basic OS functions.

- **Real-time Operating System.** An RTOS is usually designed for embedded systems (small size), but this is not necessary for it to be "real-time". An RTOS has timing constraints it must meet. If it cannot respond to events (interrupts, task switches, completing a calculation, etc.) within a specific time, then the result is **wrong**. "Soft" real-time systems have some flexibility in the timing. "Hard" real-time systems have no flexibility for critical deadlines.

- **"Regular" Operating System**s. These systems have no timing constraints and are designed for systems that do not have limited resources. Examples are the Windows variants that run on PCs, Linux, Macintosh's OS X, and main-frame operating systems.

11.4.2 Do I really need a real-time operating system (RTOS)?

If an operating system is selected for use in the safety-critical system, it will most likely be an RTOS. Even if the timing aspects aren't important, most non-real-time operating systems are not designed for safety-critical environments. What may be acceptable on your desktop (program freezes, frequent rebooting, or the blue screen of death) is not acceptable when safety is involved.

The first question to answer is: Do I need an operating system? Small projects often use just a "boot loader" to boot up the system and load an application program. "Get by without an RTOS" by Michael Melkonian [63] describes a method that provides most operating system functionality. For small projects, such a system may be the best option. It avoids the overhead of having to learn an RTOS. And since commercial operating systems are COTS software, they would require extra analysis and testing in a safety-critical application.

Once you determine that you need (or want) an operating system, the next question is: build, reuse, or buy? Do you create your own operating system, reuse an existing, proprietary one, or purchase a commercial OS? If you have an existing OS that was used in safety-critical applications before, or that has been thoroughly tested, it may be best to use that. Building your own OS is not an easy option. The advantage is that you can build in only what you need, eliminate options that might affect safety, and do formal development and/or thorough testing. For many systems, purchasing a commercial OS is the most cost-effective choice. This has the disadvantages associated with Off-The-Shelf software in general, but the advantages of time and money. The developers can spend time developing the applications, and not creating the operating system.

11.4.3 What to look for in an RTOS

What makes an OS a RTOS?

1. An RTOS (Real-Time Operating System) has to be multi-threaded and preemptible.

2. It must support a scheduling method that guarantees response time, especially to critical tasks.

3. Threads (tasks) must be able to be given a priority (static or dynamic). An alternative would be a deadline driven OS.

4. The OS has to support predictable thread synchronization mechanisms (semaphores, etc.)

5. A system of priority inheritance has to exist.

6. OS behavior should be known. This includes the interrupt latency (i.e. time from interrupt to task run), the maximum time it takes for every system call, and the maximum time the OS and drivers mask the interrupts. The developer also needs to know the system interrupt levels and device driver parameters (IRQ levels, maximum time within a device IRQ, etc.).

Every system is unique, and there is no simple universal set of criteria for selecting an operating system. Some commonly encountered issues to consider in the selection process are:

- **Memory management.** Operating systems which support a dedicated hardware MMU (Memory Management Unit) are superior from a safety viewpoint. An MMU guarantees protection of the designated memory space. In a multitasking application, it ensures the integrity of memory blocks dedicated to individual tasks by preventing tasks from writing into each others' memory space. It protects each task from errors such as bad pointers in other tasks. For small, single task systems (such as those running on a microcontroller), an MMU may not be needed. In such cases, even more than a minimal operating system may be overkill.

- **Determinism.** Determinism is the ability of the operating system to:

  o Meet deadlines

  o Minimize jitter, (i.e. variations in time stamping instants, the difference between the actual and believed time instant of a sample) o   Remain steady under dynamic occurrences, e.g. off nominal occurrences

o   Bounding of priority inversion (time the inversion is in place).

- **Priority inversion.** Priority inversion is a problem where a higher priority task is blocked by a low priority task that has exclusive access to a resource. The problem occurs when a medium priority task is running, preventing the low priority one from finishing and releasing the resource. Priority inheritance is a temporary state used to resolve priority conflicts. The low priority task is temporarily assigned a higher level priority to ensure its orderly completion prior to releasing a shared resource requested by the higher priority task. The priority change occurs when the higher priority task raises a "semaphore" flag. It is vital that the lower priority task releases its shared resource before delay of the higher priority task causes a system problem. The period of temporary increase of priority is called the "priority inheritance" time

- **Speed.** The context switching time is the most important speed issue for real-time operating systems. Context switching is how quickly a task can be saved, and the next task made ready to run. Other speed issues are the time it takes for a system call to complete.

- **Interrupt latency**. Interrupt latency is how fast an interrupt can be serviced.

- **Method of scheduling.** The method of scheduling can be predetermined logical sequences (verified by Rate Monotonic Analysis). It can be priority-based preemptive scheduling in a multitasking environment (such as UNIX, Windows NT or OS2). Another method is "Round Robin" time slice scheduling at the same priority for all tasks. "Cooperative" schedule can also be used, where the task keeps control until it completes, then relinquished control to the scheduler. Cooperative scheduling may not be a good idea in a safety-critical system, as a task can "hog" the processor, keeping the safety-critical code from running.

- **POSIX compliance(1003.1b/c).** POSIX compliance is a standard used by many operating systems to permit transportability of applications between different operating systems. For single use software, or software that will never be used on other operating systems, this is not as important.

- **Support for synchronization.** What support for synchronization and communication between tasks does the OS use? How much time does each method take?

- **Support for tools**. Does the OS have support for tools such as debuggers, ICE (In Circuit Emulation) and multi-processor debugging. Consider also the ease of use, cost and availability of tools.

- **Support for multiprocessors.** Does the OS support a multiprocessor configuration (multiple CPU's) if required.

- **Language used to create the OS.** Consider the language in which the operating system kernel is written, using the same criteria as selecting application programming languages.

- **Error handling in OS system calls.** How does the OS handle errors generated within system calls? What does the application need to check to verify that a system call operated correctly? Does the OS return an error code or can it access a user-created error handler?

- **Safety Certifications**. Some operating systems go through levels of safety-related certification, often for use in medical or aviation applications.

11.4.4 Commonly used Operating Systems

The following is a list of Operating Systems used in embedded or real-time systems. This is not a complete list, and no endorsement is meant by the ordering, inclusion, or exclusion of any OS. If the OS has been certified to any safety standard, that will be mentioned.

* VxWorks (Wind River Systems, http://www.windriver.com/) – This is a popular RTOS with a tool-rich integrated development environment. There is a version of VxWorks certified to DO-178B, a standard used for aviation software. VxWorks is available for most higher-level processors.

* OSE (http://www.enea.com) – This operating system is certified to the safety standard IEC 61508. It is also being certified to DO-178B. OSE also provides an integrated development environment with many tools useful to embedded or real-time applications. OSE supports many processors, including DSPs.

* PSOSystem 3 (http://www.windriver.com/products/psosystem_3/index.html)–This RTOS is now owned by Wind River. "pSOSystem™ 3 is a modular, high-performance, memory protected, highly reliable real-time operating system, designed specifically for embedded microprocessors" according to Wind River. pSOSystem supports the PowerPC and MIPS families of processors.

* QNX (http://www.qnx.com/) – This RTOS supports x86 (80386 and higher) processors only. It uses a microkernel with minimal required functionality that can be extended by dynamically plugging in service-providing processes. A free, non-commercial version is available for download and evaluation.

* CMX (http://www.cmx.com/) - CMX provides both a full-featured RTOS and a "tiny" one that runs on lower-level microcontrollers (with as little as 512 bytes of RAM). The RTOS supports a wide range of microprocessors.

* OS-9 (http://www.radisys.com/microware.cfm) – According to Microware, "OS-9® is a system-secure, fault-tolerant RTOS with high availability and reliability. Users can dynamically add and replace modules while the system is up and running." OS-9 supports many higher-level processors.

* AMX (http://www.kadak.com/) - This small, compact RTOS runs on x86, 68K family, Coldfire, ARM, PowerPC, and Z80 architectures. Depending on the processor, AMX can fit in 12K to 36K of ROM, with 2K to 4K of RAM needed. Besides the standard RTOS services, AMX claims rapid task context switching and fast interrupt response. Timing information is given on their website.

* LynxOS (http://www.lynuxworks.com/products/whatislos.html) - LynxOS is a Linux-compatible real-time operating system that "is a hard RTOS that combines performance, reliability, openness, and scalability together with patented technology for real-time event handling." It supports processors from Intel, Motorola, and MIPS.

* RTEMS (http://www.rtems.com/) – RTEMS is a free, open source operating system. It was originally developed for the U.S. Army Missile Command. It contains all the basics of an RTOS, and the source code is available. RTEMS supports most commonly used processors.

* Linux (http://www.linux.org and http://www.embedded-linux.org/) - Linux is the "open source" version of Unix. It is not normally a real-time operating system, but there are versions developed for embedded systems. In addition, there are extensions to Linux for real-time systems. Linux has been ported to many processors, though it is not usually available for the latest processors. You can "roll your own" version of Linux, creating a smaller system with only the elements you need.

* Windows NT/2000/XP (http://www.microsoft.com) - Windows NT (and its descendents, Windows 2000 and Windows XP) are general purpose operating systems that have many "real-time" abilities. Out of the box, neither are "hard" real-time systems, but several companies provide extensions that meet the "hard" timing criteria. Windows NT and 2000 are more robust than the desktop versions of Windows (95,98), with fewer memory leaks and greater memory protection.

* Windows CE (http://www.microsoft.com) - Microsoft describes Windows CE 3.0 as "the modular, real-time, embedded operating system for small footprint and mobile 32-bit intelligent and connected devices that enables rich applications and services.". It supports many 32-bit microprocessors. It contains many "real-time" aspects, such as task priority, priority inheritance, and nested interrupts. It is not "hard" real-time, however.

11.5 Distributed Computing

Having multiple processors working together may "share the load" of a complex calculation, or may distribute the appropriate part of a problem to a processor optimized for that particular calculation or control. Such "multi-brained" systems constitute a distributed computing system. Distributed systems can be defined as two or more independent processors, working together, and communicating across a medium that may have substantial transmission delays.

Distributed computing is used for many different purposes. For complex computational problems, parallel processors or clustered processors are used. Distributed computing is also used when high availability is required (continuing on if one processor has a hard failure).

Distributed systems may reside on the same processor board (multiprocessors), in the same system, or in widely separated areas. The processors in a distributed system usually use one of two main methods to communicate: shared memory or message passing. Shared memory systems have real or simulated RAM available to all the processors, and use this to communicate (pass values, signal use of resources, etc.). Shared memory is normally used in distributed systems that are physically compact (processors are near each other) and tightly coupled, such as multiprocessor systems.

Shared memory allows large or complex data structures to be easily communicated between processes. Issues with shared memory distributed systems are

* Data consistency. The consistency of the data in shared memory (accuracy at any given moment) is a problem because of network latency. Most processes will cache the shared memory to improve performance. The value in Process A's cache may be outdated,

because process B has updated it, but delays may lead the update information to arrive after A has read the value. Various scenarios are implement to prevent this.

- Access synchronization. Distributed systems must also provide ways to prevent multiple processes from accessing the shared data at the same time. Usually a locking mechanism is used.

- Address space structure. A system may use a single shared distributed address space, where all the processes appear as threads within this space. The advantage is that objects appear at the same addresses on all nodes. However, security and protection are a major problem in such systems. Another approach divides each process's address space into fixed regions, some of which are shared and the rest are private. Shared data may or may not appear at the same address in each process.

- Fault tolerance. Distributed shared memory systems have some problems with fault tolerance. Most systems ignore it or maintain that it is an operating system issue. If one node that is sharing data with other processes fails, all the connected sites may fail as well.

Message passing distributed systems communicate via a network, sending and receiving messages. Messages are blocks of data, usually wrapped in a protocol layer that contains information on the sender and recipient, time stamp, priority, and other parameters. A distributed system may pass messages synchronously or asynchronously. In synchronous message passing, the system has two phases: delivery and local computation. During the delivery phase, each process may send one or more messages to its immediate neighbors. The local computation phase encompasses receiving messages, state changes, and queuing messages to be sent during the next delivery phase.

Asynchronous message passing distributed system do not have phases where messages are transmitted. Any process can send or receive messages at any time. Propagation delays are arbitrary, though in real systems they are often bounded (given a maximum delay value).

The underlying network in a distributed system may or may not guarantee that all messages are eventually delivered to the correct recipient and that the messages will be without error or duplication.

A distributed computing system may be fixed (i.e. known processors and processes that never change, except for failure) or dynamic. In a dynamic system, new processes can be added to the network and other processes can leave at arbitrary times. The protocols (message passing, usually) must adapt to the changing topology.

Nodes (processes) in a distributed system can fail completely, intermittently (where the node operates correctly some of the time and at other times fails), or randomly (Byzantine). In the Byzantine failure mode, the node behaves arbitrarily, sending valid-looking messages inconsistent with the state it is in and the messages it has received. Failures can occur in the communications medium. Links between nodes can be broken. Intermittent problems may lead to the loss, garbling, reordering, or duplication of messages. Delays in message transfer may be interpreted as a lost message, or the data in the message, when it finally arrives, may be out of date. Breaking up software across (possibly) diverse multiple processors, communicating through some medium (serial line, network, etc.), creates a complex environment, full of potentially complex errors. Distributed systems have an *inherent* complexity resulting from the challenges of the latency of asynchronous communications, error recovery, service partitioning, and load balancing. Since distributed software is *concurrent* as well, it faces the possibility of race conditions, deadlock, and starvation problems. An excellent article that discusses the complexities of distributed computing is "Distributed Software Design: Challenges and Solutions" [64], which describes some problems inherent to distributed computing :

- **Processing site failures.** Each processor in a distributed system could fail. The developer must take this into account when building a fault-tolerant system. The failure must be detected, and the other processors must "pick up the slack", which may involve reallocating the functionality among the remaining processors or switching to another mode of operation with limited functionality.

- **Communication media failure (total loss, or loss between links).** If the communication medium goes down, one or more processors are isolated from the others. Depending on how they are programmed, they may undertake conflicting activities.

- **Communication media failure (intermittent).** Intermittent failures include loss of messages, reordering of messages or data (arriving in a different order than when sent), and duplicating messages. They do not imply a hardware failure.

- **Transmission delays.** A delayed message may be misconstrued as a lost message, if it does not arrive before a timeout expires. Variable delays (jitter) make it hard to specify a timeout value that is neither too long nor too short. Delayed messages may also contain out-of-date information, and could lead to miscalculations or undesirable behavior if the message is acted on.

- **Distributed agreement problems.** Synchronization between the various processors poses a problem for distributed systems. It is even more difficult when failures (intermittent or complete) are present in the system.

- **Impossibility result.** It has been formally proven that it is not possible to guarantee that two or more distributed sites will reach agreement in finite time over an asynchronous communication medium, if the medium between them is lossy or if one of the distributed sites can fail.

- **Heterogeneity.** The processors and software involved in a distributed system are likely to be very different from each other. Integration of these heterogeneous nodes can create difficulties.

- **System establishment.** A major problem is how distributed sites find and synchronize with each other.

More information on distributed computing problems and solutions can be found at:

- "Distributed Software Design: Challenges and Solutions" by Bran Selic, Embedded Systems Programming, Nov. 2000

- FINITE STATE MACHINES IN DISTRIBUTED SYSTEMS, Class 307. Speaker: Knut Odman, Telelogic

- Distrib. Syst. Eng. **3** (1996) 86–95. Printed in the UK, Implementing configuration management policies for distributed applications, Gerald Krause y and Martin Zimmermann

11.6 Programmable Logic Devices

Until recently, there was a reasonably clear distinction between hardware and software. Hardware was the pieces-parts: transistors, resistors, integrated circuits, etc. Software ran on the hardware (operating systems, applications programs) or resided *inside* the hardware (firmware). The design, construction, and testing process for hardware and software differed radically.

Programmable logic devices (PLDs) blur the lines between hardware and software. Circuitry is developed in a programming language (such as VHDL or Verilog), run on a simulator, compiled, and downloaded to the programmable device. While the resulting device is "hardware", the process of programming it is "software". Some versions of programmable devices can even be changed "on the fly" as they are running.

Programmable logic is loosely defined as a device with configurable logic and flip-flops, linked together with programmable interconnects. Memory cells control and define the function that the logic performs and how the logic functions are interconnected. PLDs come in a range of types and sizes, from Simple Programmable Logic Devices (SPLDs) to Field Programmable Gate Arrays (FPGAs).

System safety normally includes hardware (electronic) safety. However, given the hybrid nature of programmable logic devices, software safety personnel should be included in the verification of these devices. Because PLDs are hardware equivalents, they should be able to be verified (tested) in a normal "hardware" way. However, because they are programmed devices, unused or unexpected interconnections may exist within the device as a result of software errors. These "paths" may not be tested, but could cause problems if accidentally invoked (via an error condition, single event upset, or other method). As the PLDs become more complex, they cannot be fully and completely tested. As with software, the process used to develop the PLD code becomes important as a way to give confidence that the device was programmed properly.

The variety of programmable logic devices is described in the sections below. Guidance is given on the safety aspects of verifying each type of device.

"Frequently-Asked Questions (FAQ) About Programmable Logic" [65] provides good introductory information on PLDs. An article in Embedded Systems programming [66] also gives a good introduction.

11.6.1 Types of Programmable Logic Devices

Simple Programmable Logic Devices (SPLDs) are the "original" Programmable Logic Devices. These are the smallest of the PLDs – each can replace only a few logic chips. Inside a PLD is a set of macrocells, each of which are composed of some amount of logic (AND gate, for example) and a flip-flop. Each macrocell is fully connected. SPLD types include PAL (Programmable Array Logic), GAL (Generic Array Logic), PLA (Programmable Logic Array), and PLD (Programmable Logic Device).

Complex Programmable Logic Devices (CPLDs) have a higher capacity than the SPLDs, typically equivalent to 2 to 64 SPLDs. The macrocells within a CPLD may not be fully connected, so not all theoretically possible designs may be implementable in a particular CPLD. Varieties of CPLDs include EPLD (Erasable Programmable Logic Device), PEEL, EEPLD (Electrically-Erasable Programmable Logic Device) and MAX (Multiple Array matrix).

Field Programmable Gate Arrays (FPGAs) have an internal array of logic blocks, surrounded by a ring of programmable input/output blocks, connected together via programmable interconnects. These devices are more flexible than CPLDs, but may be slower for some applications because that flexibility leads to slightly longer delays within the logic.

11.6.2 "Program Once" Devices

"Program once" devices require an external programming mechanism and cannot be reprogrammed, once inserted on the electronics board. Included in this category are erasable-reprogrammable devices and "on-the-board" reprogrammable devices where the ability to reprogram is removed or not implemented, as well as true "write once" devices. Simple Programmable Logic Devices (SPLDs) nearly always are "program once". Depending on the underlying process technology used to create the devices, CPLDs and FPGAs may be "program once", "field reprogrammable", or fully configurable under operating conditions.

With "program once" devices, safety only needs to be concerned with the resulting final chip. Once the device is verified, it will not be changed during operations.

Simple Programmable Logic Devices (SPLDs) are fairly simple devices. Don't worry about the development process, just test as if they were "regular" electronic devices. Treat them as **hardware**.

Complex Programmable Logic Devices (CPLDs) and Field Programmable Gate Arrays (FPGAs) are complex enough that unexpected connections, unused but included logic, or other problems could be present. Besides a complete test program that exercises all the inputs/outputs of the devices, the software should be developed according to the same process used for regular software, tailored to the safety-criticality of the device or system. Requirements, design, code, and test processes should be planned, documented, and reviewed. For full safety effort, analyses should be performed on the documents from each stage of development.

11.6.3 "Reprogram in the Field" Devices

Both Complex Programmable Logic Devices (CPLDs) and Field Programmable Gate Arrays (FPGAs) come in a in-the-field-programmable variety. The internals of these devices is based on EEPROM (Electrically-Erasable Programmable Read Only Memory) and FLASH technology. If the circuitry is present on the board (and implemented within the chip), then these devices can be reprogrammed while on their electronics board. This is not "on-the-fly" reprogramming while in operation. Reprogramming erases what was there and totally replaces what was in the chip.

One scenario that might be used is to hook up the CPLD or FPGA "reprogramming" circuitry to an external port, such as a serial port. During development, an external computer (laptop, etc.) is connected to the port, and the device is reprogrammed. When no computer is connected, the device cannot be reprogrammed. This scenario allows for changes in the device during development or testing, without having to physically disassemble the instrument and remove the device from the electronics board.

Another scenario could be that a new CPLD or FPGA "program" is sent to a microprocessor in the system, which would then reprogram the CPLD or FPGA. The ability to do this would have to be included in the microprocessor's software, as well as the physical circuitry being present.

This scenario would allow the device to be reprogrammed in an environment where physical connection is impossible, such as in orbit around Earth.

When the device can only be reprogrammed by making a physical connection, it is relatively "safe" during operation. A software error in the main computer (processor) code, or a bad command sent by a human operator, is not going to lead to the unexpected reprogramming of the device. The main concern is that reprogramming invalidates all or most of the testing that has gone before. The later the reprogramming is done in the system development cycle, the riskier it is. A set of regression tests should be run whenever the device is reprogrammed, once the instrument is out of the development phase.

 If the device can be reprogrammed by an in-system processor, then the possibility exists that it could accidentally be reprogrammed. If the device is involved in a hazard control or can cause a hazardous condition, this could be very dangerous. The legitimate command to reprogram the device would be considered a hazardous command. Commanding in general would have to be looked at closely, and safeguards put in place to make sure the reprogramming is not accidentally commanded. Other checks should be put in place to make sure that software errors do not lead to the unintentional reprogramming of the device.

11.6.4 Configurable Computing

Some FPGAs (and CPLDs) use SRAM (Static RAM) technology inside. These SRAM-based devices are inherently re-programmable, even in-system. However, they require some form of external configuration memory source on power-up. The configuration memory holds the program that defines how each of the logic blocks functions, which I/O blocks are inputs and outputs, and how the blocks are interconnected together. The device either self-loads its configuration memory or an external processor downloads the memory into the device. The configuration time is typically less than 200 ms, depending on the device size and configuration method.

The ability to change the internal chip logic "on the fly" can be very useful in some applications, such as pattern matching, encryption, and high-speed computing. Configurable computing's key feature is the ability to perform computations in hardware to increase performance, while retaining much of the flexibility of a software solution. Applications that benefit the most from configurable computing solutions are those with extremely high I/O data rate requirements, repetitive operations on huge data sets, a large number of computational operations per input data point, or with a need to adapt quickly to a changing environment.

One strength of configurable computing machines (CCMs) is their inherent fault tolerance. By adding structures to detect faults, the hardware can be reconfigured to bypass the faults without having to shut down the instrument.

The downside of flexibility, however, is the difficulty in verifying the functionality and safety of a configurable system. When you can change the hardware in the middle of an operation, how do you assure its safety? That question has not been well addressed yet, as configurable computing is still a new concept. However, if your design uses CCMs, then consider very carefully how to test and verify them, as well as how to guard against internal and external errors or problems.

An article by Villasenor and Mangione-Smith [67] discusses various aspects of configurable computing.

11.6.5 Safety and Programmable Logic Devices

IEC 1131-3 is the international standard for programmable logic controller (PLC) programming languages. As such, it specifies the syntax, semantics and display for the following suite of PLC programming languages:

- Ladder diagram (LD)

- Sequential Function Charts (SFC)

- Function Block Diagram (FBD)

- Structured Text (ST)

- Instruction List (IL)

However, IEC 1131-3 does not address safety issues in programming PLCs. The SEMSPLC project was developed to address those issues. They have issued "SEMSPLC Guidelines: safety-related application software for programmable logic controllers" [68], available from the Institution of Electrical Engineers.

Language choice for the PLC should meet with the standard IEC 1131-3. Coding standards should be created. In addition, the language should conform to the following criteria, if possible:

- Closeness to application domain

- Definition and standardization

- Modular

- Readable and understandable

- Traceability

- Checkable

- Analyzable

- Deterministic

Standard software engineering practices should be used in the creation of PLC software. This includes requirements specification, design documentation, implementation, and rigorous testing. For safety-critical systems, Formal Inspections should be used on the products from the various stages, in particular on the requirements.

PLC development can be very formal, up to and including using Formal Methods. However, tailoring of many of the techniques for PLC development has not been done. This an emerging field that requires much more study, to determine the best development practices and the best safety verification techniques.

Besides the SEMSPLC guidelines [68], some general guidelines for better (and safer) PLC programming are:

- **Spaghetti code results in spaghetti logic.** Create a coding style or standard and stick to it. The better your code is, the faster or smaller the resulting logic will be!

* **Keep it under 85.** Don't use more than 85% of the available resources. This makes it easier to place-and-route the design and allows room for future additions or changes.

* **Modularize.** As much as possible, use modules in your PLC software. This helps avoid spaghetti code, and aids in testing and debugging.

* **Use black-and-white testing.** Use both black-box and white-box testing. Verify proper response to inputs (black-box), and also that all paths are executed (white-box), for example.

* **Research safety techniques for PLC application.** Work is being done to see which software engineering techniques are useful for PLC applications. Work by the SEMSPLC project has shown that control-flow analysis produces little information on the errors, but mutation analysis and symbolic execution have revealed a number of complex errors. [69]

11.7 Embedded Web Technology

Everything is connected to everything else...through the Internet, or so it seems. Once the realm of academics sharing research data and ideas, the Internet (and its multimedia child, the World Wide Web) is now the medium for information exchange, conversation, and connectivity.

From the Embedded Web Technology site at the NASA Glenn Research Center (http://vic.lerc.nasa.gov/): "Embedded Web Technology (EWT) is the application of software developed for the World Wide Web to embedded systems. Embedded systems contain computers, software, input sensors and output actuators all of which are dedicated to the control of a specific device. Examples of devices with embedded systems include cars, household appliances, industrial machinery, and NASA Space Experiments. EWT allows a user with a computer and Web browser to monitor and/or control a remote device with an embedded system over the Internet using a convenient, graphical user interface."

Many embedded devices are now including web servers and network hardware for communications with the outside world, instead of (or in addition to) serial or parallel ports. Some devices (Internet appliances) have no user interface hardware (keyboard, monitor). The user connects through any computer with a web browser to interact with the appliance. Embedded web servers allow remote access to the instrument (hardware) from nearly anywhere in the world.

Instruments can operate as distributed systems, with a central processor and various microcontrollers, communicating back and forth via a network. In the same way that multi-tasking operating systems "break up" the application software into various independent tasks, a distributed system "breaks up" the tasks and runs them on specialized or remote processors. A distributed instrument will have the same problems as described in Section 11.5 *Distributed Computing*.

11.7.1 Embedded Web Servers

Most web server software is designed for desktop systems, with a keyboard, monitor, file system, and large hard-disk. For embedded systems, the web server needs to be scaled down, as well as addressing some embedded-specific issues. Reduced memory footprint, increased efficiency and reliability, and source portability are important in the embedded world.

The requirements for an embedded web server include [70]:

* **Memory usage.** A small memory footprint (amount of memory used, including code, stack, and heap) is a very important requirement for an embedded web server. Memory fragmentation is also important, as frequently creating and destroying data (such as web pages) may create a myriad of tiny memory blocks that are useless when a larger memory block must be allocated. If the embedded software does not provide memory defragmentation, then embedded web servers should use only statically allocated or pre-allocated memory blocks.

* **Support for dynamic page generation.** Most of the HTML pages produced by embedded systems are generated on the fly. An embedded device will have only a few pages in memory and will often generate part or all of their content in real-time. The current status of the device, sensor values, or other information may be displayed on the dynamically generated page.

* **Software integration.** Without source code, integrating the web server with the embedded operating system and applications code may be difficult or impossible. When source code is available, ease of integration (and good documentation!) are still important factors to consider.

* **ROMable web pages.** Embedded systems without disk drives often store their data in ROM (or flash memory), sometimes within the executable file, and sometimes external to it. The ability to "pull out" an HTML file or other data from the executable, or find it on the flash disk, is lacking in most desktop-based web servers.

* **Portability.** Nothing stays the same in the embedded world. Technology changes fast, and the processor or operating system used today may be obsolete tomorrow. The ability to port the web server to different processors or operating systems is important for long-term usage.

11.7.2 Testing Techniques

Some aspects of standard web-site testing do not apply to embedded web servers. However, consider checking the following areas:

* **Load Handling Capacity.** What is the total data rate the server can provide? How many transactions per second can the server handle? Are these values in line with the expected usage? What happens when the limits are exceeded?

* **User Interface.** Even if the web pages are not meant for world-wide viewing, there is a customer or two who need to view the provided data. Review the generated web pages for clarity of communication (tone, language), accessibility (load time, easy to understand and follow links), consistency ("look and feel", repeating themes), navigation (links obvious in intent and destination, standard way to move between pages), design (page length, hyperlinks), and visual presentation (use of color, easy on the eyes).

* **Data age.** Is there a way to know how fresh the data is? Is the data time-tagged? When the data refreshes, does it show up on the web page?

* **Speed of page generation.** Since most pages are generated "on the fly" in embedded web servers, the speed at which they are constructed is important.

❖ **Can the user "break" the system?** Check all user-input elements on the web page (buttons, etc.). Try combinations of them, strange sequences, etc. to see if the user can create problems with the web server. If you have a colleague who seems to break his web client on a regular basis, put him to work testing your system.

❖ **Security testing.** If you will not be on a private network, test the security provision in your web server. Can an unauthorized user get into the system?

❖ **Link testing.** If you provide links between pages, make sure they are all operational.

❖ **HTML and XML validation.** Are the HTML and/or XML standard? Will it work with all the browsers expected to interface with the web server? All browser versions?

❖ **Control of instrumentation.** If the embedded server provides a way to control instrumentation, test this thoroughly. Look for problems that might develop from missed commands, out of sequence commands, or invalid commands.

❖ **Error handling.** Does the web page handle invalid input in a graceful way? Do any scripts used anticipate and handle errors without crashing? Are "run time" handlers included? Do they work?

Good sources for information on error handling and website testing are:

• "Handling and Avoiding Web Page Errors Part 1: The Basics" (and parts 2 and 3 as well) http://msdn.microsoft.com/workshop/author/script/weberrors.asp

• "WebSite Testing", http://www.soft.com/eValid/Technology/White.Papers/website.testing.html

11.8 AI and Autonomous Systems

Artificial Intelligence (AI) and Autonomous Systems reside on the "cutting edge" of software technology. They are two separate entities that, combined, have the potential to create systems that can operate in changing environments without human control. Space exploration, particularly in environments far from Earth, where human intervention would come far too late, is an ideal use for Intelligent Autonomous Systems.

Artificial Intelligence encompasses any system where the software must "think" like a human. This involves information gathering, information pattern recognition, planning, decision making, and execution of the decision. That's a lot for a software system to do! Various aspects of AI includes:

• **Game Playing.** Games such as chess or checkers.

• **Expert Systems**. Systems that capture a large body of information about a domain to answer a question posed to them. Diagnosing a disease based on symptoms is one example of an expert system.

• **Agents.** A computational entity which acts on behalf of other (most often human) entities in an autonomous fashion, performs its actions with proactivity and/or reactiveness and exhibits some level of learning, co-operation and mobility. For example, an agent may perform independent searches for information, on the Internet or other sources, based on subjects needed for an upcoming technical meeting you will be attending.

- **Natural Language**. Understanding and processing natural human languages.

- **Neural Networks.** Connecting the information "nodes" in ways similar to the connections within an animal brain. Neural nets "learn" with repetitive exercising.

- **Robotics.** Controlling machines that can "see" or "hear" (via sensors) and react to their environment and input stimuli. AI robots have a "thinking" capability, unlike factory robotics that perform specific functions as programmed.

Whereas several versions of AI can exist independent of "hardware" (e.g. on a desktop computer), autonomous systems almost always control real-world systems. A robot that operates without human intervention, except for the issuance of orders ("clean the first floor on Tuesday night, the second and third on Wednesday, …") is an example of an autonomous system. One definition for an autonomous system is "a combination of a computational core, sensors and motors, a finite store for energy, and a suited control allowing, roughly speaking, for flexible stand-alone operation."[71]

This section focuses on Intelligent Autonomous Systems that control hardware systems capable of causing hazards. As an immature technology, methods to design, code, test, and verify such systems are not well known or understood. The issue of assuring the safety of such systems is being researched, but the surface has barely been scratch. Hopefully, much more will be learned in the coming years about creating and verifying safety-critical Intelligent Autonomous Systems.

In the future, when you travel to Jupiter in cryogenic sleep, with an Intelligent Autonomous System operating the spacecraft and watching your vital signs, you want it to operate *correctly* and *safely*. HAL 9000 needed a bit more software verification!

11.8.1 Examples of Intelligent Autonomous Systems (IAS)

Intelligent spacecraft are one promising application of IAS. In the past, the on-board software had some "built-in intelligence" and autonomy in responding to problems, but planning for both the mission and any failures was performed by humans back on Earth. As we send probes out into the far reaches of the solar system, where communications lag time is measured in hours, having a spacecraft that can "think for itself" would be useful. Even for nearby objects, such as Mars, the communications lag time is enough to cause problems in a rover moving at speed over a varied terrain. Removing the "human" from the details of operation can increase the amount of science returned, as intelligent spacecraft and robots no longer have to wait for responses from Earth whenever a problem is encountered. The Deep Space 1 mission focused on technology validation, and contained an experiment in Intelligent Autonomous Systems. Called Remote Agent, it actually controlled the spacecraft for several days, responding to simulated faults. This experiment is described and discussed in Section 11.8.3 Case Study.

Back down to Earth, cleaning office buildings is a monotonous, dirty, dull and "low-esteem" task that does not use the higher faculties of human intelligence. Intelligent mobile cleaning robots are currently under development to automate the process [72], moving humans from "grunts" to supervisors.

"Fly-by-wire" aircraft systems have replaced hydraulic control of the aircraft with computer control (via wire to electromechanical hardware that moves the parts or surfaces). The computer keeps the aircraft stable and provides smoother motions than would be possible with a strictly mechanical system. Computers also provide information to the pilots, in the form of maps, trajectories, and aircraft status, among other items.

At this time, most of the fly-by-wire systems are not *intelligent*. Humans still direct the systems, and usually have overrides if the system misbehaves. However, the trend is to move the human pilot farther from direct control of the aircraft, leaving the details to the computerized system. At some time in the future, fly-by-wire computers could control nearly all aircraft functions, with the pilot providing guidance (where the plan should go) and oversight in the case of a malfunction.

Despite the fact that software used in aircraft is subjected to a stringent development process and thorough testing, an increasing number of accidents have "computer problems" as a contributing factor. In some cases, the computer displayed inaccurate information, which misled the flight crew. In others, the interface between the pilot and software was not well designed, leading to mistakes when under pressure. This points to the increased likelihood of aircraft accidents as computers and software become the "pilots". Finding reliable methods for creating and verifying safe software must become a priority.

The Intelligent Transportation System (ITS) is being researched and developed under the direction of the US Department of Transportation (http://www.its.dot.gov/). Major elements of ITS include:

- Advanced Traffic Management Systems (ATMS) which monitor traffic flow and provide decision support to reduce congestion on highways.

- Advanced Traveler Information Systems (ATIS) which provide travelers with directions, route assistance and real-time information on route conditions.

- Automated Highway Systems (AHS) which support and replace human functions in the driving process

- Intelligent Vehicle Initiative (IVI) which focuses efforts on developing vehicles with automated components

- Advanced commercial vehicle Systems (ACS) which provide support for commercial vehicle operations including logistics.

Software safety will obviously be important in developing ITS, though information on how it will be implemented has been difficult to come by. The DOT document on Software Acquisition for the ITS, which consists of over 250 pages, devotes only 4 pages to Software Safety issues.

11.8.2 Problems and Concerns

Like distributed systems and other complex software technologies, verifying the safety of Intelligent Autonomous Systems poses a large problem. Remember that for NASA, safety means more than just injury or death. Safety refers to the vehicle and payload as well. So even though no one can be killed by your space probe, loss of the probe would be a safety issue!

The complex interactions that occur between hardware and software must be considered for Intelligent Autonomous Systems, as for any software that controls hardware. In addition, the choices made by the software (plans and decisions based on past performance, current hardware status, and desired goals) form a subset of millions of possible "paths" the system may take. If that subset was known, it could be thoroughly tested, if not formally verified. The number of paths, and the complexities of the interactions between various software modules and the hardware, make complete testing or formal verification essentially impossible.

Various areas of concern with Intelligent Autonomous Systems (IAS) are:

- **Technology is more complicated and less mature.** Intelligent Autonomous Systems are new, and therefore not mature, software technology.

- **Sensitivity to the environment or context.** Traditional flight software (and other complicated embedded software) was designed to be *independent* of the system environment or software context. When a command was received, it was executed, regardless of what the spacecraft was doing at the time (but within the safety and fault tolerance checks). Whether or not the command made sense was the responsibilities of the humans who sent it. An IAS, on the other hand, must know what the environment and system context are when it generates a command. It must create a command appropriate to the system state, external environment, and software context.

- **Increased Subsystem interactions.** Traditional software systems strive for minimal interactions between subsystems. That allows each subsystem to be tested independently, with only a minimal "integrated" system testing. IAS subsystems, however, interact in multiple and complicated ways. This increases the number of system tests that must be performed to verify the system.

- **Complexity.** Intelligent Autonomous Systems are complex software. Increased complexity means increased errors at all levels of development – specification, design, coding, and testing.

New software technology often stresses the ability of traditional verification and validation techniques to adequately authenticate the system. You can't formally specify and verify the system without tremendous effort, you cannot test every interaction, and there is no way to know for certain that every possible failure has been identified and tested!

The state-of-the-art for Intelligent Autonomous System (IAS) verification has focused on two areas: Testing (primarily) and Formal Verification (Model Checking). Simmons, et. al. [73] discuss using model checking for one subset of IAS - application-specific programs written in a specialized, highly-abstracted language, such as used by Remote Agent. The application programs are verified for *internal* correctness only, which includes checks for liveness, safety, etc.

Testing issues with Remote Agent are discussed in 11.8.3.2. An additional testing strategy is described by Reinholtz and Patel [74]. They propose a four-pronged strategy, starting with *formal specifications* of correct system behavior. The software is tested against this specification, to verify correct operations. Transition zones (areas of change and interaction among the subsystems) are *identified* and *explored* to locate incorrect behavior. The fourth element of the strategy is to *manage risk* over the whole lifecycle.

11.8.3 Case Study – Remote Agent on Deep Space 1

Remote Agent is an experiment in Intelligent Autonomous Systems. It was part of the NASA Deep Space 1 (DS-1) mission. The experiment was designed to answer the question "Can a spacecraft function on its own nearly 120 million kilometers from Earth, without detailed instructions from the ground?"

Remote Agent was originally planned to have control of DS-1 for 6 hours (a confidence building experiment) and for 6 days. Due to various problems, the experiment was replanned for a 2 day period in May, 1999. During the experiment run, Remote Agent controlled the spacecraft and responded to various simulated problems, such as a malfunctioning spacecraft thruster. Remote Agent functioned very well, though not flawlessly, during it's two day experiment.

11.8.3.1   Remote Agent Description

"Remote Agent (RA) is a model-based, reusable, artificial intelligence (AI) software system that enables goal-based spacecraft commanding and robust fault recovery."[75] To break that statement down into its component parts:

*   **Model based.** A model is a general description of the behavior and structure of the component being controlled, such as a spacecraft, robot, or automobile. Each element of Remote Agent (RA) solves a problem by accepting goals, then using reasoning algorithms on the model to assemble a solution that meets the goals.

*   **Reusable.** Parts of the Remote Agent were designed to be system independent and can be used in other systems without modification. Other aspects are system dependent, and would need modification before being used in a different system.

*   **Artificial Intelligence.** Remote Agent *thinks* about the goals and how to reach them.

*   **Goal-based commanding.** Instead of sending Remote Agent a sequence of commands (slew to this orientation, turn on camera at this time, begin taking pictures at this time, etc.), RA accepts *goals* such as "For the next week, take pictures of the following asteroids, keeping the amount of fuel used under X." Goals may not be completely achievable (parts may conflict) and Remote Agent has to sort that out.

*   **Robust fault recovery.** Remote Agent can plan around failures. For example, if one thruster has failed, it can compensate with other thrusters to achieve the same maneuver.

The Remote Agent software system consists of 3 components: the Planner/Scheduler, the Executive, and the MIR (Mode Identification and Reconfiguration, also called Livingstone).

The Planner/Scheduler (PS) generates the plans that Remote Agent uses to control the spacecraft. It uses the initial spacecraft state and a set of goals to create a set of high-level tasks to achieve those goals. PS uses its model of the spacecraft, including constraints on operations or sequence of operations, to generate the plan.

The Executive requests plans from PS and executes them. It also requests and executes failure recoveries from MIR, executes goals and commands from human operators, manages system resources, configures system devices, provides system-level fault protection, and moves into safe-modes as necessary. It's a busy little program!

The Mode Identification and Reconfiguration (MIR) element diagnoses problems and provides a recovery mechanism. MIR needs to know what is happening to all components of the spacecraft, so it eavesdrops on commands sent to the hardware by the Executive. Using the commands and sensor information, MIR determines the current state of the system, which is reported to the

Executive. If failures occur, MIR provides a repair or workaround scenario that would allow the plan to continue execution.

11.8.3.2   *Testing and Verification of Remote Agent*

The main problem in testing Remote Agent was that the number of possible execution paths through the software was on the order of millions. Unlike traditional spacecraft flight software, where a *sequence* of operations was uplinked after ground verification, Remote Agent had to think for itself, identifying problems and taking corrective action, in order to achieve the goals. It is impossible to test all these execution paths within the software, at least within the lifetime of the tester, if not the universe!

For the Remote Agent experiment, a scenario-based verification strategy was augmented with model-based verification and validation [Smith et. al. 76]. The universe of possible inputs (goals, spacecraft state, device responses, timing, etc.) is partitioned into a manageable number of scenarios. Remote Agent is exercised on each scenario and its behavior is verified against the specifications.

Going from millions or billions of possible tests down to a manageable number (200 to 300) entails adding risk. If you test everything, you know how the system will respond in any possible scenario. When you test a small subset, there is the risk that you missed something important – some scenario where the interactions among the subsystem are not what you expected. You must be able to have confidence that the tested scenarios imply success among the untested scenarios.

The effectiveness of scenario-based testing depends largely on how well the scenarios cover the requirements. This means that not only is the requirement tested, but that the selected inputs for the tests give confidence that the requirement works for all other inputs. The Remote Agent experiment used a parameter-based approach to select the scenarios and inputs to use.

Three methods were used to achieve good coverage while maintaining manageability:

- Abstracting parameter space to focus on relevant parameters and values. Parameters and parameter values were selected to focus on areas where the software was most sensitive. Equivalence classes were used to generalize from these inputs to a collection of comparable tests that would not be performed.

- Identifying independent regions of the parameter space. Areas where there is low or no interactions mean that fewer combinations of parameters and values must be tested. When there is strong interaction among parameters, more combinations must be tested.

- Using orthogonal arrays to generate minimal-sized test suites that cover the parameter combinations. Every parameter value and every pair of values appears in at least one test case. Every parameter value appears in about the same number of cases.

One difficulty encountered during testing was that it was difficult to know what parameter value lead to failure. To overcome this, a collection of test cases identical to the faulty one was generated, with each test identical except for one parameter. This allowed the value leading to the error to be identified.

Another difficulty in any form of spacecraft software testing is the lack of high-fidelity test beds. The closer the test bed is to flight fidelity, the less time you will get on it. To deal with this issue, the Remote Agent experiment performed tests on highly abstract software (software that did not care about the underlying hardware) on low-fidelity test beds, and reserved the high-fidelity test beds for hardware-specific software and general system verification.

Remote Agent automated the testing process, and in some cases "warped" the time, so that a multi-day test could be completed in hours. Software was also written to help with understanding the test results. These not only allowed more tests to be done in the limited period of time, but increased the chance of spotting errors. Reviewing log files is very tedious, and errors can be missed.

> **Remember: Software which tests safety-critical code must also be considered safety-critical.**

Additional information on the verification and testing of the Remote Agent experiment can be found in Smith et. al. [76]. Bernard et. al. [75] discusses the testing strategy, as well as the in-flight validation of Remote Agent.

11.8.3.3   *In-flight Validation: How well did it work?*

Even before flight, problems with some aspects of the testing strategy were noted. During the last four months before flight, after the formal testing phase had ended, a large number of new problems were discovered. Most of the problems related to the planning system operating correctly, but unable to find a plan within the time constraints. Several reasons were identified:

o   Range of some parameters differed from those assumed for testing.

o   Disappearance of slack time in going from the 6 day to 2 day scenario revealed brittleness in the Planner chronological backtracking search.

o   The test generator only considered pair-wise interactions. Some problems depended on the specific values of 3 or more parameters.

During the flight experiment, a problem developed with Remote Agent not terminating the Ion Propulsion System (IPS) thrusting as expected. Plan execution appeared to be blocked, but the Remote Agent and the spacecraft were both healthy. The cause was later identified as a missing critical section in the plan-execution code. This created a race condition between two Executive threads. If the wrong thread won, a deadlock condition would occur where each thread was waiting for an event from the other. This occurred in flight, though not on the ground, despite thousands of previous races during the ground testing.

The following is drawn from the Remote Agent Lessons Learned:

•   Basic system must be thoroughly validated with a comprehensive test plan as well as formal methods, where appropriate.

•   Automatic code generation of interface code, telemetry, model interfaces, and test cases was enormously helpful.

•   Better model validation tools are needed. Automated test running capability helped increase the number of off-nominal tests that could be run. However, manual evaluation of the test results was laborious.

•   Confidence in complex autonomous behaviors can be built up from confidence in each individual component behavior.

- Ground tools need to be created early and used to test and understand how to operate the complex flight system. For Remote Agent, the ground tools were developed very late and many of them were not well integrated.

- Ensuring sufficient visibility into the executing software requires adequate information in the telemetry. Design the telemetry early and use it as the primary way of debugging and understanding the behavior of the system during integration, test, and operations.

As the problems found in late ground operations and flight operations show, the testing strategy was not 100% successful. In particular, a timing problem that rarely occurred was missed because it never happened on the ground.

More work needs to be done on the verification and validation of Intelligent Autonomous Systems, especially if they are to have control over safety-critical functions and equipment. Remote Agent had "backup" from the flight software and hardware hazard controls. It was a successful experiment that shows promise for the future. But it is not quite ready for complete control of safety-critical systems.

11.9   Human Factors in Software Safety

Humans are an integral, vital part of a safe system. Humans design the systems, build the hardware, write the software, and operate the resulting system. Even when automated processes are used in the creation of a system, humans were involved in producing that automated process.

Humans are fallible. We "break" – are forgetful, miss things, make mistakes, and even sometimes deliberately act to bring harm. Humans are also problem solvers. We design systems to catch errors, find ways to bring a broken system back to operation, and can intervene before a problem becomes a catastrophe. This mix of error-producer and error-solver creates both problems and potential benefits for the creation of safety-critical systems.

When designing a software system, consider these questions:

- What are the potential causes of human error in the system? Section 11.9.1.2 lists some errors to watch out for.

- What tasks are suitable for humans and which for computers? What training and support will operators require to perform their tasks?

- What policies and management will be required in order to develop a safe system?

- What are the "impossible", unthinkable events that can lead to a hazard?

Once you have a list of human errors you consider possible, design the system and software to minimize them. Consider the situation of a software system replacing a mostly-hardware system. A completely new user interface will likely be confusing to the operators. They may require training or at least on-the-job time to adjust. If the system is safety-critical, the new interface could delay an operator's response long enough for a hazard to occur.

There are several "design" solutions to the above problem. One is to emulate the older hardware interface within the software. This increases familiarity with the new system, though there will still be some difference. Another option is to get extensive user input as the new interface is developed. This can be as simple as talking with them, or as complex as research studies that monitor how the operators actually use the system. There are likely to be more options. This example is meant to get you thinking about human errors and how to design the software with them in mind.

No matter how well you design your software to minimize human error, someone is still going to select the wrong command from a menu or type the wrong value into a data field. How can your system recognize such errors and recover from them? Follow the principles of fault avoidance (don't let the fault happen) and fault tolerance (keep going safely even if fault occurs). Sections 6.5.2 and 7.4.2 provide more information on these topics. When all else fails, you want your system to operate in a safe mode. Of course, this requires that the parts of the system required to place the rest of the system in safe mode still work!

The "impossible", unthinkable events that lead to a hazard should have been considered during hazard analysis (PHA section 2.3.1 and SSHA section 2.3.4). However, it never hurts to think about them again. Humans are likely to come up with additional events whenever we think about the system in-depth. Consider these events from a human-error perspective. Also, remember that outsiders can often see what insiders cannot. Have someone else, from a different discipline or project, look at the system. They may well discover ways for the "impossible" events to occur.

A great deal of current software engineering is human-intensive, which increases the likelihood of errors. Determining requirements, preparing specifications, designing, programming, testing, and analysis are still mostly performed by humans. Good software engineering practice compensates for individual human error by providing processes to make error less likely (e.g. defined methods) and to locate errors when they occur (e.g. reviews, analysis, automated tools, etc.).

Much of the information in this section comes from "Human Factors in Safety-Critical Systems" [96]. This book is an excellent introduction to human errors and how to minimize them.

11.9.1 Human Error

To create a safe system, it is important to understand the role human error plays in accidents and incidents. It is also important to understand the role of humans in the development of safe software. "Software errors" are almost always actually human errors, either in the requirements (wrong, missing, etc.), the design, the implementation, or incomplete and inadequate testing.

A successful development project requires more than just a technical development team. The lack of sound project management and a failure by senior management to identify strategic goals have caused numerous software development projects to founder. In addition, management must work to create harmonious human relationships within the team.

The competence of the technical and managerial team members has a direct effect on the success of the project. Competence is both capabilities and skills, plus the applicability of those skills to the task at hand. A well-qualified team member will have experience, training in the field of knowledge, knowledge of hazards and failures the system is capable of, knowledge of practices used in the organization, and an appreciation of individual limitations and constraints. Teams need to balance the competence factors. Not everyone needs to be an expert in everything, but someone should be an expert in each area. Communication provides a means to share the expertise among the team. Task sharing or cross-training allows other team members to learn from the experts.

Human error is a very common cause of accidents and incidents. We misread signs when we are tired, select the wrong command from a menu list, press the wrong button, and fail to act appropriately when a hazard is imminent.

When it comes to an accident (hazardous event), humans can act as:

- *An initiating event.* The operator presses the wrong button, types in the wrong command, or forgets to reactivate the alarm after maintenance.

- *Escalation or control of the accident.* We can perform actions that bring the situation back under control and mitigate the hazard. We can also fail to act, or act inappropriately, and allow the situation to escalate from a minor accident into a major one.

- *Emergency evacuation, escape and rescue.* When it comes to critical and catastrophic hazards, our ability to "get out of the way" can prevent the loss of life. Poor response to an accident can lead to further loss of life.

- *Latent failure.* Indirect human error is also a concern. Programming errors, management that allows sloppiness in development or testing, or a management decision to hire barely qualified developers are all software-related examples of latent failure.

Consider the human element in these high-profile accidents:

- **Three Mile Island (1979).** This nuclear accident was caused, in part, by incomplete and misleading feedback to the operators. An indicator light showed that the command <u>was sent</u> to a valve to close it. It did not indicate whether the valve had actually closed. It was up to the human operator to remember that the indicator light might not show the actual state of the valve. When the accident occurred, the relief valve had <u>not</u> closed, though the command was sent (and the indicator light was on). The problem was not discovered for some time, and ultimately lead to the accident.

- **Kegworth M1 Air Crash (Jan. 1989).** This plane crash, which killed 47 and injured may others, was probably caused by the pilot misinterpreting the aircraft instruments and shutting down the wrong engine.

- **Mars Polar Lander (1999).** The most probable cause of the loss of the Mars Polar Lander was the premature shutdown of the descent engines. The software was intended to ignore shutdown indications prior to the enabling of touchdown sensing logic. However, the software was not properly implemented, and the spurious touchdown indication was retained (not ignored). At 40 meters altitude the touchdown sensing logic is enabled, and the software would have issued a command to shut the engines down. In addition to the probable direct cause, the investigating board found other human-related problems with the project:

  o The contractor used excessive overtime in order to complete the work on schedule and within the available workforce. Records show that much of the development staff worked 60 hours per week, and a few worked 80 hours per week, for extended periods of time.

o Some aspects of the software were created by only one person. Peers working together are the first and best line of defense against errors. The investigating board recommended adequate engineering staffing to ensure that no one individual is "single string".

o System software testing was not as adequate as it should have been. The board recommended that system testing should include stress testing and fault injection in a suitable simulation environment to determine the limits of capability and search for hidden flaws.

11.9.1.2   *Errors to Watch Out For*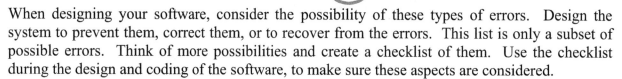

When designing your software, consider the possibility of these types of errors. Design the system to prevent them, correct them, or to recover from the errors. This list is only a subset of possible errors. Think of more possibilities and create a checklist of them. Use the checklist during the design and coding of the software, to make sure these aspects are considered.

- Confusing Information.

- Conflicting Information.

- Misleading Information (e.g. see Three Mile Island example above)

- Invalid or old Information

- Human memory limitations (unable to keep too many details at one time, unable to remember details when screen page is covered by another, etc.)

- Intentional Actions

- Tinkering (a form of Intentional Actions, user tries out the system usually in an unanticipated manner)

- Difficulty accessing required information in time (e.g. during crisis)

- Difficulty finding information on screen

- Change in Operational Mode (user interface, way of accessing information, etc. changes from previous way of doing things)

Humans make errors during the process of creating the software as well as when using it. Good software development processes help prevent such errors from occurring.

- Checklists, language restrictions and common defect lists help prevent the insertion of defects into the software.

- Editors and Integrated Development environments with language and style highlighting reduce the occurrence of some errors.

- Inspections and reviews (including software checking programs) find errors before the software is completed. Domain experts should be included on inspection teams. If a user interface is safety-critical, a human factors expert should also be included.

- Testing finds other errors, especially those that result from integration or operation.

11.9.1.3   *Process Problems*

Sometimes problems come from the environment the software was created in, or the environment the software is operated in. Many of these problems are outside the control of those creating and assuring the software. These issues are managerial, and may come from all levels of management.

Managers can create the context for accidents, within which operators merely provide the final triggering actions. Managers can also create (or perpetuate) a development environment that is detrimental to safety. There is a need to train managers to avoid these problems. There is also a need to provide independent assessment of policies and decisions as well as processes and products.

Types of problems that can be attributed (in whole or in part) to management and organizational environment include:

- *Design failures.* May be due to lack of oversight, lack of training or inadequate resources provided.

- *Poor operating procedures.*

- *Error-enforcing conditions* (e.g. "Get it done on time, any way you can.", "That requirement isn't important, focus on the functionality.", or simply working the developers 60 hours a week for more than a short time).

- *System goals incompatible with safety.*

- *Organizational failures* (e.g. undocumented processes, pressure to cut corners, pressure to break or bend rules, unrealistic schedules or workloads).

- *Communications failures.*   Management may not provide good channels of communication, keep team members isolated, or "shoot the messenger" of bad news.

- *Inadequate training.* At any level (developers, operators, project managers, etc.)

- *Lack of safety culture.* Safety is not given priority.

11.9.2 The Human-Computer Interface

The Human computer Interface (HCI) is the connection between the computer (embedded, desktop, etc.) and the person using it (operator, user, etc.). The HCI consists of all aspects of this interaction, including display screens (hardware), the information displayed on them (user interface) and input devices (keyboard, keypad, mouse, touch screen, etc.).

Why should you care about the HCI? Improved design of the HCI leads to reduced errors, which lead to reduced accidents and incidents. For safety-critical systems, this is especially important.

The user interface (UI) is not just a skin on the surface but goes very deeply into the system. The user interface is any part of the system that affects any user or through which any user can affect the system. The user interface is not just the form of display and method of information entry, but includes the information content, and the temporal and semantic structuring of that information. The UI includes such things as sensor accuracy, data processing, and database design. You want the right kinds of information available for diagnosis or decision making at any given time.

Users present the biggest problem for interface designers, mostly because of unpredictability. It is commonly known among developers that you cannot make a system foolproof, because fools are so ingenious. Most problems stem from the inherent variability between people. We also don't understand people at the level necessary to make this a science.

How the system will be used (the tasks) is also significant. The developer needs to know what the end-users of a proposed system will be doing, and **why** they will be doing it. This process (gathering information and understanding) is usually absent in software development. The designer makes guesses (or goes on what the client said, which may not be what the end-users will really be doing).

The finest detail of a user interface (such as placement of a command within a menu) can affect the error rate, search times, and learning curve for a piece of software. The naming of commands or buttons, size of icons, etc. can affect usability. The goal of good HCI design is to prevent confusion and enhance comprehensibility.

It is important that the user perspective on the system is taken into account throughout analysis and is reflected back to the user when he or she is required to make any judgment about its adequacy or completeness. Don't wait until the acceptance test to get user feedback. When user interface elements deal with safety-critical information or procedures, design the system *for the operators*, rather than assuming the operators will adapt to whatever you design.

11.9.3 Interface Design

Prototyping is one of the most useful techniques to create and verify good user interfaces. For prototyping to work, it needs to present to the end user how the system looks and acts. A prototype doesn't need the "guts" (i.e. results from computations), unless they affect how the user interacts with the system.

Once the user interface prototype is created, it needs to be tested extensively with the actual users. Part of the testing should include observation (watch them use it) and feedback from those using the system. Observation can be especially useful. In designing a new air traffic control system, observation of those using the system indicated a problem not reported by the users. During some situations the controllers were writing information on a sticky note before switching screens. The need to do this indicated a weakness in the user interface that would be trivial in a normal operating situation, but potentially deadly in a crisis situation (when the time to write the information on the note could be critical).

Good user interfaces reflect the user's model (how the user perceives the system). How can you determine who the user will actually use the system? Asking the user is the first step, of course, but the user does not always understand exactly what he wants to do. And even if the understanding is present, communicating that viewpoint may be difficult. Besides prototyping, consider these types of analyses:

- **Functional analysis** looks at the allocation of functions between people, hardware, and software. It identifies required system functionality (both normal and emergency or off-nominal operations).

- **Task analysis** identifies tasks performed by all personnel who will operate the system (both normal and emergency or off-nominal).

- **Information analysis** identifies information requirements of the operators for each task scenario. It also identifies information to be displayed on monitor, including the content of the displays (in broad terms), how the same information may be used in different tasks, and what different items of information will be required to complete a single task.

During a crisis situation, appropriate information must be provided to the operator. At the same time, the operator must not be overwhelmed with all possible information. It is also important to make sure that the information presents the true state of system (see the Three Mile Island example in 11.9.1.1). Inconsistencies are confusing, especially when under stress. A well-designed interface that keeps the user informed, that displays information in manageable ways, that indicates the amount of uncertainty in the information in ways that can be understood, and which allows control actions to be taken in a forgiving environment, can help reduce fear-induced stress during a problem.

User interfaces must be designed defensively. Humans sometimes do unorthodox things. Sometimes accidentally, sometimes with a "what does this do" attempt to understand the system, and sometimes deliberately. The software should be designed to prevent such behavior from creating a hazard.

Sometimes the user needs too independent sources of information to verify that a hazard control is working. These pieces of information should be easy to compare. For example, display them in the same units and to the same precision. Also remember that redundancy (independence) is not achieved by a single sensor displayed in two locations using separate algorithms. Separate sensor and separate algorithms must be used to make the data truly independent.

What should be considered when creating a user interface? The list below provides a starting point, but is not complete. What is important will vary between projects. Look at your own system and decide what information and operations are safety-critical, and design accordingly.

Consider the following:

- Display formats. What range of formats will be used? Consider color, coding techniques, font size, position, etc.

- How will the information be structured into "pages"? What is the allocation of information to various formats or pages? Is the information allocated to different formats based on task requirements?

- Is all required information on one page? How will the user navigate between pages and is the consistent? Is the display format consistent across pages?

- Maintain consistency throughout the display system (same colors, window layout, type sizes, etc.).

- Do not overload working memory (human memory – what they need to remember between pages).

- Make sure mapping between displays and controls matches what the user expects.

- Provide appropriate, timely feedback. If the operation is complete, indicate that. If further options or actions will occur, also specify that.

- Enable efficient information assimilation (help users *understand* the information quickly).

- Allow reversal and recovery. Actions should be able to be reversed. Errors should be recovered from.

- Anticipate and engineer for errors.

- Remember that the operator needs to feel that she has control of the system and that it will respond to her actions.

Chapter 12 Software Acquisition

Acquiring software, whether off-the-shelf, previously created, or custom made, carries with it a set of risks and rewards that differ from those related to software development. When the software will serve a safety-critical function, or be integrated with in-house developed safety-critical code, it becomes very important to select carefully. This section provides guidance on both purchased off-the-shelf and reused software as well as software acquired from a contractor.

Software safety is a concern with off-the-shelf (OTS), reused, and contract-developed software, and NASA safety standards apply to all types. NASA-STD-8719.13A, the Software Safety NASA Technical Standard, section 1.3, states (emphasis added):

"This standard is appropriate for application to **software acquired or developed by NASA** that is used as a part of a system that possesses the potential of directly or indirectly causing harm to humans or damage to property external to the system. When software is acquired by NASA, this standard applies to the level specified in contract clauses or memoranda of understanding. When software is developed by NASA, this standard applies to the level specified in the program plan, software management plan, or other controlling document."

Definitions	
Off-the-shelf (OTS)	Software not developed in-house or by a contractor for the project. The software is general purpose, or developed for a different purpose from the current project.
COTS	Commercial-off-the-shelf software. Operating systems, libraries, applications, and other software purchased from a commercial vendor. Not customized for your project. Source code and documentation are often limited.
GOTS	Government-off-the-shelf software. This was developed in-house, but for a different project. Source code is usually available. Documentation varies. Analyses and test results, including hazard analyses, may be available.
Reused software	Software developed by the current team (or GOTS) for a different project, portions of which are reused in the current software. While it is tempting to pull out a previously written function for the new project, be aware of how it will operate in the new system. Just because it worked fine in System A does not mean it will work OK in System B. A suitability analysis should be performed.
Contracted software	Software created for a project by a contractor or sub-contractor. The project defines the requirements the software must meet. Process requirements and safety analyses may be included. This is custom-made software, but not in-house.
Glueware	Software created to connect the OTS/reused software with the rest of the system. It may take the form of "adapters" that modify interfaces or add missing functionality, "firewalls" that isolate the OTS software, or "wrappers" that check inputs and outputs to the OTS software and may modify either to prevent failures.

NASA Policy Directive NPD 2820.1, NASA Software Policies, includes consideration of COTS and GOTS software that is part of a NASA system. Projects need to evaluate whether the use of COTS and GOTS would be more advantageous than developing the software. It expects proof that software providers are capable of delivering products that meet the requirements.

Off-the-shelf (OTS) software and reused software share many of the same benefits and concerns. They will be grouped together for convenience in section 12.1. "OTS" or "off-the-shelf software" will refer to both off-the-shelf (usually commercial) software and reused software. When a comment refers only to one or the other, the appropriate form of the software will be clearly designated. Software developed under contract will be discussed in section 12.2.

For off-the-shelf software, this section discusses the following areas:

- Pros and Cons of OTS software

- What to look for when purchasing off-the-shelf software

- Using OTS in your system

- Recommended extra testing for OTS software

- For contract-developed software, guidance is provided on

- What to put in the contract regarding software development.

- What to monitor of contractor processes (insight/oversight)

- What testing is recommended

12.1 Off-the-Shelf Software

The decision to use off-the-shelf (OTS) software in your system should not be made lightly. While it is becoming common to purchase software rather than create it, the process is not without pitfalls. Reusing software from other projects, even similar projects, is not a panacea either. Systems differ, and the subtle differences can lead to devastating results.

 Why is OTS software use becoming more commonplace in NASA and industry? Primarily, the prevailing "wisdom" is that it will save on cost and/or schedule. If a commercial software product can be purchased that meets the needs of the project, it is usually a less expensive alternative to developing the software in-house. Or the organization may have software from a similar project that can be reused in the new project. In addition, the OTS software is often available immediately, which helps in a tight schedule. In a project strapped for money or time, OTS software looks very attractive. However, there are risks involved in using OTS software. Some of the issues are discussed below, and reference [77] provides a method for determining the risks, as well as the cost/benefit ratio, for using COTS software in your system. Reference [78] discusses concerns as well as ways to make sure the OTS software meets your needs and is safe.

Some OTS software is so common that most developers do not even consider it. Operating Systems (OS) are one example. It is very rare for a development team to create their own operating system, rather than purchasing a commercial one. Guidance on what to look for in an operating system is given in section 11.4 *Operating Systems*. Another example of common OTS software is language libraries, such as the C standard library.

OTS software has acquired another name recently: SOUP (Software of Uncertain Pedigree). In many ways, SOUP is a better name, because it emphasizes the potential problems and pitfalls upfront. OTS software may be developed by a team that uses good software engineering practices, or by a few developers working late nights, living on pizza and soft drinks, and banging out some code. Knowing the pedigree of the OTS software can save you headaches down the road.

Carefully consider all aspects of the OTS software under consideration. It not an easy decision, choosing between creating the software in-house (with its accompanying headaches) or purchasing OTS software/reusing software (which have a different set of headaches). You must take a systems approach and consider how the OTS software will fit into your system. You must also perform an adequate analysis of the impacts of the OTS software. Don't wait until you are deep into implementation to find out that one of the extra functions in the OTS software can cause a safety hazard!

Consider the following questions:

- Will you need glueware to connect the software to your system?

- How extensive will the glueware need to be?

- Will you have to add functionality via glueware because the OTS software doesn't provide all of it?

- Is there extra functionality in the OTS software that the rest of the system needs to be protected from?

- What extra analyses will you need to perform to verify the OTS software?

- What extra tests will you need to do?

If the glueware is going to be a significant portion of the size of the OTS software, you may want to rethink the decision to use OTS. You don't save time or money if you have to created extensive wrappers, glueware, or other code to get the OTS software working in your system. Also, in a safety-critical system, the cost of extra analyses and tests may make the OTS software a costly endeavor.

In safety-critical systems, OTS software can be a burden as well as a blessing. The main problems with off-the-shelf software are:

- Inadequate documentation. Often only a user manual is provided, which describes functionality from a user point of view. In order to integrate the software into the system, more information is needed. In particular, information is required on how the software interacts within itself (between modules) and with the outside world (its application program interface (API)).

- Lack of access to source code, which precludes some safety analyses. It also precludes obtaining a better understanding of how the software actually works.

- Lack of knowledge about the software development process used to create the software.

- Lack of knowledge about the testing process used to verify the software.

- Concern that the OTS developers may not fully understand the interactions between elements of their system or may not communicate that information fully to the purchaser.

- Inadequate detail on defects, including known bugs not provided to purchaser.

- Inadequate or non-existent analyses performed on the software.

- Missing functionality. The OTS software may provide most but not all required functionality. This is one area where glueware is necessary.

- Extra functionality. The OTS software may contain functions that are not required. Sometimes these functions can be "turn off", but unless the OTS software is recompiled, the code for these functions will remain in the system. Glueware (wrappers) may be needed to shield the rest of the system from this extra functionality.

For further information on how OTS software is handled in other industries, check references [79] (FDA) and [80] (nuclear). They provide some high-level guidance on using COTS software in medical and nuclear applications, both of which are highly safety-critical venues.

The Avionics Division of the Engineering Directorate at the NASA Lyndon B. Johnson Space Center (JSC) baselined a work instruction, EA-WI-018, "Use of Off-the-Shelf Software in Flight Projects Work Instruction" that outlines a lifecycle process for OTS software projects, including safety considerations. This work instruction is based partly on the FDA's process detailed in "Guidance for Off-the-Shelf Software Use in Medical Devices." [79]

 The lifecycle described in the JSC work instruction coordinates the selection and integration of OTS software with the development and implementation of custom software. In comparing the lifecycle processes it is evident that the amount of time spent on each phase changes and the skills of the personnel need to be different. For selecting OTS products, a great deal of time is spent evaluating the functional needs of the project and the available OTS products on the market. Flexibility of requirements is needed with a clear idea of the overall system. A poor OTS selection can severely complicate or cripple a project. A series of questions are included in both the JSC work instruction and the FDA guidance document to give personnel enough information to determine whether or not to use a specific OTS software product.

The work instruction specifies that an initial determination of the criticality of the function must be accomplished. The amount of scrutiny the candidate OTS software faces is based on the criticality assessed. Experienced personnel need to determine the criticality. The JSC work instruction and the FDA guidance document list similar requirements for high criticality OTS software. A project with life threatening hazards must do the first three items of the *Checklist for Off-the-Shelf (OTS) Items* (second checklist) in Appendix H.

Some of this section, and those that follow, on Off-the-Shelf software issues, especially within NASA, comes from a whitepaper by Frances E. Simmons of JSC [81].

12.1.1 Purchasing or Reusing OTS Software: Recommendations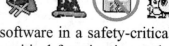

While all OTS software should be considered carefully, using OTS software in a safety-critical system "ups the ante". OTS software that directly performs a safety-critical function is not the only element that must be considered. **Any** OTS software that resides on the same platform as the safety-critical software must be analyzed, to verify that it cannot impact the safety-critical code. Since there is no independent COTS certification authority to test the safety and reliability of the COTS software, all additional analyses and tests will have to be done by you.

 Using non-safety-critical OTS software on the same platform as safety-critical software is not recommended. Certain commercial programs are known to crash regularly. Do you really want to have Word on the same system that controls your air supply? If the OTS software provides a necessary function, then it must be considered in conjunction with the safety-critical code. The hazard analysis should be updated (or at least reviewed) *before* you purchase the software.

This guidebook gives an introduction to the good software development processes that go into safety-critical software development. As much as possible, verify that the OTS software was created using good development processes. When purchasing OTS software, or deciding to reuse existing code, the following areas should also be considered:

- Does the OTS software fill the need *in this system*? Is its operational context compatible with the system under development? Consider not only the similarities between the system(s) the OTS was designed for and the current system, but also the differences. Look carefully at how those differences affect operation of the OTS software.

- How stable is the OTS product? Are bug-fixes or upgrades released so often that the product is in a constant state of flux?

- How responsive is the vendor to bug-fixes? Does the vendor inform you when a bug-fix patch or new version is available?

- How compatible are upgrades to the software? Has the API changed significantly between upgrades in the past? Will your interface to the OTS software still work, even after an upgrade? Will you have to update your glueware with each iteration?

- How mature is the software technology? OTS software is often market driven, and may be released with bugs (known and unknown) in order to meet an imposed deadline or to beat the competition to market.

- Conversely, is the software so well known that it is assumed to be error free and correct? Think about operating systems and language libraries. In a safety-critical system, you do not want to *assume* there are no errors in the software.

- What is the user base of the software? If it is a general use library, with thousands of users, you can expect that most bugs and errors will be found and reported to the vendor. Make sure the vendor keeps this information, and provides it to the users! Small software programs will have less of a "shake down" and *may* have more errors remaining.

- What level of documentation is provided with the software? Is there more information than just a user's manual? Can more information be obtained from the vendor (free or for a reasonable price)?

- Is source code included, or available for purchase at a reasonable price? Will support still be provided if the source code is purchased or if the software is slightly modified?

- Can you communicate with those who developed the software, if serious questions arise? Is the technical support available, adequate, and reachable? Will the vendor talk with you if you modify the product?

- Will the vendor support older versions of the software, if you choose not to upgrade? Many vendors will only support the newest version, or perhaps one or two previous versions.

- Is there a well-defined API (Application Program Interface), ICD (interface control document), or similar documentation that details how the user interacts with the software? Are there "undocumented" API functions?

- What are the error codes returned by the software? How can it fail (return error code, throw an exception, etc.)? Do the functions check input variables for proper range, or is it the responsibility of the user to implement?

- Can you obtain information on the internals of the software, such as the complexity of the various software modules or the interfaces between the modules? This information may be needed, depending on what analyses need to be performed on the OTS software.

- Can you get information about the software development process used to create the software? Was it developed using an accepted standard (IEEE 12207, for example)? What was the size of the developer team?

- What types of testing was the software subjected to? How thorough was the testing? Can you get copies of any test reports?

- Are there any known defects in the software? Are there any unresolved problems with the software, especially if the problems were in systems similar to yours? Look at product support groups, newsgroups, and web sites for problems unreported by the vendor. However, also keep in mind the source of the information found on the web – some is excellent and documented, other information is spurious and incorrect.

- Were there any analyses performed on the software, in particular any of the analyses described in chapters 5 through 10? Formal inspections or reviews of the code?

- How compatible is the software with your system (other software, both custom and OTS)? Will you have to write extensive glueware to interface it with your code? Are there any issues with integrating the software, such as linker incompatibility, protocol inconsistencies, or timing issues?

- Does the software provide all the functionality required? How easy is it to add any new functionality to the system, when the OTS software is integrated? Will the OTS software provide enough functionality to make it cost-effective?

- Does the OTS-to-system interface require any modification? For example, does the OTS produce output in the protocol used by the system, or will glueware need to be written to convert from the OTS to the system protocol?

- Does the software provide extra functionality? Can you "turn off" any of the functionality? If you have the source code, can you recompile with defined switches or stubs to remove the extra functionality? How much code space (disk, memory, etc.) does the extra software take up? What happens to the system if an unneeded function is accidentally invoked?

- Will the OTS software be stand-alone or integrated into your system? The level of understanding required varies with the two approaches. If stand-alone (such as an Operating System), you need to be concerned with the API/ICD primarily, and interactions with your independent software are usually minimal. If the software is to be integrated (e.g. a library), then the interaction between your code and the OTS software is more complicated. More testing and/or analyses may be needed to assure the software system.

- Does the OTS software have any "back doors" that can be exploited by others and create a security problem?

- Is the software version 1.0? If so, there is a higher risk of errors and problems. Consider waiting for at least the first bug-fix update, if not choosing another product.

- If the OTS product's interface is supposed to conform to an industry standard, verify that it does so.

Appendix H provides the above information as a checklist, and also contains another checklist of items to consider when using OTS software in your system.

IEEE 1228, the standard for Software Safety Plans, states that previously developed (reused) software and purchased software must be

- Adequately tested.

- Have an acceptable risk.

- Remains safe in the context of its planned use.

- Any software that does not meet these criteria, or for which the level of risk or consequences of failure cannot be determined, should not be used in a safety-critical system. In addition, IEEE 1228 provides a standard for a minimal approval process for reused or purchased software:

- Determine the interfaces to and functionality of the previously developed or purchased software that will be used in safety-critical systems.

- Identify relevant documents (e.g. product specifications, design documents, usage documents) that are available to the obtaining organization and determine their status.

- Determine the conformance of the previously developed or purchased software to published specifications.

- Identify the capabilities and limitations of the previously developed or purchased software with respect to the project's requirements.

- Following an approved test plan, test the safety-critical features of the previously developed or purchased software *independent* of the project's software.

- Following an approved test plan, test the safety-critical features of the previously developed or purchased software *with* the project's software.

- Perform a risk assessment to determine if the use of the previously developed or purchased software will result in undertaking an unacceptable level of risk.

12.1.2 Integrating OTS Software into your System

Okay, you've weighed all the factors (in-house development costs/time vs. OTS costs/time including glueware and extra tests/analyses), and decided to go ahead with using OTS software. Remember, OTS includes software reused from a different project as well. Now that software must be integrated into the software system, which consists of in-house developed code and/or other OTS/reused code modules. Keeping the OTS code as isolated as possible from the rest of the system is a good idea, and several approaches to doing this are presented below. Reference [82] discusses these approaches, and more.

Making sure the software system is *safe* also requires some additional tests and analyses, which are discussed in <u>section 12.1.4</u>.

12.1.2.1 *Sticky stuff: Glueware and Wrapper Functions*

It would be great if the OTS software (including reused libraries and functions from other projects) could just be plunked down into the new system with no additional work. It doesn't work that way, of course. You have to connect the OTS software to the rest of the code. The software that provides the connection is called glueware.

Glueware is a general term for any software that sits between the OTS software and the rest of the software system. Usually it is the software required to connect the two pieces (OTS and in-house) and make them work and play well together. Two specific versions of glueware are *wrappers*, which are described below, and *adapters*, which are discussed in <u>section 12.1.2.3</u>.

Wrappers are an encapsulation mechanism, where the OTS code is isolated from the rest of the system. Wrappers can prevent certain inputs from reaching the OTS component and/or check and validate outputs from the component. Restricting inputs should be done if certain values could cause the OTS/reused software to behave badly or execute dormant code. Finding those inputs can be difficult, especially when the source code is unavailable and the documentation is barely adequate. Reference [83] discusses using software fault injection with an OTS component, to determine what undesirable outputs the component can produce, and what inputs lead to those outputs. An experiment in using fault injection with wrapper functions to test the interface robustness of the system is described in reference [84].

Wrappers have several problems when they are applied to OTS software. First, the OTS component's interface must be well understood, which requires more-than-adequate documentation. Outputs that are outside the documented understanding may slip through the wrapper. Second, wrappers may be quite complex, and can approach or exceed the size of the OTS component.

Reference [85] discusses "generic software wrappers", including the development of a "wrapper description language", for wrapping COTS software in a Unix environment. The primary focus of the article is on security issues, but is of interest to anyone considering creating OTS wrappers.

Wrappers have a use outside of the operational software. During debug/testing phase, or while evaluating the OTS software, wrappers can be used to *instrument* the software system.

Essentially, the wrapper allows information about what is happening (inputs to the OTS, outputs from the OTS) to be recorded or displayed. This provides insight into what the OTS software is doing in the operational or test situations.

12.1.2.2   *Redundant Architecture*

The influence of the COTS component can be restricted by using a redundant architecture. Replication and multi-voting approaches, including N-Version programming, can be used if the software produces consistent faults. That is, for a specific input, the same fault is always produced. However, this approach (especially N-Version programming) has debatable reliability, and is not recommended.

Partitioning the system into a high-performance portion and a high-assurance kernel (or safety kernel) is another option. The high-performance portion is just that – the best, fastest, leanest, etc. code. This part of the software can contain OTS software, as well as custom-developed software. If this part fails, however, the system defaults to the high-assurance kernel. This portion maintains the system in a safe state while providing the required functionality (with reduced performance).

The Carnegie Mellon Software Engineering Institute (SEI) developed a framework of safety techniques they named Simplex Architecture. These techniques include high-assurance application-kernel technology, address-space protection mechanisms, real-time scheduling algorithms, and methods for dynamic communication among components. This process requires using analytic redundancy to separate major functions into high-assurance kernels and high-performance subsystems. Off-The-Shelf (OTS) products can be used in the high-performance subsystem and even replaced without bringing down the system. Reference [46] describes the Simplex Architecture.

Redundant architecture is no silver bullet for OTS. It suffers from the same problems as wrapper functions: complexity, and the inability to deal effectively with unknown and unexpected functionality.

12.1.2.3   *Adding or Adapting Functionality*

Sometimes the OTS software is *almost* what you want, but is missing some small piece of required functionality. Or the OTS software contains what is needed, but the interfaces don't match up. In either case, a specialized form of glueware called an *adapter* can be written.

If extra functionality is required, an adapter will intercept the input (command, function call) for that functionality, execute the new function which it contains, and return the result – all without invoking the OTS software! Or, the adapter may provide some pre- or post-processing for an OTS function. For example, the OTS software has a function to control 16-bit output ports. The function takes two parameters – port address and value to write to the port. The primary software needs to access a specialize output port. This one requires writing to two consecutive 8-bit ports instead of one 16-bit port. The adapter software intercepts the function call (by matching the port address to the special one). It breaks the 16 bit value passed into 2 8-bit values, then performs two calls to the OTS function to write the values, incrementing the output port address by one between the calls.

When the interfaces between the OTS software and the rest of the code don't match up, an adapter can be written to "translate" between the two. For example, the OTS software produces messages in one format (header, message, checksum), but the standard protocol used by the rest of the system has a different header and uses a CRC instead of a checksum. The adapter would intercept messages coming from the OTS software, modify the header, and calculate the CRC before passing the message on..

12.1.2.4 Dealing with Extra Functionality

Because OTS software was originally written for another application, or written as a general set of functions, it will often contain "extra" functionality not needed by the current project. This extra code is referred to as "dormant" code, because it should sit there in the software, undisturbed and not executing. The trick is to make sure that's what it really does!

The first step is to identify if the OTS/reused software has any dormant code within it. To adequately determine this, access to the source code is necessary. If source code is unavailable, the software provider may be able to provide information, if you supply a list of the functions you will be using. Product user groups, newsgroups, and web pages may also contain useful information, though always consider the source of the information. If nothing else is available, look through the documentation for defined functions that you will not be using. The higher the ratio of used functionality to total functionality in the OTS software, the less dormant code there is.

Once the presence of dormant code is determined, look for the stimuli that activate it (cause it to execute). That will include command invocation, function calls to specific routines, and possible invocation from required functions based on the software state or parameters passed. If the source code is available, it can be examined for undefined (i.e. not specified in the documentation) ways of entering the dormant code.

Also look at the resources the dormant code uses. How much memory space does it take up? How much disk/storage space? Will the presence of this extra code push the software system close to any prescribed limits?

In an ideal system, you will be able to identify any dormant code and verify that it cannot ever be executed. Since we never have an ideal system, contingency planning (risk mitigation) is required. Look at what happens when the dormant code is executed. What functions does it perform? Does it affect the system performance or capacity? Examine the behavior of the system if any of the dormant code is executed – can it go into an unsafe state? Will system performance be degraded, leading to a possible mission or safety issue? Can the dormant software lead to a hazard, or interfere with a hazard control or mitigation?

> WARNING: Glueware Needed! Extra Work Ahead!

 You have to protect your system (in particular your safety-critical functions) from malfunctioning OTS software. This requires wrapping the OTS software (glueware) or providing some sort of firewall. The more dormant code there is in the OTS software, the more likely it is to "trigger" accidentally.

Depending on the issue and the product, you may be able to work with the vendor to disable the dormant code, or provide some safeguards against its unintentional execution. Procedural methods to avoid accidentally invoking the dormant code can be considered, but only as a last resort. They open up many possibilities for human error to cause problems with the system.

How much extra testing will need to be done on the software system is determined by the amount of dormant code, the level of insight into the code (what can it do), and any safety problems with the code. OTS software that could interfere with a safety control, with no source code availability, and with little or no details on its development and testing, will require extra testing! Software with good documentation, well encapsulated (not integrated with the system), and with no ability to affect safety (such as no I/O capability) may not need much extra testing. The determination of the level of testing effort should be made by the software engineers and the safety engineers, with input from project management, based on the risk to the system and to safety that the OTS software imparts.

12.1.3 Special Problems with Reused Software

The greatest problem with reusing software created for a different project is psychological. You *know* what the software does, how well it was tested in the previous system, and it just fits so *perfectly* into the new system. You don't need any extra analysis or testing – it's already been done. WRONG! That's what the Ariane 5 team thought when they reused Ariane 4 software! (See reference [86] for details.)

No two systems are alike. You cannot assume that the software you wrote for System A is going to function as expected in System B. The new system may be on a faster processor, and timing problems that weren't apparent in slower System A now become critical. Or the new system may have a critical task that must be executed regularly. The reused code may tie the system up long enough that the critical task is delayed. Or the input data may be different enough that problems missed by the first system are triggered in the new one.

 It is very important to analyze the reused code in light of the capacity, capability, and requirements of the new system. Look for issues with timing, hogging the system, overwriting variables, using the same system resources for different purposes, and …. As well as other issues. Carefully consider the differences between the new and old systems, and how those differences can affect the functioning of the reused software.

It is a goal in modern software engineering to create reusable software. After all, why should the wheel have to be constantly reinvented? We recycle many things in our society – why not code? While a laudable goal, software reuse is still in its infancy, and all the problems and pitfalls haven't been found yet. Applying reused software to a new system requires a lot of thought *up front*.

> # Think *before* you reuse!

12.1.4 Who Tests the OTS? (Us vs. Them)

Hopefully, the OTS software you are about to use has been thoroughly tested, either by the vendor or by the previous project. If you're lucky, you have copies of the test reports. If you're even luckier, you have a copy of a hazard analysis for the software. You can stop now, right?

Wrong. Even the most thoroughly tested and analyzed OTS software must still be analyzed and tested for how it operates *in the new system*! Think about OTS software as a child in a playground. It may play well with the children in the sandbox and on the slide. It gets dizzy on the merry-go-round, but still keeps playing. But put it on the swing and the rope breaks, dumping itself on the ground and creating a hazard for other children in the area. **No two systems are identical.** Old software must be looked at in the new context.

 Safety-critical Off-The-Shelf (COTS, GOTS, or reused) software should be analyzed (up front) and tested **by the user**. Software that resides on the same platform as safety-critical software (and is not partitioned from that software), and any "high risk" OTS software, are included as safety-critical. These analyses and tests should be performed whether the software is modified or not. **Remember, this is YOUR system.** The OTS software may have been tested, even thoroughly tested, but not in your system environment. Ariane 5 [86] demonstrated that well tested software can cause significant problems when applied to a new system (domain).

> **Don't assume that if the software works properly,** with no hazard potentials or problems, **in the old environment it will work properly in the new system.**

Your first step is to find out what testing has already been done. Ideally, the software will be delivered with documentation that includes the tests performed and the results of those tests. If not, ask the vendor for any test or analysis documentation they have. (It never hurts to ask.) If the software is government supplied or contractor developed for a government program, hazard analyses may be available. Hazard analyses may be available for other software as well, though it is less likely for commercial software unless developed for other safety regimes (FAA, medical, automobile, etc.).

Existing hazards analyses and test results of unmodified software previously used in safety-critical systems may be used as the **basis** for certification in a new system. The existing analyses and test reports should be **reviewed for their relevance** to the reuse in the new environment. This means that you need to look at the differences in the environment between the "old" system and the system you wish to use this software in.

If the OTS software causes or affects hazards, you need to address mitigation. If source code is available, correct the software to eliminate or reduce to an acceptable level of risk any safety hazards discovered during analysis or test. The corrected software must be retested under identical conditions to ensure that these hazards have been eliminated, and that other hazards do not occur. If source code is not available, the hazards must be mitigated in another way – wrapping the OTS software, providing extra functionality in the in-house software, removing software control of a hazard cause/control, or even deciding not to use the OTS software. Thoroughly test the system to verify that the hazards have been properly mitigated.

 OTS software has taken software and system development by storm, spurred on by decreasing funds and shortened schedules. Safety engineering is trying to catch up, but the techniques and tests are still under development. Providing confidence in the safety of OTS software is still something of a black art.

12.1.5 Recommended Analyses and Tests

The hazard analysis (mentioned above) **must** be updated to include the OTS software. Any new hazards that the OTS software adds to the system must be documented, as well as any ability to control a hazard. As much as possible, consider the interactions of the OTS software with the safety-critical code. Look for ways that the OTS software can influence the safety-critical code.

For example,

- overwriting a memory location where a safety-critical variable is stored

- getting into a failure mode where the OTS software uses all the available resources and prevents the safety-critical code from executing

- clogging the message queue so that safety-critical messages do not get through in a timely manner.

Ideally, OTS software should be thoroughly tested in a "stand alone" environment, before being integrated with the rest of the software system. This may have been already done, and the vendor may have provided the documentation. The level of software testing should be determined by the criticality or risk index of the software. High-risk safety-critical software should be analyzed and tested until it is completely understood.

 If the OTS software is safety-critical, subject it to as many tests as your budget and schedule allow. The more you know about the software, the less likely it is to cause problems down the road. Since source code is often not available, the primary testing will be black box. Test the range of inputs to the OTS software, and verify that the outputs are as expected. Test the error handling abilities of the OTS software by giving it invalid inputs. Bad inputs should be rejected or set to documented values, and the software should not crash or otherwise display unacceptable behavior. See if the software throws any exceptions, gets into infinite loops, or reaches modes where it excessively uses system resources.

Software fault injection (SFI) is a technique used to determine the robustness of the software, and can be used to understand the behavior of OTS software. It *injects* faults into the software and looks at the results (Did the fault propagate? Was the end result an undesirable outcome?). Basically, the intent is to determine if the software responds gracefully to the injected faults. Traditional software fault inject used modifications of the source code to create the faults. SFI is now being used on the interfaces between components, and can be used even when the source code is unavailable. [83] and [84] discuss software fault injection with COTS software.

The following analyses, if done for the system, should be updated to include the OTS software:

- Timing, sizing and throughput – especially if the system is close to capacity/capability limits.

- Software fault tree, to include faults and dormant code in the OTS software

- Interdependence and Independence Analyses, if sufficient information available

- Design Constraint Analysis

- Code Interface Analysis

- Code Data Analysis

- Interrupt Analysis
- Test coverage Analysis

12.2 Contractor-developed Software

With government downsizing and budget cutting, a large portion of the software previously developed in-house at NASA centers is now being contracted out. Usually, whole systems are developed under the contract, including the software that runs the system.

The NASA Safety Manual (NPG 8715.3), chapter 2, discusses safety and risk management requirements for NASA contracts. Responsibilities of the Project/Program manager, Contracting Officer, and Safety and Mission Assurance personnel are described.

With a contract, especially a performance-based contract, it is usually difficult to specify *how* the contractor develops the software. The end-result is the primary criteria for successful completions. However, with safety-critical software and systems, the *how* is very important. The customer needs to have insight into the contractor development processes. This serves two purposes: to identify major problems early, so that they can be corrected; and to give confidence in the final system.

12.2.1 Selecting a Contractor

When a contractor will develop safety-critical software or systems, it is very important that the contract be awarded to a team capable of creating that safe system. Technical expertise is obviously important. The software development process used by the organization and past performance should also be factors in the selection.

Capability frameworks (see Section 4.3.8) are one way of evaluating the software development process of an organization. Such frameworks include the Software Capability Maturity Model (SW-CMM) and ISO-9000. The idea behind these frameworks is that a good process will lead to a good quality product. In general, this is true. However, factors beyond the process are also important, such as the expertise of team members, how well the team functions, and how well the process is actually followed.

If a specific process maturity level is required of the contractor (such as SW-CMM Level 3), consider how that level will be verified. Will the contractor be allowed to perform an internal assessment, or will an outside assessment be required? When the company was assessed in the past, was it for the particular sub-section of the organization that will develop your software? How will you verify throughout the contract period that the contractor's processes are being followed? These are questions to consider when you impose a capability level on a contractor.

The experience, stability, and successful past performance with similar efforts of the potential contractor are prerequisites to developing dependable safety-critical software. Past projects should be evaluated as part of the contractor selection process. This evaluation can confirm a capability determination or provide evidence to the contrary. The actual past performance, for the team that will create the software, should be rated higher than capability levels determined for a different sub-section of the company.

12.2.2 Contract Inclusions

Once the contract is awarded, both sides are usually stuck with it. Making sure that the delivered software is what you want starts with writing a good contract. According to NPG 8715.3, the following items should be considered for inclusion in any contract:

- Safety requirements

- Mission success requirements

- Risk management requirements

- Submission and evaluation of safety and risk management documentation from the contractor, such as corporate safety policies, project safety plans, and risk management plans.

- Reporting of mishaps, close calls, and lessons learned

- Surveillance by NASA. Performance-based contracts still have a requirement for surveillance!

- Sub-contracting – require that the safety requirements are passed on to sub-contractors!

Clear, concise and unambiguous requirements prevent misunderstandings between the customer and the contractor. Safety requirements should be clearly stated in the specifications. Remember that changing requirements usually involves giving the contractor more money. Do as much thinking about the system safety *up front*, and write the results into the system specification.

12.2.2.1   Safety Process

NASA has a particular process for safety verification of flight projects (both Shuttle and ISS payloads, changes to the Shuttles, Expendable Launch Vehicles, and ISS Elements). This involves creating a Safety Compliance Data Package and going through three levels of reviews at Johnson Space Center. The reviews are by phase. Phase 0/1 is the preliminary review, where the Payload Safety Review Panel (for Shuttle and ISS payloads) or the Safety Review Panel (for ISS Elements) learns about the project, reviews the safety aspects of the preliminary design, and has a chance to input any safety concerns to the project. Phase II (2) usually occurs around the Critical Design Review or during the actual implementation of the design. It is a more in-depth look at the system, hazards, and controls, as well as at the verification process to assure the hazards are mitigated. Phase III (3) must be completed 30 days prior to the delivery to the launch site. The verification of safety features must be complete, or tracked on a Verification Tracking Log (VTL) if they are still outstanding. All VTL inputs must be completed before the Flight Readiness Review, prior to launch.

It is important to specify in the contract who has responsibility for preparing and presenting the Safety Compliance Data Package to the Payload Safety Review Panel or the Safety Review Panel. Software safety will need to be addressed as part of the process.

12.2.2.2   *Analysis and Test*

The contract should also clearly state what analyses or special tests need to be done for safety and mission assurance, who will do them, and who will see the results. In a performance-based contract, usually the contractor performs all functions, including analyses. In other cases, some of the analyses may be handled from the NASA side. Regardless, the tests and analyses should be spelled out, as well as the responsible party.

Before writing the contract, review sections 5 through 10 to determine what development processes, analyses, and tests need to be included in the system specification or contract. Use the guidance on tailoring when imposing processes, analyses and tests.

12.2.2.3   *Software Assurance and Development Process*

 Software Assurance (SA) (also referred to as Software Quality Assurance or Software Product Assurance) is a vital part of successful software development. For a performance-based contract, the SA role is usually handled by a managerially independent group within the contracting company. For other contracts, SA may be performed by NASA SA personnel, if stated in the requirements. Regardless of *who* performs the SA function, the requirement for a Software Assurance function should be included in the contract. Rather than call out specific roles and responsibilities for SA, requiring use of an accepted standard (IEEE 12207 or CMM level 3, for example), or specifying that the SA responsibilities will be called out in an SA plan that is approved by the NASA project manager, is sufficient.

The contract can also state process requirements that the contractor must meet. For example, software development according to IEEE 12207 may be required. The contractor can be required to have or obtain a certain level of the Capability Maturity Model (CMM). Local ISO requirements (local to the NASA center) may also be imposed. A special method of problem reporting may be required, or the contractor may use their own, established method. It is important that a mechanism exist for NASA to be aware of problems and their corrections, once the software and system reaches a certain level of maturity. A formal Problem Reporting/Corrective Action process usually begins when the software has reached the first baseline version.

If there is question concerning the capability of the organization to perform the work, then an assessment of the organization may be necessary. The Software Assurance or IV&V engineer can provide more information. Even if the organizational makeup cannot change, some risks may be identified regarding how the software will be developed. This may lead to some form of mitigation such as requiring the use of Formal Inspections of requirements and detailed design.

12.2.2.4   *Contractor Surveillance*

It is important when imposing requirements on the contractor that a method of monitoring their compliance is also included. Metrics might be selected that will give insight into the software status. The submittal of corroborating data might be required (such as certification to ISO 9000 or CMM level 3). Surveillance of the contractor also needs to be included, and is discussed in section 12.2.3.

12.2.2.5   *Software Deliverables*

Making sure you get the software you need is important, but figuring it out *what* you need at the beginning of a project can be difficult. Some of the software deliverables are obvious. Others are often forgotten or overlooked. You also need to consider what happens after the system is delivered and the contractor is no longer part of the project. You, the customer, will have to maintain the system. Make sure you have enough information to do that!

This list encompasses many commonly required or desired software deliverables. It does not include every conceivable software deliverable, but gives a good starting point.

- Operational software – the software that is part of/runs the system. This includes flight software, ground support software, and analysis software.

- Standard project documentation for software, including Software Management Plan, Software Development Plan, Software Assurance Plan, Software Requirements Specification (if not NASA-provided), Verification and Validation Plan, Software Test Plan, and Software Configuration Management Plan. The Risk Management Plan, Safety Plan and Reliability/Maintainability Plan should address software, or point where the risk management, safety, reliability, and maintainability of the software is discussed.

- Design documentation.

- Source code.

- Any development tools used, especially if they are obscure, expensive, or difficult to obtain later.

- Any configuration files, setup files, or other information required to configure the development tools for use with the project.

- Simulators or models developed for use with the operational software. These may be needed to reproduce a test, for updates to the software after delivery, or to understand aspects of the software when errors are found during operation.

- Test software used to verify portions of the software. This includes stubs and drivers from unit and integration tests. Software that generates data for use in testing also falls under this category.

- Software Assurance reports, including process audit results and discrepancy reports.

- Formal Inspection reports.

- Test procedures and reports.

- User/operator manual.

12.2.2.6　　Independent Verification and Validation (IV&V)

All NASA projects must complete an evaluation on the need for IV&V or Independent Assessment (IA). NPD 8730.4 gives the criteria and process for this evaluation. It is important that this evaluation be completed, and agreed to, before the contract is awarded. Extra contractor resources may be needed to aid the IV&V or IA activities. Contractor cooperation with IV&V or IA personnel is expected. At a minimum, management, software development, and software assurance will need to work with the IV&V or IA personnel, providing information, answers, and understanding of the software system and the development process.

Depending on the level of IV&V levied on the project, some independent tests may be performed. These may require some contractor resources to implement.

12.2.2.7　　Software Change Process

The requirement to implement a formal software change process should be included in the contract. The process should include a change control board to consider each request. The board should have representatives from various disciplines, including software development, software assurance, systems, safety, and management. Depending on the level of software/hardware integration, someone with an electronics or mechanical understanding may be included, permanently or as the need for such expertise arises.

A NASA/customer representative should be part of the change board, or at least review the board decisions. Some of the changes may impact the ability of the system to meet the requirements, may add or remove functionality, or may impact the safety and reliability of the system.

12.2.2.8　　Requirements Specification

> **Formal inspection of the requirements specification by the NASA customer should be used to ensure that the specification is complete and unambiguous.**

 Problems found now, before the contract is written, will save money in the long run! Most software problems are actually specification problems, and the fixes become progressively more expensive as the software develops.

You should also have a mechanism in place to facilitate communication between the contractor and the customer. The requirements are rarely completely unambiguous, and some interpretation often occurs. Exchanges between contractors (and subcontractors) and the NASA customer will help to assure that misunderstanding are caught early, ambiguous requirements are clarified, and everyone is on the same page.

12.2.3　Monitoring Contractor Processes

NASA contract monitoring for Safety and Mission Assurance (S&MA) takes one of two approaches. *Oversight* is an in-line approach, where NASA personnel work with the contractor as a team member. For the software portion, NASA personnel may act as Software Assurance, perform audits, witness tests, and perform safety analyses. They may advise the project on "best practices" or make suggestions of new techniques or tools.

Insight is a more "hands off" approach and is often used with performance-based contracts. The assumption is that the contractor knows what they are doing, and NASA only needs enough insight into their processes to make sure things are functioning properly and that no major problems are brewing. In this mode, the contractor performs all SA functions. NASA software surveillance consists of reviewing the SA records, "spot auditing" the software development process and the SA process, and participating in major reviews. Other activities may be performed if requested by the contractor and NASA project management.

 Which approach is used, and the specifics of *how* to apply the approach, is called out in a **surveillance plan**. The NASA project management produces this plan once the contract is awarded. The *who* and *what* details are included in this plan. *Who* is the responsible party. For example, the contract may state that NASA will perform the Preliminary Hazard Analysis, but that the contractor will perform all subsequent analyses. *What* would be the list of analyses and special tests that must be performed. *What* is also the list of audits, records and documentation reviews, and other surveillance processes that the NASA S&MA engineer will need to perform, to verify contractor compliance with the process and SA requirements of the contract.

12.2.4 Recommended Software Testing

In addition to tests performed by the contractor, you may wish to do additional tests after software delivery. If the environment under which the software safety verification tests were performed has changed (from engineering model to flight system, for example), or if the safety verification tests were not witnessed by NASA personnel, those tests should be rerun (depending on the criticality of the hazards).

Hopefully, all desired tests will have been included in the contract, and the software will be delivered with test reports. If not, then the software should be subjected to additional tests upon delivery.

The software acceptance test should be thorough. It should include more than just functional testing. All "must work" and "must not work" functions should be exercised and verified. The error handling and fault tolerance of the software must be verified. You don't want to "break the system", but you also want to make sure that the software can safely handle the "real world" inputs and unanticipated events.

Chapter 13 Looking Ahead

Software engineering is an evolving enterprise in a fast-changing world. Innovation in languages and methodologies for software creation, along with new technologies, solve old software development problems, while often creating new ones. Keeping up with the "state of the art" is difficult for the software engineer. For Software Safety, the task is more difficult, as new analyses or techniques must be developed in parallel to the new software engineering techniques.

This guidebook does not have access to a working crystal ball. True innovations in software engineering or software safety will always take the prognosticators by surprise. However, much of the progress in software engineering and safety comes from building on the past. In that light, some areas of interest for the future are outlined below.

Object-oriented (OO) development is fairly well established in software engineering. However, the "best practices" of OO are still being determined. What is the best way to manage an OO project? How does object-orientation fit in with various lifecycles, such as the spiral or evolutionary? What are the best ways to test object-oriented software? What metrics are really the best for understanding the software and its changes? These questions, and more, will hopefully be answered in the next few years.

Some evolving technologies (distributed systems, autonomous systems, reconfigurable computing, web-based systems) were discussed in this guidebook on a superficial level. The problems associated with these technologies, and other new areas of software development, need to be understood and solved. What is the best way to develop these systems? How can you verify (through test or other means) systems that "think" or can change their programming? How can you test a distributed system with a thousand nodes? What level of security is required for web-based applications, and how can that level be achieved? How do these new technologies impact requirements management activities – how can you track the requirements and changes in highly complex systems? How can the impact of changes be accurately determined in complex systems?

New software development methodologies are being created on a regular basis. The latest methodologies include the "agile processes", which focus on short development times. Should they be used in safety-critical systems? Can they be adapted such that they would meet the requirements for such systems? With any new methodology, the problem is determining when it is safe to use, and when it should **not** be used.

"Software Engineering for Safety: A Roadmap" [105] lists some areas software safety may wish to focus on in the near future:

- Integration of informal and formal methods.

  o Automatic translation of informal notations (such as UML and fault trees) into formal models.

  o Lightweight formal methods that involve rapid, low-cost use of formal methods tailored to the immediate needs of a project.

  o Integration of previously distinct formal methods, such as theorem provers and model checkers or high-level languages and automatic verification.

- Constraints on safe product families and safe reuse.
  - Safety analyses of product families so that large aspects that are in common between systems within the same family can be analyzed only once. How can the minor variations, and especially the interaction of the variations, be characterized?
  - Safe reuse of COTS software requires a way to assess a COTS product for fitness for a particular application. It also requires ways to verify that the COTS software does not have additional, unexpected behavior.

- Testing and evaluation of safety-critical systems
  - Requirements-based testing would tightly integrate safety requirements with test cases.
  - Evaluation from multiple sources of safety evidence begs the question of how to integrate that information into a coherent whole.
  - Model consistency. How can the model of the system more accurately represent the real system?
  - Virtual environments. Using virtual environments to help design, test and certify safety-critical systems is on the horizon.

- Runtime monitoring can detect and recover from hazardous states. How can it detect unexpected hazardous states? How can it be used to identify system conditions that may threaten safety?

- Education. Current new software engineers lack exposure to the safety aspects of software creation.

- Collaboration with related fields. Software safety needs to work with others involved in software security, survivability, software architecture, theoretical computer science, human factors engineering, and other areas to exploit their advances.

Appendix A   References and Information

A.1   References

[1]   NASA-STD-8719.13A NASA Software Safety Standard, September 1997

[2]   Jet Propulsion Laboratory, Software Systems Safety Handbook

[3]   Gowen, Lon D, and Collofello, James S. "Design Phase Considerations for Safety-critical Software Systems". Professional Safety, April 1995

[4]   NPG 8715.3 NASA Safety Manual, Chapter-3, System Safety, and Appendix-D (Analysis Techniques)

[5]   NSTS 13830C Payload Safety Review and Data Submittal Requirements

[6]   NSTS-22254   Methodology for Conduct of Space Shuttle Program Hazard Analyses.
      http://wwwsrqa.jsc.nasa.gov/PCE/22254.pdf

[7]   Department of Defense, SOFTWARE SYSTEM SAFETY HANDBOOK, *A Technical & Managerial Team Approach* , Dec. 1999, by Joint Software System Safety Committee

[8]   Software Safety Hazard Analysis, J. Dennis Lawrence, Lawrence Livermore National Laboratory, Oct. 1995

[9]   Leveson, Nancy G., "Safeware - System Safety and Computers", Addison-Wesley, Appendix-A Medical Devices - The Therac-25 Story.

[10] MIL-STD-882D Military Standard - Standard Practice for System Safety

[11] NASA System Engineering Handbook, SP-610S June 1995
      http://ldcm.gsfc.nasa.gov/library/Systems_Engineering_Handbook.pdf

[12] NASA Software Assurance Guidebook, NASA-GB-A201, Sept. 1989

[13] NASA Software Management Guidebook, NASA-GB-001-96, ,   November, 1996

[14] NASA Program and Project Management Processes and Requirements, NPG 7120.5A, April, 1998

[15] Yourdon Inc., "Yourdon Systems Method-Model Driven Systems Development:, Yourdon Press, N.J., 1993.

[16] De Marco, T., Structured analysis and system specification, Prentice-Hall/Yourdon Inc., NY, NY, 1978.

[17] Peter Coad , Edward Yourdon, Object-oriented analysis (2nd ed.), Yourdon Press, Upper Saddle River, NJ, 1991

[18] Glendenning, B. E. "Creating an Object-Oriented Software System---The AIPS++ Experience", Astronomical Data Analysis Software and Systems V, ASP Conference Series, Vol. 101, 1996
      http://iraf.noao.edu/iraf/web/ADASS/adass_proc/adass_95/glendenningb/glendenningb.html

[19] Booch, G. "Object-Oriented Analysis and Design with Applications", Addison-Wesley 1994, ISBN 0-805-35340-2

[20] Shah, V., Sivitanides, M. and Martin, R. "Pitfalls of Object-Oriented Development",
      http://www.westga.edu/~bquest/1997/object.html

[21] Lubars et al, "Object-oriented Analysis For Evolving Systems", International Conference on Software Engineering, 1992 (IEEE) Page(s): 173 -185

[22] NASA-GB-A302 Formal Methods Specification and Verification Guidebook for Software and Computer Systems.

[23] Lutz, Robyn R., Ampo, Yoko, "Experience Report: Using Formal Methods for Requirements Analysis of Critical Spacecraft Software", SEL-94-006 Software Engineering Laboratory Series - Proceedings of the Nineteenth Annual Software Engineering Workshop, NASA GSFC, December 1994.

[24] Rushby, John: Formal Methods and Digital Systems Validation for Airborne Systems, NASA Contractor Report 4551, December 1993

[25] Miller, Steven P.; and Srivas, Mandayam: Formal Verification of the AAMP5 Microprocessor: A Case Study in the Industrial Use of Formal Methods, presented at WIFT '95: Workshop on Industrial-Strength Formal Specification Techniques, April 5-8, 1995, Boca Raton, Florida, USA, pp. 30-43.

[26] Butler, Ricky; Caldwell, James; Carreno, Victor; Holloway, Michael; Miner, Paul; and Di Vito, Beb: NASA Langley's Research and Technology Transfer Program in Formal Methods, in 10th Annual Conference on Computer Assurance (COMPASS 95), Gathersburg, MD, June 1995.

[27] Hall, Anthony, "Seven Myths of Formal Methods", IEEE Software, 7(5):11-19, September 1990.

[28] Kemmerer, Richard A., "Integrating Formal Methods into the Development Process", IEEE Software, 7(5):37-50, September 1990.

[29] "Process Tailoring for Software Project Plans"

[30] Brown, D., "Solving the Software Safety Paradox", Embedded Systems Programming, volume 11 number 13, Dec. 1998. http://www.embedded.com/98/9812/9812feat2.htm

[31] Stewart, D. "30 Pitfalls for Real-Time Software Developers, Part 1 ", Embedded Systems Programming, volume 12 number 10, Oct. 1999. http://www.embedded.com/1999/9910/9910feat1.htm

[32] Stewart, D. "More Pitfalls for Real-Time Software Developers", Embedded Systems Programming, volume 12 number 11, Nov. 1999 http://www.embedded.com/1999/9911/9911feat2.htm

[33] Wood, B. "Software Risk Management for Medical Devices", Medical Device & Diagnostic Industry magazine column, Jan. 1999, http://www.devicelink.com/mddi/archive/99/01/013.html

[34] NSTS 1700.7B Safety Policy and Requirements for Payloads Using the Space Transportation System.

[35] The Computer Control of Hazardous Payloads - Final Report NASA/JSC/FDSD 24 July 1991

[36] Radley, Charles, 1980, M.Sc. Thesis, Digital Control of a Small Missile, The City University, London, United Kingdom.

[37] NASA -STD-2202-93 Software Formal Inspections Standard

[38] DOD-STD-2167A Military Standard Defense Systems Software Development, Feb. 29, 1988 (this document has been replaced by DOD-STD-498, which was cancelled in 1998 when IEEE 12207 was released)

[39] Model Checking (book) E. M. Clarke, Orna Grumberg, Doron Peled; MIT Press ISBN: 0262032708; Hardcover - 314 pages (December 1999) ;Price: $50.00

[40] Leveson, N., Harvey, P., "Analyzing Software Safety", IEEE Transaction on Software Engineering, Vol. 9, SE-9, No. 5, 9/83.

[41] Leveson, N., Cha, S., and Shimeall, T., "Safety Verification of Ada Programs Using Software Fault Trees", IEEE Software, Volume 8, No. 4, 7/91.

[42] SSP 50038 Computer-Based Control System Safety Requirements International Space Station Alpha

[43] Knight, John C, and Nancy G. Leveson, "An Experimental Evaluation of the Assumption of Independence in Multiversion Programming." IEEE Transactions on Software Engineering, SE12(1986); 96-109.

[44] Butler, Ricky W.; and Finelli, George B.: The Infeasibility of Quantifying the Reliability of Life-Critical Real-Time Software' IEEE Transactions on Software Engineering, vol. 19, no. 1, Jan 1993, pp 3-12.

[45] Gowen, Lon D. and Collofello, James S. "Design Phase Considerations for Safety-Critical Software Systems". PROFESSIONAL SAFETY, April 1995.

[46] Sha, L., Goodenough, J. and Pollak, B. "Simplex Architecture: Meeting the Challenges of Using COTS in High-Reliability Systems", Crosstalk, April 1998, http://www.stsc.hill.af.mil/crosstalk/1998/04/index.html

[47] BSR/AIAA R-023A-1995 (DRAFT) "Recommended Practice for Human Computer Interfaces for Space System Operations" - Sponsor: American Institute of Aeronautics and Astronautics.

[48] Sha, Liu; Goodenough, John B. "Real-time Scheduling Theory and Ada", Computer, Vol. 23, April 1990, pp 53-62, Research Sponsored by DOD.

[49] Sha, Liu; Goodenough, John B. "Real-time Scheduling Theory and Ada", The 1989 Workshop on Operating Systems for Mission Critical Computing, Carnegie-Mellon Univ, Pittsburgh, PA.

[50] Kolcio, et. al., "Integrating Autonomous Fault Management with Conventional Flight Software: A case study", IEEE, 1999

[51] Garrett, C., M. Yau, S. Guarro, G. Apostolakais, "Assessing the Dependability of Embedded Software Systems Using the Dynamic Flowgraph Methodology". Fourth International Working Conference on Dependable Computing for Critical Applications, San Diego Jan 4-6, 1994

[52] Parnas, D., van Schouwen, A., and Kwan, S., "Evaluation of Safety-Critical Software", Communications of the ACM, p. 636648, 6/90.

[53] Horgan, et. al., "Perils of Software Reliability Modeling", SERC Technical Report, February 3, 1995, http://www.serc.net/library/publication/reportByCategory.asp?Category=Software%20Reliability%20

[54] Daconta, Michael C. "C Pointers and Dynamic Memory Management" ISBN 0-471-56152-5.

[55] Hatton, Les. "Safer C: Developing Software for High-Integrity and Safety-critical Systems." McGraw-Hill, New York, 1995. ISBN 0-07-707640-0.

[56] Plum, Thomas. "C Programming Guidelines", pub Plum Hall - Cardiff, NJ.\ISBN 0-911537-03-1.

[57] Plum, Thomas. "Reliable Data Structures in C", pub Plum Hall - Cardiff, NJ. ISBN 0-911537-04-X.

[58] Willis, C. P., and Paddon, D. J. : "Machine Learning in Software Reuse". Proceedings of the Seventh International Conference in Industrial and Engineering Application of Artificial Intelligence and Expert Systems, 1994, pp. 255-262

[59] Second Safety through quality Conference, 23rd -25th October 1995, Kennedy Space Center, Cape Canaveral, Florida

[60] Perara, Roland. "C++ Faux Pas - The C++ language has more holes in it than a string vest." EXE: The Software Developers' Magazine, Vol 10 - Issue 6/November 1995.

[61] Barbagallo, T. "Choosing The Right Embedded Software Development Tools", Integrated Systems Design, http://www.eedesign.com/design/embeddedtools/embeddedtools.html

[62] Bell, R. "Code Generation from Object Models", Embedded Systems Programming, volume 11, number 3, March 1998. http://www.embedded.com/98/9803fe3.htm

[63] Melkonian, M., "Get by Without an RTOS", Embedded Systems Programming, volume 13, number 10, Sept. 2000. http://www.embedded.com/2000/0009/0009feat4.htm

[64] Selic, B. "Distributed Software Design: Challenges and Solutions", Embedded Systems Programming, Volume 13, number 12, November, 2000   http://www.embedded.com/2000/0011/0011feat5.htm

[65] OptiMagic, Inc. "Frequently-Asked Questions (FAQ) About Programmable Logic", http://www.optimagic.com/faq.html

[66] Barr, M. "Programmable Logic: What's It To Ya?", Embedded Systems Programming, volume 9, number 6, June 1999 http://www.embedded.com/1999/9906/9906sr.htm

[67] Villasensor, J. and Mangione-Smith, W. H., "Configurable Computing", Scientific American, June, 1997

[68] "SEMSPLC Guidelines: Safety-related application software for programmable logic controllers". The Institution of Electrical Engineers. ISBN 0 85296 887 6

[69] Canning, et. al., "Sharing Ideas: the SEMSPLC Project", IEE Review , Volume: 40 Issue: 2 , 17 March 1994

[70] O'Brien, M. "Embedded Web Servers", Embedded Systems Programming, Volume 12, Number 11, November, 1999. http://www.embedded.com/internet/9911/9911ia2.htm

[71] Birk, Andreas "Autonomous Systems as distributed embedded devices", http://arti.vub.ac.be/~cyrano/AUTOSYS/

[72] Schofield, M. "Neither Master nor Slave, A Practical Case Study in the Development and Employment of Cleaning Robots", Proceeding of the 7th IEEE International Conference on Emerging Technologies and Factory Automation, Volume: 2 , 1999

[73] Simmons, et. al. "Towards Automatic Verification of Autonomous Systems", Proceedings of the 2000 IEEE/RSJ International Conference on Intelligent Robots and Systems (IROS 2000). , Volume: 2 , 2000

[74] Reinholz and Patel, "Testing Autonomous Systems for Deep Space Exploration", Aerospace Conference, 1998 IEEE , Volume: 2 , 1998

[75] Bernard, et. al. "Remote Agent Experiment DS1 Technology Validation Report", http://nmp-techval-reports.jpl.nasa.gov/DS1/Remote_Integrated_Report.pdf

[76] Smith, et. al. "Validation and Verification of the Remote Agent for Spacecraft Autonomy", Aerospace Conference, 1999. Proceedings. 1999 IEEE , Volume: 1 , 1999

[77] Fischman, L. and McRitchie, K. "Off-the-Shelf Software: Practical Evaluation", Crosstalk, Jan. 2000, http://www.stsc.hill.af.mil/crosstalk/2000/01/index.html

[78] Besnard, J., Keene, S., and Voas, J. "Assuring COTS Products for Reliability and Safety-critical Systems", 1999 Proceedings, Annual Reliability and Maintainability Symposium (IEEE)

[79] "Guidance for Industry, FDA Reviewers and Compliance on Off-the-Shelf Software Use in Medical Devices", Sept. 9, 1999, US Department of Health and Human Services, http://www.fda.gov/cdrh/ode/1252.pdf

[80] Scott, J., Preckshot, G. and Gallagher, J. "Using Commercial-Off-the-Shelf (COTS) Software in High-Consequence Safety Systems", UCRL-JC-122246, Fission Energy and Systems Safety Program (FESSP), Lawrence Livermore National Laboratory,

[81] "The Use of Commercial Off-The-Shelf Software in Safety-critical Projects" by Frances E. Simmons at Johnson Space Center, October 11, 1999. Non-published whitepaper.

[82] Lindsay, P. and Smith, G. "Safety Assurance of Commercial-Off-The-Shelf Software" Technical Report No. 00-17, May 2000, Software Verification Research Centre, School of Information Technology, The University of Queensland

[83] Voas, J. and Payne, J. "COTS Software Failures: Can Anything be Done?", IEEE Workshop on Application-Specific Software Engineering Technology, 1998.   ASSET-98. Proceedings, Page(s): 140 –144

[84] Voas, J. and Miller, K. "Interface Robustness for COTS-based Systems", IEE Colloquium on Cots and Safety-critical Systems (Digest No. 1997/013), 1996, Page(s): 7/1 –712

[85] Fraser, T., Badger, L. and Feldman, M. "Hardening COTS Software with Generic Software Wrappers", Proceedings of the 1999 IEEE Symposium on Security and Privacy

[86] European Space Agency "ARIANE 5: Flight 501 Failure", http://www.esa.int/export/esaCP/Pr_20_1996_p_EN.html

[87] Shlaer, S. and Mellor, S. "Object-Oriented System Analysis", Yourdon Press, 1988, ISBN 0-136-29023-x

[88] Jacobson, I. "Object-Oriented Software Engineering", Addison-Wesley 1992, ISBN 0-201-54435-0

[89] Stolper, S.A., "Streamlined design approach lands Mars pathfinder", IEEE Software , Volume: 16 Issue: 5 , Sept.-Oct. 1999 Page(s): 52 –62

[90] R. Lutz and R. Woodhouse, "Bi-directional analysis for Certification of Safety-Critical Software," Proceedings, International Software Assurance Certification Conference, Chantilly, VA, 1999.

[91] D. Thompson, The Literate Programming FAQ, http://shelob.ce.ttu.edu/daves/lpfaq/faq.html

[92] "Best Practices", IEEE Software, Vol. 13, No. 6, December 1996

[93] A. Watson and T. McCabe, "Structured Testing: A Testing Methodology Using the Cyclomatic Complexity Metric", NIST Special Publication 500-235

[94] J.D. Lawrence, "Software Safety Hazard Analysis", October 1995, prepared for the US Nuclear Regulatory Commission

[95] Brad Appleton [Note: link to his website is no longer valid.]

[96] F. Redmill and J. Rajan, "Human Factors in Safety-Critical Systems", 1997 ISBN 0-7506-2715-8

[97] A. Davis and D. Leffingwell, "Requirements Management in Medical Device Development", Medical and Diagnostic Industry Magazine, March 1996, http://www.devicelink.com/mddi/archive/96/03/013.html

[98] K. Wiegers, "When Telepathy Won't Do: Requirements Engineering Key Practices"

[99] Wood, J. and D. Silver, Joint Application Development, 2nd ed., New York : Wiley, 1995.

[100] C. Cruz Neira and R. Lutz, "Using Immersive Virtual Environments for Certification," IEEE Software, 16 (4) July/Aug, 1999, pp. 26-30.

[101] P. Texel and C. Williams, " Use Cases combined with Booch OMT UML: Processes and Products" , Prentice Hall 1997, ISBN: 013727405X

[102] J. Stapleton, "DSDM Dynamic Systems Development Method: The Method in Practice", Addison-Wesley 1997, ISBN: 0201178893

[103] "Maintainability Index Technique for Measuring Program Maintainability", http://www.sei.cmu.edu/activities/str/descriptions/mitmpm.html

[104] S. Bohner and R. Arnold, "Software Change Impact Analysis", IEEE Computer Society Press 1996, ISBN 0-8186-7384-2

[105] R. Lutz, "Software Engineering for Safety: A Roadmap", ICSE 2000, 22nd International Conference on Software Engineering

[106] V. Kanabar, L. Appleman, and J. Gorgone, "Object-Oriented Project Management", http://hsb.baylor.edu/ramsower/ais.ac.96/papers/OOFINI.htm

[107] D. Pitts, "Metrics: Problem Solved?", CROSSTALK 1997, http://www.stsc.hill.af.mil/crosstalk/1997/12/index.html

[108] T. Augustine and C. Schroeder, "An Effective Metrics Process Model", CROSSTALK, June 1999, http://www.stsc.hill.af.mil/crosstalk/1999/06/index.html

[109] SpecTRM product page, Safeware Engineering, http://www.safeware-eng.com/index.php/products

[110] *These quotations were taken from Imperial College, London, UK, world wide web home page "The Free On-Line Dictionary of Computing" Copyright Denis Howe, 1993-1999, (http://foldoc.doc.ic.ac.uk/foldoc/index.html), compiled by Denis Howe. It contains graphic descriptions of common problems with C. The quotations were reproduced by permission of Denis Howe <dbh@doc.ic.ac.uk>.

A.2 Information

Standards and Guidebooks

NASA Standards and Guidebooks

- NPG 8715.3   NASA Safety Manual
- NASA-CM-GDBK   NASA Software Configuration Management Guidebook
- NASA-GB-001-94   NASA Software Measurement Guidebook
- NASA-GB-001-95   NASA Software Process Improvement Guidebook
- NASA-GB-001-96   NASA Software Management Guidebook
- NASA-GB-002-95   Formal Methods Specification And verification Guidebook For Software And Computer Systems, Volume I: Planning And Technology Insertion
- NASA-GB-001-97   Formal Methods Specification And Analysis Guidebook For The verification Of software And computer Systems, volume II: A Practitioner's companion
- NASA-GB-A201   Software Assurance Guidebook
- NASA-GB-A301   Software Quality Assurance Audits guidebook
- NASA-GB-A302   Software Formal Inspections Guidebook
- NASA-STD-2100-91   NASA Software Documentation Standard
- NASA-STD-2201-93   NASA Software Assurance Standard
- NASA-STD-2202-93   Software Formal Inspection Process Standard
- NASA-STD-8719.13A   NASA Software Safety Standard
- KHB-1700.7   Space Shuttle Payload Ground Safety Handbook
- NSTS-08126   Problem Reporting and Corrective Action (PRACA) System Requirements
- NSTS-1700-7B   Safety Policy and Requirements for Payloads Using the International Space Station, Addendum
- NSTS-1700-7B   Safety Policy and Requirements for Payloads Using the Space Transportation System Change No. 6
- NSTS-22206   Requirements for Preparation and Approval of Failure Modes and Effects Analysis (FMEA) and Critical Items List (CIL)
- NSTS-22254   Methodology for Conduct of Space Shuttle Program Hazard Analyses
- NSTS-5300-4(1D-2)   Safety, Reliability, Maintainability and Quality Provisions for the Space Shuttle Program Change No. 2
- NSTS-5300.4   Safety, Reliability, Maintainability and Quality Provisions for Space Shuttle Program
- NSTS-ISS-18798   Interpretations of NSTS/ISS Payload Safety Requirements
- NSTS 13830   Payload Safety Review and Data Submittal Requirements
- NSTS 14046   Payload Verification Requirements
- NSTS 16979   Shuttle Orbiter Failure Modes & Fault Tolerances for Interface Services
- NSTS 18798   Interpretations of NSTS Payload Safety Requirements
- NSTS 22648   Flammability Configuration Analysis for Spacecraft Application
- SSP-50021   Safety Requirements Document, International Space Station Program
- SSP-50038   Computer-Based Control System Safety Requirements, International Space Station Program
- JSC 26943   Guidelines for the Preparation of Payload Flight Safety Data Packages and Hazard Report

IEEE Standards

- ISO/IEC 12207 Information Technology - Software Life Cycle Processes
- EIA 12207.0, .1, .2 Industry Implementation of International Standard ISO/IEC 12207 : 1995
- IEEE 610.12 IEEE Standard Glossary of Software Engineering Terminology
- IEEE 830-1998 IEEE Recommended Practice for Software Requirements Specifications
- IEEE 982.1 IEEE Standard Dictionary Of Measures To Produce Reliable Software
- IEEE 1016-1998 IEEE Recommended Practice for Software Design Descriptions
- IEEE 1228-1994 IEEE Standard for Software Safety Plans

US Military Standards

- DoD-STD-498 Software Development and Documentation, cancelled in 1998. Replaced by IEEE 12207.
- MIL-STD-882D Standard Practice for System Safety, February 10, 200.
- MIL-STD-882C (1993) and MIL-STD-882B (1987) are both deprecated, but include useful processes and procedures for system and software safety that are not included in 882D.

Other Standards

- DO-178B Software Considerations in Airborne Systems and Equipment Certification (Federal Aviation Administration).
- AIAA G-010 Reusable Software: Assessment Criteria for Aerospace Applications
- ANSI/AIAA R-013 Recommended Practice: Software Reliability R-013-1992
- ISO 9000-3 Quality Management And Quality Assurance Standards - Part 3: Guidelines For The Application Of ISO 9001: 1994 To The Development, Supply, Installation And Maintenance Of Computer Software Second Edition
- "Review Guidelines for Software Languages for Use in Nuclear Power Plant Safety Systems", U.S. Nuclear Regulatory Commission Contractor Report, NUREG/CR-6463, June, 1996
- UK Defence Standard 00-55 Requirements for Safety Related Software in Defence Equipment

To access NASA standards and other standards used by NASA, go to the NASA Standardization Program website at http://standards.nasa.gov/sitemap.htm.

ISS documents can be found at the PALS site (http://iss-www.jsc.nasa.gov:1532/palsagnt/plsql/palshome?db_id=ORAP).

Books

"Software Safety and Reliability : Techniques, Approaches, and Standards of Key Industrial Sectors", Debra S. Herrmann, et al., March 2000

"Safeware : System Safety and Computers", Nancy Leveson, April 1995

"Safety-Critical Computer Systems", Neil Storey, August 1996

"Software Assessment: Reliability, Safety, Testability", Michael A. Friedman and Jeffrey M. Voas (Contributor), August 16, 1995

"Semsplc Guidelines : Safety-Related Application Software for Programmable Logic Controllers", February 1999

"The Capability Maturity Model: Guidelines for Improving the Software Process", Software Engineering Institute , ISBN 0-201-54664-7, Addison-Wesley Publishing Company, Reading, MA, 1995.

Websites

NASA Websites

NASA Lessons Learned — http://llis.nasa.gov/llis/llis/main.html

NASA Technical Standards — http://standards.nasa.gov/sitemap.htm

NASA Online Directives Information System (NODIS) Library
http://nodis.gsfc.nasa.gov/library/main_lib.html

NASA Documents Online (HQ) — http://www.hq.nasa.gov/office/hqlibrary/books/nasadoc.htm

ISS Documentation (PALS) — http://iss-www.jsc.nasa.gov:1532/palsagnt/plsql/palshome

NASA Formal Methods — http://eis.jpl.nasa.gov/quality/Formal_Methods/home.html

NASA Langley Formal Methods group: — http://atb-www.larc.nasa.gov/fm/index.html

GSFC Software Engineering Laboratory — http://sel.gsfc.nasa.gov/

NASA Software Assurance Technology Center — http://satc.gsfc.nasa.gov/homepage.html

NASA IV&V Center — http://www.ivv.nasa.gov/

NASA Software Working Group — http://swg.jpl.nasa.gov/index.html

Reference Websites

Guide to the Software Engineering Body of Knowledge (SWEBOK) — http://www.swebok.org/

Standards (and 36 Cross References) — http://www.cmpcmm.com/cc/standards.html

Software Safety

Software System Safety Working Group — http://sunnyday.mit.edu/safety-club/

Safety-critical systems links: — http://archive.comlab.ox.ac.uk/safety.html

A Framework for the Development and Assurance of

High Integrity Software — http://hissa.ncsl.nist.gov/publications/sp223/

Software QA and Testing

Society for Software Quality: — http://www.ssq.org/welcome_main.html

Software Testing hotlist: — http://www.io.com/~wazmo/qa/

Guidance for Industry, General Principles of Software Validation, Draft Guidance

Version 1.1 (FDA) — http://www.fda.gov/cdrh/comp/guidance/938.html

Software Testing Stuff: — http://www.testingstuff.com/testing2.html

Software QA/Test Resource Center http://www.softwareqatest.com/

TestingCraft – tester knowledge exchange — http://www.testingcraft.com/index.html

Miscellaneous

Software Project Survival Guide — http://www.construx.com/survivalguide/chapter.htm

Software Documents, military, — http://www.pogner.demon.co.uk/mil_498/6.htm

Annals of Software Engineering — http://manta.cs.vt.edu/ase/

Software Engineering Readings — http://www.qucis.queensu.ca/Software-Engineering/reading.html

Introduction to Software Engineering — http://www.caip.rutgers.edu/~marsic/Teaching/ISE-online.html

Best Manufacturing Practices guidelines — http://www.bmpcoe.org/guideline/books/index.html

Embedded systems programming — http://www.embedded.com

Embedded systems articles — http://www.ganssle.com/

Appendix B   Glossary and Acronyms

B.1   Glossary of Terms

Various definitions contained in this Glossary are reproduced from IEEE Standard 610.12-1990, IEEE Standard Glossary of Software Engineering Terminology, copyright 81990 by the Institute of Electrical and Electronic Engineers, Inc. The IEEE takes no responsibility for and will assume no liability for damages resulting from the reader's misinterpretation of said information resulting from the placement and context in this publication.

Terminology	**Definition**
Access type	A value of an access type is either a null value or a value that designates an object created by an allocator. The designated object can be read and updated via the access value. The definition of an access type specifies the type of objects designated by values of the access type.
Accident	See Mishap.
Accreditation Certification	A formal declaration by the Accreditation Authority that a system is approved to operate in a particular manner using a prescribed set of safeguards.
Annotations	Annotations are written as Ada comments (i.e. preceded with "—" so the compiler ignores it) beginning with a special character, "#", that signals to the Static code analysis tool that special information is to be conveyed to the tool.
Anomalous Behavior	Behavior which is not in accordance with the documented requirements.
Anomaly	A state or condition which is not expected. It may or may not be hazardous, but it is the result of a transient hardware or coding error.
Architecture	The organizational structure of a system or CSCI, identifying its components, their interfaces and a concept of execution between them.
Assertions	A logical expression specifying a program state that must exist or a set of conditions that program variables must satisfy at a particular point during a program execution. Types include input assertion, loop assertion, and output assertion. (IEEE Standard 610.12-1990)
Associate Developer	An organization that is neither prime contractor nor subcontractor to the developer, but who has a development role on the same or related project.
Assurance	To provide confidence and evidence that a product or process satisfies given requirements of the integrity level and applicable national and international law(s)
Audit	An independent examination of the life cycle processes and their products for compliance, accuracy, completeness and traceability.
Audit Trail	The creation of a chronological record of system activities (audit trail) that is sufficient to enable the reconstruction, review and examination of the sequence of environments and activities surrounding or leading to an operation, procedure or an event in a transaction from its inception to its final results.

Authenticate	To verify the identity of a user, device or other entity in a system, often as a prerequisite to allowing access to resources in the system.
Authorization	The granting of access rights to a user, program or process.
Automata	A machine or controlling mechanism designed to follow automatically a predetermined sequence of operations or correct errors or deviations occurring during operation.
Baseline	The approved, documented configuration of a software or hardware configuration item, that thereafter serves as the basis for further development and that can be changed only through change control procedures.
Build	(1) A version of software that meets a specific subset of the requirements that the completed software will meet. (2) The period of time during which a version is developed. NOTE: The relationship of the terms "build" and "version" is up to the developer; for example, it may take several versions to reach a build, a build may be released in several parallel versions (such as to different sites), or the terms may be used as synonyms.
Built-In Test (BIT)	A design feature of an item which provides information on the ability of the item to perform its intended functions. BIT is implemented in software or firmware and may use or control built- in test equipment.
Built-In Test Equipment (BITE)	Hardware items that support BIT.
Catastrophic Hazard	A hazard which can result in a disabling or fatal personnel injury, loss of high-value equipment or facility, or severe environmental damage.
Caution and Warning (C&W)	Function for detection, annunciation and control of impending or imminent threats to personnel or mission success.
Certification	Legal recognition by the certification authority that a product, service, organization or person complies with the applicable requirements. Such certification comprises the activity of checking the product, service, organization or person and the formal recognition of compliance with the applicable requirements by issue of a certificate, license, approval or other document as required by national law or procedures. In particular, certification of a product involves: (a) the process of assuring the design of a product to ensure that it complies with a set of standards applicable to that type of product so as to demonstrate an acceptable level of safety; (b) the process of assessing an individual product to ensure that it conforms with the certified type design; (c) the issue of any certificate required by national laws to declare that compliance or conformity has been found with applicable standards in accordance with items (a) or (b) above.
Code Safety Analysis (CSA)	An analysis of program code and system interfaces for events, faults, and conditions that could cause or contribute to undesirable events affecting safety.
Cohesion	(1) DeMarco: Cohesion is a measure of strength of association of the elements of a module. (2) IEEE: The manner and degree to which the tasks performed by a single software module are related to one another. Types include

coincidental, communication, functional, logical, procedural, sequential and temporal.

Command	Any message that causes the receiving party to perform an action.
Computer Hardware	Devices capable of accepting and storing computer data, executing a systematic sequence of operations on computer data, or producing control outputs. Such devices can perform substantial interpretation, computation, communication, control or other logical functions.
Computer Program	A combination of computer instructions and data definitions that enable computer hardware to perform computational or control functions.
Computer Software Configuration Item	An aggregate of software that is designated for configuration management and is treated as a single entity in the configuration management process. (IEEE Standard 610.12-1990)
Concept/Conceptual	The period of time in the software development cycle during which the user needs are described and evaluated through documentation (for example, statement of needs, advance planning report, project initiation memo, feasibility studies, system definition, documentation, regulations, procedures, or policies relevant to the project).
Configuration	The requirements, design and implementation that define a particular version of a system or system component.
Configuration Control	The process of evaluating, approving or disapproving, and coordinating changes to configuration items after formal establishment of their configuration identification.
Configuration Item	(1) An item that is designated for configuration management.
	(2) A collection of hardware or software elements treated as a unit for the purpose of configuration management.
	(3) An aggregation of hardware, software or both that satisfies an end user function and is designated for separate configuration management by the acquirer.
Configuration Management	The process of identifying and defining the configuration items in a system, controlling the release and change of these items throughout the system life cycle, recording and reporting the status of configuration items and change requests, and verifying the completeness and correctness of configuration items.
Control Path	The logical sequence of flow of a control or command message from the source to the implementing effector or function. A control path may cross boundaries of two or more computers.
Controlling Application	The lower level application software that controls the particular function and its sensors and detectors.
Controlling Executive	The upper level software executive that serves as the overseer of the entire system including the lower level software.
COTS	Commercial-off-the-shelf. This refers primarily to commercial software purchased for use in a system. COTS can include operating systems, libraries, development tools, as well as complete applications. The level of documentation varies with the product. Analyses and test results are rarely available. These products are market driven, and usually contain known bugs.
Coupling	DeMarco: Coupling is a measure of the interdependence of modules The manner and degree of interdependence between software modules.

	Types include common-environment coupling, content coupling, control coupling, data coupling, hybrid coupling, and pathological coupling.
Coverage	A measure of achieving a complete assessment. 100% coverage is every one of the type specified, e.g. in the situation of test coverage, an assessment of 100% decision coverage is achieved when every one of the decisions in the software has been exercised.
Coverage Analysis	An analysis of the degree(s) of coverage assessed.
Credible Failure	A condition that has the potential of occurring based on actual failure modes in similar systems.
Critical Design Review (CDR)	A review conducted to verify that the detailed design of one or more configuration items satisfy specified requirements; to establish the compatibility among configuration items and other items of equipment, facilities, software, and personnel; to assess risk areas for each configuration item; and, as applicable, to assess the results of the producibility analyses, review preliminary hardware product specifications, evaluate preliminary test planning, and evaluate the adequacy of preliminary operation and support documents. (IEEE Standard 610.12-1990)
	For Computer Software Configuration Items (CSCIs), this review will focus on the determination of the acceptability of the detailed design, performance, and test characteristics of the design solution, and on the adequacy of the operation and support documents.
Critical Hazard	A hazard which could result in a severe injury or temporary disability, damage to high-value equipment, or environmental damage.
Critical Software Command	A command that either removes a safety inhibit or creates a hazardous condition or state. - See also Hazardous Command.
Database	A collection of related data stored in one or more computerized files in a manner that can be accessed by users or computer programs via a database management system.
Data Flow Diagram Control Flow Diagram (DFD-CFD)	DFD and CFD diagrams are a graphical representation of a system under the Structured Analysis/Structured Design methodology. Control Flow Diagrams represent the flow of control signals in the system, while Data Flow Diagrams represent the flow of data.
Deactivated Code	(1) A software program or routine or set of routines, which were specified, developed and tested for one system configuration and are disabled for a new system configuration. The disabled functions(s) is (are) fully tested in the new configuration to demonstrate that if inadvertently activated the function will result in a safe outcome within the new environment.
	(2) Executable code (or data) which by design is either (a) not intended to be executed (code) or used (data), or (b) which is only executed (code) or used (data) in certain configurations of the target system.
Dead Code	(1) Dead Code is code (1) unintentionally included in the baseline, (2) left in the system from an original software configuration, not erased or overwritten and left functional around it, or (3) deactivated code not tested for the current configuration and environment.

	(2) Executable code (or data) which, as a result of design, maintenance, or installation error cannot be executed (code) or used (data) in any operational configuration of the target system and is not traceable to a requirement (e.g., embedded identifier is OK)
Deadlock	A situation in which computer processing is suspended because two or more devices or processes are each awaiting resources assigned to the other. (IEEE Standard 610.12-1990)
Debug	The process of locating and eliminating errors that have been shown, directly or by inference, to exist in software.
Degree of Demonstration	Extent to which evidence is produced to provide confidence that specified requirements are fulfilled (ISO 8402, 4.5). Note the extent depends on criteria such as economics, complexity, innovation, safety and environmental considerations.
Developer	The organization required to carry out the requirements of this standard and the associated contract. The developer may be a contractor or a Government agency.
Development Configuration	The requirements, design and implementation that define a particular version of a system or system component.
Document/Documentation	A collection of data, regardless of the medium on which it is recorded, that generally has permanence and can be read by humans or machines.
Dormant Code	Similar to dead code, it is software instructions that are included in the executable but not meant to be used. Dormant code is usually the result of COTS or reused software that include extra functionality over what is required.
Dynamic allocation	Dynamic allocation is the process of requesting to the operating system memory storage for a data structure that is used when required by the application program's logic. Successful allocation of memory (if memory space is available) may be from the task's heap space.
Emulator	A combination of computer program and hardware that mimic the instruction and execution of another computer or system.
Environment	(1) The aggregate of the external procedures, conditions and objects that affect the development, operation and maintenance of a system.
	(2) Everything external to a system which can affect or be affected by the system.
Error	(1) Mistake in engineering, requirement specification, or design.
	(2) Mistake in design, implementation or operation which could cause a failure.
Error Handling	An implementation mechanism or design technique by which software faults are detected, isolated and recovered to allow for correct runtime program execution.
Exception	Exception is an error situation that may arise during program execution. To raise an exception is to abandon normal program execution to signal that the error has taken place.
Fail-Safe	(1) Ability to sustain a failure and retain the capability to safely terminate or control the operation.

	(2) A design feature that ensures that the system remains safe or will cause the system to revert to a state which will not cause a mishap.
Failure	The inability of a system or component to perform its required functions within specified performance requirements. (IEEE Standard 610.12-1990)
Failure Tolerance	The ability of a system or subsystem to perform its function(s) or maintain control of a hazard in the presence of failures within its hardware, firmware, or software.
Fault	Any change in state of an item that is considered to be anomalous and may warrant some type of corrective action. Examples of faults included device errors reported by Built-In Test (BIT)/Built-In Test Equipment (BITE), out-of-limits conditions on sensor values, loss of communication with devices, loss of power to a device, communication error on bus transaction, software exceptions (e.g., divide by zero, file not found), rejected commands, measured performance values outside of commanded or expected values, an incorrect step, process, or data definition in a computer program, etc. Faults are preliminary indications that a failure may have occurred.
Fault Detection	A process that discovers or is designed to discover faults; the process of determining that a fault has occurred.
Fault Isolation	The process of determining the location or source of a fault.
Fault Recovery	A process of elimination of a fault without permanent reconfiguration.
Fault Tree	A schematic representation, resembling an inverted tree, of possible sequential events (failures) that may proceed from discrete credible failures to a single undesired final event (failure). A fault tree is created retrogressively from the final event by deductive logic.
Finite State Machine	Also known as: Requirements State Machine, State of Finite Automation Transition Diagram.
	A model of a multi-state entity, depicting the different states of the entity, and showing how transitions between the states can occur. A finite state machine consists of:
	1. A finite set of states
	2. A finite set of unique transitions.
Firmware	Computer programs and data loaded in a class of memory that cannot be dynamically modified by the computer during processing (e.g. ROM).
Flight Hardware	Hardware designed and fabricated for ultimate use in a vehicle intended to fly.
Formal Methods System	(1) The use of formal logic, discrete mathematics, and machine-readable languages to specify and verify software.
	(2) The use of mathematical techniques in design and analysis of the system.
Formal Verification	(For Software) The process of evaluating the products of a given phase using formal mathematical proofs to ensure correctness and consistency with respect to the products and standards provided as input to that phase.

GOTS	Government-off-the-shelf. This refers to government created software, usually from another project. The software was not created by the current developers (see *reused software*). Usually, source code is included and all available documentation, including test and analysis results.
Graceful Degradation	(1) A planned stepwise reduction of function(s) or performance as a result of failure, while maintaining essential function(s) and performance. (2) The capability of continuing to operate with lesser capabilities in the face of faults or failures or when the number or size of tasks to be done exceeds the capability to complete.
Graph theory	An abstract notation that can be used to represent a machine that transitions through one or more states.
Ground Support Equipment (GSE)	Ground-based equipment used to store, transport, handle, test, check out, service, and/or control aircraft, launch vehicles, spacecraft, or payloads.
Hardware Configuration Item (HWCI)	An aggregation of a hardware device and computer instructions and/or computer data that reside as read-only software on a hardware device.
Hazard	The presence of a potential risk situation caused by an unsafe act or condition. A condition or changing set of circumstances that presents a potential for adverse or harmful consequences; or the inherent characteristics of any activity, condition or circumstance which can produce adverse or harmful consequences.
Hazard Analysis	The determination of potential sources of danger and recommended resolutions in a timely manner for those conditions found in either the hardware/software systems, the person/machine relationship, or both, which cause loss of personnel capability, loss of system, loss of life, or injury to the public.
Hazard Cause	A component level Fault or failure which can increase the risk of, or result in a hazard.
Hazard Control	Design or operational features used to reduce the likelihood of occurrence of a hazardous effect.
Hazardous Command	A command whose execution (including inadvertent, out-of-sequence, or incorrectly executed) could lead to an identified critical or catastrophic hazard, or a command whose execution can lead to a reduction in the control of a hazard (including reduction in failure tolerance against a hazard or the elimination of an inhibit against a hazard).
Hazardous State	A state that may lead to an unsafe state.
Hazard Report	The output of a hazard analysis for a specific hazard which documents the hazard title, description, causes, control, verification, and status.
Hazard Risk Index	A combined measure of the severity and likelihood of a hazard. See Table in Section 2.
Hazard Severity	An assessment of the consequences of the worst credible mishap that could be caused by a specific hazard.
Higher Order Logic	A functional language for specifying requirements, used in Formal Methods.

Independent Assessment (IA)	A formal process of assessing (auditing) the development, verification, and validation of the software. An IA does not perform those functions (as in IV&V), but does evaluate how well the project did in carrying them out.
Independent Inhibit	Two inhibits are independent if no SINGLE failure, error, event, or environment can eliminate more than one inhibit. Three inhibits are independent if no TWO failures, errors, events or environments (or any pair of one of each) can eliminate more than two inhibits.
Independent Verification and Validation (IV & V)	A process whereby the products of the software development life cycle phases are independently reviewed, verified, and validated by an organization that represents the acquirer of the software and is completely independent of the provider.
Inhibit	A design feature that provides a physical interruption between an energy source and a function (e.g., a relay or transistor between a battery and a pyrotechnic initiator, a latch valve between a propellant tank and a thruster, etc.).
Interface	In software development, a relationship among two or more entities (such as CSCI-CSCI, CSCI-HWCI, CSCI-User or software unit-software unit) in which the entities share, provide or exchange data. An interface is not a CSCI, software unit or other system component; it is a relationship among them.
Interface Hazard Analysis	Evaluation of hazards which cross the interfaces between a specified set of components, elements, or subsystems.
Interlock	Hardware or software function that prevents succeeding operations when specific conditions exist.
Life Cycle	The period of time that starts when a software product is conceived and ends when the software is no longer available for use. The software life cycle traditionally has eight phases: Concept and Initiation; Requirements; Architectural Design; Detailed Design; Implementation; Integration and Test; Acceptance and Delivery; and Sustaining Engineering and Operations.
Machine Code	Low level language Computer software, usually in binary notation, unique to the processor object in which it is executed. The same as object code.
Maintainability	The ability of an item to be retained in or restored to specified condition when maintenance is performed by personnel having specified skill levels, using prescribed procedures, resources and equipment at each prescribed level of maintenance and repair.
Moderate Hazard	A hazard whose occurrence would result in minor occupational injury or illness or property damage.
Memory Integrity	The assurance that the computer program or data is not altered or destroyed inadvertently or deliberately.
Mishap	An unplanned event or series of events that results in death, injury, occupational illness, or damage to or loss of equipment, property, or damage to the environment; an accident.
Must Work Function	"Must work" functions are those aspects of the system that have to work in order to for it to function correctly.

Must Not Work Function	"Must not work" functions are aspects of the system that should not occur, if the system is functioning correctly. If they do occur, they could lead to a hazardous situation or other undesired outcome.
N-Version Software	Software developed in two or more versions using different specifications, programmers, languages, platforms, compilers, or combinations of some of these. This is usually an attempt to achieve independence between redundant software items. Research has shown that this method usually does not achieve the desired reliability, and it is no longer recommended.
Negative Testing	Software Safety Testing to ensure that the software will not go to a hazardous state or generate outputs that will create a hazard in the system in response to out of bound or illegal inputs.
Negligible Hazard	Probably would not affect personnel safety (no or minor injury) or damage high-value equipment. Equipment may be stressed. Such hazards are a violation of specific criteria, rather than a major safety concern..
No-Go Testing	Software Safety Testing to ensure that the software performs known processing and will go to a known safe state in response to specific hazardous situations.
Object Code	Low level language Computer software, usually in binary notation, unique to the processor object in which it is executed. The same as machine code.
Objective Evidence	Information which can be proved true, based on facts obtained through observation, measurement, test or other means.
Operator Error	An inadvertent action by an operator that could eliminate, disable, or defeat an inhibit, redundant system, containment feature, or other design features that is provided to control a hazard.
Override	The forced bypassing of prerequisite checks on the operator-commanded execution of a function. Execution of any command (whether designated as a "hazardous command" or not) as an override is considered to be a hazardous operation requiring strict procedural controls and operator safing. (ISS)
Patch	(1) A modification to a computer sub-program that is separately compiled inserted into machine code of a host or parent program. This avoids modifying the source code of the host/parent program. Consequently the parent/host source code no longer corresponds to the combined object code. (2) A change to machine code (object code) representation of a computer program and by-passing the compiler
Path	The logical sequential structure that the program must execute to obtain a specific output.
Peer Review	An overview of a computer program presented by the author to others working on similar programs in which the author must defend his implementation of the design. Note: A phase does not imply the use of any specific life-cycle model, nor does it imply a period of time in the development of a software product.
Predicate	Predicate is any expression representing a condition of the system.

Preliminary Design Review (PDR)	A review conducted to evaluate the progress, technical adequacy, and risk resolution of the selected design approach for one or more configuration items; to determine each design's compatibility with the requirements for the configuration item; to evaluate the degree of definition and assess the technical risk associated with the selected manufacturing methods and processes; to establish the existence and compatibility of the physical and functional interfaces among the configuration items and other items of equipment, facilities, software, and personnel; and as appropriate, to evaluate the preliminary operation and support documents. (IEEE Standard 610.12-1990)

For CSCIs, the review will focus on:

(1) the evaluation of the progress, consistency, and technical adequacy of the selected architectural design and test approach,

(2) compatibility between software requirements and architectural design, and

(3) the preliminary version of the operation and support documents. |
Preliminary Hazard Analysis (PHA)	Analysis performed at the system level to identify safety-critical areas, to provide an initial assessment of hazards, and to identify requisite hazard controls and follow-on actions.
Program Description Language (PDL)	PDL is used to describe a high level design that is an intermediate step before actual code is written.
Redundancy	Provision of additional functional capability (hardware and associated software) to provide at least two means of performing the same task.
Regression Testing	The testing of software to confirm that functions, that were previously performed correctly, continue to perform correctly after a change has been made.
Reliability	The probability of a given system performing its mission adequately for a specified period of time under the expected operating conditions.
Rendezvous	A rendezvous is the interaction that occurs between two parallel tasks when one task has called an entry of the other task, and a corresponding accept statement is being executed by the other task on behalf of the calling task.
Requirement(s)	(1) Condition or capability needed by a user to solve a problem or achieve an objective.

(2) Statements describing essential, necessary or desired attributes. |
| Requirements, Derived | (1) Essential, necessary or desired attributes not explicitly documented, but logically implied by the documented requirements.

(2) Condition or capability needed, e.g. due to a design or technology constraint, to fulfill the user's requirement(s). |
Requirements, Safety	Those requirements which cover functionality or capability associated with the prevention or mitigation of a hazard.
Requirement Specification	Specification that sets forth the requirements for a system or system component.
Requirements State Machine	See Finite State Machine

Reusable Software	A software product developed for one use but having other uses, or one developed specifically to be usable on multiple project or in multiple roles on one project. Examples include, but are not limited to, commercial-off-the-shelf software (COTS) products, acquirer-furnished software products, software products in reuse libraries, and pre-existing developer software products. Each use may include all or part of the software product and may involve its modification. This term can be applied to any software product (for example, requirements, architectures, etc.), not just to software itself.
Reused Software	This is software previously written by an in-house development team and used on a different project. GOTS software would come under this category if it is supplied to another government project. Because this software was verified and validated for a previous project, it is often assumed to work correctly in the new system. Each piece of reused software should be thoroughly analyzed for its operation in the new system. Remember the problems when the Ariane 4 software was used in Ariane 5!
Risk	(1) As it applies to safety, exposure to the chance of injury or loss. It is a function of the possible frequency of occurrence of the undesired event, of the potential severity of resulting consequences, and of the uncertainties associated with the frequency and severity.
	(2) A measure of the severity and likelihood of an accident or mishap.
	(3) The probability that a specific threat will exploit a particular vulnerability of the system.
Safe (Safe State)	(1) The state of a system defined by having no identified hazards present and no active system processes which could lead to an identified hazard.
	(2) A general term denoting an acceptable level of risk, relative freedom from and low probability of: personal injury; fatality; loss or damage to vehicles, equipment or facilities; or loss or excessive degradation of the function of critical equipment.
Safety	Freedom from hazardous conditions.
Safety Analysis	A systematic and orderly process for the acquisition and evaluation of specific information pertaining to the safety of a system.
Safety Architectural Design Analysis (SADA)	Analysis performed on the high-level design to verify the correct incorporation of safety requirements and to analyze the Safety-Critical Computer Software Components (SCCSCs).
Safety-Critical	Those software operations that, if not performed, performed out-of-sequence, or performed incorrectly could result in improper control functions (or lack of control functions required for proper system operation) that could directly or indirectly cause or allow a hazardous condition to exist.
Safety-Critical Computer Software Component (SCCSC)	Those computer software components (processes, modules, functions, values or computer program states) whose errors (inadvertent or unauthorized occurrence, failure to occur when required, occurrence out of sequence, occurrence in combination with other functions, or erroneous value) can result in a potential hazard, or loss of predictability or control of a system.
Safety-Critical Computing System	A computing system containing at least one Safety-Critical Function.

Safety-Critical Computing	Those computer functions in which an error can result in a potential hazard to the user, friendly forces, materiel, third parties or the environment.
Safety-Critical Software	Software that:
	(1) Exercises direct command and control over the condition or state of hardware components; and, if not performed, performed out-of-sequence, or performed incorrectly could result in improper control functions (or lack of control functions required for proper system operation), which could cause a hazard or allow a hazardous condition to exist.
	(2) Monitors the state of hardware components; and, if not performed, performed out-of-sequence, or performed incorrectly could provide data that results in erroneous decisions by human operators or companion systems that could cause a hazard or allow a hazardous condition to exist.
	(3) Exercises direct command and control over the condition or state of hardware components; and, if performed inadvertently, out-of-sequence, or if not performed, could, in conjunction with other human, hardware, or environmental failure, cause a hazard or allow a hazardous condition to exist.
Safety Detailed Design Analysis (SDDA)	Analysis performed on Safety-Critical Computer Software Components to verify the correct incorporation of safety requirements and to identify additional hazardous conditions.
Safety Kernel	An independent computer program that monitors the state of the system to determine when potentially unsafe system states may occur or when transitions to potentially unsafe system states may occur. The Safety Kernel is designed to prevent the system from entering the unsafe state and return it to a known safe state.
Safing	The sequence of events necessary to place systems or portions thereof in predetermined safe conditions.
Sensor	A transducer that delivers a signal for input processing.
Separate Control Path	A control path which provides functional independence to a command used to control an inhibit to an identified critical or catastrophic hazard.
Software	(1) Computer programs and computer databases.
	Note: although some definitions of software include documentation, MIL-STD-498 limits the definition to programs and computer databases in accordance with Defense Federal Acquisition Regulation Supplement 227.401 (MIL-STD-498).
	(2) Organized set of information capable of controlling the operation of a device.
Software Assurance (SA)	The process of verifying that the software developed meets the quality, safety, reliability, security requirements as well as technical and performance requirements. Assurance looks at both the process used to develop the software and the analyses and tests performed to verify the software. Software Quality Assurance (SQA) and Software Product Assurance (SPA) are sometimes used interchangeably with Software Assurance.
Software Controllable Inhibit	A system-level hardware inhibit whose state is controllable by software commands.

Software Error	The difference between a computed, observed or measured value or condition and the true, specified or theoretically correct value or condition.
Software Fault	An incorrect step, process or data definition in a computer system.
Software Inhibit	A software or firmware feature that prevents a specific event function from occurring or a specific function from being available. The software may be resident in any medium. (A software inhibit is not in itself an "inhibit" in the sense of providing a physical interrupt between an energy source and a function.)
Software Partitioning	Separation, physically and/or logically, of (safety-critical) functions from other functionality.
Software Requirements Review (SRR)	A review of the requirements specified for one or more software configuration items to evaluate their responsiveness to and interpretation of system requirements and to determine whether they form a satisfactory basis for proceeding into a preliminary (architectural) design of configuration items. (IEEE Standard 610.12-1990) Same as Software Specification Review for MIL-STD-498.
Software Requirements Specification (SRS)	Documentation of the essential requirements (functions, performance, design constraints, and attributes) of the software and its external interfaces. (IEEE Standard 610.12-1990)
Software Safety Requirements Analysis (SSRA)	Analysis performed to examine system and software requirements and the conceptual design in order to identify unsafe modes for resolution, such as out-of-sequence, wrong event, deadlocking, and failure-to-command modes.
Software Specification Review (SSR)	Same as Software Requirements Review.
Software Safety	The application of the disciplines of system safety engineering techniques throughout the software life cycle to ensure that the software takes positive measures to enhance system safety and that errors that could reduce system safety have been eliminated or controlled to an acceptable level of risk.
Software Safety Engineering	The application of System Safety Engineering techniques to software development in order to ensure and verify that software design takes positive measures to enhance the safety of the system and eliminate or control errors which could reduce the safety of the system.
System Safety	Application of engineering and management principles, criteria, and techniques to optimize safety and reduce risks within the constraints of operational effectiveness, time, and cost throughout all phases of the system life cycle.
Software Specification Review (SSR)	Same as Software Requirements Review
State Transition Diagram	(See also Finite State Machine). Directed graph used in many Object Oriented methodologies, in which nodes represent system states and arcs represent transitions between states.
System	A set of components which interact to perform some function or set of functions.
System Safety	Application of engineering and management principles, criteria, and techniques to optimize safety and reduce risks within the constraints of

operational effectiveness, time, and cost throughout all phases of the system life cycle.

System Safety Engineering	An engineering discipline requiring specialized professional knowledge and skills in applying scientific and engineering principles, criteria, and techniques to identify and eliminate hazards, or reduce the associated risk.
System Safety Management	A management discipline that defines system safety program requirements and attempts to ensure the planning, implementation and accomplishment of system safety tasks and activities consistent with the overall program requirements.
System Specification	Document stating requirements for the system.
Test Case	A set of test inputs, execution conditions and expected results used to determine whether the expected response is produced.
Testing	The process of executing a series of test cases and evaluating the results.
Test Procedure	(1) Specified way to perform a test.
	(2) Detailed instructions for the set-up and execution of a given set of test cases and instructions for the evaluation of results executing the test cases.
Test Readiness Review (TRR)	A review conducted to evaluate preliminary test results for one or more configuration items; to verify that the test procedures for each configuration item are complete, comply with test plans and descriptions, and satisfy test requirements; and to verify that a project is prepared to proceed to formal test of the configuration items. (IEEE Standard 610.12-1990)
Test, Stress	For software, this is testing by subjecting the software to extreme external conditions and anomalous situations in which the software is required to perform correctly.
Test, System	A set of tests on the complete system. Includes load, stress, performance, functionality, and other tests.
Time to Criticality	The time between the occurrence of a failure, event or condition and the subsequent occurrence of a hazard or other undesired outcome.
Traceability	Traceability for software refers to documented mapping of requirements into the final product, through all development life cycles.
Transition	A transition is when an input causes a state machine to change state.
Trap	Software feature that monitors program execution and critical signals to provide additional checks over and above normal program logic. Traps provide protection against undetected software errors, hardware faults, and unexpected hazardous conditions.
Trigger	Triggers are one or more conditions that when all are true enable a specific action to take place.
Type	(As used in software design). A type characterizes both a set of values and a set of operations applicable to those values. Typing of variables can be strong or weak. Strong typing is when only defined values of a variable and defined operations are allowed. Weak typing refers to

	when the restrictions that are applied are very loose (i.e. a declaration of type integer with no range or operation definition).
Undocumented Code	Software code that is used by the system but is not documented in the software design. Usually this pertains to Commercial Off-the-Shelf Software(COTS) because the documentation is not always available.
Unified Modeling Language	UML is the defacto standard for modeling object-oriented software. It consists of a graphical notation for class definition and interaction.
Unit Test	Test performed on a software "unit" – usually a coherent, self-contained set of modules, classes, or other components. A Unit may correspond to a CSCI. Unit testing is often performed by the developer.
Unsafe State	A system state that may result in a mishap.
Unused Code	Software code that resides in the software that is not intended for use during nominal or contingency situation. Examples are test code, no-oped coded (code that is bypassed), and code that is retained by not being used from one operational increment to the next.
Validation	(1) An evaluation technique to support or corroborate safety requirements to ensure necessary functions are complete and traceable. (2) The process of evaluating software at the end of the software development process to ensure compliance with software requirements. (3) Confirmation by examination and provision of objective evidence that the particular requirements for a specific use are fulfilled (for software). The process of evaluating software to ensure compliance with specified. (4) The process of determining whether the system operates correctly and executes the correct functions.
Verification	(1) The process of determining whether the products of a given phase of the software development cycle fulfill the requirements established during the previous phase(s) (see also validation). (2) Formal proof of program correctness. (3) The act of reviewing, inspecting, testing, checking, auditing, or otherwise establishing and documenting whether items, processes, services, or documents conform to specified requirements. (4) Confirmation by examination and provision of objective evidence that specified requirements have been fulfilled (for software). (5) The process of evaluating the products of a given phase to determine the correctness and consistency of those products with respect to the products and standards provided as input to that phase.
Waiver	A variance that authorizes departure from a particular safety requirement where alternate methods are employed to mitigate risk or where an increased level of risk has been accepted by management.
Watchdog Timer	An independent, external timer that ensures the computer cannot enter an infinite loop. Watchdog timers are normally reset by the computer program. Expiration of the timer results in generation of an interrupt, program restart, or other function that terminates current program execution.

B.2   Acronyms

Acronym	Term
BIT	Built-In Test
BITE	Built-In Test Equipment
C&W	Caution and Warning
CASE	Computer Aided Software Engineering
CDR	Critical Design Review
CFD	Control Flow Diagram
COTS	Commercial Off-the-Shelf
CSA	Code Safety Analysis
CSC	Computer Software Component
CSCI	Computer Software Configuration Item
CSU	Computer Software Unit
DFD	Data Flow Diagram
DID	Data Item Description
DLA	Design Logic Analysis
DoD	Department of Defense
FDIR	Fault Detection, Isolation, and Recovery
FI	Formal Inspection
FMEA	Failure Modes and Effects Analysis
FQR	Formal Qualifications Review
FTA	Fault Tree Analysis
GFE	Government Furnished Equipment
GOTS	Government Off-the-Shelf
GSE	Ground Support Equipment
HCI	Human-Computer Interface
HOL	Higher Order Logic
HRI	Hazard Risk Index
IA	Independent Assessment
ICD	Interface Control Document
IEEE	Institute of Electrical and Electronics Engineers
IOS	International Organization for Standardization
ISO	from the Greek root isos meaning equal or standard (not an acronym). ISO standards are published by IOS
ISS	International Space Station
IV&V	Independent Verification and Validation
JPL	Jet Propulsion Laboratory, Pasadena, California
MIL-STD	Military Standard
MNWF	Must Not Work Function
MWF	Must Work Function
NDI	Non-Developmental Item
NHB	NASA Handbook

NDS	Non-Developmental Software
NMI	NASA Management Instruction
NPD	NASA Policy Directive
NPG	NASA Procedures and Guidelines
NSTS	National Space Transportation System
OO	Object Oriented
OOA	Object Oriented Analysis
OOD	Object Oriented Development
OTS	Off the Shelf
QA	Quality Assurance
PDL	Program Description Language
PHA	Preliminary Hazard Analysis
PLC	Programmable Logic Controller
PLD	Programmable Logic Device
POCC	Payload Operations Control Center
POST	Power On Self Test
ROM	Read Only Memory
S&MA	Safety and Mission Assurance
SA	Software Assurance
SADA	Safety Architectural Design Analysis
SCCSC	Safety-critical Computer Software Component
SDDA	Safety Detailed Design Analysis
SEE	Software Engineering Environment
SIS	Software Interface Specification
SFMEA	Software Failure Modes and Effects Analysis
SFTA	Software Fault Tree Analysis
SPA	Software Product Assurance
SQA	Software Quality Assurance
SRD	Software Requirements Document
SRR	Software Requirements Review
SRS	Software Requirements Specifications
SSHA	Software Subsystem Hazard Analysis
SSR	Software Specification Review
SSRA	Software Safety Requirements Analysis
TRR	Test Readiness Review
UML	Unified Modeling Language

Appendix C   Software Fault Tree Analysis (SFTA)

This section is provided to assist systems safety engineers and software developers with an introductory explanation of the Software Fault Tree Analysis technique. Most of the information presented in this entry is derived from Leveson et al. [41].

It is possible for a system to meet requirements for a correct state and be unsafe. It is unlikely that developers will be able to identify, prior to the fielding of the system, all correct but unsafe states which could occur within a complex system. In systems where the cost of failure is high, special techniques or tools such as Fault Tree Analysis (FTA) need to be used to ensure safe operation. FTA can provide insight into identifying unsafe states when developing safety-critical systems. Fault trees have advantages over standard verification procedures. Fault trees provide the focus needed to give priority to catastrophic events, and they assist in determining environmental conditions under which a correct or incorrect state becomes unsafe.

FTA was originally developed in the 1960's for safety analysis of the Minuteman missile system. It has become one of the most widely used hazard analysis techniques. In some cases FTA techniques may be mandated by civil or military authorities.

C.1   Software Fault Tree Analysis Description

A Fault Tree Analysis (FTA) is a top-down approach to failure analysis that starts with an undesirable event, such as a failure or mishap/accident or malfunction, and then determining all the ways it can happen. Fault Trees are often used to look at the hardware aspects of the system for possible failure modes. Traditionally, Fault Trees did not consider software or operations as possible causes of events.

A *Software* Fault Tree Analysis (SFTA) uses the same techniques to look at the software failures that could cause a hazard. It is a system for identifying causes of hazards, but not the hazards themselves. That should have been done previously in the Preliminary Hazard Analysis (section 2.3.1) or in the hardware FTA. Like the standard FTA, the SFTA is a systematic top down deductive approach to risk analysis within which specific software failure modes are hypothesized. The task is to identify all possible software events that can lead up to a failure mode. Like the FTA, SFTAs use a deductive approach to identify critical paths and provide minimal sets of states or critical paths which will lead to the top event.

A software FTA is a little trickier than strict hardware FTA. Software operates in many modes or states. It performs different functions at different times. There may be a lot more of inhibits and conditioning events when mapping a Software Fault Tree.

A sample fault tree is shown in Figure C- 2 *"Example of High Level Fault Tree"*. Note that much of the diagram is hardware related. Software Fault Trees will often include hardware elements. The actual hazards are a result of a hardware failure of some sort. Software can only cause the hazard through its interactions with the hardware. When tracing through the tree of causes, hardware-only causes are "non-primal" and ignored.

C.2   Goal of Software Fault Tree Analysis

SFTA is a technique to analyze the safety of a software design. The goal of SFTA is to show that the logic in a software design or in an implementation (actual code) will not produce a hazard. The design or code should be modified to compensate for those failure conditions deemed hazardous threats to the system. In this manner, a system with safer operational characteristics is produced. SFTAs are most practical to use when we know that the system has relatively few states that are hazardous

Developers typically use forward inference to design a system. That is, their analysis focuses on generating a next state from a previously safe state. The software is developed with key assumptions about the state of the system prior to entering the next state. In complex systems that rely on redundancy, parallelism, or fault tolerance, it may not be feasible to go exhaustively through the assumptions for all cases.

The SFTA technique provides an alternative perspective that uses backward inference. The experience from projects that have employed SFTA shows that this change of perspective is crucial to the issue of finding safety errors. The analyst is forced to view the system from a different perspective, one that makes finding errors more apparent.

SFTA is very useful for determining the conditions under which fault tolerance and fail safe procedures should be initiated. The analysis can help guide safety engineers in the development of safety-critical test cases by identifying those areas most likely to cause a hazard. On larger systems, this type of analysis can be used to identify safety-critical software components, if they have not already been identified.

SFTA is language independent and can be applied to any programming language (high level or low level) as long as the semantics are well defined. The SFTA is an axiomatic verification where the postconditions describe the hazard rather than the correctness condition. This analysis shows that, if the weakest precondition is false, the hazard or postcondition can never occur and conversely, if the precondition is true, then the program is inherently unsafe and needs to be changed.

Software fault trees should not be reviewed in isolation from the underlying hardware, because to do so would deny a whole class of interface and interaction problems. Simulation of human failure such as operator mistakes can also be analyzed using the SFTA technique.

The symbols used for the graphical representation of the SFTA have largely been borrowed from the hardware fault tree set (see Figure C-1 - *SFTA Graphical Representation Symbols*). This facilitates the linking of hardware and software fault trees at their interfaces to allow the entire system to be analyzed.

The SFTA makes no claim as to the reliability of the software. When reusing older components, a new safety analysis is necessary because the fundamental safety assumptions used in the original design must be validated in the new environment. The assertion that highly reliable software is safe is not necessarily true. In fact, safety and reliability at times run counter to each other. An example of this conflict can be found in the actual experience of air traffic controllers from the U.S. who attempted to port an air traffic control software application from the U.S. to Britain. The U.S. software had proved to be very reliable but certain assumptions had been made about longitude (i.e., no provision for both east and west coordinates) that caused the map of Britain to fold in half at the Greenwich meridian).

SFTA is not a substitute for the integration and test procedures that verify functional system requirements. The traditional methods that certify that requirements are correct and complete will still need to be used. The SFTA helps provide the extra assurance that is required of systems that are either safety-critical or very costly by verifying that safety axioms have been implemented through a rigorous analysis of those software components that are responsible for the safety controls of the system.

C.3   Use of Software Fault Tree Analysis

Any SFTA must be preceded by a hazard analysis of the entire system. The information in the hazard analysis identifies those undesired events in the system that can cause serious consequences. It should be noted that in complex systems not all hazards can be predetermined. In this respect the technique does not claim to produce consistent results irrespective of the analyst. It is dependent on the judgment of the individual as to when to stop the process and which hazards to analyze.

The SFTA can be used at different stages of the software life cycle, beginning at the software requirements phase. At that early stage, only the bare minimum of the software will be defined, though the system will usually have a preliminary design. Only a very high-level SFTA will be able to be performed. However, as the software design progresses, and the code is developed, the SFTA can be "fleshed out" with the new information. High-level blocks can be broken down into specific components (modules, classes, methods, etc.).

The basic procedure in an SFTA is to assume that the hazard has occurred and then to determine its set of possible causes. The technique is useless if one starts with the overly generalized hazard "system fails". A more specific failure, such as those identified from the earlier hazard analysis, has to be the starting point for the analysis. The hazard is the root of the fault tree and its leaves are the necessary preconditions for the hazard to occur. These preconditions are listed in the fault tree and connected to the root of the tree via a logical AND or logical OR of the preconditions (see Figure C- 3 - Example of High Level Fault Tree). In turn, each one of the preconditions is expanded in the same fashion as the root fault (we identify the causes of each precondition).   The expansion continues until all leaves describe events of computable probability or the event cannot be analyzed further.   The analysis also stops when the precondition is a hardware malfunction that has no dependency on software.

The fault tree is expanded from the specified system level failure to the software interface level where we have identified the software outputs or lack of them that can adversely affect system operation.   At this stage the analysis begins to take into account the behavior specific to the language.   The language constructs can be transformed into templates using preconditions, postconditions and logical connectives. (For templates of Ada constructs, see Leveson et al. [41].) All the critical code must be traced until all conditions are identified as true or false or an input statement is reached.

The technique will be illustrated with an example using a Pascal like language [40]. The code will be analyzed for the occurrence of the variable Z being output with a value greater than 100. We should assume B, X, Z are integers.

```
While B>Xdo
        begin B :=B- 1;
        Z := Z + 10;
end
if Z ~ 100 then output Z;
```

In this piece of code there are assignment statements, an "if" and a "while" construct. The templates for these statements will be applied, starting from the occurrence of the event we are searching for "output Z with Z > 100". Refer to Figure C- 3 – "Example Code Fault Tree" for the discussion that follows. The templates for the constructs will be drawn showing all the considerations that are required for the analysis to be complete. Some leaves of the tree are not expanded further because they are not relevant to the event or postcondition that we are analyzing. The "if" template shows that the event is triggered by the "then" clause. This follows from the condition in the "if" statement. At this point we need to determine the preconditions necessary for Z > 100 prior to the entry into the while construct.

In this example we have only two simple assignments within the "while" construct but they could be replaced by more complex expressions. The analysis would still be similar to that shown here in the example. The "while" construct would be analyzed as a unit and the expressions within the "while" would generate a more complex tree structure as previously described using the language templates to determine the preconditions. By analysis of the transformations in the "while" loop, we arrive at the conclusion that for the Z > 100 to be output, the weakest precondition at the beginning of the code was that for $B > X$, $Z + 1$ OB - $10X > 100$. At this point we have identified the weakest condition necessary for this code to output Z with Z > 100. More detailed examples are provided in reference [40]. Anyone interested in applying the technique should study the examples in the reference or other articles where the technique is illustrated.

The analysis that was shown in the section above determined the preconditions for the event to occur. One way to preclude a hazard from happening is to place an assertion in the code that verifies that the precondition for the hazard, as determined in the analysis, does not occur. SFTAs point out where to place assertions and the precondition to assert. If the preconditions do occur, some corrective action needs to take place to remedy the problem or, if a remedy is not possible, to mitigate the consequences.

Typically a small percentage of the total software effort on projects will be spent on safety-critical code. The Canadian Nuclear Power Plant safety-critical shutdown software was reviewed via the SFTA technique in three work months. The cost of this technique is insignificant considering the total amount spent on testing and verification. Full functional verification of the same software took 30 work years [41]. In cases where no problems are found, the benefits can still justify the investment. The resulting code is made more robust by the inclusion of the safety assertions and the analysis verifies that major hazardous states identified have been avoided.

Due to complexity, the figures from the example cited above (3 work months for 6K lines of code) will probably not scale up. The technique can be selectively applied to address only certain classes of faults in the case where a large body of safety-critical code requires a safety verification.

C.4 Benefits Of Software Fault Tree Analysis

Overall, the benefits of carrying out an SFTA are well worth the small investment that is made at either the design or code stage, or at both stages. SFTAs can provide the extra assurance required of safety-critical projects. When used in conjunction with the traditional functional verification techniques, the end product is a system with safer operational characteristics than prior to the application of the SFTA technique.

Figure C-1 SFTA Graphical Representation Symbols

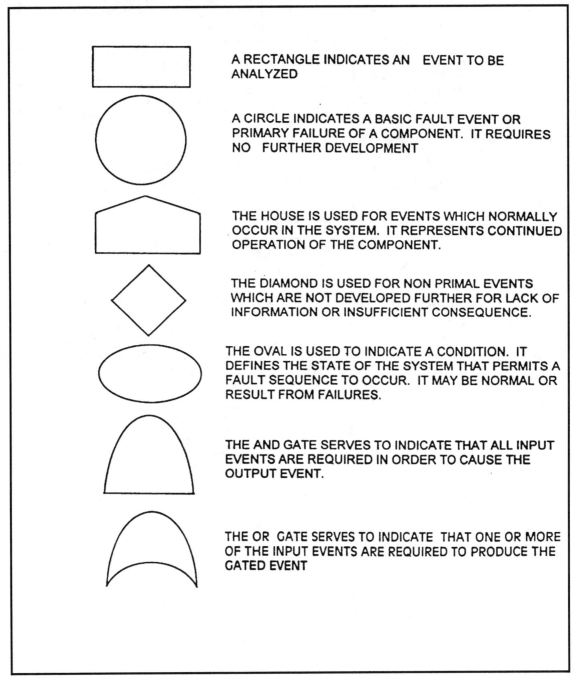

Figure C-2 Example of High Level Fault Tree

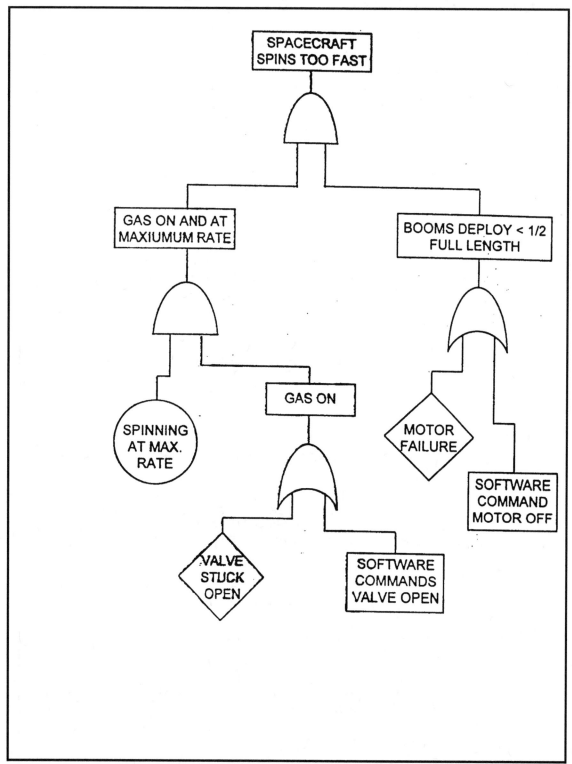

Figure C-3 Example Code Fault Tree

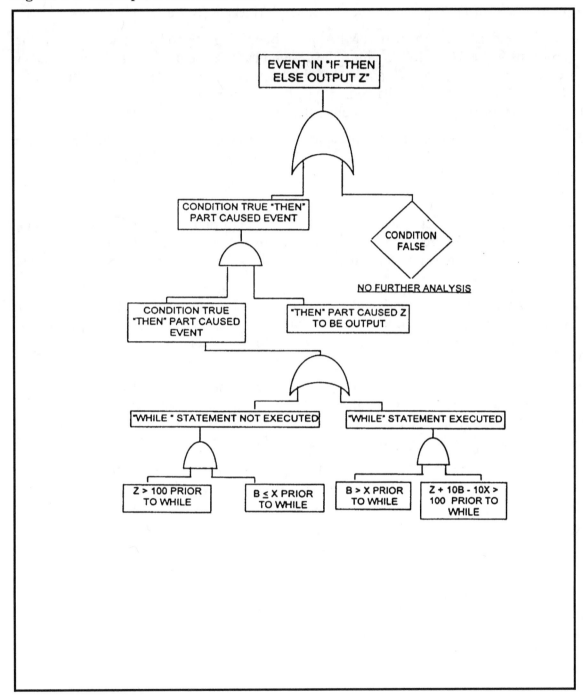

Appendix D   Software Failure Modes and Effects Analysis

This section is provided to assist systems safety engineers and software developers with an introductory explanation of the Software Failure Modes and Effects Analysis technique. The information presented here is part of the NASA Safety Critical Software Analysis course.

Failure Modes and Effects Analysis (FMEA) is a bottom-up method used to find potential system problems while the project is still in the design phase. Each component in the system is examined, and all the ways it can fail are listed. Each possible failure is traced through the system to see what effects it will have, and whether it can result in a hazardous state. The likelihood of the failure is considered, as well as the severity of the system failure.

FMEA has been used by system safety and other engineering disciplines since the 1960's. The methodology has been extended to examine the software aspects of a system (SFMEA).

D.1   Terminology

A **failure** is the inability of a system or component to perform its required functions within specified performance requirements. An event that makes the equipment deviate from the specified limits of usefulness or performance is also a failure. Failures can be complete, gradual, or intermittent.

A **complete** system failure is manifested as a system crash or lockup. At this juncture, the system is usually unusable in part, or in whole, and may need to be restarted as a minimum. - What precautions are needed to guard against this, if it is inevitable, then what can be done to insure the system is safe and can recover safely.

A **gradual** system failure may be manifested by decreasing system functionality. Functions may start to disappear and others follow or, the system may start to degrade (as in the speed with which functions are executed may decrease). Often resource management is a fault here, the CPU may be running out of memory or time slice availability.

Intermittent failures are some of the most frustrating and difficult to solve. Some of these may be cyclical or event driven or some condition periodically occurs which is unexpected and/or non-predictive. Usually an unrealized path through the software takes place under unknown conditions.

These types of failures should be kept in mind when considering failure modes (described below). Unlike most hardware failures, software faults don't usually manifest as "hard" (complete lockup of the system) type system failures. Software doesn't wear out and break. It is either functional, or already broken (but no one knows it)!

A **Failure Mode** is defined as the type of defect contributing to a failure (ASQC); the physical or functional manifestation of a failure (IEEE Std 610.12-1990). The Failure Mode is generally the manner in which a failure occurs and the degree of the failure's impact on normal required system operation. Examples of failure modes are: fracture (hardware), value of data out of limits (software), and garbled data (software).

The **Failure Effect** is the consequence(s) a failure mode has on the operation, function, or status of an item or system. Failure effects are classified as local effects (at the component), next higher level effects (portion of the system that the component resides in), and end effect (system level).

D.2   Why do an SFMEA?

SFMEA's identify key software fault modes for data and software actions. It analyzes the effects of abnormalities on other components in the system, and on the system as a whole. This technique is used to uncover system failures from the perspective of the lowest level components. It is a "bottom-up" (or "forward") analysis, propagating problems from the lowest levels, up to a failure within the broader system.

Software Fault Tree Analysis (SFTA, Appendix C) is a "top down" (or "backward") approach. It identifies possible system failures and asks what could have caused them. SFTA looks backwards from the failure to the component(s) whose defects could cause or contribute to the failure.

The SFMEA asks "What is the effect if this component operates incorrectly?" Failures for the component are postulated, and then traced through the system to see what the final result will be. Not all component failures will lead to system problems. In a good defensive design, many errors will already be managed by the error-handling part of the design.

A Software FMEA takes a systems approach, analyzing the software's response to hardware failures and the effects on the hardware of anomalous software actions. Doing an FMEA is done on software can identify:

* Hidden failure modes, system interactions, and dependencies
* Unanticipated failure modes
* Unstated assumptions
* Inconsistencies between the requirements and the design

SFMEA's are not a panacea. They will not solve all of your problems! You will probably not get all of the above results, but you should be a lot closer to a clean system than if you had not done the analysis.

It's important to interact with other members of the team as you perform an SFMEA. No one person understands all components, software or hardware. Have hardware and software designers/engineers review your analysis as you are performing it. Their point of view will help uncover the hidden assumptions or clarify the thought process that led to a requirement or design element. SFMEA is not a silver bullet, but a tool to hedge your bets (reduce your risk).

D.3   Issues with SFMEA

If SFMEA's are so wonderful, why isn't everyone doing them? The problems are the technique are that it is:

* Time consuming
* Tedious
* Manual method (for now)
* Dependent on the knowledge of the analyst

* Dependent on the accuracy of the documentation
* Questionable benefit of incomplete failure modes list
* Only considers a single failure at one time (not multiple concurrent failures)

The place to reap the greatest advantages of this technique is in requirements and design analysis. This may take some time, but it is well worth the effort in terms of the different perspectives with which you'll be able to view the project (hardware, software, operations, etc.).

The technique is considered tedious by some. However, the end result is greater and more detailed project and/or system knowledge. This is most true when used earlier (requirements and design) in the life-cycle. It is easier to use SFMEA later in the project, since components and their logical relationships are known, but at this point (i.e. detailed design and implementation) it is often too late (and expensive) to affect the requirements or design. Early in the project, lower level components are conjecture and may be wrong, but this conjecture can be used to drive out issues early. There must be balance in the approach. There is no value in trying to perform analysis on products that are not ready for examination.

The technique is dependent on how much the analyst knows and understands about the system. However, as mentioned earlier, the technique should be helpful in bringing out more information as it is being used. Include more reviewers who have diverse knowledge of the systems involved. In addition to looking at the project from different angles, the diversity of background will result in a more keen awareness of the impact of changes to all organizations.

Documentation is also very important to using this analysis technique. So, when reviewing documents, use many and different types of resources (systems and software engineers, hardware engineers, system operations personnel, etc.), so that differing perspectives have been utilized in the review process. The obvious benefit is a better product as a result of critique from numerous angles.

Again, don't work in a vacuum! Communication is paramount to success.

Where should you use the SFMEA technique? In all of the following areas, though you should focus on the safety-critical aspects.

* Single Failure Analysis
* Multiple Failure Analysis
* Hardware/Software Interfaces
* Requirements
* Design
* Detailed Design

D.4   The SFMEA Process

Figure D-1

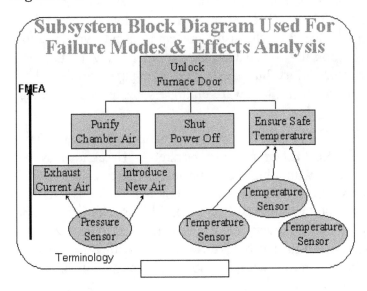

FMEA analysis begins at the bottom (the "end" items). Figure D-1 shows a subsystem, indicating how each piece interacts with the others. Logic (and's and or's) is not included on this introductory diagram. The end items are the pressure sensor and temperature sensor. The diagram shows how the failures propagate up through the system, leading to a hazardous event.

Software FMEA's follow the same procedure used for hardware FMEA's, substituting software components for the hardware. Alternately, software could be included in the system FMEA, if the systems/reliability engineer is familiar with software or if a software engineer is included in the FMEA team. MIL-STD-1629 is a widely used FMEA procedure, and this appendix is based on it.

To perform a Software Failure Modes and Effects Analysis (SFMEA), you identify:

* Project/system components

* Ground rules, guidelines, and assumptions

* Potential functional and interface failure modes

* Each failure mode in terms of potential consequences

* Failure/fault detection methods and compensating provisions

* Corrective design or actions to eliminate or mitigate failure/fault

* Impacts of corrective changes

D.4.1   Identify Project/system Components

Engineers must know the project, system, and purpose and keep the "big picture" in mind as they perform the analysis. A narrow perspective can prevent you from seeing interactions between components, particularly between software and hardware. Communicate with those of differing backgrounds and expertise.

In performing a FMEA, defining whatever is being worked on is the first order of business. The "whatever" can be a project, system, subsystem, "unit", or some other piece of the puzzle. Depending on where the project is in the development life-cycle (requirements, design, implementation), you will hopefully have some documents to work with. If the documentation is lacking, you will have to do some detective work. Often there is a collection of semi-formal paperwork on the requirements or design produced by the software team but not written into a formal requirements or design document. Look for a "Software Development Folder", talk with the developers, and accumulate whatever information you can. If little is on paper, you will have to interview the developers (and project management, hardware engineers, systems people, etc.) to create your own documentation.

Once you know what the system is and what it is supposed to do, it's time to start breaking down the system into bite size chunks. Break a project down into its subsystems. Break a subsystem down into its components. This process begins with a high level project diagram which consists of blocks of systems, functions, or objects. Each block in the system will then have its own diagram, showing the components that make up the block (subsystem). This is a lot of work, but you don't usually have to do the whole project! Not every subsystem will need to be detailed to its lowest level. Deciding what subsystems need further breakdown comes with experience. If in doubt, speak with the project members most familiar with the subsystem or component.

During the requirements phase, the lowest-level components may be functions or problem domains. At the preliminary (architectural) design phase, functions, Computer Software Configuration Items (CSCIs), or objects/classes may be the components. CSCIs, units, objects, instances, etc. may be used for the detailed design phase.

Take the "blocks" you've created and put them together in a diagram, using logic symbols to show interactions and relationships between components. You need to understand the system, how it works, and how the pieces relate to each other. It's important to lay out how one component may affect others, rippling up through the system to the highest level. Producing this diagram helps you, the analyst, put the information together. It also provides a "common ground" when you are discussing the system with other members of the team. They can provide feedback on the validity of your understanding of the system.

D.4.2 Ground Rules

Before you begin the SFMEA, you need to decide what the ground rules are. There are no right or wrong rules, but you need to know ahead of time what will be considered a failure, what kinds of failures will be included, levels of fault-tolerance, and other information. Some sample ground rules are:

1. All failure modes are to be identified at the appropriate level of detail: component, subsystem, and system.

2. Each experiment mission shall be evaluated to determine the appropriate level of analysis required.

3. The propagation of failure modes across interfaces will be considered to the extent possible based on available documentation.

4. Failures or faults resulting from defective software (code) shall be analyzed to the function & object level during detailed design.

5. Failure modes induced by human error shall not be included in this FMEA.

6. The criticality categorization of a hardware item failure mode shall be made on the basis of the worst case potential failure effect.

7. Identical Items which perform the same function, in the same environment (where the only difference is location) will be documented on a worksheet only once provided that the failure mode effects are identical.

8. Containment structures such as combustion chambers and gas cylinders will be analyzed.

9. Release of the contents in a single containment gas bottle does not constitute a hazard of any kind provided that the gases released are pre-combustion gases.(e.g., flammability, toxicity, 02 depletion)

10. Items exempt from failure modes and effects analysis are: tubing, mounting brackets, secondary structures, electrical wiring, and electronic enclosures.

Besides the ground rules, you need to identify and document the assumptions you've made. You may not have sufficient information in some areas, such as the speed at which data is expected at an interface port of the system. If the assumption is incorrect, when it is examined it will be found to be false and the correct information will be supplied (sometimes loudly). This examination will occur when you describe what you believe to be the normal operation of the system or how the system handles faults to the other project members.

Don't let assumptions go unwritten. Each one is important. In other words, "ASSUME NOTHING" unless you write it down. Once written, it serves as a focus to be further explored.

Try to think "outside the box" – beyond the obvious. Look at the project as a whole, and then at the pieces/parts. Look at the interactions between components, look for assumptions, limitations, and inconsistencies.

Figure D-2

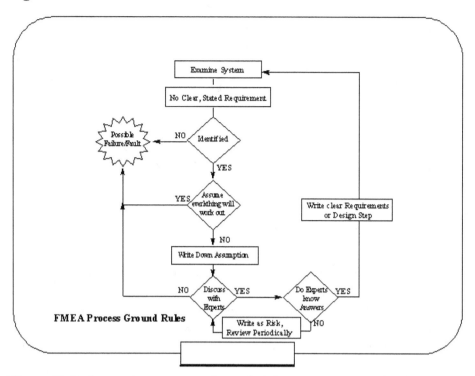

Figure D-2 shows the process of recognizing your assumptions, documenting them, finding out what the reality is, and clarifying them for future reference.

D.4.3 Identify Failures

Once you understand the system, have broken it into components, created ground rules, and documented your assumptions, it's time to get to the fun part: identifying the possible failures. Failures can be functional (it doesn't do what it was supposed to do), undesirable responses to bad data or failed hardware, or interface related.

Functional failures will be derived from the Preliminary Hazard Analysis (PHA) and subsequent Hazard Analyses, including subsystem HA's. There will probably be hardware items on this list. This analysis looks at software's relationship to hardware.

It is important to identify functions that need protecting. These functions are "must work functions" and "must not work functions". A failure may be the compromise of one of these functions by a lower-level software unit.

There are also interfaces to be dealt with. There are more problems identified with interfaces, according to some researchers, than any other aspect of software development. Interfaces are software-to-software (function calls, interprocess communication, etc.), software-to-hardware (e.g. setting a Digital-to-Analog port to a specified voltage), hardware-to-software (e.g. software reads a temperature sensor), or hardware-to-hardware. SFMEA's deal with all of these except the hardware-to-hardware interfaced. These are included in the system FMEA. Interfaces also (loosely) include transitions between states or modes of operation.

As you look at the system, you will find that you need to make more assumptions. Write them down. When all else fails, and there is no place to get useful information, sometimes a guess is in order. Again, write it down and go discuss it with others. The "others" should include people outside of your area of expertise. If you are a software person, go talk with safety and systems. If you are a safety specialist, talk with systems, software, and reliability experts.

D.4.3.1 Examination of Normal Operations as Part of the System

The normal operations of the system include it performing as designed, being able to handle known problem areas, and its fault tolerance and failure response (if designed into the system). Hopefully, the system was designed to correctly and safely handle all anticipated problems. The SFMEA will find those areas where *unanticipated* problems create failures.

This step identifies how the software responds to the failures. This step validates the sufficiency, or lack thereof, of the product "to do what its supposed to do". This has the side affect of confirming the product developers' understanding of the problem. In order to understand the operation of a system it may be necessary to work and communicate with systems engineering if you are a software engineer. Systems engineering must also communicate with software engineering, and both must talk with safety and Software Assurance (SA).

The normal operation of the software as part of the system or function is described in this part of the SFMEA.

D.4.3.2 Identify Possible Areas of Software Faults

Areas to examine for possible software faults include:

❖ **Data Sampling Rate.** Data may be changing more quickly than the sampling rate allows for, or the sampling rate may be too high for the actual rate of change, clogging the system with unneeded data.

❖ **Data Collisions.** Examples of data collisions are: transmission by many processors at the same time across a LAN, modification of a record when it shouldn't be because of similarities, and modification of data in a table by multiple users in an unorganized manner.

❖ **Command Failure to Occur.** The command was not issued or not received.

❖ **Command out of sequence.** There may be an order to the way equipment is commanded on (to an operational state). For instance, it is wise to open dampers to the duct work going to the floors, as well as the dampers to bring in outside air before turning on the air handling units of a high rise office building.

❖ **Illegal Command.** Transmission problems or other causes may lead to the reception of an unrecognized command. Also, a command may be received that is illegal for the current program state.

❖ **Timing.** Dampers take a long time to open (especially the big ones) so, timing is critical. A time delay would be necessary keep from imploding (sucking in) the outside air dampers or possibly exploding the supply air dampers, by turning on the air handler prematurely.

❖ **Safe Modes.** It is sometimes necessary to put a system which may or may not have software in a mode in where everything is safe (i.e. nothing melts down or blows up). Or the software maintains itself and other systems in a hazard free mode.

❖ **Multiple Events or Data.** What happens when you get the data for the same element twice, within a short period of time? Do you use the first or second value?

❖ **The Improbable.** The engineers or software developers will tell you that something "can't happen". Try to distinguish between truly impossible or highly improbable failures, and those that are unlikely but possible. The improbable **will** happen if you don't plan for it.

These are all sorts of things that software can do to cause system or subsystem failures. Not every software fault will lead to a system failure or shutdown, and even those failures that occur may not be safety-critical. There are lots more types of faults than these, but these are good start when looking for things that can go wrong.

D.4.3.3 Possible Failure Modes

Identify the possible failure modes and effects in an Events Table and Data Table, included in Section D.4.8.

Examples of failure modes are:

Hardware Failures/Design Flaws

* Broken sensors lead S/W down wrong path

* No sensors or not enough sensors - don't know what H/W is doing

* Stuck valves or other actuators

Software

* Memory over written (insufficient buffer or processing times).

* Missing input parameters, incorrect command, incorrect outputs, out of range values, etc.

* Unexpected path taken under previously unthought of conditions.

Operator

* Accidental input of unknown command, or proper command at wrong time.

* Failure to issue a command at required time.

* Failure to respond to error condition within a specified time period.

Environment

* Gamma Radiation

* EMI

* Cat hair in hard drive

* Power fluctuations

D.4.3.4 Start at the Bottom

Go back to the block diagrams you created earlier. Starting at the lowest level, look at a component and determine the effect of that component failing, in one of its failure modes, on the components in the level above it.

You may need to consider the effect of this component and all the effected components at the next higher level as well. This must be worked all of the way up the chain.

This is a long process. However, if the safety-critical portions are fairly isolated in a system, then the analyst will be looking at only those parts of the system that can lead to a critical failure. This is true for the detailed design and implementation phases/versions of this analysis. For the requirements and preliminary design phases, the system is more abstract (and therefore smaller and more manageable).

D.4.4 Identify Consequences of each Failure

The next thing to look at is the effect (consequences) of the defined faults/failures. It is also important to consider the criticality or severity of the failure/fault.

So far in the FMEA process, we've concentrated on the safety perspective. However, it's time to look at reliability as well. Like safety , reliability, looks at:

- ❖ **Severity** may be catastrophic, critical, moderate, or negligible.

- ❖ **Likelihood of occurrence** may be probable, occasional, remote or improbable.

Risk indices are defined as 1 through 5, with 1 being prohibitive (i.e. not allowed, must make requirements or design change). The critically categories include the added information of whether the component or function has redundancy or would be a single point of failure.

For each project and Center there may be some variation in the ranking of severity level and risk index. This is, after all, not an exact science so much as a professional best guess (best engineering judgment).

The relationship between reliability's criticality categories and the safety risk index is shown in the following table:

Criticality Category	Relative Safety Risk Index
1 – A single failure point that could result in a hazardous condition, such as the loss of life or vehicle.	Levels 1 to 2
1R – Redundant components/items for which, if all fail, could result in a hazardous condition.	Levels 1 to 2
2 – A single failure point that could result in a degree of mission failure (the loss of experiment data)	Levels 2 to 3
2R – Redundant items, all of which if failed could result in a degree of mission failure (the loss of experiment data).	Levels 2 to 3
3 – All others.	Levels 4 and 5

D.4.5 Detection and Compensation

At this step, you need to identify the methods used by the system to detect a hazardous condition, and provisions in the system that can compensate for the condition.

For each failure mode, a fault/failure detection method should be identified. A failure detection mechanism is a method by which a failure can be discovered by an operator under normal system operation or by some diagnostic. Failure detection in hardware is via sensing devices or instruments. In software this could be done by error detection software on transmitted signals, data or messages, memory checks, initial conditions, etc.

For each failure mode, a compensating provision should be identified, or the risk accepted if it is not a hazardous failure. Compensating provisions are either design provisions or operator actions which circumvent or mitigate. This step is required to record the true behavior of the item in the presence of an internal malfunction of failure. A design provision could be a redundant item or a reduced function that allows continued safe operation. An operator action could be the notification at an operator console to shut down the system in an orderly manner.

An example: The failure is the loss of data because of a power loss (hardware fault), or because other data overwrote it (a software fault) .

Detection: A critical source and CPU may be backed up by a UPS (uninterruptible power supply) or maybe not. Detect that power was lost and the system is now on this backup source. Mark data at time x as not reliable. This would be one detection scheme.

Compensation for the occurrence of this failure: Is there another source for that data.? Can it be re-read? Or just marked as suspect or thrown out and wait for next normal data overwrite it? What of having a UPS, battery backup, redundant power supply? Of course these are all hardware answers. Can software detect if the data is possibly suspect and tag it or toss it, wait for new input, request for new input, get data from alternate sources, calculate from previous data (trend) etc.?

What if input data comes in faster than expected and was overwriting pervious data before it was processed. How would this system know? What could be done about it? For example, a software system normally receives data input cyclically from 40 sources, then due to partial failures or maintenance mode, now only 20 sources are cycling and the token is passed 2 times faster. Can buffers handle the increased data rate?

D.4.6 Design Changes

Catastrophic hazards will usually have been eliminated or mitigated prior to a Software FMEA being performed. If the SFMEA uncovers catastrophic or critical hazards that were previously unidentified, these need to be eliminated or mitigated. This will usually involve more than just the software sub-system. The hardware design may also be impacted, as well as future operations scenarios. Such hazards should be immediately brought to the attention of the project manager.

After a hazard has been identified it is usually eliminated or mitigated. The result of either of these two actions is a corrective action. This corrective action may be via documented new requirements, design, process, procedure, etc. Once implemented, it must be analyzed and verified to correct the failure or hazard.

After a critical hazard has been identified, the project needs to

* Identify corrective actions
* Identify changes to the design
* Verify the changes
* Track all changes to closure

It is important to look at the new design, once the change is made, to verify that no new hazards have been created.

D.4.7 Impacts of Corrective Changes

A corrective action will have impact. Impacts can be to the schedule, design, functionality, performances, process, etc. If the corrective action results in a change to the design of the software, then some segment of that software will be impacted. Even if the corrective action is to modify the way an operator uses the system there is impact.

You need to go back and analyze the impact of the changes to the system or operating procedures to be sure that they (singularly or jointly) don't have an adverse effect and do not create a new failure mode for a safety-critical function or component.

Often fixes introduce more errors and there must be a set process to insure this does not occur in safety-critical systems. Ensure that verification procedures cover the effected areas.

D.4.8 Example forms

This worksheet is used to gather relevant information on the system. It is also a great place to put the data developed during the analysis. The ID number can be a drawing number, work break down structure number, CSCI identification, or other identification value.

FMEA Worksheet

ITEM Description	ID #	SUBSYSTEM COMPONENT	LOCAL FAILURE MODE/EFFECT	SYSTEM EFFECT	CRIT

Once elements of the system are identified, list them in this worksheet and identify their functions.

COMPONENTS

ITEM DESCRIPTION	ITEM ID	FUNCTION	FAILURE MODE	LOCAL EFFECT	SYSTEM EFFECT	DETECTABILITY	CRIT

For a Software FMEA, the **Data Table** is used to list the effects of **bad data** on the performance of the system or process being analyzed. A **Data Item** can be an input, output, or information stored, acted on, passed, received, or manipulated by the software. The **Data Fault Type** is the manner in which a flaw is manifested (**bad data**), including data that is out of range, missing, out of sequence, overwritten, or wrong.

SFMEA DATA TABLE

Mode	Data Item	Data Fault Type	Description	Effect (local and system)	Crit

The **Events Table** is used to list the effects of an event being performed. The **Event Item** is the occurrence of some action, either within the software or performed on hardware or other software. An event can be an expected and correct, expected but incorrect, unexpected and incorrect, or unexpected but correct action. **Event Fault Types** can occur locally (with a component) or on the system as a whole. Types can include halt (abnormal termination), omission (failure of the event to occur), incorrect logic/event, or timing/order (wrong time or out of sequence).

SFMEA EVENTS TABLE

Mode	Event Item	Event Fault Type	Description	Effect (local and system)	Crit

APPENDIX E   Requirements State Machines

E.1   Characteristics of State Machines

A formal description of state machines can be obtained from texts on Automata Theory. This description will only touch on those properties that are necessary for a basic understanding of the notation and limitations. State machines use graph theory notation for their representation. A state machine consists of states and transitions. The state represents the condition of the machine and the transition represent changes between states. The transitions are directed (direction is indicated by an arrow), that is, they represent a directional flow from one state to another. The transition from one state to another is induced by a trigger or input that is labeled on the transition. Generally an output is produced by the state machine.

The state machine models should be built to abstract different levels of hierarchy. The models are partitioned in a manner that is based on considerations of size and logical cohesiveness. An uppermost level model should contain at most 15 to 20 states; this limit is based on the practical consideration of comprehensibility. In turn, each of the states from the original diagram can be exploded in a fashion similar to the bubbles in a data flow diagram/control flow diagram (DFD/CFD) (from a structured analysis/structured design methodology) to the level of detail required. An RSM model of one of the lower levels contains a significant amount of detail about the system.

The states in each diagram are numbered and classified as one of the following attributes: Passive, Startup, Safe, Unsafe, Shutdown, Stranded and Hazard (see Figure E-1 *Example of State Transition Diagram*). For the state machine to represent a viable system, the diagram must obey certain properties that will be explained later in this work.

The passive state represents an inert system, that is, nothing is being produced. However, in the passive state, input sensors are considered to be operational. Every diagram of a system contains at least one passive state. A passive state may transition to an unsafe state.

The startup state represents the initialization of the system. Before any output is produced, the system must have transitioned into the startup state where all internal variables are set to known values. A startup state must be proven to be safe before continuing work on the remaining states. If the initialization fails, a time-out may be specified and a state transition to an unsafe or passive state may be defined.

The shutdown state represents the final state of the system. This state is the only path to the passive state once the state machine has begun operation. Every system must have at least one shutdown state. A time-out may be specified if the system fails to close down. If a timeout occurs, a transition to an unsafe or stranded state would be the outcome. Transition to the shutdown state does not guarantee the safety of the system. Requirements that stipulate safety properties for the shutdown state are necessary to insure that hazards do not occur while the system is being shutdown.

Figure E-1 Example of State Transition Diagram

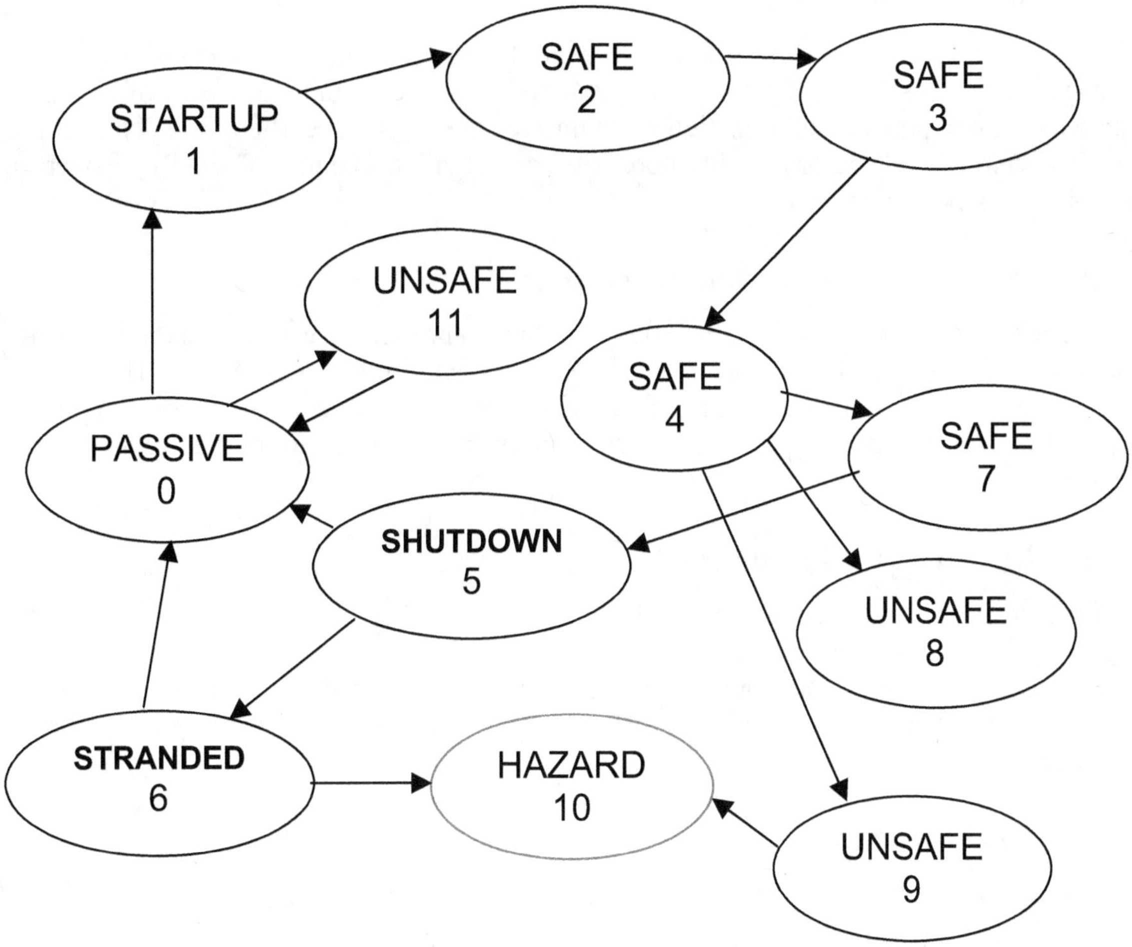

A <u>safe</u> state represents the normal operation of the system. A safe state may loop on itself for many cycles. Transitions to other safe states is a common occurrence. When the system is to be shutdown, it is expected to transition from a safe state to the shutdown state without passing through an unsafe state. A system may have zero or more safe states by definition. A safe state also has the property that the risk of an accident associated with that state is acceptable (i.e., very low).

<u>Unsafe</u> states are the precursors to accidents. As such, they represent either a malfunction of the system, as when a component has failed, or the system displays unexpected and undesired behavior. An unsafe state has an unacceptable, quantified level of risk associated with it from a system viewpoint. The system is still in a controllable state but the risk of transition to the hazard state has increased. Recovery may be achieved through an appropriate control action that leads either to an unsafe state of lesser risk or, ideally, to a safe state. A vital consideration when analyzing a path back to a safe state is the time required for the transitions to occur before an accident occurs. A system may have zero or more unsafe states.

The hazard state signals that control of the system has been lost. In this situation the loss of the system is highly probable and there is no path to recovery. The hazard state should take action where possible to contain the extent of damage.

The stranded state represents the situation, where during the course of a shutdown operation, the system has lost track of state information and cannot determine a course of action. This state has a high potential to transition to an unsafe state after a specified time depending upon what system is modeled or possibly upon environmental conditions. The only recovery from this state is a power-on restart.

E.2   Properties of Safe State Machines

There are certain properties that the state machine representation should exhibit in order to provide some degree of assurance that the design obeys certain safety rules. The criteria for the safety assertions are based on logical considerations and take into account input/output variables, states, trigger predicates, output predicates, trigger to output relationship and transitions.

E.3   Input/Output Variables

All information from the sensors should be used somewhere in the RSM. If not, either an input from a sensor is not required or, more importantly, an omission has been made from the software requirements specification. For outputs it can be stated that, if there is a legal value for an output that is never produced, then a requirement for software behavior has been omitted.

E.4   State Attributes

The state attributes of the RSM are to be labeled according to the scheme in Figure E-2 *Example RSM and Signals.*

E.5   Trigger Predicates

A necessary, but not a sufficient condition for a system to be called robust, is that there must always be a way for the RSM to leave every state of the system. This leads us to define two statements about RSMs:

1) Every state in the RSM has a defined behavior (transition) for every possible input.

2) One or more input predicates, out of all possible input predicates, must be able to trigger a transition out of any state.

Figure E-2 Example RSM and Signals

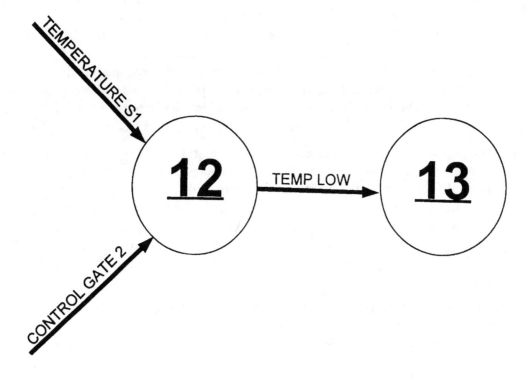

State 12 outputs a temperature low signal to State 13. Control Gate 2 is a
trigger that controls the flow of temperature S1 into State 12.

This diagram can be expressed as:
Temp Low := Temperature S1 $\leq$ Threshold when Control Gate 2 is high.

In case there is no input within a specified time, every state must have a defined transition,
such as a time-out, that triggers an action. The state machine may also express what actions
are taken if the input data is out of range. Low level functions, such as exception handling,
may be features that are required for an implementation.

A relatively simple method that provides an elementary correctness check is for range
verification of input data. The computational cost in most cases will probably not be
significant. While range checking does not provide a guarantee of correctness, it is the first
line of defense against processing bad data. Obviously, if the input data is out of range, we
have identified either a bad sensor or a bad data communication medium.[12]

The RSM technique has limitations when analyzing fault tolerant systems that contain two or
more independent lanes. In redundant systems the use of threshold logic may generate
another class of safety problems. The area where problems may arise is threshold logic used
to validate inputs coming from different sensors. Typically the value read from the different
sensors will differ by a certain percentage. Sensors are calibrated to minimize this difference,

---

[12] A third possibility may also exist: the data may truly be valid, but the understanding of the system or
environment state is incomplete and data having values outside of the expected range is regarded as invalid (e.g.
data on ozone loss in the atmosphere above Antarctica was regarded as invalid until ground based observations
confirmed the situation).

but a check must be made to verify that neither of the following situations occur: 1) a threshold may trigger one lane of the system and not the other if a value below the threshold is contrasted with a value above the threshold from the other lane; and 2) the input as processed by the control law will generate quantitatively and qualitatively different control actions. This effect can be avoided if a vote is taken at the source of the data before transmitting potentially confusing data. In the case of fully redundant, dual lane systems, each system may determine that the other is in error when in reality there is no hardware or software error. A high level RSM will not show this explicitly but it is an issue that needs to be considered in the design before any prototyping, or worse yet, coding takes place.

Timing problems are common causes of failures of real-time systems. Timing problems usually happen because either timing is poorly specified or race conditions that were not thought possible occur and cause an unwanted event to interrupt a desired sequence. All real-time data should have upper and lower bounds in time. Race conditions occur when the logic of a system has not taken into account the generation of an event ahead of the intended time. This type of error occurs when events that should be synchronized or sequenced are allowed to proceed in parallel. This discussion will not address the obvious case of an error in the sequence logic.

The ability to handle inputs will be called capacity and the ability to handle diverse types of input will be called load. A real-time system must have specifications of minimum and maximum capacity and load. Robustness requires the ability of the system to detect a malfunction when the capacity limits have been violated. Capacity limits are often tied to interrupts where hardware and software analyses are necessary to determine if the system can handle the workload (e.g., CPU execution time, memory availability, etc.). Load involves multiple input types and is a more comprehensive measure than capacity. Criteria for the system or process load limits must be specified. For a system to be robust, a minimum load specification needs to be specified, as well as a maximum (assuming that a real-time process control system has inputs of a certain period). The capacity and load constraints as developed for the RSM will help serve as a guide for designing the architecture of the system and subsequently in the final system implementation. These performance requirements have safety implications. The ability of the system to handle periodic capacity and load requirements is a fundamental safety property. If a system cannot handle the work load then the safety of the system is at risk because process control is not performed in a timely fashion.

E.6   Output Predicates

The details of when an output is valid may not be known at the time the RSM is generated but these constraints should be documented somewhere in the RSM to serve as a guideline for the implementer. In a similar fashion to inputs, outputs must have their value, and upper and lower timing bounds specified. Output capacity is limited by the ability of the actuator to respond. Compatibility must exist between the frequency of reaction to input and the capacity of the output mechanism to respond. This requires that a timing analysis be performed to be certain that potential worst case input and output rate speeds can be adequately handled by both software and hardware. For output data to be valid the input data must be from a valid time range. Control decisions must be based on data from the current state of the system, not on stale data. In the computation of the output, the delay in producing the output must not exceed the permissible latency. An example of an incorrect output timing problem occurred on the F-18 fighter plane. A wing mounted missile failed to separate from the launcher after ignition because a computer program signaled the missile retaining mechanism to close before the rocket had built up enough thrust to clear the missile from the wing. The aircraft went violently out of control, but the missile fuel was eventually expended and the pilot was able to bring the plane under control before a crash occurred.

E.7 Degraded Mode Operation

When a system cannot meet its work load requirements in the allotted time or unanticipated error processing has consumed processor resources and insufficient time is available for normal processing, the system must degrade in a graceful manner. Responses to graceful degradation include:

• Masking of nonessential interrupts	• Reduction of accuracy and/or response time
• Logging and generation of warning messages	• Signals to external world to slow down inputs
• Reduction of processing load (execute only core functionality)	• Trace of machine state to facilitate post event analysis
• Error handling	

Which of the above measures get implemented depends on the application and its specific requirements.

Where there is load shedding, a degraded mode RSM will exist that exhibits properties that in all likelihood are different from the original RSM. The same analysis that is performed for the RSM of the fully operational system should be done on the degraded mode RSM.

Special care must be taken in the implementation of performance degradation that reduces functionality and/or accuracy. A situation can arise where, because of the transition to a state machine with different properties (and therefore, the control laws of the original RSM will be affected by a reduction in accuracy or frequency of the inputs), the outputs may not transition smoothly. In systems where operator intervention is an integral part of operation, this jolt may confuse the operator and contribute to further degradation because of operator inability to predict behavior. In principle, where response time limits can be met, predictability is preferable to abrupt change.

In order to recover from degraded mode operation there needs to be a specification of the conditions required to return to normal operations. These conditions must be specific enough to avoid having the system continuously oscillate back and forth between normal and degraded mode. In practice, a minimum delay and a check of the cause of the anomaly can achieve this.

E.8 Feedback Loop Analysis

Process control models provide feedback to the controller to notify changes in state caused by manipulated variables or internal disturbances. In this manner the system can adjust its behavior to the environment. An RSM can be used to verify if feedback information is used and what signals are employed. If feedback is absent then either the design is incorrect or the requirements are faulty. The design of the system needs to incorporate a mechanism to detect the situation where a change in the input should trigger a response from the system and the response is either too slow, too fast or unexpected. For example, when a command is given to turn on a heater, a resulting temperature rise curve would be expected to follow a theoretical model within certain tolerances. If the process does not respond within a certain period of time then it can be assumed that something is wrong and the software must take an appropriate action. At a minimum, this action should be the logging of the abnormality for future analysis. The simplest, most inexpensive check for a servo loop is to verify if the reference position is different from the actual position. If the difference is non-negligible, some form of control action must be taken. If the actual position does not vary in the presence of a command to act, then it can be concluded that there is a fault in the system. RSMs can be used to help design the control process and to verify that all feedback loops are closed and that they generate the appropriate control action.

E.9 Transition Characteristics

Requirements may also involve specifications regarding transitions between states. A system may or may not possess certain properties, while some other properties are mandatory. All safe states must be reachable from the initial state. Violation of this principle leads to a contradiction of requirements or a superfluous state. No safe state should ever transition, as a result of a computer control action, to an unsafe state. In principle, an automated (i.e., computer controlled) system should never transition to a hazardous state unless a failure has occurred. In general, if operator action is considered (such as the issuing of a command), the previously stated requirement may be impossible to accomplish given the requirements of certain systems. In this latter situation, the transition into and out of the unsafe state should be done in a manner that takes the least amount of time and the system eventually reverts back to a safe state.

Once the system is in an unsafe state, either because of error conditions or unexpected input, the system may transition to another unsafe state that represents a lower risk than the previous state. If it is not possible to redesign the system so that all transitions from a hazardous state eventually end in a safe state, then the approach must be to design the transitions to the lowest possible risk, given the environment. Not all RSM diagrams will be able to achieve an intrinsically safe machine, that is, one that does not have a hazardous state. The modeling process's main virtue lies in the fact that, through analysis of the RSM, faults may be uncovered early in the life cycle. The objective and challenge is to design a system that poses a tolerable level of risk.

The design of a robust system requires that, for all unsafe states, all soft and hard failure modes be eliminated. A soft failure mode occurs when an input is required in at least one state through a chain of states to produce an output and that the loss of the ability to receive that input could potentially inhibit the software. A hard failure mode is analogous to a soft failure except that the input is required for all states in the chain and the loss of the input will inhibit the output.

If a system allows for reversible commands, then it must check that, for every transition into a state caused by the command, it can transition back to the previous state via a reverse command. While in that state, an input sequence must be able to trigger the deactivation of the command. In a similar fashion, if an alarm indicates a warning and the trigger conditions are no longer true, then the alert should also cease (if appropriate operator acknowledgment action was performed when required). State transitions do not always have to be between different states. Self loops are permissible, but eventually every real-time system must initiate a different function and exit from the self loop. Watchdog timers may be used to catch timeouts for self loops. The RSM technique helps a designer by graphically representing these constraints and assisting in specifying implementation level detail.

E.10 Conclusions

The RSM techniques described above can be used to provide analysis procedures to help find errors and omissions. Incorporating the RSM analysis into the development cycle is an important step towards a design that meets or exceeds safety requirements. Practically all the current safety oriented methodologies rely on the quality of the analyst(s) for results and the techniques mentioned above are a first attempt at formalizing a system's safety properties.

The RSM technique does not claim to guarantee the design of a 100% safe system. Inevitably some faults (primarily faults of omission) will not be caught, but the value of this methodology is in the fact that many faults can be made evident at an early stage, if the right mix of experienced people are involved in the analysis. Complexity of current software and hardware has caused a nonlinear increase in design faults due to human error. For this reason and because testing does not prove the absence of faults, it is recommended that the RSM modeling techniques be employed as early as possible in the system life cycle. The RSM methodology, if applied with system safety considerations, is a valuable step towards a partial proof to show the effects and consequences of faults on the system. If the RSM model is robust and the design can be shown to have followed the criteria in the previous sections, then a significant milestone will have been completed that demonstrates that the system is ready to proceed to the next phase in the life-cycle and developers will have a high level model that satisfies a core set of requirements.

From an overall systems perspective, the RSM model is used to provide a high level view of the actual system, and further refinements of the states can give insight into implementation detail. This model is then checked against the rules formulated in the previous sections. Deviation from the rules involves additional risk and, as such, this additional risk should be evaluated and documented. This process of documentation is necessary for a post project analysis to confirm the success of the system or to analyze the cause of any failures.

The technique of using RSMs to explore properties of safety-critical systems is a highly recommended practice that development teams should follow. Verification of the safety properties of the RSM should be performed as a team effort between software developers, systems safety and software quality assurance. If the RSM analysis or any equivalent technique has not been performed for the design of a complex system, then that project is running the risk that major design constraints will be put aside until late in the development cycle and will cause a significant cost impact.

Appendix F Preliminary Hazard Analysis (PHA)

F.1 PHA Approach

The following is an excerpt from NPG 8715.3 Appendix-D:

"In many ways the PHA is the most important of the safety analyses because it is the foundation on which the rest of the safety analyses and the system safety tasks are built. It documents which generic hazards are associated with the design and operational concept. This provides the initial framework for a master listing (or hazard catalog) of hazards and associated risks that require tracking and resolution during the course of the program design and development. The PHA also may be used to identify safety-critical systems that will require the application of failure modes and effects analysis and further hazard analysis during the design phases."

Hazards and their causes and controls are identified by using lessons learned, mishap data, PHA's from similar systems, and engineering judgment. Table F-1 *Generic Hazards Checklist* lists some generic hazards, which are also a good starting place. The last column gives some examples of how software can function as a control for a hazard. It is important to understand that this and other checklists are merely tools to encourage the thought process. Keep thinking and brainstorming for all the permutations of potential hazards, causes, and controls for a given system.

Table F-1 Generic Hazards Checklist

Generic Hazard Category	Hazards	Software Controls Example
Contamination / Corrosion	Chemical Disassociation Chemical Replacement / Combination Moisture Oxidation Organic (Fungus, Bacterial, Etc.) Particulate Inorganic (Includes Asbestos)	Receive data input from hardware sensors (gas chromatograph, particle detector, etc.). Activate caution and warning indicators if levels surpass programmed limits, and/or automatically shutdown sources or activate fans.
Electrical Discharge / Shock	External Shock Internal Shock Static Discharge Corona Short	Prevent power from being turned on while access door is open. Disable High Voltage when not in vacuum.
Environmental / Weather	Fog Lightning Precipitation (Fog, Rain, Snow, Sleet, Hail) Sand / Dust Vacuum Wind Temperature Extremes	Receive data input from sensor readings of hardware devices (particle detector, wind velocity probe, etc.). Send commands to shut down hardware if programmed limits are surpassed.

Fire / Explosion	Chemical Change (Exothermic, Endothermic)	Monitor temperature; activate fire suppression system if temperature goes over set threshold.
	Fuel & Oxidizer in Presence of Pressure and Ignition Source	
	Pressure Release / Implosion	
	High Heat Source	
Impact / Collision	Acceleration (Including Gravity)	Monitor position of rotating equipment. Keep position within defined limits, or shutdown motion if exceeding limits.
	Detached Equipment	
	Mechanical Shock / Vibration / Acoustical	
	Meteoroids / Meteorites	
	Moving / Rotating Equipment	
Loss of Habitable Environment*	Contamination	Receive data input from sensor readings of hardware devices. Send commands to operate proper sequencing of valve operation.
	High Pressure	
	Low Oxygen Content	
	Low Pressure	
	Toxicity	
	Low Temperature	
	High Temperature	
Pathological / Physiological/ Psychological	Acceleration / Shock / Impact / Vibration	Monitor pressure and rate of change. Control pressure system to keep rate of change under set limit.
	Atmospheric Pressure (High, Low, Rapid Change)	
	Humidity	
	Illness	
	Noise	
	Sharp Edges	
	Sleep, Lack of	
	Visibility (Glare, Surface Fogging)	
	Temperature	
	Workload, Excessive	
Radiation	EMI	Receive data input from sensor readings of hardware devices. Shut down high gain antenna when operational time limit is reached.
	Ionizing Radiation (Includes Radon)	
	Non-ionizing Radiation (Lasers, Etc.)	
Temperature Extremes	High	Monitor temperature. Sound warning if temperature outside of limits
	Low	
	Variations	

*Health issues require coordination with Occupational Health personnel

F.2   Identifying Hazards

Preliminary hazard analysis of the entire system is performed from the top down to identify hazards and hazardous conditions. Its goal is to identify all credible hazards up front. Initially the analysis is hardware driven, considering the hardware actuators, end effects and energy sources, and the hazards that can arise. For each identified hazard, the PHA records the hazard causes and candidate control methods. These hazards and hazard causes are mapped to system functions and their failure modes. Most of the critical functions are associated with one or more system controls. These control functions cover the operation, monitoring and/or safing of that portion of the system safety assessment and must consider the system through all the various applicable subsystems including hardware, software, and operators.

To assure full coverage of all aspects of functional safety, it can be helpful to categorize system functions as two types:

1. "Must work" functions (MWF's)
2. "Must not work" functions (MNWF's)

"Must work" functions are those aspects of the system that have to work in order to for it to function correctly. Of course, *all* elements of the system "must work" if the desired functionality is to be obtained. From the safety perspective, only those functions that "must work" in order to prevent a hazard or other safety-related event from occurring are considered. "Must not work" functions are aspects that should not occur, if the system is functioning correctly. In fact, if they do occur, they could lead to a hazardous situation or other undesired outcome. Examples of "must work" and "must not work" functions are given below.

"Must work" and "must not work" functions often depend on the state of the system. Some functions can even change from one to the other as the system state changes. When designating an aspect of the system as "must work" or "must not work", you also need to specify *when* these designations are valid. "Open furnace door" is a "must work" when changing out a test sample. but it is a "must not work" when the experiment is operating and the furnace is at full temperature.

The system specification often initially defines the criticality (e.g., safety-critical) of some system functions, but may be incomplete. This criticality is usually expressed only in terms of the Must-Work nature of the system function, and often omits the Must-Not-Work functional criticality. The PHA defines all the hazardous MNWF's as well as the MWF's.

Examples:

1. A science experiment might have a system Criticality designation of 3 (Non-critical) in terms of its system function, because loss of the primary experiment science data does not represent a hazard. However, the experiment might still be capable of generating hazards such as electric shock due to inadvertent activation of a power supply during maintenance. Activation of power during maintenance is a MNWF.

2. An experiment might release toxic gas if negative pressure (vacuum) is not maintained. Maintaining a negative pressure is a MWF.

3. An air traffic control system and aircraft flight control systems are designed to prevent collision of two aircraft flying in the same vicinity. Collision avoidance is a MWF.

4. A spacecraft rocket motor might inadvertently ignite while it is in the STS Cargo Bay. Motor ignition is a MNWF, at that time. It is apparent that the MNWF becomes a MWF when it is time for the motor to fire.

If functions identified in the PHA were not included in the system specification, that document should be amended to address control of those functions.

F.3 Preliminary Hazard Analysis (PHA) Process

Step 1: System and Safety experts **examine the proposed system concepts and requirements** and identify System Level Hazards. Areas such as power sources, chemicals usage, mechanical structures, time constraints, etc. are considered (as per Section F.2 *Identifying Hazards* and Table F-1 *Generic Hazards Checklist*).

Step 2: **Hazard cause(s) are identified.** Common hazard cause categories include: collision, contamination, corrosion, electrical shock/damage, explosion, fire, temperature extremes, radiation, illness/injury and loss of capability. Each hazard has at least one cause, such as a hardware component failure, operator error, or software fault. The PHA should identify some or all of the hazard causes, based on the system definition at that point in the development effort. Consideration of these categories as risks early in the development effort reduces the chance that any of these surface as a problem on a project.

Step 3: **Identify at least one hazard control for each hazard cause.** NASA safety standards often stipulate the methods of control required for particular hazard causes. This is not necessary for the PHA, but may become a requirement at later phases in the system development process. Each control method must be a "real feature", usually a design feature (hardware and/or software), or a procedural sequence and must be verifiable.

Step 4: **Identify at least one verification method for each hazard control.** Verification can be by analysis, test, demonstration or inspection. In some cases, the verification method is defined by established NASA safety requirements (e.g. Payload Safety Requirements NSTS 1700.1 (V1-B)).

When performing the PHA, it is important not to get sidetracked into arguments about how a hazard might occur or whether it is impossible. It is better to assume that a hazard can occur and examine the consequences. Hazards can be removed later if they are determined to be improbable and their consequences are negligible. This is the time to be creative paranoids – determine all the ways a system can create a hazard and assume that it will.

Each system hazard is documented in a "Hazard Report". The NASA Shuttle / Station Payload Hazard Report is offered as a good example. The form is included at the end of this appendix (Figure F-1). Detailed instructions for completing this form are given as an appendix when the form is downloaded from the NASA Payload Safety Homepage [http://wwwsrqa.jsc.nasa.gov/pce] and also in NPG 8715.3 NASA Safety Manual, Chapter-3, System Safety, and Appendix-D (Analysis Techniques) [1].

Typical elements in a hazard report are:

- **Hazard Description**. This describes a system hazard, such as an uncontrolled release of energy resulting in a mishap.

- **Safety Requirement**. This can be a hardware or software requirement and is usually a system level requirement. It can result in further flow-down to software functionality by identifying software Hazard Controls as described below.

- **Hazard Cause.** This is usually a fault or defect in hardware or software. Software causes include:
  - Failure to detect a problem
  - Failure to perform a function
  - Performing a function at the wrong time, out of sequence, or when the program is in the wrong state
  - Performing the wrong function
  - Performing a function incompletely
  - Failure to "pass along" information or messages

- **Hazard Control**. This is usually a design feature to control a hazard cause. The hazard control should be related to the applicable safety requirements cited by the hazard report. For example, where independence and fault tolerance are required, the hazard control block describes how the design meets these requirements.

- **Hazard Detection Method.** This is the means to detect imminent occurrence of a hazardous condition as indicated by recognizing unexpected values of measured parameters.

- **Safety Verification Method.** This identifies methods used to verify the validity of each Hazard Control. These methods include analysis, test, demonstration or inspection.

- **Status of Verification.** This identifies scheduled or actual start and completion dates of each verification item, and if the item is open or closed.

Another document that will usually be produced as part of a PHA is the Preliminary Hazard List. This is a tabulated list of all the identified hazards. Each hazard on the list will have a corresponding hazard report.

F.4   Tools and Methods for PHA

Tools and methods for performing a formal Preliminary Hazard Analysis are detailed in the following documents. In addition, many system safety books describe the process of conducting a Preliminary Hazard Analysis.

- NSTS 22254, Methodology for Conduct of Space Shuttle Program Hazard Analysis (available at http://jsc-web-pub.jsc.nasa.gov/psrp/)

- SOFTWARE SYSTEM SAFETY HANDBOOK, A Technical & Managerial Team Approach, December 1999 (Joint Software System Safety Committee) (available at http://sunnyday.mit.edu/safety-club/)

- MIL-STD-882B, Task 201 (PHL) and Task 202 (PHA) (available at http://sunnyday.mit.edu/safety-club/)

Fault Tree Analysis (FTA) and Failure Modes and Effects Analysis (FMEA) are two types of analyses that supplement a Preliminary Hazard Analysis. Descriptions of these analyses may be found in any system safety book. Appendix C provides details on Software Fault Tree

Analysis (SFTA), and Appendix D describes Software Failure Modes and Effects Analysis (SFMEA).

F.5   PHA is a Living Document

A completed Preliminary Hazard Analysis is just the beginning of the safety process. All required information is typically not available at the start of the development lifecycle. Details for the various items are filled in and expanded during the development lifecycle as the Hazard Analysis process continues. Usually, hazard causes and controls are identified early in the development process and verifications are addressed in later lifecycle phases. Hazard reports are revisited and updated on subsequent Safety Analyses throughout the life cycle of the system. As the design matures, hazards may be added or deleted, and additional hazard analysis performed.

 The PHA provides an initial set of hazards early in the development cycle. This allows safety engineering tasks to begin in a timely manner, avoiding costly design impacts later in the process. The PHA is also required before software subsystem hazard analysis can begin. Those hazard causes residing in the software portion of a control system become the subject of the software subsystem hazard analysis. **It is important to reexamine software's role and safety impact throughout the system development phases.** Software is often relied on to work around hardware problems encountered which result in additions and/or changes to functionality.

Figure F-1 Example Payload Hazard Report Form (from JSC)

PAYLOAD HAZARD REPORT		a. NO:
b. PAYLOAD:		c. PHASE:
d. SUBSYSTEM:	e. HAZARD GROUP:	f. DATE:
g. HAZARD TITLE:		i. HAZARD CATEGORY ☐ CATASTROPHIC ☐ CRITICAL
h. APPLICABLE SAFETY REQUIREMENTS:		
j. DESCRIPTION OF HAZARD:		
k. HAZARD CAUSES:		
l. HAZARD CONTROLS:		
m. SAFETY VERIFICATION METHODS:		
n. STATUS OF VERIFICATION:		
o. APPROVAL	PAYLOAD ORGANIZATION	SSP/ISS
PHASE I		
PHASE II		
PHASE III		

JSC Form 542B (Rev November 22, 1999) (MS Word September 1997)

Appendix G   Reliability Modeling

G.1   Criteria for Selecting a Reliability Model

- **Model validity.** How good is the model at accurately measuring the current failure rate? At predicting the time to finish testing with associated date and cost? At predicting the operational failure rate?

- **Ease of measuring parameters.** What are the cost and schedule impacts for data (metrics) collection? How physically significant are the parameters to the software development process?

- **Quality of assumptions.** How close are the model assumptions to the real world? Is the model adaptable to a special environment?

- **Applicability.** Can the model handle program evolution and change in test and operational environments?

- **Simplicity.** Is the model simple in concept, data collection, program implementation, and validation?

- **Insensitivity to noise.** Is the model insensitive to insignificant changes in input data and parameters, without losing responsiveness to significant differences?

- **Usefulness**. Does the model estimate quantities that are useful to project personnel?

G.2   Issues and Concerns

Ideally, one simple reliability model would be available, with great tool support, that would easily and accurately predict or estimate the reliability of the software under development. The current situation, however is that

- Over 40 models have been published in the literature.

- The accuracy of the models is variable.

- You can't know ahead of time which model is best for your situation.

Some aspects of the models that are a cause for concern are:

- How accurate is the data collected during testing? How easy is it to collect that data?

- Models are primarily used during the testing phase, which is late in the development cycle.

- Estimation of parameters is not always possible, and sometimes it is mathematically intractable.

- Reliable models for multiple systems have not been developed.

- There is no well-established criteria for model selection.

G.3   Tools

In the last decade, tools have become available to aid in software reliability modeling. Most of the established models have tools that support them. Resources for information on available tools are:

1. "Applying Software Reliability Engineering in the 1990s", W. Everett, S. Keene, and A. Nikora, *IEEE Transaction on Reliability*, Vol. 47, No. 3-SP, September 1998

2. "Software Reliability Engineering Study of a Large-Scale Telecommunications Software System", Carman et. al., *Proc. 1995 International Symposium on Software Reliability Engineering*, Toulouse, France, Oct. 1995, pp. 350-.

3. MEADEP tool. http://www.meadep.com/

4. Reliability Modeling, Developed by C. Chay and W. Leyu, http://www.icaen.uiowa.edu/~ankusiak/reli.html

G.4   Dissenting Views

Not everyone agrees that software reliability modeling is a useful technique. Some are concerned about the applicability of the models to real-world situations. Most models assume random failures, but is that true? The models do not usually address the fact that fixing a failure may add other errors to the software. The fact that software is often "unique" (one-of-a-kind) makes statistics about the error rates difficult to apply across a broad spectrum of programs. Unlike hardware, you are dealing with one part, not one of many identical units.

A critique of software reliability modeling is found in [53]. The authors assert that current models do not adequately deal with these factors:

*   **Difficulties in estimating Operational Profiles**, such as the input distribution (what is input, when, in what order). New software may have no history or customer base to use to determine typical operations. It is non-trivial to determine how the system will be used, but such an operational profile is a key element for most reliability models.

*   **Problems with reliability estimation.** Inadequate test sets, failure to exercise each feature in testing, and skewed operational profile (critical functions may not be part of the "typical" profile) make reliability difficult to estimate accurately.

*   **Reliability estimation occurs near the end of development.** Individual component reliability is not known, just for the full system. There is no information to feed back that may lead to process improvement and better reliability in future projects.

*   **Saturation effects lead to reliability overestimation.** Most testing techniques reach a saturation point past which they are unable to find defects. These limits can lead to an overestimate of the software reliability.

G.5   Resources

The following papers and websites provide useful information on software reliability modeling:

* "Software Reliability Assurance Handbook", http://www.cs.colostate.edu/~cs630/rh/

* "Software Reliability Modeling Techniques and Tools", Michael R. Lyu and Allen P. Nikora, ISSRE'93 Tutorial, November, 1993 http://techreports.jpl.nasa.gov/1993/93-1886.pdf

* "Software Reliability: To Use or Not To Use?", a panel discussion chaired by Michael Lyu, http://www.stsc.hill.af.mil/crosstalk/1995/02/index.html

* "Applying Software Reliability Engineering in the 1990s", W. Everett, S. Keene, and A. Nikora, *IEEE Transaction on Reliability*, Vol. 47, No. 3-SP, September 1998

* "Software Reliability: Assumptions, Realities and Data", Michel Defamie, Patrick Jacobs, and Jacques Thollembeck, *Proceedings of the IEEE International Conference on Software Maintenance*, 1998

* "Software Reliability Engineering Study of a Large-Scale Telecommunications Software System", Carman et. al., *Proc. 1995 International Symposium on Software Reliability Engineering*, Toulouse, France, Oct. 1995, pp. 350-.

* "Predicting Software Reliability", Alan Wood, *IEEE Computer*, Vol. 29, No. 11, November 1996

* "Software Metrics and Reliability", Dr. Linda Rosenberg, Ted Hammer, and Jack Shaw, http://satc.gsfc.nasa.gov/support/ISSRE_NOV98/software_metrics_and_reliability.html

* "Reliability Modeling for Safety-Critical Software", Norman F. Schneidewind, *IEEE Transactions on Reliability*, Vol. 46, No.1, March 1997, pp. 88-98

* "Handbook of Software Reliability Engineering" (Book), Edited by Michael R. Lyu, Published by IEEE Computer Society Press and McGraw-Hill Book Company, http://www.cse.cuhk.edu.hk/~lyu/book/reliability/

Appendix H   Checklists

H.1   Checklist 1 for Off-the-Shelf (OTS) Items

Item to consider	Answer or Comment
Does the OTS software fill the need *in this system*? Is its operational context compatible with the system under development? Consider not only the similarities between the system(s) the OTS was designed for and the current system, but also the differences. Look carefully at how those differences affect operation of the OTS software.	
How stable is the OTS product? Are bug-fixes or upgrades released so often that the product is in a constant state of flux?	
How responsive is the vendor to bug-fixes? Does the vendor inform you when a bug-fix patch or new version is available?	
How compatible are upgrades to the software? Has the API changed significantly between upgrades in the past? Will your interface to the OTS software still work, even after an upgrade?	
How mature is the software technology? OTS software is often market driven, and may be released with bugs (known and unknown) in order to meet an imposed deadline or to beat the competition to market.	
Conversely, **is the software so well known that it is assumed to be error free and correct?** Think about operating systems and language libraries. In a safety-critical system, you do not want to *assume* there are no errors in the software.	

Item to consider	Answer or Comment
What is the user base of the software? If it is a general use library, with thousands of users, you can expect that most bugs and errors will be found and reported to the vendor. Make sure the vendor keeps this information, and provides it to the users! Small software programs will have less of a "shake down" and *may* have more errors remaining.	
What level of documentation is provided with the software? Is there more information than just a user's manual? Can more information be obtained from the vendor (free or for a reasonable price)?	
Is source code included, or available for purchase at a reasonable price? Will support still be provided if the source code is purchased or if the software is slightly modified?	
Can you communicate with those who developed the software, if serious questions arise? Is the technical support available, adequate, and reachable? Will the vendor talk with you if you modify the product?	
Will the vendor support older versions of the software, if you choose not to upgrade? Many vendors will only support the newest version, or perhaps one or two previous versions.	
Is there a well-defined API (Application Program Interface), ICD (interface control document), or similar documentation that details how the user interacts with the software? Are there "undocumented" API functions?	
What are the error codes returned by the software? How can it fail (return error code, throw an exception, etc.)? Do the functions check input variables for proper range, or it is the responsibility of the user to implement?	

Item to consider	Answer or Comment
Can you obtain information on the internals of the software, such as the complexity of the various software components or the interfaces between the components? This information may be needed, depending on what analyses need to be performed on the OTS software.	
Can you get information about the software development process used to create the software? Was it developed using an accepted standard (IEEE 12207, for example)? What was the size of the developer team?	
What types of testing was the software subjected to? How thorough was the testing? Can you get copies of any test reports?	
Are there any known defects in the software? Are there any unresolved problems with the software, especially if the problems were in systems similar to yours? Look at product support groups, newsgroups, and web sites for problems unreported by the vendor. However, also keep in mind the source of the information found on the web – some is excellent and documented, other information is spurious and incorrect.	
Were there any analyses performed on the software, in particular any of the analyses described in Chapters 5 through 10? Formal inspections or reviews of the code?	
How compatible is the software with your system? Will you have to write extensive glueware to interface it with your code? Are there any issues with integrating the software, such as linker incompatibility, protocol inconsistencies, or timing issues?	

Item to consider	Answer or Comment
Does the software provide all the functionality required? How easy is it to add any new functionality to the system, when the OTS software is integrated? Will the OTS software provide enough functionality to make it cost-effective?	
Does the OTS-to-system interface require any modification? For example, does the OTS produce output in the protocol used by the system, or will glueware need to be written to convert from the OTS to the system protocol?	
Does the software provide extra functionality? Can you "turn off" any of the functionality? If you have the source code, can you recompile with defined switches or stubs to remove the extra functionality? How much code space (disk, memory, etc.) does the extra software take up? What happens to the system if an unneeded function is accidentally invoked?	

H.2 Checklist 2 for Off-the-Shelf (OTS) Items

Lessons learned from earlier projects using OTS software are useful. The following checklist can be used to reduce the risk of using OTS software:

No.	Items To Be Considered	Does It Apply? (yes/no)	Planned Action
1*	**Has the vendor's facilities and processes been audited?** Allow an audit of their facility and processes. If for any reason an audit cannot be conducted then the OTS software is considered an unmitigated significant hazard, and as such, the OTS software may be inappropriate for the intended device.		
2*	**Are the verification and validation activities for the OTS appropriate?** Demonstrate that the verification and validation activities performed for the OTS software are appropriate and sufficient to fulfill the safety and effectiveness requirements for the device.		
3*	**Can the project maintain the OTS independent of vendor support?** Ensure that the project can maintain the OTS software even if the original developer ceases support.		
4	**Does software contain interfaces, firewalls, wrappers, etc.?** Consider interfaces, firewalls, wrappers and glue early in the process. When creating wrappers avoid dependency on internal product interfaces and functionality or isolate the dependencies.		
4	**Does software provide diagnostics?** Look for built-in diagnostics and error handling.		
5	**Any key products influencing choices?** Identify key products (or strategies or standards) that can influence other choices before product evaluation.		
6	**Has the software vendor been used before?** Employ any past experience with vendor/product. Ask for information from other projects. Use databases of information, keeping in mind that the behavior of a product can change depending on how it is used.		
7	**Is this the initial version?** Do not buy a version 1.0.		
8	**Have competitors been researched?** Ask competitors of the products about the other products.		
9	**Is the source code available?** Consider buying the source code so you can perform your own testing. Note that this is expensive and will usually require waiving technical support and/or the warranty.		
10	**Are industry standard interfaces available?** Ensure the product uses industry standard interfaces.		
11	**Has product research been thorough?** Base product selection on analysis of the facts.		

No.	Items To Be Considered	Does It Apply? (yes/no)	Planned Action
12	**Is the validation for the OTS driver software package available?** Include the validation process for the OTS driver software package as part of the system interface validation process. This includes the verification of the data values in both directions for the data signals; various mode settings for control signals in both directions (if applicable); and the input/output interrupt and timing functions of the driver with the CPU and operating system.		
13	**Are there features that will not be used?** Determine how to handle unused features.		
14	**Have tools for automatic code generation been independently validated?** Determine whether tools for automatic code generation have been independently validated. OTS tool selection should follow the same process as component selection.		
15	**Can previous configurations be recovered?** Reevaluate each version and ensure that the previous configuration can be restored.		
16	**Will a processor require a recompile?** Perform a complete and comprehensive retest of the system replacing a processor that requires a recompile.		
17	**Has a safety impact assessment been performed?** Perform a safety impact assessment when new or modified OTS components are placed in a baselined system. Document hazards in a Failure Modes and Effects Analysis (FMEA) table. Ensure there is traceability between the hazard reports, the design requirements, and the test reports. Analysis should include the review of known problem reports, user manuals, specifications, patches, literature and internet searches for other user's experience with this OTS Software.		
18	**Will the OTS tools affect safety?** Keep in mind the tool's purpose when selecting OTS tools. Determine whether the results are easy to verify and whether the results of the tool's use will influence decisions that affect safety.		
19	**Is the OTS being used for the proper application?** Use OTS products for the purpose for which they were created.		
20	**Is there compatibility between the OTS hardware and software?** Realize that not all OTS hardware can run all OTS software.		
21	**Does the vendor have ISO certification?** Determine whether the vendor is ISO certified or has been awarded a SEI rating of 3 or higher. This provides confidence that their development process is adequate.		
22	**Does the vendor receive quality products from their suppliers?** Ensure that vendors are aware that they are responsible for the product quality from their contractors and subcontractors.		

* A PROJECT WITH LIFE THREATENING HAZARDS MUST DO THESE ITEMS

H.3   Generic Software Safety Requirements From MSFC

REQUIREMENT TO BE MET	APPLICABILITY Yes/No/Partial	ACTION Accept/Work
The failure of safety-critical software functions shall be detected, isolated, and recovered from such that catastrophic and critical hazardous events are prevented from occurring.		
Software shall perform automatic Failure Detection, Isolation, and Recovery (FDIR) for identified safety-critical functions with a time to criticality under 24 hours.		
Automatic recovery actions taken shall be reported to the crew, ground, or controlling executive. There shall be no necessary response from crew or ground operators to proceed with the recovery action.		
The FDIR switch over software shall be resident on an available, non-failed control platform which is different from the one with the function being monitored.		
Override commands shall require multiple operator actions.		
Software shall process the necessary commands within the time to criticality of a hazardous event.		
Hazardous commands shall only be issued by the controlling application, or by the crew, ground, or controlling executive.		
Software that executes hazardous commands shall notify the initiating crew, ground operator, or controlling executive upon execution or provide the reason for failure to execute a hazardous command.		
Prerequisite conditions (e.g., correct mode, correct configuration, component availability, proper sequence, and parameters in range) for the safe execution of an identified hazardous command shall be met before execution.		
In the event that prerequisite conditions have not been met, the software shall reject the command and alert the crew, ground operators, or the controlling executive.		
Software shall make available status of all software controllable inhibits to the crew, ground operators, or the controlling executive.		
Software shall accept and process crew, ground operator, or controlling executive commands to activate/deactivate software controllable inhibits.		
Software shall provide an independent and unique command to control each software controllable inhibit.		
Software shall incorporate the capability to identify and status each software inhibit associated with hazardous commands.		
Software shall make available current status on software inhibits associated with hazardous commands to the crew, ground operators, or controlling executive.		
All software inhibits associated with a hazardous command shall have a unique identifier.		

REQUIREMENT TO BE MET	APPLICABILITY Yes/No/Partial	ACTION Accept/Work
Each software inhibit command associated with a hazardous command shall be consistently identified using the rules and legal values.		
If an automated sequence is already running when a software inhibit associated with a hazardous command is activated, the sequence shall complete before the software inhibit is executed.		
Software shall have the ability to resume control of an inhibited operation after deactivation of a software inhibit associated with a hazardous command.		
The state of software inhibits shall remain unchanged after the execution of an override.		
Software shall provide error handling to support safety-critical functions.		
Software shall provide caution and warning status to the crew, ground operators, or the controlling executive.		
Software shall provide for crew/ground forced execution of any automatic safing, isolation, or switch over functions.		
Software shall provide for crew/ground forced termination of any automatic safing, isolation, or switch over functions.		
Software shall provide procession for crew/ground commands in return to the previous mode or configuration of any automatic safing, isolation, or switch over function.		
Software shall provide for crew/ground forced override of any automatic safing, isolation, or switch over functions.		
Software shall provide fault containment mechanisms to prevent error propagation across replaceable unit interfaces.		
Hazardous payloads shall provide failure status and data to core software systems. Core software systems shall process hazardous payload status and data to provide status monitoring and failure annunciation.		
Software (including firmware) Power On Self Test (POST) utilized within any replaceable unit or component shall be confined to that single system process controlled by the replaceable unit or component.		
Software (including firmware) POST utilized within any replaceable unit or component shall terminate in a safe state.		
Software shall initialize, start, and restart replaceable units to a safe state.		
For systems solely using software for hazard risk mitigation, software shall require two independent command messages for a commanded system action that could result in a critical or catastrophic hazard.		
Software shall require two independent operator actions to initiate or terminate a system function that could result in a critical hazard.		
Software shall require three independent operator actions to initiate or terminate a system function that could result in a catastrophic hazard.		
Operational software functions shall allow only authorized access.		
Software shall provide proper sequencing (including timing) of safety-critical		

REQUIREMENT TO BE MET	APPLICABILITY Yes/No/Partial	ACTION Accept/Work
commands.		
Software termination shall result in a safe system state.		
In the event of hardware failure, software faults that lead to system failures, or when the software detects a configuration inconsistent with the current mode of operation, the software shall have the capability to place the system into a safe state.		
When the software is notified of or detects hardware failures, software faults that lead to system failures, or a configuration inconsistent with the current mode of operation, the software shall notify the crew, ground operators, or the controlling executive.		
Hazardous processes and safing processes with a time to criticality such that timely human intervention may not be available, shall be automated (i.e., not require crew intervention to begin or complete).		
The software shall notify crew, ground, or the controlling executive during or immediately after execution of an automated hazardous or safing process.		
Unused or undocumented codes shall be incapable of producing a critical or catastrophic hazard.		
All safety-critical elements (requirements, design elements, code components, and interfaces) shall be identified as "safety-critical."		
An application software set shall ensure proper configuration of inhibits, interlocks, and safing logic, and exception limits at initialization.		

H.4   Design for Safety Checklist

From a paper given at a talk to the Forth Interest Group (UK) in London during May 1992. Paul E. Bennett.

- Keep the design simple and highly modular. Modularity aids in the isolation of systematic failure modes.

- Minimize common failure modes. The calculation time for failure probabilities can be extended as by the cube of common mode entries in a fault tree. [GB: This means that the more common failure modes there are, the longer it takes to calculate the failure probabilities.]

- Identify safe states early in the design. Have these fully checked and verified for completeness and correctness.

- Ensure that failures of dynamic system activities result in the system achieving a known and clearly identified safe state within a specified time limit.

- Specify system interfaces clearly and thoroughly. Include, as part of the documentation, the required action or actions should the interface fail.

- Diagrams convey the most meaning. They can often achieve more than words alone and should be used when presenting design ideas to the customer.

- Design all systems using the same methodologies framework wherever possible. A well practiced craft helps minimize errors.

H.5 Checklist of generic (language independent) programming practices

Derived from NUREG/CR-6463, appendix B, "Review Guidelines on Software languages for Use in Nuclear Power Plant Safety Systems" Final Report.

- Minimize use of dynamic memory. Using dynamic memory can lead to memory leaks. To mitigate the problem, release allocated memory as soon as possible. Also track the allocations and deallocations closely.

- Minimize memory paging and swapping. In a real-time system, this can cause significant delays in response time.

- Avoid *goto*'s. *Goto*'s make execution time behavior difficult to fully predict as well as introducing uncertainty into the control flow. When used, clearly document the control flow, the justification for using *goto*'s, and thoroughly test them.

- Minimize control flow complexity. Excessive complexity makes it difficult to predict the program flow and impedes review and maintenance. Project guidelines or coding standards should set specific limits on nesting levels.

- Initialize variables before use! Using uninitialized variables can cause anomalous behavior. Using uninitialized pointers can lead to exceptions or core dumps.

- In larger routines, use single entry and exit points in subprograms. Multiple entry or exit points introduce control flow uncertainties. In small subprograms, multiple exit points may actually make the routine more readable, and should be allowed. Document any secondary entry and exit points.

- Minimize interface ambiguities. Interface errors account for many design and coding errors. Look at the interfaces to hardware, other software, and to human operators.

- Use data typing. If the language does not enforce it, include it in the coding standards and look for it during formal inspections.

- Provide adequate precision and accuracy in calculations, especially within safety-critical components.

- Use parentheses to specify precedence order, rather than relying on the order inherent in the language. Assumptions about precedence often lead to errors, and the source code can be misinterpreted when reviewing it.

- Avoid functions or procedures with side effects. Side effects can lead to unplanned dependencies, and ultimately to bugs.

- Separate assignments from evaluation statements. Mixing them can cause unanticipated side effects. An example of a mixed assignment/evaluation statement is:

- y = toupper(x=getchar());   // x=getchar() should be on separate line

- Instrumentation (debugging statements, etc) should be highly visible. If left in the run-time system, it should be minimized to avoid timing perturbations. Visibility allows the "real code" to be obvious when the source code is reviewed, and it makes it easier to be sure all instrumentation is removed for the run-time system.

- Minimize dynamic binding. Dynamic binding is a necessary part of polymorphism. When used, it should be justified. Keep in mind that it causes unpredictability in name/class association and reduces run-time predictability.

- Be careful when using operator overloading. While it can help achieve uniformity across different data types (which is good), it can also confuse the reader (and programmers) if used in a non-intuitive way.

- Use tasking with care. While it adds many good features to programs (e.g. splitting the work into logical units, each of which can be tested independently), it can also lead to timing uncertainties, sequence of execution uncertainties, vulnerability to race conditions, and deadlocks.

- Minimize the use of interrupt driven processing. Interrupts lead to non-deterministic response times, which is very important in real-time systems. The best way to handle this is to have the interrupt processing do the bare minimum, and return to primary program control as soon as possible. Check how the operating system does time slicing (usually using clock interrupts), and what overhead or problems may be inherent in their implementation.

- Handle exceptions locally, when possible. Local exception handling helps isolate problems more easily and more accurately. If it is not possible to do this, then thorough testing and analysis to verify the software's behavior during exception testing is recommended.

- Check input data validity. Checking reduces the probability of incorrect results, which could lead to further errors or even system crashes. If the input can be "trusted", then checking is not necessary.

- Check the output data validity, if downstream input checking is not performed. This reduces incorrect results, which can have mild to major effects on the software.

- Control the use of built-in functions through project specific guidelines. Built-in functions (usually in the language library) have unknown internal structure, limitations, precision, and exception handling. Thoroughly test the functions that will be used, use a certified compiler, or review formal testing done on the compiler.

- Create coding standards for naming, indentation, commenting, subprogram size, etc. These factors affect the readability of the source code, and influence how well reviews and inspections can find errors.

- When doing mixed-language programming, separate out the "foreign" code, to enhance readability. Also document it well, including the justification. Mixed-language programming should be used only when necessary (such as accessing hardware with C, from a Java program).

- Use single purpose functions and procedures. This facilitates review and maintenance of the code.

- Use each variable for a single purpose only. "Reusing" a variable (usually a local) makes the source code confusing to read and maintain. If the variable is named properly for its original purpose, it will be misnamed for the new purpose.

- If the hardware configuration may change, for this project or in the future, isolate hardware-dependent code.

- Check for dead code. Unreachable code may indicate an error. It also causes confusion when reading the code.

- Use version control tools (configuration management).

- Utilize a bug tracking tool or database. Once a bug is found, it should be tracked until eliminated. Bug databases are also good sources to use when creating checklists for code inspections.

- Avoid large if-then-else and case statements. Such statements are extremely difficult to debug, because code ends up having so many different paths. The difference between best-case and worst-case execution time becomes significant. Also, the difficulty of structured code coverage testing grows exponentially with the number of branches.

- Avoid implementing delays as no-ops or empty loops. If this code is used on a different processor, or even the same processor running at a different rate (for example, a 25MHz vs. 33MHz CPU), the code may stop working or work incorrectly on the faster processor.

H.6 Checklist of assembly programming practices for safety

- Use the macro facility of the assembler, if it exists, to simplify the code and make it more readable. Use if/else and loop control of the macro facility.

- If using labels, make the names meaningful. Label1 is not meaningful.

- Be careful to check the base of numbers (decimal, octal, hexadecimal)

- Use comments to describe WHAT the procedure or section is meant to do. It is not always clear from the assembly code.

- Update comments when the code changes, if the intent of the procedure or section changes as well.

- Use named code segments if possible. Consider separate segments for reset, non-volatile memory initialization, timer interrupts, and other special-purpose code

H.7   Checklist of Ada programming practices for safety

Guidelines for Ada programming can be found in the book "Ada 95, Quality and Style: Guidelines for Professional Programmers, Vol. 134". The checklist below lists some common errors to look for.

- *Reading Uninitialized variables.* Access values are always initialized to null, but other types are not specifically given an initial value and might have an arbitrary set of "garbage" bits set

- *Off-by-one boundary conditions* (for loop conditions, array indexing, and comparisons). This is the error of having almost the right boundary. For example, did you use < when you meant <=?

- *Access type (pointer) and storage management errors* (especially boundary conditions like null lists).

- *Incorrect return values handling.* For example, if a function returns a range, make sure every value in the range will be handled appropriately by your program.

- *Incorrect special condition handling.* Have you handled all cases? If you're reading from a sensor, do you deal with bogus sensor values? Do you handle all appropriate exceptions?

- *Incorrect array bound handling.* An array's lower bound is not always one, so use 'First, 'Last, 'Length, and 'Range when you're passed an array.

- *Instantiated unconstrained arrays.* Arrays with large array indices (like Integer or Positive), or records containing them, must have their bounds set.

- *Missing "reverse" keyword in a backward "for" loop.*

- *Tasks exposed to unexpected exceptions.* If a task does not catch exceptions the task will terminate on one.

- *Invalid fairness assumptions in tasking.* Some tasking operations are not guaranteed to be "fair". For example, in a selective wait with several open alternatives, Ada is free to pick between any of them each time; it need not pick between them "fairly".

H.8   Checklist of C programming practices for safety

Derived from NUREG/CR-6463, appendix B. Refer to generic list (H.5) as well.

- Limit the number and size of parameters passed to routines. Too many parameters affect readability and testability of the routine. Large structures or arrays, if passed by value, can overflow the stack, causing unpredictable results. Always pass large elements via pointers.

- Use recursive functions with great care. Stack overflows are common. Verify that there is a finite recursion!

- Utilize functions for boundary checking. Since C does not do this automatically, create routines that perform the same function. Accessing arrays or strings out-of-bounds is a common problem with unpredictable, and often major, results.

- Do not use the *gets* function, or related functions. These do not have adequate limit checks. Writing your own routine allows better error handling to be included.

- Use *memmove*, not *memcpy*. *Memcpy* has problems if the memory overlaps.

- Create wrappers for built-in functions to include error checking.

- If "*if…else if…else if…*" gets beyond two levels, use a *switch…case* instead. This increases readability.

- When using *switch…case*, always explicitly define *default*. If a *break* is omitted, to allow flow from one case to another, explicitly document it.

- Initialize local (automatic) variable. They contain garbage before explicit initialization. Pay special attention to pointers, since they can have the most dangerous effects.

- Initialize global variables in a separate routine. This ensures that variables are properly set at warm reboot.

- Check pointers to make sure they don't reference variables outside of scope. Once a variable goes out of scope, what it contains is undefined.

- Only use *setjmp* and *longjmp* for exception handling. These commands jump outside function boundaries and deviate from normal control flow.

- Avoid pointers to functions. These pointers cannot be initialized and may point to non-executable code. If they must be used, document the justification.

- Prototype all functions and procedures! This allows the compiler to catch errors, rather than having to debug them at run-time. Also, when possible, use a tool or other method to verify that the prototype matches the function.

- Minimize interface ambiguities, such as using expressions as parameters to subroutines, or changing the order of arguments between similar functions. Also justify (and document) any use of functions with an indefinite number of arguments. These functions cannot be checked by the compiler, and are difficult to verify.

- Do no use ++ or – operators on parameters being passed to subroutines or macros. These can create unexpected side effects.

- Use bit masks instead of bit fields, which are implementation dependent.

- Always explicitly cast variables. This enforces stronger typing. Casting pointers from one type to another should be justified and documented.

- Avoid the use of typedef's for unsized arrays. This feature is badly supported and error-prone.

- Avoid mixing signed and unsigned variables. Use explicit casts when necessary.

- Don't compare floating point numbers to 0, or expect exact equality. Allow some small differences due to the precision of floating point calculations.

- Enable and read compiler warnings. If an option, have warnings issued as errors. Warnings indicate deviation that may be fine, but may also indicate a subtle error.

- Be cautious if using standard library functions in a multitasking environment. Library functions may not be re-entrant, and could lead to unspecified results.

- Do not call functions within interrupt service routines. If it is necessary to do so, make sure the functions are small and re-entrant.

- Avoid the use of the ?: operator. The operator makes the code more difficult to read. Add comments explaining it, if it is used.

- Place #include directives at the beginning of a file. This makes it easier to know what files are actually included. When tracing dependencies, this information is needed.

- Use #define instead of numeric literals. This allows the reader or maintainer to know what the number actually represents (RADIUS_OF_EARTH_IN_KM, instead of 6356.91). It also allows the number to be changed in **one** place, if a change is necessitated later.

- Do not make assumptions about the sizes of dependent types, such as *int*. The size is often platform and compiler dependent.

- Avoid using reserved words or library function names as variable names. This could lead to serious errors. Also, avoid using names that are close to standard names, to improve the readability of the source code.

H.9   Checklist of C++ programming practices for safety

Derived from NUREG/CR-6463, appendix B. Refer to generic list (H.5) as well. Also, as C++ is a superset of the C language, refer to that checklist (H.8) for C-type errors.

- Always pass large parameters (structures, arrays, etc.) via reference. If it will not be changed, pass it as const.

- Group related parameters within a class, to minimize the number of parameters to be passed to a routine.

- Avoid multiple inheritance, which can cause ambiguities and maintenance problems.

- When overloading an operator, make sure that its usage is natural, not clever. Obscure overloading can reduce readability and induce errors. Using + to add two structures is natural. Using + with structures to perform a square of each element is not natural.

- Explicitly define class operators (assignment, etc.). Declare them private if they are not to be used.

- For all classes, define the following: Default constructor, copy constructor, destructor, operator=.

- Declare the destructor virtual. This is necessary to avoid problems if the class is inherited.

- Use *throw* and *catch* for exception handling, not C's *setjmp* and *longjmp*, which are difficult to recover from.

- Avoid pointers to members. These unnecessarily complicate the code.

- Use *const* variables and functions whenever possible. When something should not change, or a function should not change anything outside of itself, use *const*.

From the High Integrity Software Systems Assurance (HISSA) group of the National Institute of Standards and Technology (NIST) [http://hissa.ncsl.nist.gov/effProject/handbook/c++/]:

Errors associated with Variables

- Over estimation of predefined type's size.(In C++ there is no guarantee that a particular type has a particular number of bits)

- Inadequate floating point precision or accuracy

- No initialization of variable before use

- Pointer initialization errors

- Input data out of range

- Incorrect use of global variables

- Function's output data needs more processing before reuse

- Inappropriate variable type conversion especially with use of pointers (e.g., pointer casting to a different type of pointer)

- Multiple declarations of one identifier with several types
- Mixing signed and unsigned variables
- Reuse of variables without reinitialization
- Use of reserved words

Errors associated with Memory

- Violation of available memory restrictions
- Allocating memory without subsequently freeing it
- Attempting to access memory that has not been allocated
- Utilizing memory that has already been freed
- Insufficient memory to meet dynamic memory requirement
- Errors due to improper attention to dynamic memory allocation functions' different services that depend on the value of input parameter
- Memory leaks due to non-use of class destructor or improper constructors or other functions that may cause leaks
- Unauthorized use of memory blocks
- Stack overflow due to passing of many parameters or large structures
- Stack overflow due to unbounded recursive function calls
- Overlapping source and destination memory areas used with memory related functions
- Use of memory related functions without bounds checking
- Out of bounds array index
- System running on unreliable data

Errors associated with Control Flow

- Improper use of error associated instructions like **goto, setjmp, longjmp**
- Use of complicated control flow (many **if …else if …else if** statements)
- Mismatch between **if** and **else**
- Forgotten **default** case in a **switch** statement
- Forgotten **break** when using **switch**
- Dead code inside the **switch** construct that does not belong to any of specified branch
- Control flow uncertainty due to multiple entry and exit points in subprograms
- Inappropriate use of **throw** and **catch** exception handling mechanism
- Interface errors (e.g., inaccurately ordering or reversing the order of parameters passed to a function)

- Inappropriate use of functions that accept indefinite number of parameters
- Parameters of incompatible type with the function prototype
- Incorrect precedence assumptions
- Inappropriate expression calculation in function or macro parameter
- Uncertainties in execution, timing and resource utilization due to multitasking

Errors associated with Functions

- Unwanted side effects in a function
- Improper use of the same function for assignment and evaluation
- Improper use of built in functions and/or compiled libraries
- Inappropriate evaluation of expressions in parameter list (e.g., in "CalcArea(length=2,width=length+2)" width's evaluation may lead to unintended error)
- Unwanted implicit calls to the default constructor, copy constructor, destructor, or other compiler supplied function
- Errors due to too many functional dependences

Errors associated with Operators

- Undefined expressions due to inappropriate use of increment (++) and decrement (- -) operators
- Incorrect precedence assumption for operators
- Inappropriate behavior of default class operators such as **operators =, operator&**, and **operator,** (i.e., operator-comma)
- Errors due to inconsistency of pointer operators

H.10 Checklist of Fortran programming practices for safety

Derived from NUREG/CR-6463, appendix B. Refer to generic list (H.5) as well.

- Unreachable code. This reduces the readability and therefore maintainability.

- Unreferenced labels. Confuses readability.

- The EQUIVALENCE statement except with the project manager's permission. This statement is responsible for many questionable practices in Fortran giving both reliability and readability problems. Permission should not be given lightly. A really brave manager will unequivocally forbid its use. Some programming standards do precisely this.

- Implicit reliance on SAVE. (This prejudices re-usability). A particular nasty problem to debug. Some compilers give you SAVE whether you specify it or not. Moving to any machine which implements the ANSI definition from one which SAVE's by default may lead to particularly nasty run and environment sensitive problems. This is an example of a statically detectable error which is almost impossible to find in a source debugger at run-time.

- The computed GOTO except with the project manager's permission. Often used for efficiency reasons when not justified. Efficiency should never precede clarity as a programming goal. The motto is "tune it when you can read it".

- Any Hollerith. This is non-ANSI, error-prone and difficult to manipulate.

- Non-generic intrinsics. Use generic intrinsics only on safety grounds. For example, use REAL() instead of FLOAT().

- Use of the ENTRY statement. This statement is responsible for unpredictable behavior in a number of compilers. For example, the relationship between dummy arguments specified in the SUBROUTINE or FUNCTION statement and in the ENTRY statements leads to a number of dangerous practices which often defeat even symbolic debuggers.

- BN and BZ descriptors in FORMAT statements. These reduce the reliability of user input.

- Mixing the number of array dimensions in calling sequences. Although commonly done, it is poor practice to mix array dimensions and can easily lead to improper access of n-dimensional arrays. It also inhibits any possibility of array-bound checking which may be part of the machine's environment. Unfortunately this practice is very widespread in Fortran code.

- Use of BLANK='ZERO' in I/O. This degrades the reliability of user input.

- Putting DO loop variables in COMMON. Forbidden because they can be inadvertently changed or even lead to bugs in some optimizing compilers.

- Declarations like REAL R(1). An old-fashioned practice which is frequently abused and leads almost immediately to array-bound violations whether planned or not. Array-bound violations are responsible for a significant number of bugs in Fortran.

- Passing an actual argument more than once in a calling sequence. Causes reliability problems in some compilers especially if one of the arguments is an output argument.

- A main program without a PROGRAM statement. Use of the program statement allows a programmer to give a module a name avoiding system defaults such as main and potential link clashes.

- Undeclared variables. Variables must be explicitly declared and their function described with suitable comment. Not declaring variables is actually forbidden in C and C++.

- The IMPLICIT statement. Implicit declaration is too sweeping unless it is one of the non-standard versions such as IMPLICIT NONE or IMPLICIT UNDEFINED.

- Labeling any other statement but FORMAT or CONTINUE. Stylistically it is poor practice to label executable statements as inserting code may change the logic, for example, if the target of a DO loop is an executable statement. This latter practice is also obsolescent in Fortran 90.

- The DIMENSION statement. It is redundant and on some machines improperly implemented. Use REAL etc. instead.

- READ or WRITE statements without an IOSTAT clause. All READ and WRITE statements should have an error status requested and tested for error-occurrence.

- SAVE in a main program. It merely clutters and achieves nothing.

- All referenced subroutines or functions must be declared as EXTERNAL. All EXTERNALS must be used. Unless EXTERNAL is used, names can collide surprisingly often with compiler supplied non-standard intrinsics with strange results which are difficult to detect. Unused EXTERNALS cause link problems with some machines, leading to spurious unresolved external references.

- Blank COMMON. Use of blank COMMON can conflict with 3rd. party packages which also use it in many strange ways. Also the rules are different for blank COMMON than for named COMMON.

- Named COMMON except with the project manager's permission. COMMON is a dangerous statement. It is contrary to modern information hiding techniques and used freely, can rapidly destroy the maintainability of a package. The author has bitter, personal experience of this ! Some company's safety-critical standards for Fortran explicitly forbid its use.

- Use of BACKSPACE, ENDFILE, REWIND, OPEN, INQUIRE and CLOSE. Existing routines for each of these actions should be designed and must always be used. Many portability problems arise from their explicit use, for example, the position of the file after an OPEN is not defined. It could be at the beginning or the end of the file. The OPEN should always therefore be followed by a REWIND, which has no effect if the file is already positioned at the beginning. OPEN and INQUIRE cause many portability problems, especially with sequential files.

- DO loops using non-INTEGER variables. The loop may execute a different number of times on some machines due to round-off differences. This practice is obsolescent in Fortran 90.

- Logical comparison of non-INTEGERS. Existing routines for this should be designed which understand the granularity of the floating point arithmetic on each machine to which they are ported and must always be used. Many portability problems arise from its explicit use. The author has personal experience whereby a single comparison of two reals for inequality executed occasionally in a 70,000 line program caused a very expensive portability problem.

- Any initialization of COMMON variables or dummy arguments is forbidden inside a FUNCTION, (possibility of side-effects). Expression evaluation order is not defined for Fortran. If an expression contains a function which affects other variables in the expression, the answer may be different on different machines. Such problems are exceedingly difficult to debug.

- Use of explicit unit numbers in I/O statements. Existing routines to manipulate these should be designed and must always be used. Many portability problems arise from their explicit use. The ANSI standard only requires them to be non-negative. What they are connected to differs wildly from machine to machine. Don't be surprised if your output comes out on a FAX machine !

- CHARACTER*(N) where N>255. A number of compilers do not support character elements longer than 255 characters.

- FORMAT repeat counts > 255. A number of compilers do not support FORMAT repeat counts of more than 255.

- COMMON blocks called EXIT. On one or two machines, this can cause a program to halt unexpectedly.

- Comparison of strings by other than the LLE functions. Only a restricted collating sequence is defined by the ANSI standard. The above functions guarantee portability of comparison.

- Using the same character variable on both sides of an assignment. If character positions overlap, this is actually forbidden by the standard but some compilers allow it and others don't. It should simply be avoided. The restriction has been removed in Fortran 90.

- Tab to a continuation line. Tabs are not part of the ANSI Fortran definition. They are however easily removable if used only to code lines and for indentation. If they are also used for continuation (like the VAX for example), it means they become syntactic and if your compiler does not support them, removing them is non-trivial.

- Use of PAUSE. An obsolescent feature with essentially undefined behavior.

- Use of '/' or '!' in a string initialized by DATA. Some compilers have actually complained at this !

- Using variables in PARAMETER, COMMON or array dimensions without typing them explicitly before such use. e.g. PARAMETER (R=3) INTEGER R Some compilers get it wrong.

- Use of CHAR or ICHAR. These depend on the character set of the host. Best to map onto ASCII using wrapper functions, but almost always safe today.

- Use of ASSIGN or assigned GOTO. An obsolescent feature legendary for producing unreadable code.

- Use of Arithmetic IF. An obsolescent feature legendary for producing unreadable code.

- Non-CONTINUE DO termination. An obsolescent feature which makes enhancement more difficult.

- Shared DO termination for nested DO loops. An obsolescent feature which makes enhancement more difficult.

- Alternate RETURN. An obsolescent feature which can easily produce unreadable code.

- Use of Fortran keywords or intrinsic names as identifier names. Keywords may be reserved in future Fortran standards. The practice also confuses readability, for example, IF (IF(CALL)) STOP=2 Some people delight in this sort of thing. Such people do not take programming seriously.

- Use of the INTRINSIC statement. The ANSI standard is particularly complex for this statement with many exceptions. Avoid.

- Use of END= or ERR= in I/O statements. (IOSTAT should be used instead). Using END= and ERR= with associated jumps leads to unstructured and therefore less readable code.

- Declaring and not using variables. This just confuses readability and therefore maintainability.

- Using COMMON block names as general identifiers, where use of COMMON has been approved. This practice confuses readability and unfortunately, compilers from time to time.

- Using variables without initializing them. Reliance on the machine to zero memory for you before running is not portable. It also produces unreliable effects if character strings are initialized to zero, (rather than blank). Always initialize variables explicitly.

- Use of manufacturer specific utilities unless specifically approved by the project manager. This simply reduces portability, in some cases pathologically.

- Use of non-significant blanks or continuation lines within user-supplied identifiers. This leads both to poor readability and to a certain class of error when lists are parsed, (it may have been a missing comma).

- Use of continuation lines in strings. It is not clear if blank-padding to the end of each partial line is required or not.

- Passing COMMON block variables through COMMON and through a calling sequence. This practice is both illegal and unsafe as it may confuse optimizing compilers and in some compilers simply not work. It is a very common error.

- An IF..ELSEIF block IF with no ELSE. This produces a logically incomplete structure whose behavior may change if the external environment changes. A frequent source of "unexpected software functionality".

- DATA statements within subroutines or functions. These can lead to non-reusability and therefore higher maintenance and development costs. If constants are to be initialized, use PARAMETER.

- DO loop variables passed as dummy arguments.

- Equivalencing any arrays other than at their base, even if use of EQUIVALENCE has been approved. Some machines still have alignment problems and also modern RISC platforms rely on good alignment for efficiency. So at best, it will be slow and at worst, it will be wrong.

- Equivalencing any variable with COMMON, even if use of EQUIVALENCE and COMMON has been approved. This rapidly leads to unreadable code.

- Type conversions using the default rules, either in DATA or assignment statements. Type conversions should be performed by the programmer - state what you mean. For example: R = I Wrong R = REAL(I) Right

- Use of mixed-type arithmetic in expressions.

- Use of precedence in any kind of expression. Parenthesize to show what you mean. Although Fortran precedence is relatively simple compared with C which has 15 levels of precedence, it is still easy to get it wrong.

- Concatenated exponentiation without parenthesizing, e.g. a**b**c. People too often forget what this means. Exponentiation associates from the right.

- Calling sequence matching. Make sure that calling sequence arguments match in type number and direction. Inconsistencies here are responsible for many unreliability problems in Fortran.

H.11 Checklist of Pascal programming practices for safety

Derived from NUREG/CR-6463, appendix B. Refer to generic list (H.5) as well.

- If using pointers, use handles whenever possible. Handles allow the memory management to recapture and compact free memory.

- Use care with multiple-condition flow statements. The order of evaluation cannot be guaranteed.

- Isolate interrupt receiving tasks into implementation dependent packages. Pass the interrupt to the main tasks via a normal entry. Interrupt entries are implementation dependent features that may not be supported.

- Use symbolic constants instead of numeric literals. This increases readability and maintainability.

- Avoid the use of the *mod* operator. Not all compilers follow the Standard, and this will create portability problems.

H.12 Checklist for Visual Basic

From "An Evaluation of Object-Based Programming with Visual Basic", James M. Dukovic and Daniel T. Joyce, 0-7803-2492-7/95 IEEE

1. If you want to add a public function or subroutine to a form, place it in a code module having the same name as the form. Place private functions and subroutines inside the general procedure section of the form. This is required because general procedures inside forms are not visible to other objects.

2. Do not use global variables. Use procedure-level variables for temporary variables and module-level variables for object data. This will require you to pass parameters to all methods ensuring a cleaner interface.

3. Do not use the *static* statement to declare variables or procedures. Use module-level variables for all object data. Static variables can become lost in your code.

4. Create handles to access properties declared in code modules. You may access properties in forms and controls directly. This will help hide the implementation of the object.

5. Code modules should be objects. They should have data and methods (subroutines and functions) to access and manipulated the data. Use object-oriented design techniques to define your objects.

6. Forms should only contain code that is unique to the form. Most code should be placed in modules. Forms are likely to change. Modules are much more stable.

7. Set the Visual Basic Environment Option called *Require Variable Declaration* to *Yes*. This will force you to declare variables explicitly. It does not, however, force you to specify a type.

8. Explicitly declare data types for all variables and functions. This will improve readability and reduce the risk of data type errors.

9. Hide the implementation of an object as much as possible. The object's interface should reveal as little about the implementation and underlying data structure as possible. This will allow you to make changes to an object without impacting other objects.

10. Avoid using environment specific parameters in the object's interface. For example, small, medium or large is preferable to passing pixels or twips.

11. Use the variant data type sparingly. Although it allows a form of parametric polymorphism, the resultant code can be difficult to understand and its use will increase the risk of data type errors.

12. Declare subroutines and functions as private whenever possible. Subroutines and functions should only be public if they are used by other objects. This will make the code more readable and it will prevent other objects from accessing private methods directly.

13. Document your interfaces at the top of each method. Include variable types, sizes, and allowable values.

14. Use standard objects whenever possible. For example, use message boxes and dialogue boxes instead of creating specific forms.

15. Do not use the OptionBase statement to alter the lower bound of array subscripts. Altering the lower bound may make reuse more difficult.

16. Design your objects with weak coupling. That is, create your object so its dependency on other objects is minimal. This will make it easier to understand your objects.

H.13 Checklist for selecting an RTOS

From "Selecting a Real-Time Operating System", Greg Hawley, Embedded Systems Programming, March, 1999

Criteria	Considerations
Language/Microprocessor Support	The first step in finding an RTOS for your project is to look at those vendors supporting the language and microprocessor you'll be using.
Tool Compatibility	Make sure your RTOS works with your ICE, compiler, assembler, linker, and source code debuggers.
Services	Operating systems provide a variety of services. Make sure your OS supports the services (queues, times, semaphores) you expect to use in your design.
Footprint	RTOSes are often scalable, including only those services you end up needing in your applications. Based on what services you'll need, and the number of tasks, semaphores, and everything else you expect to use, make sure your RTOS will work in the RAM and ROM you have
Performance	Can your RTOS meet your performance requirements? Make sure you understand benchmarks vendors give you and how they apply to the hardware you will really be using.
Software Components	Are required components (protocol stacks, communications services, real-time databases, Web services, virtual machines, graphics libraries, and so on) available for your RTOS? How much effort will it be to integrate them?
Device Drivers	If you're using common hardware, are device drivers available for your RTOS?
Debugging Tools	RTOS vendors may have debugging tools that help find defects that are harder to find with source-level debuggers (such as deadlocks, forgotten semaphore puts, and so on).
Standards Compatibility	Are there safety or compatibility standards your application demands? Make sure your RTOS complies.
Technical Support	Phone support is typically covered for a limited time after your purchase or on a year-to-year basis through support. Sometimes applications engineers are available. Additionally, some vendors provide training and consulting.
Source vs. Object Code	With some RTOSes you get the source code to the operating system when you buy a license. In other cases, you get only object code or linkable libraries.
Licensing	Make sure you understand how the RTOS vendor licenses their RTOS. With some vendors, run-time licenses are required for each board shipped and development tool licenses are required for each developer.
Reputation	Make sure you're dealing with someone you'll be happy with.
Services	Real-time operating systems provide developers a full complement of features: several types of semaphores (counting, mutual exclusion), times, mailboxes, queues, buffer managers, memory system managers, events, and more.
Priority Inheritance	Must support, or priority inversion can result

H.14 Good Programming Practices Checklist

These items should be considered when creating a Coding Standard or when beginning a software project.

Programming Practice	Yes/No/NA	Comment or Justification
General Suggestions		
CPU self test. Test the CPU on boot up.		
Fill ROM/RAM/flash with a known pattern (halt, illegal instruction, return) to guard against illegal jumps.		
ROM tests. Verify integrity of ROM (EEPROM, Flash disk, etc.) prior to executing the software stored in it.		
Watchdog Timers. Implement a watchdog timer to reboot software if it gets "stuck".		
Guard against Variable Corruption. Store multiple copies of critical variables, especially on different storage media or physically separate memory.		
Stack Checks. Checking the stack guards against stack overflow or corruption. By initializing the stack to a known pattern, a stack monitor function can be used to watch the amount of available stack space.		
Write what you need, and use what you write! Don't make unnecessarily verbose or lengthy documentation, unless contractually required. It is better to have short documents that the developers will actually read and use.		
Initialize all **unused memory** locations to a pattern that, if executed as an instruction, will cause the system to revert to a known safe state.		
Don't use a stop or halt instruction. The CPU should be always executing, whether idling or actively processing		
When possible, put safety-critical operational software instructions in nonvolatile read-only memory.		
Don't use scratch files for storing or transferring safety-critical information between computers or tasks within a computer.		
Keep Interface Control Documents up to date. Out-of-date information usually leads to one programmer creating a module or unit that will not interface correctly with another unit. The problem isn't found until late in the testing phase, when it is expensive to fix.		

Programming Practice	Yes/No/NA	Comment or Justification
Prohibit program patches. During development, patching a program is a bad idea. During operations, patching may be a necessity, but should still be carefully considered.		
Follow the two person rule. At least two people should be thoroughly familiar with the design, code, testing and operation of each software module of the system. If one person leaves the project, someone else understands what is going on.		
Design Issues		
Program Calculation Checks. Simple checks can be used to give confidence in the results from calculations.		
Verify all reused code was designed for reuse.		
Do not implement program as "One big loop". A single large loop forces all parts of the software to operate at the same rate.		
Analyze hardware peculiarities before starting software design.		
Avoid inter-module dependencies when possible. This maximizes software reusability.		
Create more than a single design diagram. Getting the entire design on paper is essential.		
Design in error detection and handling! Tailor the effort to the level of the code – don't put it everywhere!		
Perform a memory analysis of the design. Estimate how much memory your system uses and adjust the design if the system is bumping up against its limits.		
Avoid indiscriminate use of interrupts. Use of interrupts can cause priority inversion in real-time systems if not implemented carefully.		
Use come-from checks. For safety-critical modules, make sure that the correct module called it, and that it was not called accidentally by a malfunctioning module.		
Provide **separate authorization and separate control functions** to initiate a critical or hazardous function. This includes separate "arm" and "fire" commands for critical capabilities.		
Do not use input/output ports for both critical and non-critical functions.		

Programming Practice	Yes/No/NA	Comment or Justification
Provide **sufficient difference in addresses** between critical I/O ports and non-critical I/O ports, such that a single address bit failure does not allow access to critical functions or ports.		
Make sure all **interrupt priorities** and responses are defined. All interrupts should be initialized to a return, if not used by the software.		
Provide for an **orderly shutdown** (or other acceptable response) upon the detection of **unsafe conditions**.		
Provide for an **orderly system shutdown** as the result of a **command shutdown**, power interruptions, or other failures.		
Protect against **out-of-sequence transmission** of safety-critical function messages by detecting and deviation from the normal sequence of transmission. Revert to a known safe state when out-of-sequence messages are detected.		
Hazardous sequences should not be initiated by a single keyboard entry.		
Prevent **inadvertent entry into a critical routine**. Detect such entry if it occurs, and revert to a known safe state.		
When **safety interlocks** are removed/bypassed for a test, the software should verify the reinstatement of the interlocks at the completion of the testing.		
Critical data communicated from one CPU to another should be verified prior to operational use.		
Set a **dedicated status flag** that is updated between each step of a hazardous operation.		
Verify critical commands prior to transmission, and upon reception. It never hurts to check twice!		
Make sure all flags used are unique and single purpose.		
Put the majority of **safety-critical decisions and algorithms** in a single (or few) software development module(s).		
Decision logic using data from hardware or other software modules should not be based on values of all ones or all zeros. Use specific binary patterns to reduce the likelihood of malfunctioning hardware/software satisfying the decision logic.		
Perform reasonableness checks on all safety-critical inputs.		
Perform a **status check** of critical system elements prior to executing a potentially hazardous sequence.		

Programming Practice	Yes/No/NA	Comment or Justification
Always **initialize the software into a known safe state.** This implies making sure all variables are set to an initial value, and not the previous value prior to reset.		
Don't allow the operator to change safety-critical time limits in decision logic.		
When the system is safed, usually in response to an anomalous condition or problem, provide the **current system configuration** to the operator.		
Create a list of possible hardware failures that may impact the software. The list will be invaluable when testing the error handling capabilities of the software, as well as making sure hardware failures have been considered in the design.		
Be careful if using multi-threaded programs. Subtle program errors can result from unforeseen interactions among multiple threads.		
Consider the stability of the requirements. If the requirements are likely to change, design as much flexibility as possible into the system.		
Design for weak coupling between modules (classes, etc.). The more independent the modules are, the fewer undesired side effects there are.		
Reduce complexity. Calculate a complexity metric. Look at modules that are very complex and reduce them if possible.		
Implementation (Coding) Issues		
Do not implement delays as empty loops. This can create problems (and timing difficulties) if the code is run on faster or slower machines, or even if recompiled with a newer, optimizing compiler.		
Avoid fine-grain optimizing during first implementation.		
Check variables for reasonableness before use. If the value is out of range, there is a problem – memory corruption, incorrect calculation, hardware problems (if sensor), etc.		
Use read-backs to check values. When a value is written to memory, the display, or hardware, another function should read it back and verify that the correct value was written.		
Safety-critical modules should have only one entry and one exit point.		

Programming Practice	Yes/No/NA	Comment or Justification
Create a dependency graph. Given such a diagram, it's easy to identify what parts of the software can be reused, create a strategy for incremental testing of modules, and develop a method to limit error propagation through the entire system.		
Consider compiler optimization carefully. Debuggers may not work well with optimized code.		
Testing Issues		
Plan and script all tests. Do not rely on interactive and incomplete test programs.		
Measure the execution time of your code. Determine if there are any bottlenecks, or any modules that should be considered for optimization.		
Use execution logging, with independent checking, to find software runaway, illegal functions, or out-of-sequence execution.		
Test for memory leakage. Instrument the code and run it under load and stress tests.		
Use a simulator or ICE (In-circuit Emulator) system for debugging in embedded systems.		

110

www.ingramcontent.com/pod-product-compliance
Lightning Source LLC
LaVergne TN
LVHW081656050326
832903LV00026B/1780

* 9 7 8 1 7 3 1 0 8 9 2 7 4 *